A SHORT HISTORY OF THE
INTERNATIONAL ECONOMY SINCE 1850

A short history of the international economy since 1850

FOURTH EDITION

William Ashworth

Emeritus Professor of Economic and Social History in the
University of Bristol

Longman
London and New York

Longman Group UK Limited
Longman House, Burnt Mill, Harlow
Essex CM20 2JE, England
Associated companies throughout the world

*Published in the United States of America
by Longman Inc., New York*

First published 1952
Second edition 1962
Third edition 1975
Fourth edition 1987

British Library Cataloguing in Publication Data
Ashworth, William
  A short history of the international
  economy since 1850. —— 4th ed.
  1. Economic history
  I. Title
  330.9'034   HC51

ISBN 0-582-49383-8

Library of Congress Cataloging-in-Publication Data
Ashworth, William.
  A short history of the international economy since 1850.
  Bibliography: p.
  Includes index.
   1. Economic history.   2. International economic
relations.   I. Title.
HC53.A8   1987   337'.09   86–7181
ISBN 0-582-49383-8 (pbk.)

Set in Linotron 202 10/12 pt Bembo
Produced by Longman Group (FE) Limited
Printed in Hong Kong

Contents

List of tables

Preface to the Second edition

The passage of ten years since the original version of this book was completed has made a fairly extensive revision seem appropriate. The purpose and general scope of the book remain unaltered. It is intended to provide the university student and the interested general reader with an introduction to the history of the modern world economy. It tries to do this by concentrating on two main fields of study. The first is concerned with the common features in the economic development and organization of those nations whose activities have had a dominant influence on the course of world economic history since the mid-nineteenth century. The other deals with the economic relations between nations.

Though the general nature of the book remains as it was, the detailed content has been considerably changed. Approximately one-third of this second edition is new. The objects of the revision have been threefold: to give some brief account of events since the original edition was completed; to take note of more recent work that has been done on the subject; and to give an opportunity to express my own second thoughts. A section on minerals has been introduced in Chapter II and a new chapter on the growth of incomes has been included. Chapter VII (which corresponds to Chapter VI in the first edition) has been entirely rewritten and the final chapter has been revised and extended in order to bring it nearer to the present. Minor revisions and corrections have been made in the remaining chapters. The bibliographical note at the end has been extended and brought up to date.

It is unnecessary to repeat here the acknowledgements which I made in the first edition. Those from whose help I benefited will know that my gratitude has not diminished. But I cannot refrain from adding my thanks to Dr Olga Crisp for her help in trying to guide me through some of the intricacies of Soviet data, when I was preparing this second edition.

W. ASHWORTH
January 1962

Preface to the Third edition

In this edition the main changes have been made with the object of bringing the subject-matter once again as nearly down to date as practicable. A new chapter has been added, incorporating part of the last chapter of the previous edition and extending the history of international economic relations to the early nineteen-seventies. In Chapters II to VI the opportunity has been taken to introduce more recent figures and some brief discussion, where appropriate, of new developments since 1950. A few passages relating to earlier periods have been revised in the light of more recent knowledge. The bibliographical note, which it is hoped will assist students who wish to pursue the subject further, has been completely rewritten in order to take account of the vast number of new publications which have appeared in the last dozen years.

W. A.
October 1974

Preface to the Fourth edition

The purposes of the changes incorporated in this new edition are to extend the period covered, so that (as in previous editions) it comes nearly down to date, and to revise the presentation and interpretation of some subjects already dealt with. No chapter is completely unaltered. The most extensive changes are in Chapters 2 and 10. The latter has been subdivided and appreciably extended in order to examine the course of events since the third edition was prepared. Some material in the thematic chapters has also been updated to include reference to very recent years. The opportunity has been taken to introduce some additional tables and to make the bibliographical note more concise and more concentrated on fairly recent work.

W. A.
September 1985

CHAPTER ONE

The mid-nineteenth century

In 1850 there were probably about 1,200 million people living in the world. For almost all of them, as soon as they had emerged from infancy, the gaining of a bare subsistence absorbed practically their entire effort. In most communities the pattern of economic activities was a simple one, although it varied enormously from one region to another, according to the state of technical knowledge and the bounty or niggardliness of nature. Nevertheless, among the greater part of the world's population, technical skill and equipment and the variety of natural resources easily available were all so limited that a simple economic pattern was the only one possible. On the other hand, the means of carrying out the narrow range of indispensable activities were abundant enough in relation to the size of the population for economies of simple structure to support a life not without notable achievements and high enjoyments, although for most individuals it was usually short, often nasty, and occasionally brutish.

But there were clear signs of change in progress and greater change impending. The proportions in which different productive resources were needed were subject to continuous alteration as a result of changes in the size of the population. World population had been expanding for a long time, but by the nineteenth century the expansion had reached a new and formidable degree. In the hundred years ending in 1850, perhaps 450 million people had been added to the total of world population, an increase of 60 per cent on the numbers in 1750. In a world of perfect mobility that would not have mattered very much, since life was sustained principally by human beings working the soil with the aid of a few implements and domestic animals, and enormous areas of fertile land still remained unoccupied. But the population was very unevenly distributed. Most of the world's people lived in Europe and Asia, and it was in the comparatively small continent of Europe that the natural increase of population was most striking, for Europe's total of about 270 million inhabitants in 1850 was probably nearly double that of a hundred years earlier. There were areas where population obviously pressed on the means of subsistence in years of poor harvest and seemed to be approaching the point at which it would do so even when harvests were good. The fact that in the nineteenth century the Malthusian problem was not insoluble does not mean, as some writers seem to imply, that it was not a problem.

There were two ways of overcoming the impending difficulties: the expanding populations could take possession of the unoccupied or thinly occupied areas, or productive techniques could be improved and diffused so as to make land already in use yield a far greater return than before in the form of consumable goods. Neither type of development was in the least new, but the pressure of external forces on economic life was becoming so great that both were induced in a new degree.

The intricate ethnological map of the world is clear enough indication of people's ability, throughout historic times and before them, to migrate long distances by land and (though perhaps only in recent millennia) by sea, and successfully to establish new settlements far from their places of origin. But the size of the migratory or colonizing bands and the duration of their wanderings is far less certain. Except over fairly short distances it is probable that the process of migration and settlement was usually a protracted one, with many temporary halting-places, occupied perhaps for years, and that the numbers involved in any one movement at the same time were, by modern standards, small. The greatest expansions of settlement had been achieved by the gradual colonization of waste lands close to areas already occupied. But by the nineteenth century many of the most densely settled regions were completely surrounded by occupied lands. What was then becoming necessary was migration on a new scale: the movement of large numbers of people over long distances in a short time without the establishment of intermediate temporary settlements. For that to be possible, and above all for it to be possible peacefully, it was necessary for a fairly full geographical knowledge to be available, a knowledge of what lands existed, where they were situated in relation to one another, whether or not they were populous, whether they seemed barren or fertile. In the possession of this knowledge the nineteenth century held one of its great advantages over all preceding ages. In the latter half of the eighteenth century and the earlier years of the nineteenth the great work of maritime exploration, intermittently pursued by Europeans from Renaissance times, was, except in the polar regions, largely completed – thanks especially to the famous voyages of Wallis, Bougainville, Cook, Vancouver, and others in the hitherto little known Pacific Ocean. The vast emptiness of New Holland (now renamed Australia), the insular structure and natural attractions of New Zealand, the position and nature of the west coast of America north of California, and the non-existence of the long-awaited *Terra Australis* bounding the South Atlantic and Pacific in temperate latitudes, were all clearly revealed for the first time. Much exploration remained to be done in the interior of every continent except Europe, but the outline map of the world could at last be accurately drawn. That was one of the essential first steps in the process which transformed the world from a multitude of autarchic and culturally self-sufficient groups into something approaching an economic unit and a single strategic conception.

Accurate knowledge of the location and nature of the world's empty spaces and unused resources was one prerequisite of the more extensive use of the natural endowments which could support mankind in greater numbers and at a more prosperous level. The other was the achievement of some means whereby people and goods might be transported more swiftly and in greater quantity. Even before steam power was applied to transport, these two influences had widened the area of economic interdependence. Trade with the Americas had a relatively growing share in the economy of Western Europe in the eighteenth century, and so, too, at least for the British, did trade with India. Growing transatlantic trade was accompanied by some increase in American settlement. Although the growth in the relative weight of transatlantic dealings was interrupted for a time in the earlier nineteenth century, the absolute increase continued. There was also in the mid-nineteenth century some further geographical extension of the area of international dealings. Australia and New Zealand, discoveries of not much above half a century earlier, already had small but firmly established colonies of British settlers, actively engaged in trade with the home country. But the numbers involved were small, too small as yet to make more than a very modest contribution to the prevention of population pressure or to increasing the material prosperity of much of the world. All these and other areas remained underpopulated, with their natural resources used inadequately, or not at all, until they were affected by the coming of mechanical transport, the railway and the steamship, which enabled new settlers and supplies to come to them and their own produce to be carried away to existing markets, easily, cheaply, and in bulk.

It is at this point that the two types of economic change, extensive and intensive, which had to occur if the rapid growth of population was not to be disastrous, were linked. For the development of mechanical transport, which was an essential part of the extensive solution of the problem, sprang from the same line of technological advance that made possible an intensive solution also. Of all the aspects of historical change in the nineteenth century the technological was, in fact, probably the most fundamental. It not only made it possible for the expansion of the world's population to be maintained and increased, but it was also, in itself, an immense force making directly for the expansion of economic activity. This was because, in so many cases, the application of new techniques on even a small scale was enough to demonstrate that they would achieve far greater results in proportion to effort if they could be applied on a scale that required an enormous widening of the market for the products which were created with their aid; and also because they drew, for their successful application, on a much widened range of productive resources. In addition, technological developments so changed the way in which the various factors of production were combined that they caused a fundamental change in the everyday experience and environment of a very large proportion of mankind.

The levels of technical achievement in different parts of the world before the nineteenth century differed enormously. But, despite the attainment elsewhere of superlative skill in the production of small quantities of some specialized items, the general standard was undoubtedly highest in Western Europe. Everywhere production was dependent mainly on what hand labour was able to do with such materials as were obtainable. In Western Europe, however, the number and variety of tools and instruments available to assist in production were greater than elsewhere, their adaptation to particular functions more complete in most cases. Technical achievements had already done something to improve living standards and thus to make it easier to set aside more and more for the purpose of raising the quantity and quality of the tools of production. This superiority of the West was not of long standing. Despite its notable achievements in the crafts as well as the art of building, its introduction of clockwork and the spinning-wheel, its numerous tiny watermills and windmills, it would be difficult to claim for medieval Europe a greater mastery of productive techniques than existed contemporaneously in the Oriental civilizations. But from at least the seventeenth century there had been in the West economic pressure for technical improvement, as the supply of some of the most essential industrial materials, especially timber, began to dwindle, and as the range of international commerce outgrew the supply of saleable goods. At the same time the conditions of intellectual enquiry and industrial practice were favourable to a marked technical advance. The immense gains in knowledge of physical principles in the Newtonian period, and the constant refinement in the accuracy of workmanship in many different crafts, those of the clock-maker and the millwright for example, all contributed to a condition in which multitudinous small but cumulative improvements were made in a large part of industry, especially, but not exclusively, in Great Britain. These improvements were not of a kind which completely transformed methods of production; but they prepared the way for more far-reaching changes which began to appear late in the eighteenth century.

On the whole, Western Europe throughout the eighteenth century was still, technically, in a handicraft era. Though handicraft production had been brought to an all-round level of efficiency never previously attained, everything was done on a very small scale and almost every finished article was, in some sense, unique. Because each workman could make only one thing at a time, the total volume of production was severely limited, its cost kept high. The characteristic which specially distinguished production in the ensuing period was the ability to turn out identical commodities in large batches, which caused enormous expansion and cheapening. This ability, which involved a drastic reorganization of the economic relationships of society, rested on fundamental technological changes which, with suitable adaptation, eventually permeated almost the whole of industry. The change was in part a matter of exercising greater ingenuity, such as had been done within the old handicraft system. When, for example, Hargreaves' spinning-jenny was adapted to function with a larger and larger number of spindles, that was a step (though a small one) in the direction away from unit production and towards mass production in the textile industries without destroying their handicraft basis.

But the main change was in the source and transmission of motive power, and this change necessitated the abandonment of handicraft methods. As long as the supply of power available was small and difficult to regulate, it was impossible for a workman to operate more than one machine at a time, or to keep in use large and elaborate machines that would turn out great quantities of goods. Up to the end of the eighteenth century the motive power for most operations was that of the workman himself or of some domestic animal. Other sources of power, notably the wind and swift-running streams had been successfully harnessed for particular purposes, but their action was apt to be irregular. The invention of the steam-engine and of a method of rotary transmission of its power remedied a great deficiency in productive ability. It enabled power to be applied in larger amounts than before, with much greater regularity, so that many machines could be gathered into one place and operated simultaneously from a single power unit, and larger, more complex machines could be devised without being hampered by the absence of anything both strong enough and sufficiently controllable to drive them.

The steam-engine alone did not, of course, effect a complete transformation of industry. Innumerable improvements were called for in the machines which it drove and in the hand tools which supplemented them. Indeed, the speeding up of production through the use of new or improved machines created fresh problems as fast as it solved old ones. The challenge to ingenuity which any productive activity always exerts was experienced in more various ways than ever before and found a response in the form of countless lines of rapid technical change. There was thus a cumulative process of technical development, and this was accompanied simultaneously by great changes in economic organization. It became increasingly common for production to be carried on in large units, with a larger proportion of the work done by power-driven machinery, and the power itself generated and applied by mechanical means; and all this involved the complementary change of greater division of labour. It is these developments (commonly but rather loosely summarized in the phrase 'the rise of the factory system') that, more than anything else, distinguish modern economic life from that of earlier periods. Their ultimate effect was tremendous, and almost universal, but their first stages were hesitant and narrowly localized. The production of the new machines needed knowledge, skill, and equipment which were scarce and could only gradually be augmented. The introduction of new methods and machines created problems which it took time to solve satisfactorily. The initial cost of transferring production from handicraft to mechanized methods was for long higher than the demand for most commodities could support. For all these reasons the victory of the new methods over the old was a protracted achievement.

6

How slow it was may be observed by surveying briefly the economic structure of some of the principal countries in the middle of the nineteenth century. A number of the most far-reaching inventions and discoveries had been made and brought into use in the eighteenth century: the steam-engine was already serving industry; power-driven factories had already begun to operate. But many years passed before these things became the commonplaces of daily life. The new mechanical techniques and factory methods of organization were at first confined almost entirely to Western Europe and the USA, and even within that area there was by 1850 no country in which they had come to dominate industry. Indeed, it was only in Great Britain and Belgium that they had then brought about a high degree of change in the national life. Great Britain was the pioneer and a portent for the world's future economic organization.

An industrial revolution in Great Britain, conventionally confined between 1760 and 1830, has become an established landmark in economic historiography. But closer acquaintance suggests that it may be such a landmark as serves to decoy rather than to guide. Our picture of economic development has been distorted by concentrating attention on too few industries. It would be truer to say that between 1760 and 1830 many of the essential foundations of an industrial revolution were laid in Great Britain, and that on a very limited part of them a notable structure was erected; but a large part of the building was left for completion later. This is not incompatible with recognition that in the seventy years after 1760 economic change was already proceeding much more rapidly than before.

The British industries which underwent an early transformation in technique and organization were characterized by the possession of large and expanding markets and by suitability to the application of power developed and transmitted in the new ways, though not every industry which fulfilled these conditions was affected. Iron, cotton and one or two other consumption goods, such as beer and pottery, and coal, the demand for which grew rapidly as the use of the steam-engine increased – these were the outstanding examples of commodities produced by new methods. But even in the production of these, change was not always rapid. Cotton-spinning and the finishing trades moved to the factories before the end of the eighteenth century, but only after the Napoleonic Wars did the power-loom in the weaving-shed make much headway, and its improvement was so slow as to permit the old hand methods under the putting-out system to carry on in painful competition for a generation. As late as 1834 there were still twice as many hand-looms as power-looms in the British cotton industry, which still also drew a quarter of its power from rivers and streams. Only after the eighteen-thirties was the hand-loom weaver driven by economic pressure out of the industry, and though in 1850 the cotton industry could stand forth as a triumphant example of the almost completely mechanized factory industry, it had only recently attained that position. The iron industry also had undergone a fairly comprehensive change, though many very small furnaces still existed. But some of the industries where steam power had been introduced very early and where a larger scale of production had been tried still included large sectors which were almost unaffected. Brewers, for instance, had been among the chief customers for the steam-engines of Boulton and Watt before 1800, but by 1850 the large power-operated brewery was still to be found only in London and one or two other large cities. Most of the provinces were served by large numbers of very small establishments and by the surviving practice of home-brewing.

The mechanized industries, few though they were in number, were of great importance in the nation's economy. The cotton industry, for example, was the mainstay of the United Kingdom's export trade. Throughout the eighteen-fifties, textiles (of which cotton yarn and cotton piece-goods formed an overwhelming proportion) constituted about 60 per cent (in terms of value) of the exports of all home-produced goods. Production for export was only a minor part of total economic activity, but even in terms of numbers employed, the mechanized industries were of considerable relative significance. In 1851 the textile industries employed 935,000 people in England and Wales, 11.1 per cent of the occupied population and, though many domestic workers were included in the figure, the majority must have been factory hands. Moreover, in this early stage of industrialization, mechanical progress was showing itself in the more rapid expansion of the few mechanized industries. In 1841 textile employees had formed only 9.1 per cent of the occupied population, and between 1841 and 1851 there had also been large proportionate increases in the numbers employed in metal-working and in engineering.

But when all this has been recognized, the picture that emerges from the figures of employment is not one of a country largely given up to factory production. Of the major groups of manufacturing industries in 1851 the one with the largest number of employees, apart from textiles, consisted of the clothing trades, which were completely untouched by factory organization. Nor had manufacture as a whole achieved an overwhelming place in economic life. By far the largest single industry in 1851 was agriculture, which in England and Wales employed 1,760,000 people, 20.9 per cent of the total occupied population. In Scotland the proportion was even higher, 22.7 per cent (299,000 people), but there the proportion engaged in manufacturing occupations was also higher, 36.5 per cent as compared with 32.7 per cent in England and Wales. In neither country did agriculture any longer outweigh manufacture as a source of employment, but, when the many home workers and tiny workshops have been considered, there can be little doubt that the farms employed more than the factories and the mines. As a source and store of wealth the land still retained its pre-eminence. It is probable that in mid-century, at current values, landed property and farm capital together formed about 40 per cent of the total capital owned in Great Britain. This cannot be attributed simply to agriculture having become one of the most technically advanced industries. It is true that many remarkable improvements in farming had been discovered, but in 1850 their adoption was only just becoming general.

Agriculture had undoubtedly increased its production very considerably during the preceding hundred years, partly as a result of improved methods, partly because it was using more land and more labour, without always departing very far from traditional practice. Something very similar was true of a large part of British economic activity. The level of production in the mid-nineteenth century was unprecedentedly high and its magnitude fascinated contemporaries. But in many branches the increase of production reflected little more than the increase in population: more people were doing the same things as before in very much the same way, though small new improvements continued to be introduced. In the production of a few items, however, including some which occupied a key position in the foundation of an industrial economy, it was because radically new methods had been adopted in a large proportion of the establishments that a far more spectacular expansion of output had been achieved and was still continuing. Between 1830 and 1850 the annual production of iron rose from about 700,000 tonnes to over 2 million tonnes. The annual output of coal, which was somewhere between 20 million and 30 million tonnes in 1830, probably rather more than doubled in the next twenty years; and the consumption of raw cotton, 122,500 tonnes in 1830, had been doubled by 1843, despite the severe depression of the early eighteen-forties, and went on steadily increasing. It is changes of this character that suggest an industrial revolution in progress. They were noteworthy at the time, though their influence should not be exaggerated. On a larger view their importance lies in the clear indication that they give of the direction in which industrial change was developing, rather than in the amount of difference they had made to economic life before 1850. Other happenings of the first half of the century helped to make clearer the trend of development. Though the factory system spread slowly, it did spread. Mainly between 1830 and 1850 worsted followed cotton into the factories, and an increasing proportion of the woollen industry was in factories, though in 1850 much still remained outside them. Once the factory system had established itself in any occupation it was not superseded. Moreover, the early nineteenth century saw the rise of one or two new industries which were conducted from the very beginning on lines unknown in any previous period, with heavy capitalization and a high degree of mechanization. The gas industry and the railway, which was advancing rapidly in the eighteen-forties, were probably the outstanding examples.

Elsewhere, though there were many signs of promise for the future of industrial development, actual performance was, by the middle of the nineteenth century, much less. Belgian industry, in the first half of the nineteenth century, developed on lines comparable to those of British industry. In this it was aided by both political and natural advantages, of which the most important was the possession of abundant coal, and by the presence of numerous British managers and skilled workmen, well versed in the new methods adopted in their own country. Some of the Belgian coal-mines were well established long before the nineteenth century, when the number of pits began to increase rapidly. By 1830 an annual output of 6 million tonnes of coal had been achieved, and such steam-operated factories as existed in other parts of the Continent were often dependent on Belgian coal. Some of them were dependent on Belgium for the supply of machines as well, for this was one of the very few regions where a thriving and skilful engineering industry grew up in the early nineteenth century. There appeared one or two large integrated concerns, combining coal-mining, iron manufacture, and machine-making, and there were also numerous smaller machine-shops. Nevertheless, there was still a substantial handicraft and agricultural basis to the Belgian economy, and the advance of some of the more modern activities was by no means smooth. Before 1840, for example, the output of coal was beginning to fall short of domestic requirements.

In any case, Belgium was a very small country to serve as the base for the industrialization of a continent. Outside it, however, continental Europe had little mechanized industry to show. Switzerland had made some early and rapid advances, especially in textiles, and, in proportion to its population, was probably the largest continental cotton manufacturer around 1840. But Switzerland, too, was very small and, lacking the mineral resources of Belgium, it did not yet make comparable progress in metal-working and engineering. Its abundant water power also discouraged early introduction of steam-engines. Some of the Swiss progress in textiles spread over the Austrian border into the Vorarlberg; but it was chiefly the developments in Bohemia and, to a rather less extent, in the adjoining provinces of Lower Austria and Moravia-Silesia which enabled Austria to become Europe's third largest producer of cotton yarn, a rather long way behind Britain and France. Here also, however, the same features were to be found. Equipment and methods had greatly improved since the mid-eighteenth century but were still much inferior to those of the British. Steam-engines were a rarity and progress was slow in metal working and slower still in engineering. There were other expanding industries, notably in the manufacture of food and drink, but there was nothing else which approached even the limited modernization of the textiles.

New machines and new methods were adopted in France by individual pioneers almost as quickly as in Great Britain, but their use did not spread rapidly. The very limited extent to which steam-engines were used is indicative of the slow rate of industrialization. Until about 1840 a steam-engine was an extreme rarity, and the larger numbers installed in the eighteen-forties seem to have been mostly of very small size. In 1830 there were in France 625 steam-engines developing an estimated 10,000 h.p.; in 1848 there were 5,200 of about 65,000 h.p. The main problem was domestic scarcity of fuel and the high cost of importing it, which meant that steam operation was much slower to offer the advantage of reduced costs than it was in Britain. The coal resources of France were small in proportion to its size, and considerable parts of them were still unknown in the first half of the nineteenth century. Though the output of the mines was increasing rapidly after 1830, it was still not much above 5 million tonnes a year by 1850.

There was, however, some development of factory industry and of large establishments using up-to-date techniques in France. The iron industry expanded steadily, but in the middle of the century its output was only about a quarter of that of Britain; and though there were a few large works with puddling furnaces and rolling-mills, the small charcoal furnace, found wherever wood was plentiful, remained characteristic. As in Britain, it was in the cotton industry that the factory system made most headway at first. In Alsace the spinning and weaving of cotton were adopted as entirely new industries in the early nineteenth century, and they very quickly came to be organized in factories, although they depended far more on water-power than on the steam-engine. In other, less important, cotton manufacturing districts also, numerous factories were established in the first half of the century, especially for spinning, but weaving was still generally carried out on hand-looms under the domestic system. The other textile industries were much less affected by new machinery and new forms of organization. The woollen industry expanded appreciably in the first half of the century, partly through the establishment of power-driven spinning-mills, but the other processes continued to be carried out by hand at home or in small workshops, and most of the industry remained in the control of large numbers of small merchant capitalists. In the silk and linen industries the use of power was scarcely known before the eighteen-forties, though during that decade it increased perceptibly. French industry as a whole underwent a gradual expansion in the first half of the nineteenth century, mainly, but not entirely, by continuing along well-established lines. In 1850 it was still manned largely by small masters and working craftsmen, a considerable minority of the latter being independent of any employer. Factories were far from typical, though their numbers were growing.

In Germany the story of the first half of the nineteenth century was one of even slower development. The natural resources suited to the encouragement of modern industry were greater than in France, but in many states the surviving legal and institutional obstacles to economic change, such as the burdens of serfdom and the exclusive rules of the gilds, were also much greater. Industry, almost without exception, was conducted on the smallest scale. In the towns the typical figure was the small master employing one or two workmen or, in many cases, relying entirely on his own labour. Though the proportion of wage-earners was slowly increasing, there remained more independent masters than apprentices and journeymen in Prussia in 1843. A great deal of such manufacture as existed was carried on in the countryside by a population partly dependent also on agriculture. Iron-making and the textile industries were to a great extent subsidiary employments of agriculturists, though woollen weaving was more often conducted by independent masters in the towns.

The steam-engine and the new techniques made only slight headway. By the middle of the century Prussia possessed only about a third as much steam-power as France, and though coal existed abundantly, it was not very extensively worked: the total Prussian output in 1846 was only 3,250,000 tonnes. From about 1840 there were important signs of change. New coal-mines were being sunk, mostly in the Ruhr field, and these were highly capitalized. A few large iron-works using methods comparable to those of British firms were established in the Rhine provinces of Prussia, and some of them extended their activities into engineering. The cotton industry was growing both in the Rhine provinces and in Saxony, and it included a few power-operated factories. But the cotton industry in 1850 still depended mainly on handwork, and most of it was organized in a putting-out system. Mechanical power and the factory system had by that time not made much difference to the basic structure of German industry.

They had had even less effect in the rest of Europe. As population increased, so did the number of workmen employed in traditional handicrafts. Many of these workmen were gathered into the small number of large cities, and many of them were employed on a wage basis by small masters. As their numbers grew, their strength and prominence increased, and in various places they were able to take a significant part in the revolutionary movements of the time. But they were not a factory proletariat. Metropolitan centres had long required a multitude of different crafts, many of which could not readily be superseded by mechanical methods. They still needed them and still possessed them in the middle of the nineteenth century; and the rural areas still met many of their basic needs through long-established handicraft methods.

In the United States of America, which was still only lightly peopled in relation to its vast area and thus did not yet outweigh the countries of Western Europe, the progress of mechanical power and the factory system before 1840 was little more striking than in France and Germany. Much of the manufacture that existed in the eighteenth century was carried on by households for their own consumption, though in some districts and industries the putting-out system existed in various forms to serve the market. America, which kept its colonial economy for a generation after it had achieved political independence, thus began the nineteenth century with less of an industrial tradition on which to build than Europe. Available capital, even in the less completely agricultural north, was more accustomed to go into land-purchase, trade, and shipowning than into manufacture. In the south, economic life was completely dominated by agriculture and the marketing of commercial crops. On the other hand, there were fewer industrial vested interests in any section of the country to resist the adoption of new methods of production.

A few textile factories were established before 1800 and others during the period of non-intercourse and the war of 1812, and steam-engines were being not only used but built before hostilities broke out. But many of the early factories succumbed to British competition immediately after 1815, and it was only in the eighteen-twenties that progress was resumed. Moreover, ·despite the early adoption of the steam-engine and its improvement by American inventors, American industrial expansion before the Civil War depended more on water-power than steam-power. Although the output of coal, which in 1820 was negligible, expanded enormously, it was far behind that of Britain, and in 1860 was still only about 14 million tonnes. In spite of this, the factory system made rapid progress in a few industries, of which cotton, as elsewhere, was the most important By 1840 the United States was the second largest cotton-manufacturing country in the world, but its output was only about one-third that of Great Britain. After 1840, the smaller woollen industry also began to transfer itself more rapidly to the factory. About the same time another of the basic needs of an industrial society, iron, began to be much more abundantly supplied as the small charcoal furnaces were superseded by larger furnaces smelting with mineral fuel. But in this field also the United States lagged behind Britain, and in 1860 its annual output of pig-iron was still not quite 1 million tonnes.

The United States before the Civil War was very far from being a highly industrialized country. Household production remained common, especially in the frontier regions. Manufacture was conducted on a small scale and played only a minor part in economic life. Even the largest industries could not compare with the largest British industries. But there were respects in which the American industrial development was specially significant. Though less in magnitude than contemporary British development, it was at least as varied. Much less than that of continental Europe was early American industrialization confined to small-scale copying of some of the leading British innovations. Mechanization and factory organization were beginning to be adapted in the United States in the mid-nineteenth century to industries which they had scarcely touched elsewhere, to the making of furniture and of watches, for example. Flour-milling, too, one of the chief American industries, was more fully mechanized than elsewhere, and meat-packing, though it used little machinery, was being conducted on factory lines at a time when in other countries it was almost exclusively a household or handicraft occupation. The small engineering industry also adapted itself to the special needs of the country, particularly in the production of agricultural machinery of a type superior to any in Europe. In the important field of communications, too, though American railways developed more slowly (relatively to the size of the country) than those of Britain, and depended on Britain for the supply of much of their equipment, yet in the uses of another major innovation, the electric telegraph, America was far ahead of Britain in 1850.

This demonstration of the way in which mechanization could be applied to new uses was, in its way, as significant a portent for the future as the British creation of some larger industries. But in 1850 the significance of both was more for the future than the present. Most American industries were unmechanized, most British industries were not large. Technical knowledge and methods of industrial organization were everywhere such as to limit severely the possibilities of economic specialization. The great contribution of mechanization was, in fact, to enable the basic material needs of mankind to be satisfied through the expenditure of a smaller quantity of the scarcer productive resources, thus releasing some of these for the production of new types of goods and of larger amounts of old types. When this ability was supplemented by easy exchange of the products of different regions, a great extension was possible in local specialization on branches of production in which local superiority was most marked.

Quite apart from the influence of the physical ease or difficulty of moving goods over long distances, there were close links between the powers of production and the extent of economic interdependence among different regions and countries. As long as its productive efficiency remained low, any community was likely to be able to afford only a small volume of purchases from outside. As long as this state of affairs persisted, most of its efforts must be put into the production of necessities, especially food, for local consumption. In the majority of places, if there were sufficient concentration of workers on agriculture, it was possible to provide for subsistence and something more out of local production, however monotonous, and even repellent, some local diets might seem to strangers.

But in few localities was self-sufficiency nearly complete. The need for buildings and manufactured goods, necessities as well as luxuries, gave rise to much trade, some of it over long distances. Even with handicraft techniques, fairly big differences in the cost and quality of product could arise in different centres of production, and essential raw materials were often widely dispersed. For many centuries before the nineteenth, international trade in woollen cloth had been an essential part of Europe's economic life, and the raw materials for its manufacture, dyestuffs and mordants as well as wool itself, were bought and sold internationally. Among other important raw materials timber was one of the chief commodities of international trade.

Even the supply of foodstuffs was dependent to some extent on an international market. National self-sufficiency in foodstuffs was made more difficult and less attractive by climatic factors which prevented the production of some goods in the regions where consumers wanted them. Among the items which, for these reasons, became of international importance was wine, in which France had long done a valuable export trade. Others were tropical and subtropical products that were required in temperate countries: cotton, sugar, tea and tobacco. Sugar, indeed, may have been the most valuable commodity of all in the world's trade in the eighteenth century. Complementary to such movements were those in the opposite direction which brought grain from the more temperate parts of Europe to various tropical colonies and to some of the Mediterranean lands. There was also some international trade in basic foodstuffs within similar climatic regions. The lands along the south of the Baltic, for example, had long made a livelihood from the export of grain, and even England had had a regular export of grain until the last quarter of the eighteenth century. But trade of this kind was of permanent importance to only a small proportion of the population in most places. Its purpose was mainly to make good temporary shortages, which always existed somewhere, and it went on (with minor exceptions) over fairly short distances.

A certain amount of international trade was thus quite indispensable. But, in proportion to the volume of its production, agriculture gave rise to much less international trade than manufacture did. As long as primitive techniques and low incomes dictated the universal predominance of agriculture among productive activities, the incentives to specialize were limited and the growth of international trade was retarded. But, as the powers of production increased with technical improvement, several related influences were released which all tended to increase economic interdependence more rapidly. Technical and organizational changes led to the expansion of manufacture not only absolutely but relatively to other branches of production; i.e. they stimulated most of all the activities which had always been most closely bound up with international trade. But, because they helped both to increase income and to keep a bigger population alive, the same changes made a more general increase in international trade very likely. More specifically, in the long run, they encouraged the international marketing of a bigger proportion of the world's output of food; for where improvements in manufacture had been carried furthest, as in Britain, the competitive superiority so attained fostered a degree of specialization that might impair the ability of home agriculture to keep pace with rising demand.

Before 1850 these influences, though very evident, had not attained their maximum. Most localities probably still provided the greater part of their necessities out of local production. But, especially after 1830, economic interdependence was obviously increasing rapidly, not only within nations but internationally as well. One rough estimate suggests that world trade rose from £280 million in 1800 to £380 million 1830 and to £800 million in 1850. Whether these figures are accurate or not (there are only imperfect data on which to base them), it is clear that a considerable part of the expansion arose because some countries were looking abroad for the supply of some of their necessities, while they themselves exported other essential goods of which they made an increasing surplus.

Changes of this kind had their repercussions beyond the regions which mechanization had directly invaded. In the seventeenth and eighteenth centuries, for instance, Britain was able to supply few commodities except bullion that were acceptable in large quantities in India, from which it desired so much. But in the nineteenth century it was able to build up a much bigger and growing merchandise trade, in which the export of cheap cotton goods had the central, but by no means exclusive, role. India, in turn, experienced losses of export opportunities previously available on a modest scale to its own handicraft cotton industry; but it was also enabled to develop other commodities for export and gradually brought into a more influential position in the world's trading system.

In the mid-nineteenth century a new economic order, based on increasing mechanization, greater division of labour and specialization of function, and more complex methods of organization, was coming into being, but was still in its early stages. A new economic order could function only through new institutions, most of which still remained to be devised. Technical and institutional change had in the short run often been very imperfectly matched. The French Revolution and its repercussions in some parts of Western Europe had had the effect of weakening or abolishing institutions which impeded industrial expansion: serfdom, which was the great barrier to the recruitment of an industrial labour force, the privileges of the gilds, which had a vested opposition to technical change. But this institutional change was not in many cases followed at all quickly by industrial expansion. On the other hand, such industrial expansion as there had been was often achieved in spite of, yet limited by, the absence of appropriate new institutions and laws: a banking system (as distinct from a collection of small, shaky banks of restricted function), a free labour market, the privileges of legal incorporation.

Only in Great Britain had there been by 1850 a fairly thorough reshaping of laws and institutions in such a way as greatly to facilitate the expansion of economic activity. Some of the institutions firmly established there, such as the stock exchange or the London money market, were especially appropriate, not only to British internal needs, but also to the service of a unified economy with international ramifications, which current events were already fore-shadowing. Elsewhere the more expansive industries still had to function in large part through the institutions of the old *régime*, while in a larger area there were no expansive industries at all. In the greater part of the world the local economic situation did not require any appreciable change in institutions. Rapid expansion was neither experienced nor expected, and there was little to offset the advantage of stability which was given by a fairly rigid control over economic activity. In much of Europe, serfdom still survived or was only just in process of termination. In the tropics and sub-tropics some of the small amount of Western enterprise depended on the not very adaptable labour of slaves. In countries of widely differing traditions, Russia or Japan or Java for example, the survival of communal rights over the use of land narrowly limited the scope of individual prac-tice. Thus agriculture, the world's leading occupation, was in general conducted within a framework of law, custom, and institutions which was inimical to rapid change; and manifold restrictions of many kinds, ranging from the almost total exclusion of European merchants by Japan to the surviving gild rules in Germany, severely restricted the development of other occupations. In a few areas the local development of industry made necessary the reshaping of ideas, laws, and institutions. In the rest of the world comparable influences were brought in from outside through commerce which was un-sought, but which proved to be inescapable. The framework of society changed, not because local needs changed spontaneously, but because new economic demands were imposed by a smaller but more highly developed area. The process of economic expansion and institutional and ideological readjustment was a continuous one. Its working out constitutes the main theme of the economic history of the last hundred and forty years and is still far from complete.

CHAPTER TWO

Technological progress and its diffusion

MANUFACTURING INDUSTRY

In the second half of the nineteenth century, economic changes, the beginnings of which were just discernible in 1850, became far more marked. In Great Britain, where agriculture and manufacture had been fairly evenly poised, the balance shifted decisively against the land. Yet, despite the great increase in manufacturing production there, the extensive use of the most advanced mechanical techniques ceased to be a near-monopoly of Great Britain. The USA, Germany, and, to a rather less extent, France, all turned increasingly to manufacture, adopted, and in some fields surpassed, the methods used in Britain, developed their own new types of product, and raised their total productive capacity to a level unprecedented in their own experience and unchallenged by the rest of the world. Some of the smaller countries, notably Belgium and Switzerland, which had been among the earliest to industrialize, had continued to build up their industry, widen its range and increase its efficiency. One or two others, such as Denmark and Sweden, were industrializing fast in the late nineteenth century. But in manufacture most of the rest of the world was still at a much lower level in 1900 than Britain, the USA, Germany and France. Several large countries, notably Austria, Italy, Russia, and Japan, could show the beginnings of industrialization, but their economic life was far less completely transformed. Bohemia was one of Europe's advanced industrial regions but the rest of Austria lagged behind the European average in industrial development. More striking still was the contrast in Russia. Though that country had a few advanced industrial regions, such as Moscow and its surroundings, and though these were responsible for very high rates of national industrial growth at the end of the nineteenth century, Russia as a whole nevertheless remained a poor agricultural country.

Yet the direct impact of mechanization was by no means confined to the small group of important manufacturing countries. The application of mechanical techniques to transport affected the greater part of the world by changing completely the accessibility of markets and raw materials and by spreading some branches of the engineering industry, on however small a scale, to almost all countries. Moreover, the much heavier concentration of even a small part of the world's economic resources on the output of manufactures was possible only because it was accompanied by a massive expansion of primary production, which was due in part to the use of machinery.

Throughout the second half of the nineteenth century the expansion of output depended both on the further improvement of productive methods in the established mechanical industries and on the introduction of more and more machinery into occupations which had previously been conducted by handicraft methods. The details and variety of technical improvement in the period are endless. But in some important respects the most influential change was the adaptation of certain basic technical devices to an ever-widening range of uses. The use of steam became the most characteristic feature of industrialization wherever it took place, and coal became the one great raw material the consumption of which was basic to nearly every branch of manufacture. The coal industry was therefore of growing relative importance and its output provides one of the most telling illustrations of the increase of industrialization. The

TABLE 1   COAL PRODUCTION, 1860–1913 (ANNUAL AVERAGES FOR QUINQUENNIA) (*million tonnes*)

Period	UK	France	Germany	USA
1860–4	86.3	10.0	15.6	17.0
1865–9	104.6	12.6	23.9	27.1
1870–4	122.6	15.3	32.3	43.8
1875–9	135.4	16.6	39.0	53.0
1880–4	158.9	19.6	52.1	90.1
1885–9	167.8	21.0	61.9	117.1
1890–4	183.2	25.8	73.2	155.8
1896–9	205.1	30.0	90.7	192.1
1900–4	230.4	32.3	112.5	285.5
1905–9	265.0	34.6	138.8	392.5
1910–3	275.4	39.1	168.6	476.6

N.B. The figures exclude brown coal and lignite

magnitude of the change is shown by the figures of output in the chief industrial countries.

The same point is emphasized by statistics of the amount of power developed, where they are available. In France, steam-engines developed 178,000 h.p. in 1860, 544,000 h.p. in 1880, 1,791,000 h.p. in 1900, and 3,539,000 h.p. in 1913. In the USA the total amount of power used in industry in 1870 was 2,346,000 h.p., of which probably about half was supplied by steam-engines; by 1900 the total was 10 million h.p., most of it developed by steam.

In another respect the expansion of manufacture in the later nineteenth century was marked by a feature characteristic of its previous development. This was the extensive use of iron, and notably the substitution of iron for timber, in both consumer and capital goods. But iron was being used in new forms and for new purposes. The invention of cheap methods of making steel was one of the major technological contributions to economic activity. The Bessemer process, which came into commercial use in 1856, was the first great advance, though its general adoption was for some time restricted by suspicions about its effectiveness and by high royalty charges. By the eighteen-seventies both this process and the Siemens open-hearth process, perfected in 1866, were making possible a large expansion in steel production. Still more influential was the discovery by Thomas and Gilchrist in 1878 of a means of adapting either process to the making of steel from phosphoric ore, which previously had been useless for the purpose. Effective use of the large Lorraine iron-ore field thus became possible, and Germany was enabled to build up the great steel industry which was one of the

TABLE 2   STEEL PRODUCTION, 1870–1929 (ANNUAL AVERAGES FOR QUINQUENNIA) *(million tonnes)*

Period	UK	France	Germany	USA	World
1870–4	0.5	0.1	0.3	0.1	1.0
1875–9	0.9	0.3	0.4	0.6	2.5
1880–4	1.8	0.4	0.8	1.6	5.6
1885–9	3.0	0.5	1.1	2.8	8.9
1890–4	3.2	0.8	2.8	4.4	13.0
1895–9	4.3	1.3	5.2	7.7	21.8
1900–4	5.0	1.7	7.4	13.6	33.2
1905–9	6.1	2.6	10.8	21.2	49.0
1910–4	7.1	3.8	15.0	27.0	66.0
1915–9	9.0	1.8	12.9	40.4	72.5
1920–4	7.2	4.6	9.0	36.7	68.3
1925–9	7.8	8.6	14.3	50.1	103.0

fundamental elements in its rapid industrialization. Cheap and abundant steel transformed the situation of the engineering industries. New constructional feats became possible and machinery could be designed for special purposes not previously contemplated. Steel made possible enormous widening of the range of goods which could be economically produced by mechanical methods. The rapid increase in its use is shown in Table 2.

It was not only in new uses of metal that the productive advance of the time was marked. Major developments were made in the application of chemistry to industry. Gas manufacture and the production of sulphuric acid in rapidly growing quantities had been noteworthy features of industrial growth in the first half of the nineteenth century, but later the scope of industrial chemistry increased enormously. New products of many kinds, including synthetic dyestuffs and fertilizers, and explosives of previously unequalled force, began to be manufactured in large quantities; and between 1900 and 1914 rayon production was commercially established and the new synthetic fibre became a significant competitor of silk. In all the chief industrial countries the chemical manufactures were of growing relative importance, but in Germany this was particularly so. By 1913 a quarter of the world's chemical output was produced in Germany.

Machinery and a larger scale of production on factory lines became more and more common in industries which had previously been only partially affected by them. Until about 1870, the most striking advances continued to be made in Great Britain. By that time the work of mechanizing the textile industries, which everywhere took an outstanding part in the early stages of industrialization, had been almost completed there. Elsewhere much still remained to be done, but there was rapid change before the end of the century. In 1875 nearly two-thirds of the cotton weavers in Germany were domestic outworkers, but twenty years later the proportion had fallen to less than one-quarter. The other textile industries, after clinging persistently to hand methods, were transferred to power-driven factories within the space of one generation. The change was especially rapid in the eighteen-nineties. In France, although the most technically advanced cotton factories, those in Alsace, were lost to Germany,. the industry resumed steady growth, and its mechanization was practically completed between 1890 and 1900. The other textile industries, except the declining linen industry, also underwent after 1870 a great increase in mechanization, which accelerated after 1890. In the United States the cotton industry had moved into the factories before the Civil War, and by the eighteen-seventies the same process was practically completed for the woollen and silk industries.

At the same time machinery was being introduced in various branches of production hitherto little affected by it. In some cases this had the effect of prolonging the existence or increasing the numbers of small workshops and outworkers. This, for example, was what the sewing-machine, produced by Howe in the USA in 1846, did for the clothing industry. But more commonly the results were that one more industry had to organize itself into larger units, and that an increasing proportion of its members became dependent wage-earners, much of whose work was merely repetitive. Crafts as diverse as those of the shoemaker, the locksmith, the cabinet-maker, and the compositor were all in part superseded because of new mechanical inventions made during the second half of the nineteenth century. Even the office began to be invaded by the machine when really efficient typewriters were put on the market in the eighteen-seventies. And without very startling mechanical innovations some of the commonest of household tasks, such as baking and the making of preserves, were, to a limited extent, taken away into factories.

For the time being, however, the spread of machinery and the factory system to such occupations as these was probably of less importance than the further mechanization and expansion of the small number of basic industries. Although the number of mechanized industries greatly increased, a very large proportion of total effort was concentrated in only a few of them. Wherever there was a large expansion of manufacture, the textile industries took a prominent part in it, though their share began to decline as the expansion proceeded. The relative importance of different manufactures changed as conditions of international competition and of demand changed, but the process was gradual, especially where years of unchallenged supremacy had enabled a few major industries to root themselves with exceptional tenacity. By the second quarter of the nineteenth century the British economy was already dependent on a few basic industries, of which the chief was cotton. That situation remained throughout the century. In 1900 the economy was firmly based on textiles, coal, iron and steel, and engineering. Other industries, including chemicals, the production of non-ferrous metals, and confectionery, were probably expanding relatively to the older staples, but not so rapidly as to challenge the dominance of the latter. Where the most rapid adoption of machinery came a little later, there was opportunity for the growth of industrial production to be spread over a wider range of industries, though both technical differences and the nature of demand favoured the special prominence of a few of them. In the USA in 1860 the six leading manufacturing industries (in terms of value of product) were, in order: flour and meal, cotton goods, lumber planed and sawn, boots and shoes, iron-founding and machinery, and clothing, including furnishing. By 1914, when a somewhat different classification was in use, the order had changed to: slaughtering and meat-packing, iron and steel, flourmill and gristmill products, foundry and machine-shop products, lumber and timber products, and cotton goods. At this time there were several industries not much smaller than the cotton manufacture which, before the Civil War, had been easily the most important apart from the agricultural processing industries, in which the contribution of manufacture to the value of the final product was small. Specially significant was the rise of some branches of the engineering industry. This was noticeable in every country where mechanized industry had been established for some time. Ability not merely to use but to make machines was becoming a characteristic of industrialization wherever it spread. In the USA this characteristic was more marked than anywhere else, as the application of machinery to manufacture was already carried to a higher degree than elsewhere.

The general picture of manufacture in the latter half of the nineteenth century is one of very rapid increase in the world's capacity to produce, but one in which that increase was largely confined to a very few countries. The ability to produce goods cheaply and in quantity by mechanical methods extended to many more commodities, but the main productive effort was concentrated on a small number of these, though this characteristic was becoming less marked. A rough quantitative expression of the extent of expansion can be given. Between 1870 and 1913 the world's output of manufactures increased more than fourfold; that of the USA was multiplied by seven, that of Germany by five, that of Britain doubled. In 1870, 79 per cent of the world's manufactures were produced in the UK, the USA, Germany, and France. By 1913 the proportion had fallen only to 72 per cent, though the relative amount of manufacture in the four countries had changed completely: the share of the UK had fallen from 32 per cent to 14 per cent, that of the USA had risen from 23 per cent to 36 per cent.

One consequence of this advance in manufacturing capacity was a large increase in incomes in the more industrialized countries. This, in turn, led to further great changes in their industrial activities in the years which followed. As productivity and incomes rose, the old basic needs of much of the population in manufacturing countries became more completely satisfied. But incomes were big enough to create valuable markets for new types of goods. At the same time continuous technical advance made it possible to meet many of these demands and indeed to suggest particular new channels into which a general demand for goods and services, which would improve the quality of living, could be turned. So in countries where economic activity had become most thoroughly mechanized, further industrialization was marked by less emphasis on the simpler basic manufactures, the production of a wider range of commodities (of which a large proportion were the products of increasingly complex manufacturing processes) and a relative (as well as absolute) rise in the amount of resources devoted to tertiary occupations, i.e. to transport, communications, professional services, and other activities which do not contribute directly to the production of goods. In other words, further advance in productive ability was in part applied in ways that did not add measurably to the physical volume of goods, and the increase of manufacturing output, taken by itself, was a less reliable guide than in earlier years to the degree of technical and economic improvement. Not only were some new needs met by the provision of more services rather than more goods, but some old needs were satisfied more effectively, not by an increased supply of familiar commodities, but by a supply, perhaps not significantly expanded in quantity, of new types of goods which fulfilled old functions more conveniently.

But at the beginning of the twentieth century most countries in the world had not achieved a level of income at which a very striking development along these lines was practicable. Even the simpler kinds of mechanized manufacturing industries had been established within their borders either not at all or only to a very limited extent, and the expansion of these types was the most prominent feature of industrialization in the early twentieth century outside the areas in which manufacture had already become dominant. When these simpler manufactures had become firmly established and had contributed to an increase of national income and a more abundant supply of capital at home, some of even the most recently industrialized countries were able to introduce also in rapidly growing amounts the production of more complex items in which the older industrial countries had kept their lead. In the nineteen-thirties the productive capacity of the USSR and of Japan was transformed in this way by the addition of large, heavy industries to a more primitive manufacturing structure.

There were many reasons why manufacture should have become more widespread in the first half of the twentieth century. In a world of ever closer international relationships, diffusion of knowledge, both of the material contribution made by manufacture to better living and of the technical basis on which that achievement rested, was swift. It was natural that non-industrial countries should wish to share in the material benefits of manufacture when they became aware of them, especially when the pecuniary reward for their own activities was increasingly uncertain. In an age dominated by wars and threats of wars on the largest scale, when the efficient conduct of war rested on a more and more elaborate economic basis, a high degree of industrialization was essential for any nation which wished to take a decisive and autonomous part in international politics.

Not only did non-industrial countries have strong motives for introducing manufacturing industries, but the older industrial countries in many cases assisted them in doing so. Earlier industrialization had been partly dependent on growing export markets in non-industrial areas, whose economic life gradually became accustomed to a regular supply of certain machine-made goods which came to be essential. As conditions changed, it sometimes became more profitable to invest further capital in the production of such goods locally rather than in commercial activity which would bring them in from abroad. Temporary diminution of foreign supplies because of war was one influence encouraging a change of this kind.

The industrialization which was sought for these various reasons was becoming more practicable over a wider area. Already by 1914 mechanical techniques had progressed a long way from simpler to much more complex processes. This was illustrated by the way in which a dominant role in the leading industrial countries was played first by textiles and agricultural processing industries, then by heavier industries led by iron and steel, and later by an ever more elaborately differentiated group of engineering industries. It might seem that this progression was making it harder for countries which had remained in a handicraft era to start copying the leaders, but for many of them it was not so. The much greater variety of manufactured goods created new opportunities of international specialization, with newly industrializing regions concentrating initially on some of the simpler types of product. And the recent advances of engineering had some simplifying effects. New machines made many processes more automatic than they had been and permitted the employment of labour with fewer trained skills. The cotton industry which Japan was building up in the early twentieth century was technically very

27

different from that which grew in Lancashire in the first half of the nineteenth. As time went on, the same sort of influence from building skills into the machine, and thereby lowering costs and reducing demands on the initiative and judgement of the operative, affected more advanced industries, including engineering, and assisted their wider diffusion.

Another achievement of the more advanced technology concerned the supply and application of energy, which was basic to all industrial expansion. The invention of new types of power-unit and their adaptation to different uses enabled manufacture to develop in places where it could not earlier have been conducted profitably. Coal remained the principal source of energy until well into the third quarter of the twentieth century, though the consumption of oil grew faster than that of coal. But the proportion of coal that was used directly for heating or steam-raising gradually declined, and industrial countries depended increasingly on electricity. In many ways the production and consumption of electricity became, after the First World War, a better indicator of economic advance than the statistics of the use of coal.

TABLE 3   ELECTRICITY PRODUCTION, 1920–1950 (*milliard kwh*)

Year	Europe	USA
1920	52.8	56.6
1925	79.9	84.7
1929	114.0	116.7
1937	171.5	146.5
1939	199.0	161.3
1948	248.4	336.8
1950	301.2	388.7

Yet, for various reasons, the potential for spreading industrialization over a much larger part of the world was only slowly turned into achievement. The years between the two world wars were financially disturbed and there were, consequently, checks to the growth of the market for new industrial products even in the most advanced countries. International trade was also seriously hampered, with the result that, for countries that might have set out on the path of industrialization, both earning power and the supply of outside finance were restricted. So, although world manufacturing output continued to grow substantially, much of the increase was still in the older industrial countries, despite their devotion of a rather bigger proportion of resources to non-manufacturing uses. This was particularly true of the USA which easily maintained its position as the leading industrial country, thanks to rapid expansion between 1914 and 1929, which counterbalanced the setbacks of the nineteen-thirties. The older industrial countries of Europe, however, failed to increase their manufacture as fast as the rest of the industrialized world, though they all achieved further growth. So there was some alteration in the international location of industry. The great changes arose from the continued rapid growth of industry in Japan and the implementation of intensive programmes of industrialization in the USSR after 1928. Japanese output of manufactures rose fivefold between 1914 and 1939. Expansion in the USSR is more difficult to indicate because the methods used at the time to compile official statistics almost certainly gave them an upward bias. The industrial output of the USSR at the start of the first five-year plan in 1928 may not have differed much from that of pre-war Tsarist Russia. Non-Russian estimates of subsequent growth differ appreciably, but three-and-a-half times to 1937 or four-and-a-half times to 1940 may not be too far out. The official figure of six-and-a-half times to 1940 is not credible.

The other main centres of spreading industrialization were in some of the smaller, partly industrialized countries of Europe. Between 1914 and 1939, for instance, Finland's industrial output nearly trebled and Sweden's more than doubled. But in absolute terms the figures were not big enough to alter the balance more than slightly. This was true also of some non-European countries which showed large expansions in percentage terms but were starting from too low a level of industrialization to have much effect on the global balance. The industrial output of India doubled. China, which at the end of the nineteenth century had been a major importer of cotton textiles, became in the nineteen-twenties a net exporter of cotton yarn and in the nineteen-thirties came near to an export–import balance in cotton piece-goods. But both these large countries remained overwhelmingly agricultural.

For the world as a whole, industrial output probably rose by about 80 per cent between 1914 and 1939, though the uncertainty of the Russian figures makes it difficult to be sure. This growth was somewhat slower than in the quarter century from 1890 to 1914. The change was attributable mainly to the slower progress of the larger European industrial countries and the inability of most of the rest of the world to seize more than a very small proportion of the opportunities indicated by technological change. The share of the USA, the UK, Germany, and France in the world total had dropped by 1939 to about 60 per cent, the percentage figures for each being roughly 35, 10, 10, and 5. But if the USSR, which also had about 10 per cent, is added in, the concentration of some 70 per cent of the world's industrial output in a very small group of larger countries was fairly similar to what it had been in 1914, except that the group had grown from four to five. And the circumstances of the Second World War gave only very limited assistance to further diffusion, mainly to non-European countries, notably Canada, which were already relatively wealthy without having been fully industrialized.

Despite the limited spread of industry, the continued growth was accompanied by structural changes which were a clear response to the progress of technology and the more varied demands which accompany rising incomes per head. Locational shifts were probably more striking within already industrialized countries than between nations. In these older industrial countries the emphasis generally was on more highly processed products, both capital equipment and consumer goods. These countries moved further away from the earlier dependence on textiles, though they by no means abandoned textile manufacture. But it was noticeable that, in the textile group, the pioneering of the established producing countries was in synthetic fibres and the mass production of clothing in factories (particularly marked in the USA), whereas the old staples, such as cotton yarn and piece-goods declined relatively. Thus the opportunities for new lines of international specilization did become reality. This was the main source of industrial growth for India and China and, until some time in the 'thirties, for Japan also. As late as 1929, 50 per cent of Japanese factory workers were in the textile industries. But Japan then went on to attempt much more in heavier and more complex industries, and thus provided additional illustration of the tendency to shift the lines of specialization after the simpler activities had established a large industrial sector in the economy.

This characteristic of industrial evolution ensured that industry continued to increase its dependence on the mechanical generation and application of power, which has already been illustrated by the rapid increase of electricity output in Europe and the USA, and on the building and use of machines for an ever-widening range of processes. One major associated feature was a growing need for steel, the principal material in almost all types of industrial and transport equipment. The slowness which most countries showed in establishing a steel industry of any size, despite its continually growing relevance to the creation of a modernized economy, is an indication of the difficulties encountered in industrialization in the interwar years. It is particularly remarkable that, outside the five main industrial countries, steel output on the eve of the Second

World War was only about 12½ million tonnes more than on the eve of the First.

TABLE 4   WORLD PRODUCTION OF STEEL, 1913–1950 *(million tonnes)*

	1913	1927–8	1936–7	1949–50
UK	7.8	8.9	12.6	16.2
Germany	14.3	17.4	19.5	13.3
France	7.0	8.9	7.3	8.9
Belgium & Luxembourg	3.8	6.3	5.8	6.1
Rest of Europe	6.2	7.4	8.2	13.3
USSR	4.2	3.9	17.0	25.3
USA	31.8	49.0	50.0	79.2
Rest of World	1.2	4.0	9.6	12.5
Total	76.3	105.8	130.0	174.8

N.B. The figure for 'USSR' in 1913 is for the Russian Empire minus Poland. That for Germany in 1949–50 covers both West and East Germany. All figures relate to boundaries at the date stated.

The full benefits of the technological opportunities apparent in the interwar years, especially in the USA, came to widespread fruition only after recovery from the Second World War was well in train. From about 1950 to the early nineteen-seventies industrial output in the world grew exceptionally fast as employment and market demand were sustained at rising levels in most countries. Though the older industrial countries were responsible for much of the growth, the number of countries that were appreciably industrialized increased much more rapidly than before, and the predominant character of industry became more and more what had been foreshadowed by the USA in the nineteen-twenties. For the most part, only countries that had recently begun to industrialize from a rather low level concentrated on textiles and other simple types of consumer goods. A few of these, with Hong Kong as a notable example, achieved a large and specialized output which replaced some of the production of the older industrial countries as the latter turned to manufactures requiring higher technology. And even some of the new industrial countries were gradually able to enlarge their repertoire, particularly as the complexities of making some more sophisticated goods were incorporated into the design of equipment with an automatically controlled sequence of processes. The chemical and engineering industries took a more and more prominent place in most of the advanced countries, and in some that were trying to catch them up. Synthetic materials, transport equipment (especially motor vehicles and aircraft), more elaborate and more differentiated industrial plant and machinery, and long production runs of an increasing variety of

31

durable consumer goods – all were established as typical elements in a modern industrial economy. The production and movement of all types of goods depended on a constantly growing quantity of machinery, capable, whenever required, of operating more continuously and often at higher speed. So the faster growth and wider spread of industrial output had to have as a major part of its base a much larger use of energy and of steel, with both of them more readily available to a larger part of the world than before.

Although there was a rapid adoption of the use of electricity for many purposes in the industrial countries in the interwar years, a good deal was in substitution for the direct use of steam and for animal and human power. The total increase in the consumption of energy was steady rather than spectacular. In Europe (excluding the USSR) it was probably only about 25 per cent higher in 1949 than in 1913. After that the increase was much faster and, though the absolute increase in energy consumption was greatest in the older industrial countries, notably the USA, the rate of increase was higher where industrialization had previously made good progress but was very incomplete.

TABLE 5   ENERGY CONSUMPTION PER HEAD, 1950 AND 1975 (*tonnes of coal equivalent*)

Area	1950	1975
World	1.00	2.06
USA	7.32	11.49
UK	4.36	5.46
EEC (members in 1975)	2.37	4.88
USSR	1.59	5.25
Japan	0.55	3.84
Latin America	0.34	0.85

Comparable trends, but with greater relative gains outside the former leading industrial areas, could be seen in steel production. In 1949–50 the four leading producers of Western and Central Europe, as shown in Table 4, together had an output of 44.5 million tonnes, and this had risen in 1970 to 119.9 million. But in the same period the output of the USSR rose from 25.3 to 115.9 million tonnes and that of all other European countries from 13.3 to 79.7 million tonnes. Before 1950 only the USA, the USSR, the UK, and Germany attained a steel output over 10 million tonnes a year. By 1970 such a level of output was almost commonplace. Not only these countries, but Japan, France, Italy, Poland, and Czechoslovakia exceeded it then.

Yet, in some ways, this was a response to the technological

creativity of the preceding generation as much as to that of contemporaries. There were signs of changing conditions in the sixties and they became much more apparent in the course of the seventies. In the wealthier countries the growth of demand was increasingly for services and highly sophisticated goods more than for bulky items incorporating large quantities of materials and demanding ever-increasing quantities of energy for their production. Energy itself became more expensive after 1970, so there was an economic incentive to be less profligate in its consumption. New lines of technological advance were becoming prominent, not only in research but in practical applications. Biological research was no longer seen as a contributor mainly to improved agriculture, but also to a variety of industrial purposes. Biological washing powders were probably the resultant product most familiar to a large public, but there were many other affected industries. The design and operation of waste-disposal plants and many branches of the pharmaceuticals industry provide examples. More pervasive in its obvious influence was the great development of electronics. Processes which had been regulated mechanically or by continual human intervention became precisely controllable by electronic equipment. Electronics provided the means of recording, storing, processing, retrieving, and transferring information on a scale, with a degree of elaboration, and at a speed all unknown before. Equipment for these purposes became more multifunctional yet physically smaller and more compact, and it consumed only small amounts of energy. Another line of technological advance came from the applications of nuclear physics, military, medical, and industrial. The most notable industrial use was the production of electricity. In this case the incorporation of heavy materials and the initial input of energy were very large, in order to obtain a many times larger output of usable energy, but here also operation and precise control of the plant permitted large economies in man power and energy.

Demand, costs, and technological innovation were thus working in the same direction in advanced countries and altering their economic structure. Major branches of technology were becoming common to industry, agriculture, transport, and services, with novel implications for existing lines of economic specialization. The increases in labour, materials, and fuel required for a given increase in the value of total output were apparently becoming smaller, and this meant changes in the nature and level of employment and in the relative size of industries. The basic industries of earlier economic growth were becoming rather less basic, or, at any rate, were having to share their basic position with others. As the nature of the most advanced type of economy was changing, so there were bound to be changes in the relations between the advanced countries and the rest. Some of the ingenuities of the new technologies were so deeply embodied in the equipment which resulted from them that operations could be simplified to the point of being readily transferable. But continuous progress in the new industries depended on such a sustained application of advanced knowledge that it was likely to be achievable only where there were the wealth, experience and equipment to support higher education, research and development on a large scale. Where progress in these fields was achieved, the results had such a widening variety of economic applications that it tended to be self-reinforcing. Thus it was hardly to be expected that there would be many large changes in economic leadership among the nations.

It was estimated that in 1981 a quarter of the world's total output (not just its industrial output) came from the USA, almost another quarter from the USSR and Japan, and rather more than 15 per cent from West Germany, France and the UK. That left only some 36 per cent for all the rest of the world, with the largest country, China, contributing less than 3 per cent of the global total. The relative rise of the USSR and Japan, especially since 1950, showed what could be accomplished in reshaping the international pattern, particularly with the aid of a very large population. The spread of industrialization and the stimulus it gave to other kinds of economic activity, and the widespread associated rise of productivity, established new and higher standards of consumption and production in much of the world. There were countries lumped together under the label 'rest of the world' which were in that category only because they had fairly small populations, and which had matched or surpassed in productivity the early industrializers. But nearly all of them were in Europe or were countries of European settlement. The great centres of nineteenth-century industrialization remained among the most advanced economic regions. Their achievements had spread to their neighbours and offspring, who had made their own contributions to further improvement. The USSR and Japan, first by emulation and then (especially in Japan) by their own originality, had carried the economic advance into new regions with different cultures. But most other countries, though their standards and expectations had been raised and their familiarity with modern techniques much extended, still had very different and much less productive economies. The obvious gap stimulated their aspirations to follow the same road as their predecessors and the third quarter of the twentieth century saw much movement along it. But in only a very few cases did the movement do much to lessen the gap, even where it brought noticeable improvement in absolute levels. And if further advances were to depend on new methods and new products, rather than on consolidation of the progress of the recent past, there were signs by the early eighties that the disadvantages of those who had not already gone a long way in modernizing their technology might be increasing.

AGRICULTURE

Though the growth and the increasing efficiency of manufacture were basic factors in the raising of living standards, this achievement depended also on complementary economic changes of a hardly less striking kind. Changes in the extent, technique, and organization of agriculture were fundamental. An increase in manufacture necessitated an increase in the quantity and variety of agricultural production to feed those workers who in earlier conditions would have raised most of their own food and had ceased to do so; to provide raw materials for manufacture; and to contribute, through a process of exchange, to an increase of consumption which new productive methods made possible.

Much of the required increase in agricultural productivity took place in the industrializing countries themselves. This was particularly so in the earlier stages of industrialization and again in the middle of the twentieth century. In the third quarter of the nineteenth century it was England, the leading manufacturing country, that was also held up to the rest of the world as a model of good farming. Some of the tributes paid to its agriculture were undoubtedly more fulsome than its achievement justified, but improved farming in this period certainly contributed a good deal to the raising of the standard of living of a considerable proportion of the population. British agricultural advance at this time depended on the concentration of land ownership in the hands of a small wealthy class, the members of which were willing to invest heavily in their estates; on the widespread adoption of new technical methods; and on the abundance of cheap labour. Concentration of land ownership had been increasing intermittently since the seventeenth century as a result of judicious matrimonial alliances, the existence of the law and custom of primogeniture, the widespread practice among the aristocracy of entailing their estates and making strict family settlements, renewed in every generation, and the investment of commercial fortunes in the land. The great enclosure movement after 1760 carried it to its peak by putting many small landowners in a position in which their choice lay between retaining an uneconomic holding and selling out to a wealthier neighbour. By 1873 concentration had gone so far that 1,688 people owned 14,200,000 acres of England and Wales; 40,400,000 acres of the whole 77 million acres of the UK were owned by only 2,500 people. A small part of these vast estates was farmed by the owners, but most of the area was occupied by tenants, in Great Britain usually with substantial holdings. The quality of agriculture, however, depended greatly on the landlords, because they provided all the fixed capital on their estates, and most of them exercised a fairly close control over the farming practices of their tenants.

Some agricultural improvements, through the adoption of new crop rotations, the greater use of root crops (especially potatoes and turnips), the practice of hoeing and drilling, attempts at scientific stock-breeding, and the reclamation of waste land, had been achieved in the eighteenth century, when their adoption was mainly due to some of the large landlords. But the evidence does not suggest that most of these improvements were in any way general. Enclosure was not accompanied by a large and universal change in the efficiency of English farming. But enclosure and, more especially, the extinction of communal control over farming practice, which accompanied where it had not preceded it, facilitated the adoption of new methods later. Knowledge and acceptance of new methods were diffused only gradually, but as experience sifted the genuinely improving from the merely odd, and as the size of the market increased, general changes were accomplished, especially between 1840 and 1880. At this time technical advances of new kinds were made and extensively adopted far more quickly than earlier discoveries had been. Besides many improvements in agricultural implements and machines, new methods of drainage were devised, and great advances were made in the application of chemistry to agriculture. British landlords spent large sums on drainage. In this they were assisted, after the repeal of the Corn Laws, by state provision for loans at low rates of interest; in thirty years these loans exceeded £12 million. But much was also provided out of landlords' own financial resources. The application of artificial fertilizers increased rapidly, and there was a steady extension of the use of farm machinery, most of it operated by horses, but some by steam. Only a few activities were mechanized, however. The large labour force, which was increasing in size until the eighteen-fifties and declined rapidly only after 1880, made it possible to obtain heavy yields from the land without a high degree of mechanization. Yet the total input to agriculture was unprecedentedly high, and it was this which made possible a high average output in proportion to area.

But however great the improvement of agriculture, it could not keep pace with all the demands of an industrial society in the same area. Britain was becoming more and more dependent on foreign food supplies at the same time as its home agriculture was making its greatest advances. Moreover, a point was soon reached at which foreign supplies could not merely supplement but could profitably replace much of the home production of some foodstuffs, especially cereals. In these circumstances British agriculture had to adapt itself to a more limited role while attempting nevertheless to remain profitable. The development of the country's own manufacturing economy was helping it to do this by contributing, through a general expansion of incomes, to the great growth of demand for those foodstuffs in which home farmers were at much less competitive disadvantage: dairy produce, fruit, and vegetables. By devoting more attention to these, by reducing investment and the labour force, yet using the diminished resources more carefully so as to maintain previous high yields per acre, and by heavily cutting returns to landlords (whose ability to put new capital into their estates and whose control over farming practice were both greatly impaired), British agriculture was, not without difficulty, successfully kept going.

Though many individual farmers suffered great losses, agriculture as a whole enjoyed moderate prosperity in the early years of the twentieth century. It was still possible, in an emergency, to obtain a greater yield from the land by putting more effort and capital into it, though government assistance was necessary in securing these additions, owing to the weakened economic position of landlords. In the First World War an appreciable increase in production was achieved in this way. Within a few years, however, agriculture had reverted to its pre-war condition, so that, for example, production of grain was once again less than one-fifth of consumption, instead of one-third as at the end of the war. The deterioration of Britain's international trading position in the nineteen-thirties prompted some encouragement to the expansion of home agriculture through the assurance of minimum prices and the grant of subsidies for some commodities and the partial reservation of markets through tariffs and quotas. But

37

it was only the needs arising once again from world war, and afterwards a change in international competitive conditions as the cost of buying food elsewhere rose rapidly, that led to any significant expansion. Once more, with the aid of much government financial assistance, there was a marked increase in input, both of labour and, more especially, of capital, as British agriculture became one of the most highly mechanized in the world; and output increased greatly, although Britain remained heavily dependent on production in many parts of the world for the supply of most of its foodstuffs.

In no other country was there an equally sharp transition from a rapid expansion of home agriculture to overwhelming dependence on cheaper expansion elsewhere. But fundamental problems of food supply similar to those experienced by Britain arose in many other places, and the new opportunities of production and sale arising from industrialization affected agriculture in most parts of the world.

The need to increase agricultural productivity in some European countries as population and manufacture increased in the nineteenth century could be and was in part met by copying and adapting English technical improvements, though not the English agrarian system. Land reclamation (particularly important in France in the second half of the century), the introduction of chemical fertilizers, the use of more numerous and better designed farm implements and machines, better stock-breeding, new methods of checking plant and animal diseases, all made great contributions to the expansion of farm output. Enclosure and consolidation of scattered holdings, which are often erroneously regarded as the foundation of English agricultural improvement, were clearly less important. In both France and Germany, physical enclosure went on only very slowly, consolidation of holdings only a little less so, but the decline in communal use of land and communal control of crop rotation was quicker, and institutional obstacles to technical innovation greatly diminished towards the end of the nineteenth century. Home agriculture in most European industrial countries was sheltered by tariffs from the severest competition which developed after 1870, and succeeded in meeting a large proportion of the increasing home demand for food. Indeed, where, as in France, the country did not divert most of its resources to secondary and tertiary activities, it was able to remain practically self-sufficient in food supply. But where industrialization was carried further, the output of home agriculture and the demand for imported food increased simultaneously.

Much of this imported food came from comparatively close at hand, partly because of the saving in transport costs, partly because various regions deliberately adapted their agriculture to supply the new needs arising in their more highly industrialized neighbours. Because industrialization led to a reduction in self-sufficiency, it completely transformed market conditions for agriculture over a very wide area. Although the rapid growth of manufacturing was confined in Western Europe to a very few regions in the second half of the nineteenth century, it stimulated a great increase in the commercialization of agriculture throughout most of Central and Western Europe and parts of Eastern Europe as well.

The production in this area of a large surplus of food for sale was achieved in an institutional setting which had arisen quite independently and was not specially adapted to this purpose. The forms of agrarian organization were mainly determined by the arrangements which had existed when serfdom was in force and by the relative political strengths of the various rural classes at the time of emancipation, which was taking place in various parts of Europe from the late eighteenth to the end of the nineteenth century. In post-feudal Europe in the later nineteenth century, though there were innumerable variations of detail, two principal land systems had emerged: peasant proprietorship of small farms, and large estates cultivated by their owners with hired labour. Peasant holdings were for the most part the successors of what had been held under servile tenures in the feudal system; the great estates were the successors of the feudal demesnes. But in the course of emancipation in some countries, France for example, the peasants were able to increase their holdings from demesne lands; in others, including Prussia and Russia, the lords' estates were increased by compulsory cessions of land by the freed serfs. After emancipation, most of the land in Western Europe belonged to peasants, and most of the great estates were in Central and Eastern Europe, though there were parts of Spain, southern Italy, and Sicily where these predominated, and there were large parts of Central and Eastern Europe in which peasant ownership prevailed. After the great continental empires had collapsed in the First World War and the balance of political power had changed within their former territories, peasant proprietorship was further extended by breaking up the great estates, so that by 1930 Hungary and western Poland were the only parts of Central and Eastern Europe where these still predominated.

Some large estates, while they were still feudal demesnes, had been organized to supply a national or international market; those of East Prussia were of considerable importance to international trade long before the nineteenth century. But peasant holdings in most places were not accustomed to supply more than a small surplus for a local market. Yet in the late nineteenth and the twentieth centuries peasant agriculture was making a major contribution to the feeding of industrialized Europe. The opportunity was there because the agriculture of the regions closest to the growing industrial markets was mostly in the hands of peasants. The farmer's own family provided sufficient labour; emancipation had provided land, and the growth of industrial employment and of emigration prevented the necessity for subdividing holdings. The real problems were whether the expense of introducing improved methods of farming could be recovered from a smallholding, whether knowledge of such improved methods could be thoroughly diffused, and whether the finance which their introduction involved could be obtained on reasonable terms. In Western Europe all these problems were solved.

The relation of technique to scale did not for a long time involve very great difficulties. Most of the greatest improvements in farming productivity did not call for great additions of indivisible capital equipment which imposed overhead charges needing to be spread over a very large output. Innovations of this kind were more important, however, in processing, and there the problem of expense was overcome by co-operation. This had its greatest development in Denmark which, from about 1880, transformed its economic life in order to take advantage of the industrial areas' demand for dairy produce. Between 1880 and 1909, 3,600 agricultural co-operative societies were founded in Denmark. They were concerned not only with the production of butter and bacon and the packing of eggs, but with the purchase of supplies and the shipping and sale of produce, thereby effecting a great saving in overheads for the individual farmer. The Danish achievement in co-operation served as a model for much of the rest of Europe, and in the opening years of the twentieth century the number of co-operative societies was growing very rapidly in almost all peasant communities which were in easy contact with industrial markets.

Experience of co-operation was one factor helping to spread knowledge of the best productive methods. Other privately organized societies contributed to the same end, and so did the activities of governments in providing not only schools of agricultural education but also the means of more general education on which the success of any technical training must rest. Co-operation also played a large part in making it possible to finance agricultural improvement. In Germany, various types of co-operative bank were developed in the nineteenth century, the most influential being the Raiffeisen village banks, first formed in 1894, and subsequently copied, with local adaptations, in many parts of Europe, Asia, and Africa. The essential feature of these banks was that all their members pledged all their possessions as security for the banks' solvency. The banks were able to raise a certain amount of capital by borrowing, and this, together with deposits received and any share capital (the earliest German examples had none), provided a fund from which loans at reasonable rates of interest could be made to reliable members for sound schemes of improvement. Co-operative banks of this kind, operated very cheaply by honorary officials, proved extremely successful, and for innumerable farmers made possible the first steps towards more intensive production. Once some intensification had been achieved and more produce had been put on the market, the resultant increase in income made easier the accumulation of capital for further improvement.

All these changes helped to make it possible in the twentieth century for intensive farming on family holdings of not more than about fifty acres, with fairly high capitalization in proportion to area and a small amount of hired labour, to be firmly established in many parts of Western Europe, including the rural areas of the more industrialized countries. Farming of this kind supplied a large and increasing part of the food requirements, chiefly of dairy and livestock products, of the industrial regions. Denmark, the Netherlands, and Switzerland, in particular, established prosperous agricultures of this type, appreciably dependent on export markets, and providing the rural population with relatively high living standards.

Peasant farming in Europe made much less contribution to satisfying the industrial regions' rising demand for grain. Most of the cereals grown on small farms were consumed locally. But during the nineteenth century the great estates of Eastern Europe, especially in Hungary, Romania, and Russia, made a larger and larger contribution to the international grain trade. From about 1880 the expansion of exports was particularly rapid, and on the eve of the First World War Russia and the Danubian countries were supplying over 26 million quarters of wheat per year to the rest of the world, more than 40 per cent of the total amount of wheat traded internationally. The increase of production was probably attributable not so much to improved methods and equipment, though they had their part, as to the more intensive application of labour which the growth of population, without a corresponding increase in alternative means of employment, made possible.

The breaking up of the great estates after the First World War led to a large increase in the proportion of produce consumed locally and a corresponding diminution of the supplies which this region put on the international market. In much of the area, arable farming predominated, and the rate of capital accumulation was very low. Because of this, and because the development of more expensive machinery offered greater efficiency, doubts arose as to whether new demands which grew later as a result of increased industrialization nearer home could be satisfied by peasant farmers.

In the USSR, where uniformity of soil conditions over large areas made the advantages of mechanization specially great, the assumption was made that they could not. The problem that posed itself there with the adoption of the first five-year plan in 1928 was to increase output per man in agriculture, so that more labour might be put into manufacturing work and more food made available. This was needed both for consumption in the growing industrial regions and for export as a means of payment for some of the essential equipment of industrialization which had to be imported. The answer was sought in collectivization, which was extended much more quickly than had originally been intended. Between 1929 and 1934, 18 million peasant farms were organized into 250,000 collective farms using up-to-date machinery.

At first the experiment was a failure in economic as well as human terms. The peasants resisted collectivization both passively and actively, especially by slaughtering great numbers of their farm animals rather than hand them over to the new collective farms. The required surplus for the market could not be obtained from increased output and was sought instead by using tighter organization to press down the amount of the peasants' own consumption, at times to near starvation level. Gradually things improved, though much less than was suggested by contemporary official statistics. Much labour was released for work in industry and, partly because the agricultural population had been so huge as to encourage its wasteful employment, this loss was offset by greater output per man among the remainder. But further progress was hampered because investment in agriculture was subordinated to that in industry. The livestock losses of the early days of collectivization were not fully replaced during the nineteen-thirties. A later official index of production, which appears to be uninfluenced by the political inhibitions that determined the form in which statistics were presented at the time, shows (with 1913 as the base year) a decline in livestock output from 129 in 1929 to 119 in 1939. The corresponding index for crop production rose from 116 in 1929 to 125 in 1939, but even for crops the physical yield per hectare, though it had revived appreciably in the thirties, was still a little below the level of 1913. To ensure the supply of urban needs the government therefore continued to keep consumption by the farm population at a very low level. This, in turn, minimized the incentives given to those in agriculture and helped to keep down farming efficiency. Twenty years of such policies, together with wartime losses, left agriculture in a condition in which it was becoming increasingly hard to keep pace with the needs of industry and the towns, even though output and productivity had risen absolutely. After 1953 the agricultural population was encouraged by reductions in compulsory levies, wage increases and very great increases in the prices paid for farm products, while investment and the cultivated area were expanded more rapidly than before. As a result, despite some serious failures (for example, in the output of the new lands) agricultural production appears to have risen fairly fast for a few years, the figures for grain, milk and meat production in 1960 all being more than 50 per cent above those for 1953. But the growth of output was soon checked again and still lagged behind industrial needs. Even in the late 'seventies and early 'eighties an adequate food supply still required large imports, particularly of grain. Thus the economic achievements of collectivization were not very impressive. Nevertheless, when, after the Second World War, there was the same problem of increasing food output in other parts of Eastern Europe in order to assist industrialization, a solution was sought by somewhat similar means. The motives were no doubt political and ideological. The economic results were mixed, but in many places they appeared to have a good deal in common with those of the earlier stages of Russian collectivization.

Internal colonization and intensification of farming enabled the old lands of Europe to meet many of the increasing needs of industrialization, but by no means all of them. There were for the first time both the need and the means to bring into use the great fertile spaces, hitherto almost unoccupied, of the USA, Canada, Brazil, Uruguay, Argentina, Australia, New Zealand, and Siberia. Here the problems were quite different. There was no need to seek means of wresting the utmost yield from a limited and crowded land. For most of the nineteenth century, land was so abundant in these countries (except in so far as its supply was restricted by government ordinance, which was not normally to any serious extent), that neither its cost nor the need to maintain its fertility was a major agricultural consideration.

What was sought was some means, other than a large labour supply, of securing what the land would yield with a suitable minimum of human guidance.

The methods adopted varied greatly according to natural conditions, the accessibility of markets, and the extent of settlers' resources. Even in these new areas the first settlers on any frontier could usually do nothing beyond providing for their own subsistence. But where there were good natural communications and as artificial communications were extended, specialization became possible. In areas of much open land and few settlers, in contact with more populous regions, one possibility which became increasingly attractive as the industrial areas' demand for wool, hides, and meat expanded, was extensive livestock-raising. In Australia, for example, the earlier nineteenth-century areas of settlement were near the coast and were characterized by much large-scale sheep-farming which was gradually pushed into the interior by cattle-ranging. As settlement increased, this in its turn was replaced in some regions by arable cultivation, and the cattle rangers moved north to other coastal districts and parts of the interior. There was a great abundance of land, and very large tracts could be leased for a trifling sum – the nominal rent was often only about £1 per square mile per year and, in the absence of accurate surveying, it might in fact be much less than that. In these conditions it was possible for large flocks and herds to be kept on a semi-nomadic system. Once a few permanent settlements with regular communications had been established, this system could be, and was, operated over a very wide area, because cattle rangers maintained their own communications on horseback and animals could be driven long distances on the hoof.

Similar conditions led to extensive ranching elsewhere. In North America it had existed near many of the fringes of settlement in colonial times, and in the first half of the nineteenth century it increased considerably, especially in Texas. Its greatest development came in the twenty years after the American Civil War. The lands beyond the Mississippi were then becoming better known, but permanent settlement of the west was only just beginning; the American market was rapidly expanding, and the westward movement of the railheads and the meat-packing industry helped western cattlemen to keep in touch with it. From western Texas to the Manitoba boundary a great open stretch of land, costing no rent, was available for cattle ranging, and a single herd could wander over huge tracts. In Texas in the eighteen-seventies one rancher had the run of 4 million acres on which to keep 225,000 cattle. Farther west, on more arid lands, there was considerable sheep-farming by squatters with large flocks roaming over wide areas. The end of this system came with the increase of permanent settlement, when squatters' lands were occupied by others and gradually brought under cultivation, and the invention of cheap barbed wire made it easy to confine ranging cattle to a smaller and smaller area. But under more settled and defined conditions, much large-scale livestock-raising still went on in the USA. In various other parts of the world, notably Argentina, Uruguay, and Brazil, it was extending rapidly at the end of the nineteenth century, and industrial Europe became dependent on them for a considerable proportion of its meat supply.

The new lands also contributed much to satisfy the industrial regions' demands for grain from about 1870 onwards. The earliest important new sources of supply were the Canadian prairies and the trans-Mississippi lands of the USA. The settlement of the American West in the last third of the nineteenth century went on in conditions which permitted specialized production from the outset. Railways were already open, and farmers were in touch with the rapidly growing markets of the eastern states and, beyond them, those of Western Europe, which were as important as the home market until the end of the nineteenth century. In the northern states of the American West, and in the Canadian provinces over the border, there was specialization in wheat production from the beginnings of substantial settlement. Immediately to the south, specialization was directed to the cultivation of maize for stock-raising.

It was where there was large arable cultivation, with a limited labour supply and easy access to valuable markets, that mechanization made its greatest contributions to agriculture in the latter half of the nineteenth century. Primary attention was given to economy in the use of labour, and most serviceable of all were machines which reduced the need for human labour at times of peak demand, such as harvest. Though effective reaping and threshing machines had been introduced in the first half of the nineteenth century, they were nowhere in general use in 1850. In the next half-century the mechanization of agriculture was greatly extended. Reapers were supplemented by binders, and before the end of the century reapers, binders, and threshing machines together were developed into effective combine-harvesters. New machines were invented for planting and harrowing and for all the operations of haymaking and stacking. In the USA, above all, very great use was made of these inventions. The value of farm implements and machinery there increased from $246 million in 1860 to $761 million in 1900, and $1,265 million in

1910. In the twentieth century it soon became possible to bring mechanical power on to the farm. Horse-drawn machines were replaced by others driven by petrol engines, and the use of electricity enabled more tasks, especially within the farm buildings, to be given over to machinery. The increase of mechanization continued. In the USA the value of farm machinery reached $3,600 million in 1930, and there was a rapid growth in the twentieth century in the use of machinery in every leading agricultural country. It contributed much to a great increase in the productivity of agricultural labour, which in the USA was estimated to have quadrupled (in terms of net ouput per man-hour) between 1869 and 1955.

The introduction of extensive agriculture into enormous unused areas of land was perhaps the most important factor of all in enabling the world to support a population which doubled in a century, while a smaller proportion of the total was directly engaged in food production. But though on balance there was an enormous gain in output, there were some losses to be set against it. Some land which had been potentially a permanent source of production was made to yield for a time and then left incapable, temporarily at least, of producing more. The great abundance of land in new countries with a moving frontier tempted many men to use it wastefully. Successive exhausting crops were taken off it with no attempt at a scientific rotation and without adequate application of manure or other fertilizers. Other activities on the land, such as rapid deforestation with no replanting, also contributed to declining fertility in some regions. The extent of such damage in the world as a whole is a matter of much doubt and controversy. In the USA alone investigation in 1930 suggested that, in a crop area of 413 million acres, 35 million acres were unfit for further cultivation, and a further 125 million acres had suffered some decline in productivity through loss of topsoil. Though there can be no question that what was done to change the nature and extent of agriculture enormously increased the world's capacity to meet its increasing basic needs, it is clear that the way in which it was done prevented the improvement from being as great as it could have been.

Neither the more intensive use of land near to the new manufacturing regions nor the agricultural settlement of the empty, fertile lands in temperate latitudes was sufficient to meet all the demands which a manufacturing economy made on primary production. A greater contribution than before was sought from the tropical and subtropical regions. The few commodities, such as sugar, tea, and tobacco, which they had formerly supplied to Europe in significant quantities, were in much greater demand as population and the average level of incomes rose. A widening range of manufacture was necessarily dependent on a supply of raw materials which were entirely new or had previously been little used. Early in the nineteenth century raw cotton was becoming one of the chief commodities of international trade. A hundred years later rubber was achieving comparable importance, though by that time it was becoming unusual for industry to take up new agricultural raw materials, and in the mid-twentieth century rubber began to be partly replaced by synthetic substitutes. Rising incomes led also to a demand for a more varied food supply, which was partly met by tropical production. Former luxuries, such as coffee and cocoa, became articles of mass consumption. Exotic fruits, such as the banana and the pineapple, which until well on in the nineteenth century few people in Western Europe had even seen, came in the twentieth century to be shipped there by the million.

Many of the economic problems which had to be overcome in securing an adequate output from tropical regions were fundamentally the same as existed for agriculture elsewhere, but they manifested themselves in different forms. One difficulty was that, as in many temperate regions, much good land was underutilized or left entirely to nature because of lack of labour. But this could not be easily remedied by attracting from surplus populations elsewhere free settlers with sufficient possessions and knowledge to make effective use of the land. The solution in the limited amount of tropical colonial agriculture in the seventeenth and eighteenth centuries had been to import and breed slaves and employ them under white supervision. But, in the raising of some tropical crops at least, slavery was a costly and inefficient system; by the end of the eighteenth century the experience of both Virginian tobacco planters and West Indian sugar planters was showing the difficulty of maintaining the productivity of slave labour at an economic level. A suggested solution was an increased used of machines, and where, for a key operation, something very simple could be devised, great improvements resulted. Whitney's cotton gin, invented in 1793, was the outstanding example of such a contribution, specially valuable because it could be operated by mechanical power. But suitable labour-saving machinery for use in raising many types of tropical crop was difficult to devise and made demands on the skill of those using it to which most slaves were unequal. The increased use of machinery ultimately made an important contribution to the output of tropical agriculture, but the usual result of early nineteenth-century experiments in greater mechanization was that the machines suffered more than the crops benefited. For most of the nineteenth century the old-established tropical regions of European enterprise had to rely mainly on the use of more efficient and more abundant labour. Slavery gradually gave way before the combined pressures of its own economic inefficiency in some of its traditional tasks and of stronger humanitarian feeling. Slave labour was supplemented or replaced to a great extent by other labour brought in from outside (above all from China) under contract for a specified period, and subject to rigorous supervision and to criminal conviction for breach of contract. The degree of success which old areas had in maintaining or increasing production, as conditions of marketing and labour supply changed, varied greatly. Among the British Caribbean sugar colonies in the second half of the nineteenth century, Trinidad and British Guiana expanded their output considerably, but Jamaica did not, and remained in a state of economic stagnation and distress.

On the whole, the increased supplies which were required from the tropics were obtained to only a small extent from the old colonies. A more important contribution came from bringing large new areas into production. Shortage of labour and a desire to economize in capital investment both contributed to attempts to make fuller use of what was provided by nature. In the late nineteenth century various European trading companies obtained very large concessions, notably in tropical Africa, either from their own governments or from native chiefs, and within the areas thus conceded secured whatever was naturally available and readily marketable by inducing or compelling the natives to collect it. But this system made no contribution whatever to productive expansion, rather the reverse. It was economically inefficient, and could not keep pace with the growing demand for tropical produce, because it did nothing to modify the subsistence basis of the local economic life and to widen the range of commodities available. It also created political and social frictions which brought it into increasing disfavour as experience brought changing views of the function of colonial administration. For these various reasons its use rapidly diminished in the first half of the twentieth century.

Far more important economically was the spread of European agricultural enterprise. This was achieved mainly by the establishment of plantations in hitherto uncultivated areas, through the use of Western capital and supervision and large quantities of local or imported coloured labour. In many ways, such as their dependence on a large labour supply and the sources from which and terms on which it was recruited, the plantations in new areas resembled those in old colonies. But the modern plantation was unhampered by the traditions and the debts of the earlier system, and, though individually many ventures failed, the extension of plantation agriculture to new regions led to a great increase in output. The contributions which the plantations made to agricultural improvement were of many kinds. The difficult and expensive work of clearing large areas for agricultural use for the first time was one; it was work which needed more capital than was available locally. Another was the introduction of crops which were entirely unknown locally, but which were in increasing demand and could conveniently be grown there. The creation of the great Asiatic output of rubber in the twentieth century, for example, was due to the pioneering work of plantations, even though small native producers soon came to supply an appreciable part of the output after the plantations had demonstrated the value of the crop. It was not until 1877 that the rubber tree was introduced to Malaya, and not until just after 1900 that it began to be planted there on a large scale. But it quickly began to replace the local food crops, for which imports were substituted, and by 1938 nearly two-thirds of the total crop area was under rubber trees. The rubber tree was similarly introduced by plantations to the Netherlands East Indies and French Indo-China, and the three countries established themselves as the main sources of the world's rubber supply.

Some plantations played an important part in the introduction of more intensive production through the use of better farming methods, higher-yielding plant strains, and more machinery, not merely in cultivation, but more particularly in the preliminary processing operations performed on certain crops, notably sugar, tea, and sisal, soon after harvesting. There were increasing incentives for such intensification. By the second quarter of the twentieth century the indignities associated with the recruitment of contract labour had led to the imposition of restrictions on it in the chief sources of supply, and a number of plantation areas found cheap labour less plentiful than before. Others, of which Java was the outstanding example, were in a situation where the local population had expanded so much as to limit severely the amount of land available for use by plantations. In both cases it was necessary to seek technical improvements to maintain yields, although less of one of the chief factors of production could be used. On the whole, the technical problems thus posed were effectively solved; sometimes, perhaps, too effectively: the sugar production of Java in the nineteen-twenties underwent such technical improvement as to contribute a good deal to the temporary glutting of the world market.

The intensification of cultivation was something which native producers also in many countries began to be encouraged to achieve in the twentieth century, although earlier their methods of farming had been nobody's concern but their own. In many tropical areas, especially in Southeast Asia, the size of the population grew rapidly under colonial rule, and merely in order to maintain current standards of local consumption it was becoming impossible, as the supply of unused land diminished, to continue reliance on traditional extensive methods of shifting cultivation under which land, once abandoned, was often exposed more to the destructive than the restorative influences of nature. Moreover, as the economies of colonial areas became more commercialized, there was increasing need for native farmers to produce a surplus above their own subsistence needs, either directly for export or else for sale to those who were engaged entirely in production for export. It became part of the policy of many colonial governments to demonstrate new techniques to native farmers and encourage them to use them, to help them to obtain better strains of seed, and to assist them to grow new commercial crops. In various cases also native producers took up spontaneously the cultivation of crops introduced to their vicinity by plantations. It was particularly easy for them to do this where it involved only the planting of a few trees which required little attention and made no serious encroachment on land used for raising subsistence crops. Peasant production for the market, in fact, underwent a great expansion in the tropics in the first half of the twentieth century. By the nineteen-thirties the only important tropical crops in the supply of which peasant farming had no appreciable share were tea, coffee, sugar, bananas, and sisal, which were difficult to produce and sell without an amount of capital beyond the reach of peasants. There were some crops, for example cocoa, the overwhelming proportion of which was supplied by small native producers. The rest of the world had become more dependent than before on tropical supplies. The enterprise and technical improvement which were needed in order to create them came from outside, from the industrial and commercial regions in which the demand was concentrated. Much of the necessary labour was also imported. But an increasing contribution came also from the more effective application of the human resources of the productive areas themselves.

These features of tropical agriculture show how it had maintained a place in a system of international specialization and trade. Much of this continued without fundamental change because it was based on differences in natural conditions. But there were developments in market conditions and in technology which greatly modified the state of international specialization. These were apparent in the nineteen-thirties and became very powerful by the nineteen-sixties. Markets for foodstuffs changed because the wealthier and more industrial countries had slower population growth and many of the poorer agricultural countries increased their populations faster than ever before. So increased needs for foodstuffs were differently located. Technologically, agriculture came to resemble manufacturing industry more closely. Great increases were achieved in the productivity of both land and labour by selective breeding, especially of plants, by the heavy use of chemicals to control weeds, pests, and diseases and to improve the fertility of the land, and by the use of machinery adapted to almost every kind of agricultural activity. The most up-to-date methods and equipment for recording and using business information also became available in agricultural management. Some of the technological advances were widely diffused, for instance the results of specialized plant breeding; but many of them were not readily transferable to a different cultural environment.

The combined effect of these various developments was to limit the growth of international trade in agricultural produce below what it would have been a little earlier, relative to the growth of population and incomes. Many of the predominantly agricultural countries needed a bigger proportion of their own output to feed their own people. The 'industrialization' of agriculture meant that the great industrial countries (with the partial exception of the USSR) became not only the most efficient agricultural producers but some of the biggest. They were able to produce large surpluses of some basic foods above their own needs. Thus by the nineteen-eighties the countries of the EEC had achieved the notoriety of stockpiling 'mountains' of grain and butter and 'lakes' of wine. This was just one of the most vivid illustrations of the way technology had altered the environment in which agricultural production and trade had to be carried on.

MINERALS

The contribution which primary production made to the rapid growth of output was not limited to agriculture. Indeed, it is evident from the utility of the figures of coal and steel production as indicators of the extent of nineteenth-century industrialization that certain minerals had the most direct possible influence. Technically, the most pervasive feature of industrialization was the use of ever-increasing amounts of energy, developed and applied by mechanical means. The immediate source of most of this energy was the burning of mineral fuels, principally coal, coke, and lignite, with a steadily growing proportion of oil in the twentieth century. The winds, the natural flow of water, human and animal effort counted for much less than they had done when the total consumption of energy was very much smaller. A continually increasing variety of manufactured goods was also dependent on the introduction of more and more processes which involved the application of heat as a means of altering the chemical constitution or physical characteristics of industrial materials. So the demand for mineral fuels was further augmented.

It was the huge need for fuel, more than anything else, which kept up the demand for minerals more or less proportionately to the growth of manufactures. In general, especially in the twentieth century, an increasing proportion of manufactured goods has come to result from elaborate productive processes. Thus more of their value has been attributable to the manufacturing work put into them, and the amount and value of the raw materials which they embody has not increased as much. But the consumption of energy has not been subject to quite the same influence. Large economies have been made in the twentieth century in the consumption of fuel, but, until recently, they have been offset by other changes. At the same time as greater efficiency was being obtained from furnaces, boilers, generators and internal-combustion engines, energy developed mechanically was being applied to new purposes – to replace human physical effort in a greater number of manufacturing processes and to carry out economic functions outside manufacture, above all in transport but also in construction and in household services. As these non-manufacturing activities grew, most of the raw materials which they used directly were minerals, so that in another way they helped to raise the demand for minerals relatively to the demand for raw materials of all kinds. The consumption of raw materials in manufactures showed a similar tendency. As manufacture expanded, capital goods came to form more and more of its total output and most of these, by their very nature, had to be made mainly from metals, especially iron. But, more generally, manufacturing industry gradually relied relatively more on mineral and relatively less on agricultural raw materials. This was mainly because minerals were physically adaptable to a wider variety of technical needs, but there may also have been some supplementary influence through prices, since the use of land to produce agricultural raw materials was bound to be affected by the competing need for more food for a rapidly increasing world population.

On the whole, therefore, the tendency of manufacture to become more economical in its use of raw materials has imposed only a minor check on the growth of the demand for minerals, especially as the minerals needed in the largest quantities, the fuels, are those which are consumed at one use and cannot be re-used after reverting to scrap. The rather rough and ready figures of world output which exist suggest that from 1880 to about 1920, the great age of the universal adoption of steam power, the use of minerals was growing faster than the output of manufactures and that since then the divergence, though not a large one, has been in the opposite direction. Recent tendencies can be clearly illustrated by a few figures. Between 1938 and 1968 the world's output of manufactures is estimated to have risen four and two-thirds times, its output of minerals was rather less than trebled, its output of agricultural raw materials increased by 85 per cent. Even though the growth of mineral output was beginning to lag a little behind that of manufactures it was absolutely very large. In 1968 it was probably about twenty-three times as great as in 1880. The beginning of the lag, however, was by then almost certainly a sign of something significant. The chemical industries had been creating a widening range of synthetic materials, some of which substituted for metals or reduced the wear and tear on metals. The performance of some functions electronically instead of mechanically reduced the use of heavy materials; and a reduced use of heavy materials caused some savings in fuel. But until then the trend towards increased mineral use had been strong for a very long time.

This great increase in the dependence of production on the exploitation of mineral resources involved both a widening of the variety of minerals for which a commercial use was found and the development of mass consumption of a few of them. Before the nineteenth century the range of minerals regularly used in industry was fairly narrow. Iron, copper, tin, lead, and zinc were the chief metals, with the addition of silver and gold for ornamental and monetary purposes. Stone was of the first importance for building and various clays were used abundantly for pottery and brick-making. Some of the manufacturing industries found a few other naturally occurring compounds essential: potash, for example, or alum which was used in dyeing. Coal was increasingly used in Europe, especially in Britain, but in general it could scarcely be regarded as more than a minor fuel. Except for the building materials hardly any of these commodities was needed in great quantities. None of the rest could compare in importance with wood, which had a threefold value, as a fuel, as a building material and as the most variously used constituent of non-textile manufactures.

The earliest technical innovations of rapid industrialization fundamentally changed this state of affairs by making coal and iron into key materials which replaced or supplemented wood in a great many of its uses, and which had also to meet independent new demands that soared from year to year. Requirements of other familiar minerals also rose more quickly than before though much less than those of coal and iron. But for many years the range of minerals used in industry was increased hardly at all. It was in the late nineteenth century that clearer signs of a different sort of change began to appear. Coal and iron remained, in terms of sheer quantity, the great mineral raw materials, though iron was being treated and used in new ways. But the use of some of the well-known metals, notably copper and zinc, began to grow a good deal faster even than that of coal and iron; and two other commodities, oil and aluminium, which had been quite without industrial significance in the mid-nineteenth century, came to be used in bulk. More novel was the great widening of the variety of minerals wanted in industry, especially from the nineteen-twenties onwards. A few, of which nickel was probably the most important, were used for quite a variety of purposes and in substantial quantities. Many others had only one or two highly specialized functions and total consumption throughout the world might amount to no more than a few thousand tonnes per year. Yet they were meeting industrial needs that often had repercussions over a wide range of manufactures and which must have remained unsatisfied without them. Borax, bromine, chromium, molybdenum, titanium, and tungsten are only a few of the minerals which became industrial essentials in the twentieth century.

The origins of this diversification of demand were to be found both in the nature of industrial technology and in the sheer size of the increase which took place in the total requirements of materials. The combination of these two types of influence is best illustrated by the changing demand for fuel. As the consumption of energy grew so rapidly it was likely to stimulate the search for new sources of supply, especially as it became more difficult to keep down the cost

TABLE 6   WORLD ENERGY CONSUMPTION, 1950–1972 (*million tonnes of coal equivalent*)

Energy source	1950	1957	1964	1972
Solid fuels (coal and lignite)	1,544	1,926	2,223	2,406
Liquid fuels	732	1,223	1,966	3,574
Natural gas	244	447	828	1,555
Hydro electricity	42	68	103	159
Nuclear electricity	—	—	2	18
Total	2,562	3,664	5,122	7,712

of mining coal. New scientific knowledge had already made internal-combustion engines a practical possibility while the steam engine was coming to dominate the world's industry in the late nineteenth century. A drastic change in the relative importance of different fuels was promoted by continued improvements in the efficiency and power of internal-combustion engines thereafter, their adaptation to every form of transport, and advances in the design of oil-burning furnaces. It is possible to make reasonably approximate comparisons by estimating the amount of coal that would have to be burned to produce the same amount of energy as is being derived from any other specified source. On this basis in 1900 only about 5 per cent of the world's commercial use of energy was derived from oil and natural gas, and even in 1938 not much more than 25 per cent. After the Second World War there were rapid changes in the sources from which the accelerating demand for energy was met, as is evident from Table 6. Many new discoveries of oil and natural gas were made and for a long period their prices were falling in real terms. By the late fifties they ranked together nearly equal with coal as energy sources. In 1967 the world, for the first time, took more of its energy from oil than from solid fuel, and from the end of the fifties there were small but gradually increasing supplies of energy from nuclear power stations. Only from 1973 did the situation change significantly. Then the cost of energy began to rise and the price of oil rose much more than that of other fuels. At the same time the additional energy needed to produce a given increment of output was falling. So the growth of energy consumption and the share of oil in its supply were both checked, though the rising trend in the share of nuclear power continued.

More varied demands for non-fuel minerals were often derived from closely related technological developments. More powerful engines and hotter furnaces were dependent on improvements in metallurgy, as were many other advances in engineering, and several of the new minerals were needed mainly in association with the old, especially in steel alloys, to provide new properties. Materials were needed that would have greater strength or hardness or cutting-power or immunity to physical and chemical change at higher temperatures or lightness without undue sacrifice of strength; and in meeting these needs minerals hitherto neglected were found ideal. Molybdenum became one of the main requirements for harder steel alloys. Chromium also became an important constituent of steel alloys and chromite ore came into use as a refractory in furnace linings. Aluminium and, to a less extent, magnesium were employed where lightness was a major consideration, as, for example, in the building of aircraft. The rise of other new industries also had a disproportionate effect on the use of particular minerals. It was, for instance, the rapid twentieth-century growth of the electrical indus-tries that caused the demand for copper and brass to rise faster than that for other familiar metals. And by the nineteen-forties there was a lesser but noticeable supplement to the fuel demand for oil as petroleum came to be the main material from which were synthe-sized the thermoplastic materials that were entering into an ever-widening variety of finished goods.

The nature and extent of the demands suggest the possibility of serious strain in meeting them. When some of the general descrip-tions of growth are translated into detailed figures of the output of particular materials that was actually achieved, the effort put into the task becomes all the more obvious. The world's annual output of coal (excluding brown coal or lignite), which was only just over 135 million tonnes in 1860, had passed 700 million by 1900 and 2,000 million by 1969, even though the rate of growth of its output slowed down markedly in the third quarter of the twentieth century. The world's old production was still below 1 million tonnes in 1870, but the annual figure had just surpassed 50 million tonnes by 1913. Output doubled from 1913 to 1921, doubled again from 1921 to 1929, then fell back for several years and did not double the 1929 total until 1947. By 1956 output had passed 800 million tonnes and in the next fifteen years it almost trebled, to reach 2,399 million tonnes in 1971. In 1974 it reached 2,905 million tonnes but subsequently fluctuated round a nearly static trend and was 2,835 million tonnes in 1984. Iron ore production, just over 40 million tonnes in 1880, doubled by 1898 and continued in the twentieth century to rise at rapid, though decelerating rates. In 1970 it reached 417 million tonnes, a tenfold increase in ninety years. Output of nickel (to take as an example one of the newer minerals) was negligible until after 1875 but was approaching 10,000 tonnes a year by the end of the century and passed 90,000 tonnes in 1936. The next thirty-five years saw an increase of more than sevenfold to a total of 681,000 tonnes in 1971.

Yet for many years the task of keeping up adequate mineral supplies was among the more straightforward of those imposed by industrialization. The main need was to extract more of familiar minerals in familiar places. As late as 1880 the three chief industrial countries, Britain, the USA, and Germany, with much smaller contributions from France and Belgium, accounted for all but a tiny fraction of the world's coal output, and major changes in the countries supplying other minerals were rare, though not unknown. As more was required it could often be obtained by carrying existing workings deeper or by starting new ones in the vicinity of those already in use. On the technical side the cumulative effect of piece-meal, empirical improvements was usually enough: more powerful winding and pumping engines, stronger ropes for winding equipment, more effective drilling and boring machinery, and so on.

In the late nineteenth century the situation was changed by the approaching shortage of some of the familiar minerals in what had been the main producing districts and by the demand for new minerals that were not to be found in familiar places and were sometimes not obtainable at all by existing techniques of mining and quarrying. Activities in the old producing areas had already indicated one of the main ways to resolve the new problems, for in some of these, chiefly in Western Europe, the mid-nineteenth century had seen the inauguration of geological surveying on an extensive scale and this helped to make mineral prospecting a less chancy business. In the next fifty years the improvement of survey techniques, their illumination by accumulating new knowledge in the geological sciences, and their application to many large areas previously of little commercial significance showed the existence of enormous and varied mineral resources and made it much easier to judge where it would be worth while to invest in their development. In some cases it became evident that many different minerals were to be found in the same region. But, in addition to the more general search, special survey techniques were devised in seeking particular minerals often located far from other commercially useful resources. This was particularly true of oil. Most oilfields were almost certain to remain undiscovered until exploration could be guided by specialized geological knowledge, and the huge finds made since the First World War have depended very much on the application of new geophysical methods to prospecting.

Supplementing the results of more scientific exploration were continued improvements in the technique and equipment of mining and extraction. Many of these were great extensions of the sort of improvements that had been built up gradually over a long period in the past. Many were strictly comparable to changes taking place at the same time in manufacturing industry: the mechanization of actions formerly done by hand, the application of electric power, the recording and control of physical conditions by automatic instruments. Others, however, were more novel in kind. The drilling of an oil-well and the control of its flow exemplified the adoption of a new technique to meet a new need. To obtain supplies of some of the new minerals economically the most important technical advances needed were in the methods of extraction and refining rather than in mining. Some that were wanted in only fairly small amounts were to be found in ores that were worked for the sake of other metals contained more abundantly in them and, when the price justified it, these minor elements could be extracted as by-products instead of being dispersed in the waste gases or solid spoil. Thus between the two world wars cadmium came to be obtained mainly in the course of purifying zinc ore, and in the nineteen-forties the demand for uranium became such as to make it worth while to extract it from the waste dumps of South African gold mines. Improvements in processing also effectively added to the commercial supply of those minerals that had a bigger market, by making it profitable to mine ores of lower grade. In particular, the twentieth-century development of the flotation process of concentrating ores made it practicable to use immense supplies of low-grade copper ores that must otherwise have been neglected and also to begin the exploitation of new Australian supplies of lead and zinc.

These new influences on supply helped to bring about great changes in the location of the world's mineral production and in the relation between mineral producers and the main industrialized regions. Before the coming of mechanical transport the sheer bulk of most minerals greatly restricted trade in them except between points close to the sea or navigable rivers. The presence of coal and iron ore within a country, not too distant from each other, was one of the major influences on the international distribution of industry in the ninetenth century. But the scope for new mineral discoveries within the more densely populated industrial countries was diminishing by 1900 and widened again only with new demands and new methods of exploration in the later twentieth century. The best opportunities were in large industrial countries with extensive territories awaiting development. The USA was the supreme example and, with the aid of some European enterprise and capital, particularly in the mountain states of the west in the late nineteenth century, created a vast and varied mineral output sufficient to meet most of the needs of its own expanding industry and providing also a surplus of many commodities for sale to industrial producers elsewhere. Russia also had great, though widely dispersed, mineral resources which were developed more slowly while its own manufacturing activity was small, but much more quickly in the mid-twentieth century. The main effort in mineral production, outside these two countries, went for many years into some of the other large territories of white settlement where incomes and skills were relatively high, promising geological conditions were noted, and it was possible to attract enterprise and capital from abroad, especially from Britain. Canada, South Africa, and Australia all emerged as international mineral suppliers and all had enough supplementary attributes to be able to use their mineral development fairly promptly to assist their own industrialization. Among other comparable areas Brazil developed large newly discovered fields of iron ore.

But some particular minerals were sought and found in still more remote places, some of which had previously had hardly any connexion with the world's general commercial activities, and in these almost the whole enterprise of mineral production and its ancillary services had to be initiated and for many years maintained from abroad. New Caledonia in the eighteen-seventies was the first place to supply nickel in commercially useful quantities. Tin mining in Malaya was begun in small undertakings by Chinese immigrants, but its rapid development did not come until a much larger scale of operations was introduced by European companies, of which the first was established there in 1892. By the nineteen-thirties European-owned mines accounted for nearly 70 per cent of Malaya's tin output, which was about one-third of the world total. It was, however, the search for oil which took European and American enterprise most frequently into remote and economically backward areas. The USA was consistently the biggest oil producer as well as oil consumer. Indeed, down to the early nineteen-fifties there was hardly any year in which United States production did not exceed that of all the rest of the world. But, except for Russia, no other appreciably industrialized country produced much oil in the early twentieth century and by the nineteen-fifties even the USA was consuming more than its current output. Supplies were sought from all over the world, wherever geological conditions suggested exploration might be worth while and practicable arrangements could-be made for working – from Romania, Iran, Burma, the East Indies, and the southern Caribbean. As demand increased so did the intensity of exploration, which naturally concentrated more and more on the areas where experience showed that the most abundant cheaply worked supplies were likely to be found. These conditions meant that while the number of sources tended to increase, their relative importance could change with astonishing rapidity. Particularly striking was the rise of the Middle East in the nineteen-forties and 'fifties to become the main source of oil for consumers outside America and the communist bloc. Commercial production of oil began only in 1939 in Sa'udi Arabia and in 1946 in Kuwait, yet in the later fifties these two countries were providing over one-third of the world total of exports and in 1971 they still had over one-third of the world's known oil reserves. In the 'sixties Libya and Nigeria also emerged as new producers which quickly became major exporters, with Nigerian output rising from 7 million tonnes in 1968 to 76 million in 1971. In the latter year, apart from the USA and USSR which produced mainly for their own vast consumption, Libya and Nigeria were fifth and seventh among the oil-producing countries, with Sa'udi Arabia and Kuwait as second and fourth. (Iran and Venezuela were first and third, though the margin between Iran and Sa'udi Arabia was negligible.) The same experience of rapid change was seen again from the mid-seventies in the growth of North Sea output. In 1974 the UK produced only 0.4 million tonnes, but in 1984 UK output was 125 million tonnes, which was much more than half the output of Sa'udi Arabia.

The continually rising consumption of minerals and the dispersion of the areas of supply might have seemed to be gradually shifting industrialization on to a more precarious foundation, especially in the twentieth century. Minerals may be regarded as wasting assets, liable to be consumed once for all, in contrast to vegetable raw materials which may be renewed regularly, often annually, by new growth. To have become increasingly dependent on the former and less on the latter looks a little like straying from the path of prudence into courses which inevitably create their own impassable limits of scarcity. And for many of the older industrialized countries the use of new minerals meant dependence on supplies beyond their own control, which might be jeopardized by fiscal or military action.

In practice, however, industry was for a long time not hampered by these conditions. The physical adequacy of mineral supplies appeared to be safeguarded in various ways, particularly by the sheer quantity of unworked materials and by the possibility of re-using those already worked. Only the fossil fuels are consumed in use. The materials embodied in structures and manufactured goods revert to scrap, and much scrap can be and has been reprocessed for productive use again. Moreover, in the twentieth century, a rising proportion of the materials of industry has been made by chemical synthesis, so that if some particular natural material becomes scarce or inaccessible a more plentiful one may be substituted for it. Nevertheless, by the late nineteen-sixties, there was a good deal of alarmed discussion (as there had been about coal supplies a century before) of the possibility that industrial expansion would soon be halted or reversed because of a lack of raw materials. The basis of the most pessimistic conclusions appears to have been a comparison of figures of known reserves of some materials (without allowance for new discoveries or the re-use of scrap or the use of substitutes) with estimates of demand reached by extrapolating recent trends, or recent rates of acceleration, in consumption. The doomsday of mineral famine was unlikely to be as imminent as such exercises suggested. But they provided a forcible reminder that existing patterns of mineral usage could not be projected forward indefinitely and that it was impracticable within those patterns to meet the industrial aspirations of the expanding populations of the non-industrial world.

Much of the argument was specifically about the supply of energy, on which all else depends. Industrialization brought a soaring use of energy and depended on a continuous rapid growth of supply which kept energy cheap. For most of the twentieth century that cheapness was unmodified by any concern to extend the life of fuel reserves as these seemed abundant enough to let the future take care of itself. In the late nineteen-fifties the world's estimated reserves of coal were more than a thousand times its annual energy consumption, which was then around 4,000 million tonnes of coal equivalent. The situation was less favourable for crude petroleum, which had been found generally more convenient for use. The known reserves then were over 26,000 million tonnes and, on general geological grounds, were expected to reach 100,000 million tonnes, and each tonne would yield roughly 1.3 times as much energy as a tonne of coal. But other sources of energy (those in atomic nuclei, for example) were being brought into use; and over the long term there was the expectation that technical ingenuity would find new ways of drawing on the continual lavish augmentation of the earth's energy supply from solar radiation. By the early nineteen-seventies the situation did not look quite so favourable. Energy consumption had continued its rapid rise and it was assumed that this would go on. The discovery of new reserves was no longer proceeding fast enough to take care of this. From 1951 to 1966 world oil production slightly exceeded the 1951 total of proved reserves, yet in 1966 the proved reserves were several times larger than in 1951. But in the early 'seventies it was estimated that the level of reserves was such that, even if demand stabilized, production would be bound to decline at the beginning of the next century, and much earlier if demand went on rising. Things did not turn out quite so badly. World oil reserves increased by just over 10 per cent between 1974 and 1984 while consumption upset the earlier forecasts by falling slightly. The production of atomic energy seemed to be reversing the previous disappointments about high costs, and claims that a large proportion of the world's coal reserves could not be economically extracted appeared to have been exaggerated, though some long-term rise in costs seemed probable. By the 'eighties, even if the safety margin had increased, it was not very large for oil; but concern about imminent energy shortage was less acute, whereas the level of energy costs remained a matter of concern, which it had not been before 1970.

There were also worries arising from new political factors, which previously had had little direct effect on the security of material supplies for industry. The diversification of mineral needs in conjunction with the geographical dispersal of supply did little damage to the position of countries which had industrialized earlier on the basis of a narrower range of domestically produced minerals. Though many minerals are unevenly distributed, only rarely was one country able to monopolize for long the known supplies of any important industrial material; and few countries have reserved mineral supplies for their own industrial production, without being ready to export part of them. International competition in supply constantly stimulated trade, even to the extent of creating in the mineral markets, at most times between 1880 and 1970, more favourable conditions for consumers than for producers; and the increasing range of substitutes among industrial materials acted in a similar way. In the early nineteen-seventies, however, this situation changed, not because of any great scarcity of supplies in most cases, but because of a deliberate lessening of competition among suppliers, sometimes under government influence. This was most obvious in 1973–4 and again in 1979 when the governments of the states producing a large proportion of the world's oil acted collectively to impose very large increases in price, which they were able to obtain because of the high cost (political as well as financial) that consumers would have incurred as a result of even a fairly short interruption of their supplies. Thus the long and short-term market conditions often differed and, most frequently , the short-term conditions were decisive. In the nineteen-fifties and 'sixties energy policies and consumption habits were based on the assumption that competition would keep the day-to-day market in line with what was believed about long-term supplies. Mainly because of the abundance of energy on offer North America and, above all, Western Europe were then using more than their own current output of energy. Asia, apart from the Middle East, was acting similarly because of shortage of developed energy supplies, but in North America and Western Europe this adverse balance was maintained on current commercial grounds, despite the possession of large reserves. A high proportion of the world's known coal reserves was in these two regions and North America had large oil reserves. In the 'seventies there was a further strengthening of the long-term supply position from the discovery of large oil deposits under the seas of Northwest Europe. But when political action and commercial monopoly shifted the market relationships it needed a period of readjustment, through changed policies, investment and technical ingenuity, to alter the balance of short-term and long-term influences. The period did not always have to be long, as was shown in the early 'eighties, when the failure of demand to continue as anticipated prevented the producers from maintaining the real value of the price increases they had imposed in 1979. But this benefit was won by consumers partly through economic recession and slow growth. In more prosperous times adjustment took longer.

None of these considerations does much to reduce the advantages that accrued from the growing dependence on minerals which was observable in industrial technology from the eighteenth century onward. As the pace of industrialization increased it was difficult, if the world was to be fed, to accelerate the production of agricultural raw materials to keep up with it; and the development of industrial techniques created new qualitative requirements that the old materials could not always meet. The major industries probably had greater doubts about the adequacy of their future raw material supplies in the mid-eighteenth century than they had in the early nineteen-seventies. There were some signs then that further industrial growth depended on the continued reduction of the proportion of raw material in the value of the final product, but this was already being achieved more easily than before. There were also some uncertainties about the ability of technology to keep down or offset the cost of raw materials even when they were used more economically. But this meant only that mineral supplies and prices had to be continuously watched, with a view to adaptations when required; it did not mean that minerals had started to impose any immediate constraint on economic progress.

TRANSPORT AND COMMUNICATIONS

Much of the increased output of both primary and secondary industries was possible only because complementary resources, previously far separated in space, could be brought together. Still more of it was worth while commercially only because new and growing markets could be supplied from centres of production far away. A revolutionary improvement in the efficiency of transport was thus an essential element in the achievement of great productive expansion. Such an improvement was brought about mainly by applying mechanical power to the movement of men and goods. In some of the wealthier countries many non-mechanical improvements in transport were introduced in the eighteenth and early nineteenth centuries. New roads with better surfaces, more smoothly running carts and carriages to use them, river-improvement schemes and the cutting of artificial inland waterways, larger and faster sailing-ships, were among the contributions to economic improvement. They facilitated and cheapened the movement of both passengers and freight, particularly over fairly short distances, though better sailing-ships improved communication across the Atlantic, and the European roads could carry a bigger volume of traffic than before. For a time the improvements appeared dramatic, simply because, down to the eighteenth century, the road systems had been so bad (or, in many districts, non-existent) and so little had been done to reduce the natural hazards of rivers. To be able to send wagons where previously only pack horses or packmen could pass often led to a great proportionate increase in traffic. Yet, wherever mechanized methods of industrial production became established, even the improved non-mechanical modes of transport came to be seen as inadequate. Their restricted physical capacity and their level of costs tended to keep markets appreciably below the size which up-to-date manufacturers believed they could satisfy. So there was a growing demand for the application of machinery to transport as well as production, and, when mechanical transport was widely supplied, as it was mainly in the second half of the nineteenth century, its economic contribution was much greater than that of the non-mechanical methods. The latter still played an important ancillary part, but it was the railways and steam shipping that now took the bulk of new transport investment. The roads and navigable waterways were mostly restricted to local traffic and to acting as feeders to the railways and seaports. Only when mechanical propulsion became generally possible on roads and rivers did this situation change once again.

The railway was an innovation with a long period of slow development followed by one of sudden tremendous growth. The potentialities of railways were obscured both by their technical unfamiliarity and by the economic difficulty of experimenting with them on an appreciable scale, owing to the very heavy initial outlay which was involved. It was therefore only to be expected that the introduction of public railways operated by steam locomotives should have been over short distances in districts where economic advance was most marked, and where, consequently, the need for better transport was most urgently felt and the cost of providing it could best be met. The earliest developments were in Great Britain and the eastern United States, but the success of local lines encouraged larger schemes there and, as soon as railways had demonstrated how much difference they could make to economic life, railway building was taken up rapidly in most European countries. In the half-century before the First World War new railway construction reached its maximum, and railways spread far into the interior of some parts of every continent as a meant of extending commerce. Their growth is shown in Table 7.

TABLE 7   LENGTH OF RAILWAY ROUTES, 1840–1930 (*kilometres*)

	1840	1870	1900	1930
World	7,678	209,751	789,976	1,279,499
North America	4,753	90,275	359,537	513,432
Europe	2,925	104,894	283,472	420,826
Asia	—	8,183	60,289	132,722
South America	—	2,848	42,558	94,624
Africa	—	1,786	20,111	68,302
Australasia	—	1,765	24,009	49,593

Railway systems were created gradually. Small networks of purely local importance were linked by longer lines, until nationwide systems existed. Small links across national frontiers were multiplied, with the result that national systems formed part of a greater whole which served a continent.

Britain was the first country in which a reasonably comprehensive railway system was created. By the end of 1850, 10,653 kilometres were in operation, and these included most of the main routes. Subsequent expansion went on through the construction of many branch lines, cross links, and short cuts, by a great increase of suburban lines, and by the addition of one or two more main routes between major towns. There was at first no conception of a national railway system, and railways were built and operated by a multitude of independent enterprises. Yet the result of the effort was reasonably systematic, for this was one activity in which there really was some similarity of private, local, and national interest, and a few leading promoters soon realized that, in railway enterprise, system paid. There were, however, some serious disadvantages which arose as a result of the haphazard growth. Competing lines were provided in some localities in which there was little traffic. In other places, though only one line was actually completed, rival schemes were initiated, and their competitive approach to landowners and others had the effect of forcing up the cost of the successful company, thus affecting adversely its subsequent profitability and efficiency. Various minor inconveniences also arose, such as the duplication of terminal facilities, which was another source of unnecessary additional expense.

In some other countries railway development was more systematic, partly because of a different political environment, partly, in some cases, because it was possible to benefit from British experience. Belgium planned a railway system at the outset in 1834. There the state undertook the construction and called in expert advice. Two main routes running north–south and east–west, the former providing a link with France and the latter with Germany, were built, and cross lines were added to connect the major towns on one line with those on the other. The original scheme was practically completed by 1844, and formed a basic pattern on which much further construction was superimposed later by private companies.

French railway construction began with a few local lines built by private companies, but a plan for a national system was prepared in 1837, and, after much discussion, was embodied in the Railway Law of 1842. This plan provided for six main routes radiating from Paris, with a total length of 4,425 kilometres. It was carried out during the eighteen-fifties by private contractors with state assistance, and formed a skeleton to which many subsidiary lines were added both by the original companies and by others.

Germany seized the advantages of railways more quickly and thoroughly than France. This was partly because Germany suffered from greater geographical disadvantages and had previously done less to overcome them by building roads and canals, and partly because the railway was used as one instrument of national unification. From the eighteen-thirties onwards there were private proposals for the creation of a general German railway system. Though this depended on the gradual accretion of small schemes promoted by individual states and private entrepreneurs, common interest led to the provision of something reasonably systematic; and the activities of neighbouring states, especially Austria and Belgium, helped to integrate German railways into a wider network for Western and Central Europe. By 1850 railway travel was already possible by somewhat roundabout routes across Germany from east to west and from the north coast to Vienna. By this time nearly 5,000 kilometres of railway were in operation in Germany and well over 1,500 kilometres in Austria. In the early eighteen-forties Austria had already begun work in taking the railway across Europe's greatest natural barrier, the Alps, and this first transalpine main line was opened in stages until in 1857 the whole route from Vienna To Trieste via Graz and Ljubljana was in operation. Ten years later came the second transalpine route over the Brenner pass. Menwhile the German and Austrian railway systems both grew apace, and in 1882, with the completion of the St Gotthard Line in Switzerland, the chief industrial regions of Germany obtained their most direct railway link with the Mediterranean. Between then and the end of the century several new links with Russia and Turkey were built. Before 1900 most European national railway systems had been so much extended as to contribute to an important international service. Perhaps the most striking symbol of this international achievement was the introduction in 1888 of throught passenger service from Paris to Constantinople.

The USA experienced two very different phases of railway development, one in which separate local lines were being built and gradually connected with each other, and one in which a trans-continental system was deliberately and quickly created, instead of emerging slowly from the connexion of numerous smaller enterprises. At first, railway development was very similar to that in Britain. It began in the later eighteen-twenties and went on steadily in the eastern states. The early lines were localized and short, but many of them soon became part of longer routes. By the middle of the century longer lines were being built as single enterprises and many were being carried far inland, especially in the north, between the coast and the upper valley of the Ohio and the Great Lakes.

The unique phase of American railway building came after the

Civil War. In the eastern part of the country, as in Europe, railways had been built to meet an immediate demand, but the penetration by the railways of the lands between the Mississippi and the Rockies occurred while the region was still economically undeveloped and very sparsely inhabited. There could be no strong effective demand for transport until the land was settled, but settlement on a large scale was impossible until the railways provided easy access. The Union Pacific and the Central Pacific, which together provided the first trans-continental route, received their charters in 1862, and, with the aid of lavish land grants and loans from the federal government, were able to complete construction in 1869. By that time the Kansas Pacific, the Northern Pacific, and the Atlantic and Pacific had already been begun. In the next few years other trans-continental lines, including the Southern Pacific and the Texas and Pacific, were chartered. Of these later lines only the Kansas Pacific, which had built westward from Kansas City to a junction with the Union Pacific at Cheyenne, Wyoming, had made a substantial contribution before financial crisis in 1873 brought a check to railroad extension. Progress was slow for several years and some large schemes were abandoned or modified. The Atlantic and Pacific, even after reorganization, was unable to complete its line. But in the early eighties its projected route beyond Albuquerque to the Pacific coast was constructed by the Atchison, Topeka and Santa Fe as a westward continuation of its own system. Throughout the eighteen-eighties trans-continental railroad building was going on rapidly, in Canada as well as the USA. By 1884 there were seven different routes westward to the Rockies. In 1885 the Atchison, Topeka and Santa Fe gained its own outlet to the Pacific coast and three years later had a through route all the way from there to Chicago. In 1886 the first through passenger train from Montreal to Vancouver ran on the Canadian Pacific line. Two years later the Northern Pacific's main line was completed. Subsequently the trans-continental services were further increased by the completion of the Great Northern in the USA and, in the early years of the twentieth century, by the building of two more lines in Canada, the Canadian Northern and the Grand Trunk Pacific.

Russia presented some of the same opportunities as North America for spectacular railway development, but the challenge was not taken up. Railway construction went on very slowly at first, even in the most heavily populated parts of the Russian Empire, and by 1855 only about 1,350 kilometres had been built. But the Crimean War revealed some of the penalties of economic backwardness, and the government began to offer assistance for railway construction. By 1867, 4,000 kilometres of line were in operation, and in 1882 the total reached 24,000 kilometres. But the railways were badly distributed. In a few districts there was acute competition between rival lines, yet most of the country was still without any railway service. From 1881 onwards the government itself began to build railways, and private construction continued, with the result that by 1914 about 74,000 kilometres were in operation. Yet even this was still inadequate for needs. The most remarkable additions were the Trans-Caspian line to Samarkand, begun in 1883 and completed in 1888, and the Trans-Siberian railway, which, after existing as a project on paper for thirty years, was constructed between 1891 and 1904, and at once had an important influence in stimulating the free settlement and economic development of Siberia. After the Revolution, at a time when most countries had little need to add to their railway systems, the extension of lines in the USSR was an urgent economic necessity. The completion of the Turksib line in 1930 provided a third long-distance route which assisted the growth of economic activity in Central Asia, and, after the ravages of war and revolution had been repaired, additional construction was undertaken in European as well as Asiatic Russia. By the late nineteen-thirties about 88,500 kilometres of railway were in use.

Wherever they were built, railways widened the range of possibilities in economic activity. Their immediate effects were not always foreseen. Most early railways, for example, were promoted with the primary object of facilitating the movement of goods, but most of them at first derived the greater part of their revenue from passenger traffic. Very soon, however, they were contributing to a great increase in both the production and marketing of goods, and became primarily concerned with freight traffic. Railways changed the relations between town and country and between different regions. One of their most significant characteristics was that, for the first time, they made it as quick and easy to move heavy loads overland as by water. So they were able to open new and direct routes for transport and to lessen the economic advantages which sites on natural harbours and navigable rivers had hitherto enjoyed. Changes in the location of industry and population took place as a result, and, in particular, the industrialization of inland regions was facilitated. In this way railways encouraged greater local specialization and an increase of domestic trade; and although their more immediate influence was shown in the internal activities of individual countries, railways were also in many places extensions of main routes of international commerce, in the expansion of which they were supremely important. In-directly they contributed to economic expansion in countless ways. The construction and operation of railways created a new demand for the products of various other industries: iron and steel, engineer-ing, timber, and quarrying; they created new types of employment, and called into being new towns to serve their special needs; and in so doing they set up a long chain of economic repercussions. Much of the stimulus given by railway building was felt locally. But from the less developed areas economic reactions were conveyed to distant sources of supply. The building of railways in South America or Asia meant a demand for iron and steel, rolling-stock and other specialized engineering products, even for skilled workers, from Europe, especially from Great Britain. But within the less developed areas the railways had a particularly important influence on the growth of mechanized industry, because in many places they were pioneers of the heavy engineering industry. Once a railway was in operation, repairs and maintenance had to be done locally, and the works established in order to do this became in some places the nucleus of a more general engineering industry. It was at railway junctions that the first engineering works in India were set up towards the end of the nineteenth century; and in several Latin American countries foundries and machine-shops which began by doing repairs and supplying spare parts for railways, tramways, and mines, went on to build rolling-stock and machines of various kinds.

Except for very short local journeys the railway, for more than half a century, was practically unchallenged as a means of inland transport. From about the time of the First World War it had to meet stronger competition. One source of this was the revival of a few inland waterways as motor-driven vessels brought new cost re-ductions, but this was of no great general significance. The main influence was that of the automobile, which had its greatest effect on the wealthiest countries. Where a good road system was available, or could be created, motor vehicles became increasingly convenient for passenger journeys of moderate length and for the carriage of most of the lighter types of merchandise. They could not claim a technical or economic advantage over the railway for all types of traffic, but where they became very numerous they were bound to take business away from the railway, despite the continued increase of the total demand for transport. The change was most evident in the USA, which has consistently had in use a larger number of motor vehicles than all the rest of the world together and which, by constructing great trans-continental highways, enabled the motor vehicles to compete for more of the longest-distance traffic than was practicable elsewhere. As early as 1922 there were in the USA 85 passenger cars and 12 commercial vehicles for every 1,000 inhabitants, a proportion that no other country could approach until the late nineteen-fifties. The 1 million motor vehicles registered in the USA in 1914 had grown to over 31 million by 1940 and in 1971 to 111.2 million, of which 92.3 million were passenger cars. Elsewhere the diffusion of private car ownership was slower and the long-distance lorry was less used, but the expansion of road transport was steady and cumulative, and after the Second World War reached very large absolute dimensions. In the world as a whole (excluding the communist countries, for which figures are not available) the number of passenger cars doubled between 1948 and 1958 and continued to grow at about the same rate up to the early seventies. In 1971 there were 204.1 million passenger cars and 53.4 million commercial vehicles. Such developments provided entirely new facilities as well as substitutes for some which the railway had long maintained. They contributed to a great increase of movement and helped in the rapid extension of a process in which railways had had a large part: the gathering of more and more of the population of the wealthier countries into great cities ringed with dormitory suburbs.

The automobile, though the greatest, was not the only important competitor in inland transport. Much traffic in fuel, a substantial element in railway business, had in the USA been transferred to long-distance oil pipe lines by the nineteen-thirties, and after the Second World War pipe lines were greatly extended elsewhere. In this period, too, civil aviation became a serious challenger for long-distance passenger transport. Only in North America had this challenge become really formidable in domestic transport before 1960. Elsewhere it was the international sea-routes that were mainly affected, but the European railways certainly suffered some loss.

In view of all these circumstances it might have been expected that the economic influence of railways would have begun to wane, and by the nineteen-twenties many old-established lines were experiencing financial difficulty and an inability to find new traffic to replace what their competitors had taken from them. But this was not the beginning of the end for the railways. Great technical improvements could still be, and were, made in traction and in traffic control. As business expanded there was an increase of heavy and fairly standardized traffic which, even in old and wealthy countries, railways were well suited to carry. In less wealthy countries that were beginning to use greater quantities of heavy equipment and to turn out more industrial goods, especially those countries with long inland distances to cover, nothing could cope with the resulting increase in traffic so easily as the railway. So it was that the world's railway freight traffic, which had undergone no sustained expansion in the decade preceding the Second World War, rose steadily from 1939 to the 'seventies at the rate of about 50 per cent per decade. The growth was particularly large in Asia, the USSR, and Eastern Europe, but in the 'sixties railway freight traffic revived even in the USA and there was modest expansion in most of the highly developed countries except Great Britain. Passenger traffic also continued to increase in the world as a whole, though the trend was very different in some of the most advanced regions, notably the USA, where the railways lost passenger traffic at a catastrophic rate. In general, in the most highly developed countries, the railways usually maintained and somewhat increased the absolute amount of their traffic (counting both passengers and freight) though their share of the total diminished. In some less developed countries which were undergoing productive expansion railway traffic was growing very rapidly indeed. It was evident that the railway was still a major factor in the growth of production and in industrialization, as it had been a hundred years earlier.

To the increased movement of goods internationally after the middle of the nineteenth century the outstanding contributions came from technical improvement in shipping and from the achievements of civil engineers in expanding port facilities. In the second half of the nineteenth century the chief improvements in shipping were the replacement of wood by iron and later by steel in construction, and the substitution of steam for sail. The steamship was in process of development throughout the nineteenth century, but came only slowly into general use, mainly because of the extravagant fuel consumption of early marine engines, which raised costs very much on long voyages, so that the steamship was for many years used for little but river, coastal, and ferry traffic, and for such ocean traffic as could afford high charges. Nothing of any importance except the North Atlantic passenger services came within this last category. But there was a great change from the eighteen-sixties, when the compound engine, which sharply reduced fuel consumption and costs, came into use. The potentialities of the steamship for general use were clearly demonstrated in 1865, when the Holt Line introduced a service between Liverpool and Mauritius, a distance of 8,500 miles, without any intermediate port of call. The opening of the Suez Canal in 1869 gave further encouragement to the adoption of the steamship, for it could not be used by sailing-ships, yet it offered great savings for traffic between Europe or America and the Far East. From this time steamship services began to be concerned mainly with cargo traffic.

For a time the sailing-ship retained an economic advantage for long voyages that passed through parts of the world which were remote from sources of coal supply, at any rate in the carriage of low-grade cargoes not subject to deterioration. But in the late nineteenth century steam was rapidly replacing sail. The proportion of the total shipping tonnage operated by steam in the chief maritime countries was 12.5 per cent in 1870, 25.1 per cent in 1880, 45.7 per cent in 1890, and 63.9 per cent in 1900, and a steamship could in a given time carry about three times as much cargo as a sailing-ship of the same gross tonnage. In the same period the use of iron in construction was making possible a great increase in the size of ships whenever the volume of traffic justified it, and this bestowed a further advantage on the steamship, as the optimum size of sailing-ships was limited by the difficulty of handling very large sails and spars.

Not only was the proportion of steamships to sailing-ships increasing, but the total amount of shipping of all kinds in use was growing rapidly. The size of the world's merchant fleets increased from 9 million net tons in 1850 to 20 million net tons in 1880, and 34,600,000 net tons in 1910. In this period British shipbuilders and shipowners established complete predominance. By 1914, 42 per cent of merchant shipping (measured in gross tons) was registered in the United Kingdom, and it performed more than half of the world's seaborne trade. During the First World War, 12 million gross tons of shipping were sunk, but at the same time great effort was put into new construction, and this was maintained after the restoration of peace. Merchant shipping fleets continued to grow rapidly, and by 1931 the world supply, 68 million gross tons, was more than half as much again as in 1914, although no comparable expansion in the volume of maritime trade had taken place. After the Second World War the revival of trade stimulated a renewed expansion in the supply of shipping, though the full extent of the increase depended also on uneconomic subsidies provided for political reasons. The world supply reached 80 million gross tons in 1948, 118 million in 1958 and 268 million in 1972.

Some of the twentieth-century increase was attributable to continued rapid technical change, especially to the development of oil-burning and motor-driven ships, which were introduced before there

73

was any physical need to scrap the coal-burning ships that operated on the same routes. In 1914, less than 1,500,000 gross tons of steamers burnt oil, and there were less than 250,000 tons of motor vessels. By 1939 there were 21 million tons of oil-burning steamers and 15,250,000 tons of motor vessels. The rapid growth of merchant fleets was also partly due to greater specialization. Some commodities which had for the first time achieved major importance in international trade could be carried only in specially designed ships. Oil was the outstanding example of such a commodity, and there was much construction of oil-tankers even when most branches of the shipbuilding industry were plunged in depression. The world's fleet of tankers grew from 1,500,000 gross tons in 1914, to 6 million in 1927, 9 million in 1931, 11 million in 1939, 15 million in 1948, 22 million in 1953, 55 million in 1965 and 105 million in 1972. At the same time a growing demand for a greater variety of foodstuffs also led to a great expansion of other kinds of highly specialized shipping capacity. Refrigerator ships, for example, had been undergoing continuous development since the later years of the nineteenth century and specialization had been carried to great lengths. Many new refrigerator ships were built which were adapted to the carriage of only one type of commodity.

The great technical improvement of shipping and the increase of its supply were able to exert their full effect on trade only because they were accompanied by comparable developments in ancillary activities: the improvement of harbours, the building of docks and warehouses, the erection of landing equipment, the cutting of ship canals. Few ports had much dock and warehouse accommodation in 1800, but during the nineteenth century there was great expansion in the provision of these. Port facilities had to match shipping, not only in scale, but also in degree of specialization. This was achieved in part by equipping some ports to deal with only one or two types of cargo, according to local conditions; in part, where the total traffic was very large, by making specialized divisions within ports. London provided an outstanding example of the way in which port facilities were expanded and differentiated as the volume of shipping increased. Before the nineteenth century, it possessed only one small wet dock. By 1914 its docks had a water area of 750 acres and a land area of 2,200 acres with accommodation at different groups for the most varied types of cargo: the Surrey Docks, for example, were specially equipped to deal with timber and grain, the St Katharine Dock with wool and wine, the West India Docks with rum and frozen meat.

The cutting of ship canals was also a major contribution to the improvement of some of the leading ports, which in this way gained easier, quicker, and cheaper access to the open sea. Amsterdam had improved its position by means of a ship canal in 1825, and the completion in 1872 of the New Waterway connecting Rotterdam with the North Sea showed how vast a difference such an enterprise could make to the activity of a port. It enabled Rotterdam to become the chief outlet for the trade of western Germany, which was then beginning its rapid industrialization, with the result that Rotterdam came to handle a larger volume of trade than any other European port except London. A little later the construction of the Manchester Ship Canal, completed in 1894, gave to an important inland commercial and manufacturing centre the advantage of direct communication with the oceans.

But the most spectacular contribution of ship canals was in providing new short links between seas and thereby making possible great reductions in long-distance freight costs. The Suez Canal, at the time of its completion in 1869, was a speculative enterprise, for the majority of existing ships were unable to use it. But its advantages were soon clear, and it came to be used by a steadily growing number of ships. The Panama Canal was a more formidable engineering problem, and the savings that it offered were in trans-Pacific trade, which, in the nineteenth century, was much less than that of Europe and the east coast of North America with the Far East, which the Suez Canal was built to serve. But, by the end of the nineteenth century, trade had grown sufficiently to justify building a Panama Canal, even if considerations of American defence had not required it. The canal was opened to traffic in 1915, and during the interwar period it was used by about 25 million gross tons of shipping per year, not very much less than passed through the Suez Canal.

Shipping suffered far less in the first half of the twentieth century from the competition of other modes of transport than did the railway. The rapid technical development of aircraft gave promise that a formidable competitor might eventually appear, but for many years their high operational cost and small carrying capacity restricted their commercial effectiveness to a very few classes of traffic. Regular airline operation began in 1919, though there had previously been small experiments. The early services were for the most part along inland routes over fairly short distances, but many of them provided useful international connexions, especially between the chief European countries. From 1927, when Pan-American Airways

75

began to develop services between the USA and the countries of Latin America, longer international routes quickly became more feasible and more important. In 1929 a service began between England and India, in 1930 one from the Netherlands to the Netherlands East Indies. Regular services between Cairo and the Cape began in 1932, and in 1938 a route was opened across half the world, from London to Sydney. In 1939 the first regularly scheduled transatlantic service began operation from New York to Southampton and Marseilles. In 1938 the 1,792 aircraft of the world's airlines flew 374 million kilometres. The Second World War gave a great fillip to research in aircraft design and made possible the technical basis of a far larger air transport industry, which began to appear in the next few years. Continued technical advances brought rapid improvements in speed, carrying capacity and comfort, and, because much of the ultimate cost of these advances could be charged against the defence needs of the more powerful countries, the convenience of air travel was reinforced by greater financial competitiveness. Flying on scheduled air services increased to 1,270 million kilometres in 1948 and 7,070 million kilometres in 1971. Passenger traffic grew nearly twentyfold between these two dates and reached 407,000 million passenger-kilometres in 1971. Cargo traffic remained on a much smaller scale but was growing just as quickly, and air services took a high proportion of the international mail.

The speeding up which air services gave to the delivery of long-distance mail was only a late stage in a long process of steady improvement. The railway and the steamship, together with more efficient organization of national postal services, had already reduced greatly the time taken to transmit mail, and had made possible the handling of a rapidly increasing quantity of letters and parcels. Mechanization, indeed, made contributions to the transmission of information no less striking than those to the movement of men and goods, and both were of great effect on the efficiency of business as well as on the amenities of life. The expansion of mail services was accompanied by the development of nationwide and international telegraph systems. Practical telegraphic apparatus was first designed by Samuel Morse in the eighteen-thirties, and the first line was opened in 1844 between Baltimore and Washington. The new system of communication spread fairly quickly in the USA where, by 1861, 80,000 kilometres of line were in use, and where, a year later, a trans-continental link was completed. In Europe, telegraphy was at first used less extensively, but a beginning was made in Great Britain in 1846, and in 1851 an important advance was made with the laying of the first submarine cable across the Strait of Dover. Overland lines were extended, and by 1865 Great Britain was linked with Calcutta. The first attempts to provide long-distance connexions by submarine cable failed, but in 1866 a successful transatlantic cable came into operation. It was the forerunner of several others laid before the end of the nineteenth century. Shorter cable links brought Australia into telegraphic communication with Great Britain across Asia and Europe by 1871, and early in the twentieth century two trans-Pacific cables were laid, one connecting Canada with Australia, the other joining the USA and China through Honolulu and Manila. By 1918, 521,000 kilometres of cable linked the chief ports of the world. Overland telegraph lines also continued to be extended, especially in the most industrialized countries. By 1937, the USA alone contained 400,000 kilometres of telegraph line transmitting 200 million telegrams annually.

Late in the nineteenth century communication facilities were augmented by another new invention. Bell produced the first successful telephone in 1876, but for many years it did not provide a very effective service. In the USA its use slowly extended, and by 1900 the American Telephone and Telegraph Company controlled 855,000 telephones; but elsewhere the telephone made little headway until the twentieth century. After 1900, however, telephone installations extended much more rapidly in all the wealthier countries, though the USA remained far more active in this field than any other country. The American Telephone and Telegraph Company, which practically monopolized telephone services in the USA, controlled over 9 million telephones in 1915, and over 17 million in 1940. After this other countries began to make good more of their arrears. The number of telephones in use in the world grew at almost 100 per cent per decade after 1948 and reached 291 million in 1971. The telephone continued to be of service mainly to local communication and to the internal administration of business. But long-distance telephone services gradually developed – in 1915 it became possible to telephone from the Atlantic to the Pacific coast of the USA – and, by saving time and by providing a more direct form of contact between those addressing each other, began to make inroads on telegraphic business. Indeed, by the nineteen-fifties, it was only in the Asiatic countries that the number of inland telegrams still showed a fairly general tendency to rise. In some of the more advanced countries, such as the USA and the UK, the trend was steeply downwards.

A greater contribution to long-range communication came with the development of wireless. About the turn of the century this was establishing itself as a practical proposition, and its potentialities were spectacularly demonstrated at the end of 1901, when Marconi succeeded in picking up a signal sent across the Atlantic. Before the outbreak of the First World War wireless telegraphy was established as a means of regular communication with ships at sea, and provided a valuable supplement to existing telegraph lines and cables. In the next two decades rapid technical progress was made in the transmission of speech and other series of sounds with varying pitch. One achievement was to give to telephony the same possibilities of long-distance international communication as existed for telegraphy. In 1927, a radio telephone service was begun between London and New York, and in the next few years the telephone systems of all the chief countries were connected with each other by radio. The use of these new facilities, however, grew only slowly for many years, though by the nineteen-fifties it had gone far enough for the number of telegrams and cables despatched abroad from the USA and the UK to begin to decline. Far more immediate was the influence that radio had through broadcasting, which in the late nineteen-twenties and the 'thirties began to pervade most of the homes of the westernized world and a great number elsewhere, and by television, which followed it at an interval of about twenty-five years. Instruction, indoctrination, information, lies plausible and implausible, and entertainment became continuously available to myriads. In no way did the influence of the machine more intimately mingle itself with the common experience of every day and hour.

THE UNEVEN DIFFUSION OF TECHNOLOGY

The increasingly productive techniques, which were based (mainly but not exclusively) in mechanical, electrical, and electronic engineering and in many branches of chemistry, became dominant in the world's economic activities, but they were never to be found in general use over most of the world. It was inevitable that there should be such contrasts for a time. New inventions and discoveries were made at a particular place and often successfully tried out there earlier than anywhere else. The requisite knowledge and specific resources were not immediately available in many other locations. But it might be expected that, with the passage of time, observation and experience would make good the deficiencies. More and more people would become aware of the qualities of the best products and aware also of the most efficient ways of making them. In their own interest they would seek to copy them and, if possible, to improve on them. In an increasing minority of countries such a course of events could be observed from at least the mid-nineteenth century onwards. The tendency, particularly by the mid-twentieth century, for all other kinds of economic activity to make influential use of the sort of technology which had once seemed characteristically and almost exclusively industrial, apparently had the potentiality to reduce the contrasts still further. To a very limited extent the minority of countries that shared a common sophisticated technology was enlarged. But the contrasts of technological character between a very advanced minority and a much less advanced majority remained. Indeed, after 150 or more years of spreading industrialization, some of the most influential contrasts appeared greater than ever.

There were many reasons for the slow and very incomplete diffusion of improved technology. Remoteness of situation was a major influence. Knowledge of superior achievement elsewhere came most easily along the routes of transport and trade; but, where backward methods had left an impoverished people or where natural obstacles were particularly difficult and costly to overcome, improved transport routes were least likely to appear. Aircraft did something by the middle of the twentieth century to increase contact with places never reached by earlier forms of mechanical transport, but the benefits were sometimes confined to the airport towns, and by that time there was a bigger technological gap to be crossed. Where access was easier there were often other adverse influences from the terrain. Regions of inefficient agriculture found sometimes that better methods developed elsewhere did not suit their conditions; or a life spent always with no margin above subsistence left them without means to adopt either better methods of farming or a more diversified economy. Twentieth-century research made it more likely that some kind of improvement adapted to local needs would be available, but the problem remained that the poor lacked the resources of both knowledge and wealth to take up the methods available to end the inefficiencies that helped to perpetuate their own poverty.

Governmental status could also have an effect. In some colonies it was only in the production of a few export commodities that the most efficient methods and equipment were introduced, whereas there was not a comparable change in the methods of activities carried on for local consumption. Colonial governments were also often unwilling to encourage the foundation of mechanized industries that might compete with imports from the home country. The objectives of policy became more liberal in this respect in the course of time, but then there was often the difficulty that outside technologies were not ideal for local conditions. This was particularly so where an acceleration of population growth made it immediately preferable to set up industries needing plenty of labour rather than a lot of imported machinery. In the nineteen-thirties, for example, the governments of French Indo-China and the Netherlands East Indies supported industrial development to try to offset the results of much reduced prices of exports of primary produce. Both favoured expansions of native handicrafts and did little to introduce new types of manufacture with up-to-date mechanized methods. When colonies had achieved independence later in the twentieth century the basic problem of population growth had usually got more difficult and was exerting more influence than the form of government. The general trend of technology had been towards capital-intensive methods. But to follow that trend without modification many former colonies (and some other countries) risked, in the short term at least, creating unemployment at home while running into debt for imports of machinery.

It might be argued that there was some mismatch between the course of technology and the economic structure of many of the countries to which it was not native. Where it worked successfully, as it did in most of the appreciably industrialized countries, the technology brought marvellous increases in productivity and material well-being. It also created, or facilitated, many of the conditions for its own continuous improvement and its adaptation to meet more varied needs. Thus, societies that mastered and adopted new technology early not only started with productive ability superior to that of most others, but were favourably placed to maintain or even increase that superiority. To take advantage of the opportunity they needed to plough back some of their increasing output into research and development and the education of their people, and they needed institutions and an outlook that led them regularly to invest in ways that made practical use of invention, and led them also to administer their businesses so as to make them as efficient as possible. Any country that showed similar characteristics and applied them in similar ways could join the small group of the technologically advanced and start to accumulate the benefits, even if it had lagged for a generation or so in the nineteenth century. The history of much of Europe bears this out. A country with much lower incomes, few educated people, and few people experienced in the requirements of risk bearing enterprise, was certain to start outside the charmed circle and to find it difficult to enter. In the course of the twentieth century some changes helped some of the outsiders. It became possible for production with highly sophisticated technology to be carried out by workers of whom only a very small proportion of managers and technicians had more than very elementary training and skills, provided that the appropriate equipment could be bought or borrowed. Even then the workers needed to apply consistently the virtues of patience and discipline. Without this, little progress was achieved. And, to catch up with the leaders, the early fruits of higher productivity had to be used to spread more advanced training to more people, to encourage creativity, and to acquire a constantly enlarging and improving stock of equipment.

In such circumstances advanced technology began to be integral to the economies of regions beyond Europe and the lands of European settlement. Most notable was the industrial rise of parts of east and southeast Asia, especially Japan and, from the nineteen-sixties, the much smaller countries of Hong Kong, South Korea, and Taiwan. Elsewhere there were countries which showed they had absorbed advanced technology into some sectors of the economy without having been able to make its results spill over very thoroughly into the rest of their activities. India, China, and some Latin American countries provide illustrations. But, even in the late twentieth century, there was still much of the rest of the world where advanced technology was very scarce, though it might show in a small industrial sector, a national airport, and a few showpieces for a capital city, and might also be embodied to some extent in schemes of agricultural and medical improvement encouraged by foreign aid.

At all times international economic dealings were moulded by conditions involving great and persistent inequalities which were associated with contrasts in productive ability and resources. The most obvious signs of the contrast, apart from levels of income, were the levels of the technology that was understood and used. But the explanations of the contrasts, and of some modifications of them, are far more complex. Changes in institutions, market organization, the ingrained habits and ideas of every type of worker (including employers and managers) were essential accompaniments of technical progress. They were an integral part of the history of economic advance, complementary to the contribution of technology. Only when they are included in the picture does the increasingly productive but wildly unequal course of the international economy start to become explicable.

CHAPTER THREE
Business management and organization

MANAGERIAL METHODS

Among the problems most closely related to the introduction of machinery was that of administration and control, a problem of ensuring that the potential advantages bestowed by technical improvement were realized in practice, that all the various divisions of the productive process were so combined as to contribute most effectively to the final result. The gathering together of wage-earners in a factory or workshop where they worked side by side under the constant observation of an overseer, instead of as and when they chose in their own homes, has often been described in general terms. The details of the internal arrangement of work within early factories are far less fully known. Study of the surviving records of some firms has revealed that very close attention and careful investigation were devoted to fundamental managerial problems, but there is little to suggest that this was typical of early factory industry as a whole anywhere. It seems more likely (though the present state of research precludes certainty) that in most factories questions of organization and layout were settled empirically, as they arose, on the basis of what seemed immediately convenient and practicable, without any elaborate or continuous attempt to estimate the relative efficiency of alternative measures. If a business prospered, then there was little incentive to seek internal administrative improvements until new technical developments or a great increase in size made some reconsideration unavoidable. In these circumstances the term 'factory system' covered a multitude of most varied practices.

There were nevertheless common elements in the problems facing early factory owners (who were usually the managers of their own factories) even in industries with considerable differences in technical conditions. Apart from the general problems of obtaining sufficient capital and labour to enable the business to be established and carried on, there were problems of ensuring that the work of men and of machines kept pace with one another and problems in the co-ordination of successive processes so as to obtain a smooth flow of work throughout the factory. It is to the need to make labour, which was accustomed to work unevenly, with many spurts and many pauses, serve the regular demands of machines that the introduction in early nineteenth-century England and New England of elaborate and often harsh codes of factory discipline, with their fines and other punishments for lateness, absence, frivolity, or other symptoms of inattention, is chiefly to be attributed. Longer experience by both employers and labourers of the nature and methods of the work which they were doing made it possible to simplify such disciplinary codes and mitigate their harshness, but it appears to have been slow to change the negative character of the contribution which adminis-tration made to the productive process. There continued to be more concern with the imposition of a variety of prohibitions than with an attempt to discover and apply a particular way in which each process could be most efficiently carried out. Emphasis was on continuous technical improvement rather than on the better adaptation of pro-ductive organization to each technical level while it existed. One of the most earnest early students of the factory system, Andrew Ure, whose surfeit of didactic clap-trap tends to distract attention from the abundance and reliability of his information, suggested in 1835 that the constant aim of mechanical improvement was to make it possible either to dispense with human labour or to use labour of less and less skill. The problem of organization would in fact gradually become incorporated in the problem of machine design.

But possibilities of better or worse organization existed and were susceptible of objective study. Ure's contemporary, Charles Babbage, made the first notable contribution to such a study. He examined the cost of each step in the productive process by taking a long series of observations of the time which individual workmen took to perform it, in different conditions, thus drawing attention to those elements which seemed to involve the greatest waste. He considered the savings which might accrue from applying the principle of division of labour as thoroughly to supervisory as to manual work. He investigated the relation between the profitable extent of division of function and the optimum size of the business unit. At every stage he tried to deduce from his abundant empirical observations general principles which might guide the management of factories. Babbage was never a practising manufacturer, but his work was fairly widely read in England in the eighteen-thirties. It is unlikely that his exposition had no practical influence, but the applications must have been of a piecemeal character. His work did not promote any generalized study of business management.

The laying out of a workshop and the combining of productive resources in such a way as to ensure a continuous flow of work was not a novelty imposed by the introduction of machinery. It was something inherent in the extension of the division of labour which had been proceeding steadily in Western Europe in the seventeenth and eighteenth centuries without very much increase in mechaniz-ation. Its importance is clear from Adam Smith's description of the work of production. The first stages of mechanization probably did not make very much difference to the extent of division of labour in most cases. They did not fundamentally change the problem of co-ordinating the successive stages of the productive process, though they changed it in detail, since the balancing of resources had to be altered when one stage was partly mechanized and others not at all. What mechanization did was to display economies, obtained by precision and regularity of working, such as had never been achieved by division of labour alone. It suggested by example new standards of exactitude which might be reached by a more careful deployment and further division of labour where, for the time being, the applica-tion of machinery was technically or economically impossible. This was important in the mid-nineteenth century when, in a number of countries, mechanization had conclusively demonstrated its material advantages, but had still been applied successfully to only a relatively small proportion of economic activities. It was most important of all where skilled labour was scarce and there was consequently the greatest incentive for managers to ensure that it was enabled to work to its maximum efficiency.

These conditions existed in many places in the USA until some time after the Civil War, and it is not surprising that the attempts made there to mechanize occupations which remained handicrafts in Europe should have been accompanied by striking developments in workshop layout so as to facilitate a quasi-mechanical use of labour itself. These developments probably achieved their most perfect manifestation in the rapidly growing meat-packing industry of Cin-cinnati in the middle of the century. Mr Giedion has described how there the live pigs were driven up an inclined plane to the top storey of a building where they were slaughtered, after which each successive group of processes was carried out at a lower level, to which the carcasses dropped under their own weight, thus saving much effort. On the level they were moved in trucks and dumb-waiters and placed with the utmost regularity before those who constantly repeated the same few operations on each carcass. It was the crude beginning, with little mechanical aid, of a continuous line of production on which, as material moves uninterruptedly through the workshop, the time in which it is not receiving any productive attention is cut to a minimum, with a consequent increase in the rate of output and reduction in prime cost.

During the later years of the nineteenth century, in a wide variety of activities in all the more highly industrialized countries, the fundamental problems of business administration began to change, partly because the questions posed separately by the use of machines and by the redeployment of labour reinforced each other much more completely than before. As mechanization increased, it led to further and further subdivision of the productive process; thus it brought a renewed emphasis, which the first stages of mechanization had not done, to the old problems of the division of labour: the necessity of ensuring that waste of time and effort in transferring a partly finished product from one stage to another was minimized, and the necessity for more than offsetting any such waste by securing maximum efficiency in the performance of each stage of the subdivided productive process. At the same time the economic conditions which made it worth while to adopt technical changes of this kind were coming into existence. There was a growing demand for many classes of goods which could be satisfied by uniform products. But the firm which adopted new methods, though it had the hope of greater rewards, exposed itself to new risks. More machinery and more administration, which was made necessary by a larger scale and more complex method of production, meant a heavier burden of overhead costs, which was temporarily increased for those firms (of which the British iron industry in the eighteen-eighties provided many examples) which, in order to maintain their competitive position, had to scrap working plant before its value had been written off by normal depreciation. The imposition of increased costs from one source was a direct incentive to seek the maximum economies obtainable in other ways, and for industries which underwent profound technical change in the last quarter of the nineteenth century it was reinforced by the pressure of falling prices and, in some cases, of difficulty in maintaining previous rates of profit on capital. Where technical change came a little later, this influence was much less common.

There were various ways in which economies could be sought, of which more efficient production through better internal administration and control of work was only one. But it was one which, in some important respects, was more feasible than it had been, because some firms had fuller and more exact information than they used to have about the economic aspects of the various elements in their activities. This was mainly due to an improvement in methods of book-keeping and of cost accounting, which made it possible to know the way in which total costs were made up and the way in which the costs of different operations varied through time, thus drawing attention to particular elements of possible weakness or strength. It is not the case, however, that in any country precise knowledge of the component elements in costs was general in business before 1900 or, indeed, much later. But awareness of the need for greater efficiency and economy was widespread even if precise information on some subjects which were relevant to achieving them was not. Within factories and workshops in many places and industries, piecemeal adjustments were made on a basis of trial and error, and among what was, at first, a very small minority an attempt was begun to reform radically the whole system of business management.

The successful rise, late in the nineteenth century, of a movement for what came to be known as scientific management was a response to the wider spread and more complete application of mechanization. This had made clearer (what Babbage had foreshadowed) that there were fundamental common principles in the administration of factories and workshops, however diverse the forms in which they presented themselves. The movement was strengthened because, as markets and the size of firms grew, the rewards for a small superiority in efficiency increased. It is significant that the pursuit of scientific management was at first largely confined to the USA, where markets for standardized products and the degree of mechanization were both increasing faster than anywhere else.

Scientific management was an attempt to apply to the organization of business the same repeated and precise observation, the same spirit of dispassionate enquiry, the same generalization from abundant and tested experiment which characterized the development of technology. Its object was to ensure that every worker, every tool and machine in a firm was used to its maximum efficiency. This it sought to achieve by giving each worker an incentive to do his best instead of spinning out his job, by discovering the best way in which each operation could be performed and then insisting on the uniform application of that method, and by planning in advance the day's work to be done by everyone so that there should be no interruption in the flow of work from one stage to another.

The leading figures in the introduction of scientific management in the USA were Taylor, Gantt, and Gilbreth, each of whom eventually established himself in the new profession of management consultant. Taylor was the pioneer whose experience as workman and foreman in engineering shops had taught him that most men tried not to work with determined effort, that even those whose intentions were good were far from efficient, and that under existing forms of management an attempt to get a fair day's work out of men created bitterness and strife. From the early eighteen-eighties he was trying to combine the increase in the productivity of labour in the various engineering works which employed him with the revision of managerial methods there. His concern was especially to remove the obstacles to efficient work which were imposed by faulty arrangements for which the worker himself was not responsible. The leading element of his reform was the division of work into set tasks. The management planned every man's work at least a day in advance and gave him complete written instructions describing in detail the task he was to accomplish, the method he was to use, and the time allowed. If he accomplished the task in the set time he received a large addition to his normal rate of wages; if he failed the rate was reduced. Taylor was also interested in discovering the most efficient way in which various operations could be performed by men and machines and enforcing that method uniformly. Thus he studied such a common manual task as shovelling, and by prescribing the design and size of shovel to be used for different purposes, the way it was to be used, the amount of time to be spent working and the amount resting, he secured an enormous increase in the quantity of material moved. Gilbreth carried investigations of this kind much further, making the most elaborate studies of movement, recorded photographically for subsequent analysis, in a constant quest for what he called 'the one best way' to do work. Gantt sought to remove the dangers to the position of labour which the close control involved in scientific management might bring. He tried to do this by introducing bonus methods of payment, by making the systematic training of operatives and provision for their upgrading an integral part of the system of management, and by suggesting an increase of industrial democracy.

Scientific management was, of course, not a static concept applied in its entirety from the beginning. New ideas and methods were continually being incorporated within it, and the type of records and charts which were best suited to its application were developed gradually out of thinking and experience. It was used by only a minority, even in the USA. In 1911, after thirty years of effort, Taylor claimed no more than that at least 50,000 people were employed under scientific management in the USA. Elsewhere the American experiments had up to that time attracted little attention. But there had been some approaches by different methods to the achievement of similar results. The outstanding example was provided by Henri Fayol in France. He was in the service of a large coal-mining combine for fifty-eight years, for the last thirty of which, from 1888 to 1918, he acted as general manager with conspicuous success. He set himself the task of devising an administrative structure based on division and relation of function which would enable the manager to have the clearest record of what was happening throughout his undertaking and enable decisions of policy, based on the fullest and clearest knowledge, to be most effectively translated into action. Towards the end of his career he began to publicize the principles of administration which he had developed.

In the first quarter of the twentieth century there were, then, both in the USA and Europe, efforts in progress to increase the whole efficiency of business by internal administrative as well as by technological means. Though these efforts were not widely copied, the influences which had stimulated a minority to devise systems of scientific management were steadily becoming more general in highly industrialized countries. Discussion of problems of industrial administration was becoming more widespread. Individual experiments in management, made empirically and without conscious reference to general principles, were increasing. The commercial and technical environment of industry was changing in such a way as to make efficient management more obviously important, and as this happened, the influence of the pioneers of improved industrial administration was gradually absorbed into more general practice. Even where there was no attempt to copy the more advanced methods, management was becoming a more specialized and subdivided occupation.

A new stimulus came from the needs of war, which called for the most efficient use of inferior productive resources. They revealed the great diversity of the contributions which existing managements could make to the achievement of this aim and at the same time they presented the opportunity of revealing to the worst managements the superior practices of the best. In the years immediately afterwards, more articles became the objects of mass consumption in a standardized form and, in conjunction with the further rapid progress of machine technology, this made profitable a fuller development of continuous assembly lines where the uninterrupted movement of conveyor systems must be matched by a comparable frictionless precision in the sequence of administrative planning. In many countries new institutions were established which facilitated the discussion of problems and experiments in management.

For all these and other reasons the years after 1914 witnessed a profound change in the internal arrangements of business. Earlier systems of scientific management were not taken over generally as they stood. They were developed in all kinds of ways, some of which proved disastrous and had to be abandoned, while others brought lasting improvements. In particular, far more attention began to be paid to increasing the welfare and enlisting the support of labour in industry, and personnel management became an important branch of industrial administration. But whatever developments were made, they rested on the wider application of the practice taken over from the foundation period of scientific management, the practice of tackling industrial problems by rational investigation and applying uniformly the conclusions thus reached.

This more rational approach to the fundamentals of industrial administration was developed mainly in manufacturing business, especially in the engineering industries, but it gradually extended to wider fields in the twentieth century. The distributive trades, financial institutions, even to some extent the military and civil administration of governments were all affected by it. Yet scientific management (in its widest sense as something more than the principles propounded and practised by Taylor) was very far from universal, even in the most highly industrialized countries. It was on the whole applied much more in the largest undertakings than in smaller ones, many of which continued to be administered by rule-of-thumb methods, and some of which still relied on the crudest and most approximate methods of costing.

In the period after 1950 there were further drastic changes in methods of business administration. They were possible partly because the proportion of business which was in the hands of very large undertakings continued to increase, and partly because of technological innovation. The effect of the latter was repeatedly to improve the facility and speed with which information could be supplied, recorded, retrieved, analysed, and communicated. There was a progression from rather clumsy data processing equipment to the use of ever more compact and adaptable computers, and then to the development of increasingly comprehensive information technology. It became possible for business decisions to be made on the basis of fuller and more up-to-date information from which more exact knowledge of inter-relationships and current trends of change had been drawn. The combination of rapid and more precise analysis of information with synchronous communication of the results created new possibilities of centralized control with decentralized location of operations. This had large implications for business structure and organization. Change of this kind increased the relative advantages of the highly sophisticated economies. The wide range of opportunities was not apparent before the late nineteen-seventies, and they did not turn management into a foolproof profession. More complex problems were tackled with more confidence, but more precise analysis of more recent data was not always a protection against spectacular errors of judgement; and all through the third quarter of the century there was much business which prospered without great sophistication of management. But the influence of the new methods grew steadily and they contributed to a great change in the characteristics of business institutions, and in the location of power within them, in the thirty years after 1950.

THE STRUCTURE OF FIRMS

The control and co-ordination of the various activities and sections within a business formed only one side of its administrative problems. There was a distinct, though not completely unrelated, set of questions concerning the business as a whole: who should own it? how could it obtain the necessary capital? how big should it be? how many types of goods should it make? what should be its relations with competitors and suppliers? Every business had to answer these questions continuously, and the answers which were commonest changed as commercial, legal, and technical conditions changed.

Until well on in the nineteenth century most businesses in all countries were small, mainly because technical and marketing conditions were such that there was seldom any advantage to be derived from a larger organization. Even where a larger unit was economically desirable, it was frequently unattainable because of lack of access to large sources of capital. In the third quarter of the nineteenth century a high proportion of European industry was still conducted on the domestic system, in many cases (for example in most of German industry) with a large number of very small masters; and the family was often of major importance as a productive unit. This state of affairs continued to characterize a substantial though declining proportion of economic activity into the twentieth century. The mechanized factories and workshops which became increasingly numerous were also at first usually small. Most of them numbered their employees in tens and their capital in no more than hundreds of pounds. They were owned by one man or a small number of partners who ran the business themselves. The owners often contributed as much of the capital as they themselves could. The rest they had to borrow from their family or acquaintances or from persons with whom mutual business contacts might have brought them in touch.

The investment of profits in the expansion of the business enabled many undertakings to grow to considerable size while still organized as partnerships. With patience, skill, and good fortune, it was often not too difficult to achieve this so long as the gradual addition of small increments of capital was an effective method of expansion, as it was when capital was needed mainly to pay for labour and material and to finance stocks of finished goods and only a small proportion of it needed to be spent on buildings, plant, and administration. The gradual expansion of businesses was still more practicable where much of the working capital was obtainable by short-term borrowing from banks that would regularly grant a renewal of loans to any business which remained in a sound condition. In England, in the first half of the nineteenth century, the many country banks made a useful contribution to business expansion in this way, though the shaky state of many of them was a source of intermittent difficulty to their borrowers and depositors, especially in the recurrent financial panics. Elsewhere banking facilities were less developed, and the channels of short-term borrowing for business were consequently fewer. But in the latter half of the century there was a great increase in the number and strength of banks in all the leading industrial and commercial countries, and they went far to meet the needs of business for working capital which, moreover, probably grew (on the average) more slowly than turnover, since improvements in transport and communication reduced the time during which materials and finished goods were in transit and reduced the volume of stocks which it was necessary for a prudent business to hold.

The small partnership providing for further expansion out of its own private means and past profits was at a disadvantage where much of the necessary investment had to go into indivisible items of fixed capital. In such conditions new capital had to be added in increments so large as often to be beyond the means of the partners themselves. In the middle of the nineteenth century there were already several industries in which these conditions existed, the outstanding examples being the chief public utilities: railways, gas, and water-supply. The course of technical change made similar conditions applicable to many manufacturing industries before 1900 and still more in the twentieth century.

The need to invest larger amounts at a time was felt simultaneously by a high proportion of the firms in several different industries in any rapidly expanding economy. Not only the size of capital increments but also the total national investment had to increase. Both changes made it necessary for business to gain access to fresh sources of capital. A partial solution of the problem was the development of investment banking, i.e. the creation of institutions which would accumulate capital by the sale of stock and bonds and, in some cases, by conducting deposit-banking business as well, and which would use the capital in making long-term loans to business enterprises. In Great Britain investment banking never became very important, though in the eighteen-sixties several highly speculative finance companies were formed, ostensibly to perform this function, and some of the existing merchant bankers made some long-term investments, chiefly overseas. But in France the example was provided by the *Crédit Mobilier* which was established in 1852 and financed a good deal of railway construction as well as some dock companies and gas companies before 1867, when its activities began rapidly to decline as a result of financial difficulties. The example was copied in several countries, including the USA, and was especially influential in Germany. There the provision of long-term capital for industry and trade was always accepted as a normal function by the deposit banks which were springing up from the eighteen-fifties onward.

If a business could obtain from a bank or finance house the extra capital that it needed, it was in many cases spared the necessity of changing its structure. Investment banking was a device which assisted the family business or partnership to survive as a unit of organization while the task of capitalization became increasingly heavy. But when a bank provided a large proportion of the capital of a business, it was able to demand some control over its organization and, in the interests of its own security, it often did so. The accompaniment of increased investment banking was participation by representatives of the banks in the government of the businesses of their borrowers. This development was particularly marked in Germany where, for example, one of the largest banks, the *Deutsche Bank*, was connected in 1920 with the administration of more than 200 businesses.

But investment banking was in any case able to supply only a small proportion of the capital needed by business, and it became necessary for more and more enterprises to seek capital from fresh sources. The easiest solution of the difficulty, where the law allowed it, was the formation of joint-stock companies which would enable outside persons to subscribe capital to a business in return for a share in its profits, without necessarily increasing the number of partners who took an active part in day-to-day administration. But a share in profits was not by itself enough to attract most potential investors. They wanted also a certain amount of liquidity and security for their investment. To satisfy the desire for liquidity it was necessary not only that shares should be legally transferable at any time, but also that there should be a permanent market on which they could be bought and sold at a known price. For the stock of a few large and famous companies these conditions were fulfilled in the eighteenth century, but investors in the earlier manufacturing and public utility companies of the nineteenth century often took the risk of tying up their money for a long period or of being able to sell their holding to only a limited circle of interested people who might be in a position to name their own price. It was only as the number of investors and of companies increased that the securities of all types of business became the subject of regular stock exchange dealings. After about 1840 existing stock exchanges rapidly extended the range and volume of their dealings, and stock exchanges were established in many places where they had not previously existed. The appearance in any centre of a sudden and unprecedentedly large demand for capital, such as occurred in one place after another in connexion with railway promotion, usually resulted in the formation of new institutions essential to the existence of a long-term capital market, and these institutions remained permanently to serve the needs of business as a whole. The telegraph and the cable made information about prices and business conditions available almost simultaneously in business centres in all parts of the world, and by the last quarter of the nineteenth century the investor in any commercially important country could rely on being able to sell his holding at any time at a competitive price.

The desire for security made necessary important changes in the position and constitution of companies themselves. The investor's first safeguard was that the company using his money should be efficient and honest, and in order to have a check on this before committing his money, he needed access to a minimum amount of information about its affairs, such as could be obtained if it were required to published its prospectus, articles of association and annual audited balance-sheet and profit and loss account. Beyond this the investor wanted to be sure that if things went wrong he would not be involved in any loss in addition to the amount of his investment; i.e. he wanted limited liability in order to ensure that his private means could not be called on to meet the debts of any company in which he had invested. Company organization with limited liability was just as much an advantage to the investor as to the expanding business enterprise, and it would be wrong to suppose that pressure for a change in the law so as to permit the general use of this type of organization came only from business as it was confronted with the need for greatly increased capitalization. In Britain, in the second quarter of the nineteenth century, the pressure came at least as strongly from a growing potential investing public which had little access, except at what seemed inordinate risk, to the more profitable branches of business enterprise. The legal privilege of incorporation with limited liability was in fact made general there while most enterprises were still able to obtain all the capital they needed without recourse to this form of organization. Elsewhere, fewer active partners could command such large amounts of capital, but on the other hand there was for a good many years less demand than in Britain for capital in large increments, so that the economic need for limited liability companies developed no more quickly than in Britain. In general the facilities for the formation of limited liability companies appear to have kept up very adequately with the need for them in almost all countries.

The steps by which the general grant of the right, on certain conditions, to incorporation with limited liability was reached differed considerably among the various countries. In England, at the beginning of the nineteenth century, a company, with limited or unlimited liability, could acquire legal existence only by Act of Parliament or the grant of a royal charter. In the second quarter of the century there was less opposition to the formation of companies and in 1834 an additional and less expensive method of sanctioning their creation, by the grant of letters patent, was introduced. But all the members of a company continued to have unlimited liability unless limited liability were specifically conferred on them. During the next twenty years there was a strong agitation for a change in this position, and a series of Acts in 1855, 1856, 1858, and 1862 established the right of any seven or more persons to become a corporate body with limited liability, on condition that they deposited a memorandum of association with the registrar of companies and subsequently filed articles of association, supplied annual statements of their capital, directors, and shareholders, and published properly audited accounts of their financial position. Until 1907 only one form of limited liability company was recognized by statute, but in that year private limited companies which, in small numbers, had for many years existed as a distinct type, became the subject of legislation. The number of their shareholders was restricted to a maximum of fifty, and they were forbidden to make a public offer of shares, but they were exempt from the obligation to publish statements of their financial position. This form of company quickly became popular, and the number of private soon far exceeded the number of public companies.

The USA inherited English company law, but the revolution had destroyed the idea that the power to grant charters rested solely in the Crown, and thus had removed one of the influences restricting the formation of new joint-stock companies. There was indeed much less opposition in the early nineteenth century to the extension of company organization than in Britain. The legal difficulties were generally less, though the position varied because of differences in the legislation of the various states. By the middle of the nineteenth century the establishment of companies was a steadily increasing practice and few legal obstacles to the adoption of limited liability remained.

In France a new body of company law had been adopted in 1807. A true joint-stock company (*société anonyme*), whether it had limited liability or not, could be established only if it obtained an individual authorization from the government. But an alternative form, known as *société en commandite par actions*, in which the active partners had unlimited liability and the sleeping partners limited liability, was subject to much less official supervision and formality and in the mid-nineteenth century was much the more widely used type. But in 1856 the *société en commandite par actions* was put under stricter official supervision. In 1867 the necessity for the individual authorization of every *société anonyme* was abolished, and limited liability was granted generally as in Britain. After that the *société anonyme* became the usual type of company in France.

In Germany there was no general system of commercial law until the latter half of the nineteenth century, and few of the individual states had any statutory code of company law before then. Prussia issued a general law for joint-stock companies in 1843, but in most states any commercial organization which wished to assume corporate form had to apply for a charter or obtain a special law. Even in Prussia after 1843, every company had to be individually authorized by the government, although authorization could always be obtained if the company conformed to a standard set of conditions. A common code of company law for all Germany was established by a series of measures adopted between 1870 and 1872. Its effect was to abolish the requirement of individual authorization for companies and to make limited liability generally available, thus facilitating the formation of the normal type of public company, known as *Aktiengesellschaft*. These measures were supplemented in 1892 by the legalization of another type of company, the *Gesellschaft mit beschränkter Haftung*, which was very similar to the private company in Great Britain. As its name indicates, it had limited liability, but the number of shareholders was restricted, there was no body of generally marketable shares, and there was no obligation to publish much about its affairs.

Although all the leading industrial countries made limited liability generally available to businesses in the second half of the nineteenth century, the limited liability company did not immediately become the usual form of business organization. In so far as the grant of general limited liability was a response to the needs of business rather than to those of potential investors, it served the interest and convenience of a minority. It was still practicable for the greater part of business to be conducted by small partnerships for many years after the grant of general limited liability. Moreover, limited liability did not by itself help the incorporated firm to tap the savings of the general public. The costs of making a public offer of shares were everywhere more than the smaller firms could afford. The adoption of corporate form depended as much on the gradually increasing worth of the legal privileges which it conferred as on financial need.

Company organization became usual in the USA earlier than anywhere else. In Europe it made very slow progress until the end of the nineteenth century. Even in Great Britain corporate organization was exceptional in business as late as 1880, but a few years later it began to be adopted rapidly, and had become the normal form of business organization some years before 1914. The number of companies registered in the United Kingdom increased from 9,344 in 1885 to 62,762 in 1914. In France, company organization did not begin to spread widely until after 1895, and nowhere on the European mainland did it become as common as in the USA or, at least until 1914, in Great Britain.

But, although its spread was delayed, company organization had become indispensable to some sections of industrial activity before the end of the nineteenth century. The greater mechanization, which has already been mentioned, stimulated a steady increase in the average size of businesses of many types in the second half of the century. So, too, did the greater abundance of information about market conditions over a wide area. Improved transport and communications made it practicable and profitable for many more enterprises to interest themselves in new markets, to establish agents and commercial travellers for the purpose of gaining a footing in them, to elaborate their systems of administration in order to be constantly responsive to changes in market conditions, and to expand their whole business to grasp the opportunity of selling more.

This growth in the size of firms was one major factor encouraging the adoption of corporate organization, but the influence was reciprocal. The establishment of general limited liability made it much easier to build up firms to a very large size. It was thus a contributory factor to the development of business concentration, i.e. the consolidation of activity into the hands of a smaller number of separately controlled firms, relatively to the total volume of business.

Concentration was not an entirely new phenomenon in the late nineteenth century. There had earlier been important industries in which it had been marked at particular times and places; in the Lancashire cotton industry, for example, in the second quarter of the century, when economies in the application of power led temporarily to the growth of composite spinning and weaving firms at the expense of smaller specialized mills. But it was only at a rather later date that a rapid increase in concentration became a feature common to many activities in all important industrial countries.

Its extent in economic activity as a whole in the late nineteenth century is difficult to assess quantitatively, but there is no doubt that it was very considerable. In thirteen leading manufacturing industries in the USA the average amount of capital of each manufacturing plant was multiplied by thirty-nine between 1850 and 1910, and the value of the average output was multiplied by nineteen. Even in so

97

widely competitive an industry as the cotton spinning of Lancashire, the number of firms remained practically unchanged between 1884 and 1911, while the number of spindles almost doubled. In newer industries, where there were fewer small firms with deep roots, concentration went on more easily and to a greater extent. In the twentieth century it proceeded more quickly, and affected a wider range of activities almost everywhere. In the USA establishments with an annual output of $5,000 to $20,000 employed 6.9 per cent of the manufacturing wage-earners and produced 3.7 per cent of the manufacturing output (in terms of value) in 1914, but by 1929 these proportions were reduced to 2.3 per cent of the wage-earners and 1.1 per cent of the output. On the other hand, establishments with an annual output of more than $1 million employed 35.3 per cent of the wage-earners and produced 48.7 per cent of the output in 1914, but in 1929 employed 58.3 per cent of the wage-earners and produced 69.2 per cent of the output. Establishments with an annual output of less than $500,000 were making a declining proportionate contribution to the nation's manufacturing activity.

Concentration was closely related to industrial combination. Although increased concentration came about partly because many smaller firms were unfitted to meet new economic and technical conditions and passed out of existence, leaving the field to their larger, expanding competitors, the process was in most cases helped on by the making of agreements or some form of complete or partial fusion between rival firms. There was a number of important industrial combinations in various countries in the eighteen-seventies, but it was in the last few years of the century that the movement really began to gather strength. In Great Britain between 1896 and 1901 large combines were formed in the manufacture of sewing cotton, bleaching powder, Portland cement, wallpaper, and tobacco, and in most branches of textile finishing. At the same time there was in Germany an increase in the formation of cartels which had begun to be prominent rather earlier; by 1906 nearly 400 were in existence. In the USA also industrial combination was rapidly extending, particularly through the formation of holding companies, which were purely financial bodies created for the purpose of exercising common control, through the ownership of stock, over the policies of previously competing enterprises. In 1904 there were in the country 318 industrial combines, in which were consolidated nearly 5,300 separate establishments, and which were capitalized at more than $7,000 million. Of these combines, 236, with a capital of about $6,000 million, had been incorporated since 1897. The combination movement slackened almost everywhere in the ten years or so preceding the First World War, though not to the same extent in all countries. In Great Britain it became temporarily of small importance, but in Germany and the USA numerous important combines continued to be made. In the period between the two world wars combination went on rapidly in all industrialized countries. The number of cartels in Germany rose to 2,400 by 1932. Estimates made on somewhat different bases suggested that in Great Britain in 1927 about 20 per cent of mining and manufacturing workers were employed by firms which formed part of some combine, and that in 1935 29 per cent of the workers in factory trades were in industries from which competition had practically disappeared.

As industrialization spread and competition in more activities became international in scope, some combines also became international. The earliest important attempt to share out markets among the producers of different countries was the foundation of the European rail-makers' cartel in 1883, and by 1914 there were over 100 agreements concerning firms in more than one country. In a smaller number of cases there were closer fusions of firms in different countries, the earliest being the Nobel Dynamite Trust, formed in 1886. Early in the twentieth century a number of the leading new industries came under the control of international combines. They included oil, rayon, and margarine. International combines were also formed in some older industries, including the manufacture of armaments; and numerous other combines which were controlled from only one country took a leading part in the business of other countries. In the interwar years, international combines, like national combines, increased steadily in numbers, but they still remained the exception rather than the rule, whereas national combines were beginning to control a major part of economic activity. After the Second World War the development of international combines became a good deal more prominent. In the most rapidly growing industries, where each firm had large overheads and most of the products were expensive and standardized items with a common appeal to consumers in all the wealthier countries, access to a multinational market was vital. This was often most easily gained by direct involvement in, or association with, producing and distributing organizations in each of several countries. The multinational firm therefore became increasingly characteristic in such industries as automobile production, electronic and electrical engineering, heavy chemicals and pharmaceuticals.

Combines included many different types of structure. Most of the business associations formed in the late nineteenth century were of a horizontal type, i.e. they were agreements or fusions among firms making similar products, and they usually included among their objects an attempt to monopolize all or part of the market for their goods. Vertical integration, by which several successive stages in the production of a finished article (ranging in extreme cases from the mining or growing of all the raw materials to the operation of chain stores in which the completed goods were sold) were brought under the control of a single organization, was rare, though not unknown, before 1900. In the early twentieth century it was developed to a much greater extent. This type of organization was in practice less concerned to secure a monopoly or near-monopoly. Its rise was more closely connected with changing methods of business management, and it was in fact an extension of the attempts to ensure the most economical transition between successive stages of the productive process which, within the individual factory, were among the chief concerns of scientific management.

There was indeed a very close connexion between the rise of scientific management and that of industrial concentration in all its aspects. In part they were complementary responses to the same environmental changes. More mechanization, greater subdivision of processes and the consequent increasing proportion which overheads bore to total costs, characteristics of industry which began to be prominent in the last quarter of the nineteenth century and became more and more so in the course of the twentieth century, eventually compelled a change, not merely in the internal administration of firms, but in their whole structure. The rewards for introducing new techniques and methods of organization were potentially great, provided that the increased overheads could be spread over a much larger output. Those rewards could be grasped only by firms which were not merely bigger than they had been, but in some cases had grown faster than the market, so that they could survive only by securing a proportion of sales which had previously been effected by others. Moreover, the increase of one group of costs was a stimulus to a search for savings elsewhere. Most of this effort in the nineteenth century appeared to be directed towards the improvement of technology so as to bring prime costs lower and lower; some of it went, as noted earlier, into securing more efficient internal management. But some efforts were put forth in other directions also, differing partly according to the opportunities available in industries with widely differing technical and commercial conditions. Some firms sought the economies of vertical integration. Some sought by agreement to reduce the expenditure which was devoted mainly to defeating their competitors, either by lavish advertisement and other methods of sales promotion, or by the provision of services and concessions to consumers which would be unnecessary in conditions of less intense competition. Some, in making similar agreements, concerned themselves less with economies than with assuring themselves an adequate net return by obtaining control of the market. Some looked for savings to the abolition of many duplicated administrative activities by bringing a number of separate establishments under a single financial control.

The incentive to do any or all of these things was particularly strong when large organizations found themselves confronted by falling prices and increased difficulty in maintaining previous rates of profit, as many of them did in the eighteen-nineties and the nineteen-thirties, two periods in which a response in the form of combination was specially facilitated because the new capital needed for financial reorganization was obtainable at fairly low rates of interest. A similar tendency was also very prominent, however, in the years of rapidly rising prices and interest rates in the third quarter of the twentieth century. In part, this was simply the response to the powerful technological and marketing factors which called for a larger scale of organization. But it was reinforced by an increased attention to the wide disparities of performance between different firms. It was often found that additional resources for a growing business could most cheaply be obtained by taking over another firm whose existing assets (especially the most flexible asset, cash) were under-employed or used unprofitably. Such assets could then be redeployed in the growing business, and this became a common practice. Indeed, takeovers and the general pursuit of larger scale became so common that their advantages seem to have been assumed by some to be so general as not to need careful demonstration in each particular case. So the movement in this direction was increased by various examples of growth, usually through mergers of some kind, which were based on misjudgement or sheer irrationality, under the influence of a prevailing fashion. Such errors, of course, encouraged some counter movement in the fashion. This could be observed in the later 'seventies and early 'eighties, when more difficult business conditions caused a pruning of unrewarding appendages. At the same time the relatively greater scope for service industries and some of the wider applications of electronics both increased the opportunities to operate successfully on a smaller scale. There was thus some restraint on recent tendencies.

To some extent, however, a rational incentive to achieve greater concentration was always present wherever there was a high or increasing degree of mechanization or standardization. This was the common factor influencing the development of concentration in all advanced industrial communities, though its influence was, of course, exerted more strongly on some activities than others, and those most affected were of differing importance in the economic structure of different countries.

There were, however, other influences. Among the most general of them was the prevalence of excess capacity in many industries in the interwar period. This prompted the introduction of many schemes of rationalization under which large groups of firms made joint financial provision to compensate those among them who closed down plant. The seriousness of this problem was the result partly of the general increase in the proportionate burden of overhead costs, but partly also of circumstances peculiar to the time. For example, the special needs imposed by the First World War had caused an expansion of capacity in some industries, such as shipbuilding in Britain and various branches of engineering in several countries, which peacetime demand could not keep employed. There were also, at the same time, as a result of higher incomes in industrialized countries, important changes in the pattern of demand which adversely affected some of the old basic industries, especially those of Britain; and the political obstacles to the maintenance of international trade, which became more serious in the nineteen-thirties, aggravated the problem of surplus capacity in some of those same industries.

But concentration, though it persistently increased, was by no means a uniform or steady process. It advanced everywhere much more rapidly in some years than others; it increased considerably in some industrial countries at times when it had temporarily slackened in others; it led to the establishment of different types of organization in different countries. No explanation of the manifold individual variations within a general movement could ever hope to be complete. Here it is necessary only to indicate some of the more important temporary or local influences: differences both in time and place in the movement of economic activity; differences in the relative importance of industries particularly suited or unsuited to concentration; differences in the available markets arising from differences of geographical position and transport facilities; differences in fiscal legislation and the law of contract. This last group of factors, arising from the policies of governments, was especially influential on the forms of organization in concentrated industries. Though the tariff was described in the USA before the end of the nineteenth century as 'the mother of trusts', it is quite clear from what happened later, especially in Britain, that much concentration and combination could take place without a protective fiscal policy. What the tariff did was to make it easier for combines catering almost entirely for the home market to reap the advantages of domestic monopoly. The influence of the law of contract was probably stronger. The readier enforceability at law of contracts in restraint of trade was undoubtedly a major reason why cartels became commoner in Germany than elsewhere. The very lax company laws in force in New Jersey at the end of the nineteenth century made it easy for the great new American holding companies to establish themselves, and similar 'liberality' in some tiny European states, including Liechtenstein and Luxembourg, seeking revenue from outside, facilitated the formation of some of the ramshackle structures of international holding companies in the interwar years.

Concentration affected particularly finance, public utilities, and manufacturing industry, the three major branches of activity in which a high degree of standardization was most commonly profitable. In manufacture the number of small establishments continued everywhere to be far greater than the number of very large ones, but the latter became responsible in the twentieth century for a preponderant and growing proportion of total output. In banking and insurance, which, it is often overlooked, are concerned with a narrow range of highly standardized functions repeated myriads of times, amalgamation was particularly rapid in the first third of the twentieth century. In public utilities concentration went very far in the interwar period: in one country after another the railways passed into the control of fewer and larger bodies; the generation of electric power was similarly treated; and in other fields the same process was repeated as services were organized on a regional or nationwide instead of a local basis. Distribution was much less affected, especially its retail side. About 1900, department stores and chain stores began to appear in the wealthier countries, and chain stores in particular became steadily more prominent in the next half-century. But the small independent shopkeeper retreated only gradually before them and retained a large share of retail trade. Of all the major economic activities, agriculture was the least subject to concentration, yet in some branches even of this it was noticeable in the interwar years. A large part of the more heavily capitalized types of tropical plantation agriculture, such as the raising of sugar-cane and rubber, passed into the control of a few large companies; and a gradual increase in the size of the unit was evident in some temperate arable regions.

However numerous were the exceptions to the increase of business concentration, they were too few to diminish the significance of the general trend. The large unit was becoming increasingly representative of business, and, as it did so, was fundamentally changing the environment of political and social life. By combining concentration in the control of wealth with dispersion in its ownership, it was modifying the nature of one of the most elemental social institutions: property. By 1930, 22 per cent of the national wealth of the world's richest country, the USA, was owned by 200 corporations, in the biggest of which no individual owned as much as 1 per cent of the stock. In highly concentrated business the nominal owner of property was neither responsible for it nor in control of it. Its value was determined by factors which he could nor influence, yet was ascertainable at any moment. Its form was highly liquid and, within a limited range, it could readily be transferred to an alternative use. By contrast, those who were given control of vast wealth often owned only a tiny fraction of it. Indeed, a large measure of control was exercised by people who owned none, for a wide range of business decisions was left to professional administrators, who in the twentieth century formed a steadily expanding class in all industrialized countries.

The great and impersonal concentration of power which accompanied changes in business organization naturally aroused some suspicion and hostility, but legal and administrative attempts to diminish it by enforcing a reversal of the process of combination were never pursued more than half-heartedly, except for short periods, in any country. It was clear that in many branches of activity profitable production was impossible without a high degree of concentration, and that adaptation, through concentration, to new technical and economic conditions had contributed much to an increase of realized wealth, some part of which was widely diffused.

The prestige of free competition declined, particularly in the depressed conditions of the nineteen-thirties, and this lessened one of the sources of resistance to the rapid increase of industrial concentration. In the much more expansive business climate of the fifties and sixties competition again looked to have great merits and there was renewed attention to efforts to prevent the emergence of new monopolies and to exercise some political and legal control over those that already existed. For a time there may even have been a temporary check to the growth of concentration. Immediately after the Second World War some small firms found that years of full order books and inflationary prices had enabled them for the time being to hold their own in rivalry with bigger undertakings. In the ensuing period output and sales in the most successful industries grew so fast that even a large increase in the size of the principal firms did not always raise the degree of concentration in their particular industry. Nevertheless, despite these qualifications, the trend towards larger scale and greater concentration continued in advanced industrial countries. Any stiffer legal restrictions were directed against monopoly rather than against imperfect competition, and the kind of competition which was restored to favour was often that in which a fairly small number of large and highly integrated businesses operated in rivalry in a wide (usually international) market and bought their own supplies in markets which similarly were not monopolized but included only a small number of competing sellers. Economic growth was rated as more important than perfect competition, and, for a long time, it appeared that in most sectors of an advanced economy maximum growth was not feasible without a high degree of business concentration. Moreover, the large firm, building up big reserves of its own, was best able to preserve autonomy in its financial policy, and was also most likely to be able to associate on equal terms with large financial institutions. So the big firm usually appeared best placed to adjust to changing needs and opportunities.

The widespread experience of lower growth rates from the late seventies raised doubts whether the existing features of business structure were all conducive to efficiency and rapid growth. There was some reaction in favour of attempts to promote greater competition. Services, in some of which the optimum scale remained fairly small, were allotted a larger role in policies for economic growth. The replacement, or supplementation, of mechanical by electronic techniques enlarged the importance of some manufacturing activities in which enormous scale had no rational justification. So there was some check to the continuing trend towards larger scale and more imperfect competition, and there was some increased scope for the small business, even in the most advanced economies. But the recent tendencies were not noticeably put into reverse and the new technological influences did not operate only in one direction. Besides establishing conditions for some highly sophisticated industries and services to operate in small units, they also made it easier for one central controlling organization to direct a large number of possibly dispersed subordinate undertakings, even though the dispersal extended over several countries. So a high degree of business concentration remained, outside the lands of peasant agriculture, one of the striking organizational features of economic life. And the sustained increase in the number of commodities for which there was a more standardized market throughout the industrialized world meant that improved methods of controlling dispersed operations had special advantages for multinational firms, which therefore gained and retained a still more prominent position in the most highly concentrated activities.

CHAPTER FOUR
Labour

Labour has a dual character, springing from its existence as a factor of production and, at the same time, as one of the principal sources of individual experience, an outstanding direct influence on the quality of life of almost every human being. To the manager of any business it has always been among the prime necessities that he should have an adequate number of workers of various types and grades of skill, that they should be both able and willing to carry out specified functions, and that he should be able to retain their services as long as he wished, or replace them by others, at a price low enough to enable him to sell his final product profitably. But to the individual with labour to sell, the most important considerations were quite different. There was a whole way of life with which he was familiar and which he wished to maintain with incidental improvements, or there was some different mode of life to which he aspired, and his pay and working conditions largely determined how far his hopes and expectations could be fulfilled. Often they determined even how long he was likely to live. Because of this difference of interest, the history of labour is marked by alternations between seemingly divergent courses. There were attempts by each interested party to subordinate the concerns of the other to its own. But the interdependence of labour as a way of life and labour as a commodity essential to business was permanently inescapable, and consequently gave rise to attempts to devise new systems and terms of employment which would benefit each party, not at the expense of the other, but through the sharing of improvements jointly created.

The local environments in which labour has had to function in the last hundred years have been of the most varied character. The type of occupation which predominated, the technical methods and managerial systems in use, the opportunities to change employment, the rate of growth and the age structure of the population, the extent of urbanization, and the state of the law on labour questions all differed from place to place and from time to time, and consequently the history of labour in different countries and industries had marked individual features. It is not possible here to trace out any but a few of the most outstanding of these contrasts. All that can be done is to discuss the way in which the most fundamental economic changes, as their influence spread over a larger part of the world and an increasing range of activities, created certain common basic labour problems and led to the adoption of solutions in many of which there were important common elements though they were not completely identical.

The first labour problem to arise in the course of industrialization was the need to recruit workers for a body of new and expanding occupations. In few communities before the nineteenth century was there much mobility of labour. It was not economically necessary, and prevailing institutions were on the whole discouraging to it. Everywhere the most important occupation was agriculture, and the proportion of the population engaged in it changed only slowly. When other occupations expanded, the absolute number of additional labourers which they required was small in proportion to the total population. The commonest experience was for members of the same family through succeeding generations to follow the same occupation, and the path of entry to most occupations in many countries was closely prescribed by status, law, or custom. It was exceptional for a person to be in a particular job simply because he received a wage which was as good as or better than he could obtain by doing something else within his capabilities.

Increasing industrialization caused more rapid change in labour requirements. Some means had to be found, either by inducement or compulsion, of diverting to work in the new mechanized manufacturing industries and the expanding commercial activities people who, under previous conditions, would have had little opportunity or incentive to escape from the occupational destiny which custom laid down for them. Compulsion, except towards a small minority, was impracticable, not only because of the humanitarian opposition which it aroused, but also on strictly economic grounds. A large, organized traffic in forced labour was, in nineteenth-century conditions, too expensive. It imposed an overhead burden which few businesses could bear without difficulty. In addition, most of the tasks awaiting operatives in early factories were not sufficiently stereotyped to be safely left to the sullen and unresponsive labour of those who had nothing to gain by doing them well and little to lose by doing them badly. The recruitment of virtually forced labour for factories was therefore practically limited to small groups, such as the pauper children in Britain in the late eighteenth and early nineteenth centuries, who could be gathered in cheaply because circumstances had already delivered them *en masse* into the hands of public authority, and who could be employed on tasks which were simple and often trivial though essential.

Inducement, however, was not easy to apply. Conditions had first to be created in which labour was free to respond to the inducements which employers could offer. Agriculture was the principal source from which an army of industrial workers had to be recruited; but as long as serfdom survived, it imposed on the mass of the rural population the obligation of remaining tied to the soil, and also offered them the security of having the soil permanently tied to them. The transfer of labour out of agriculture on a large scale was impossible in Europe until serfdom was abolished. Other surviving restrictions placed by legislation or administrative practice on freedom of occupation or movement also had to disappear. In Europe in the early nineteenth century a great many such restrictions still remained. So did others of a slightly different kind. Occupations which were expanding and in which it was desired to introduce competitive bidding for labour were still subject to wage-fixing by administrative decision or by legislation, and found the size of their labour force still limited by strict conditions of entry. During the first half of the nineteenth century many restrictions were repealed or fell into disuse. Some had disappeared even earlier. But their influence survived them. People who had grown up in an environment in which particular regulations and restrictions were part of the background of everyday life usually retained the habits and outlook appropriate to that environment unless some catastrophe broke up their existence. It was not until a new generation emerged which had never been accustomed to the old regulations that the abolition of these made its full contribution to the establishment of an unrestricted labour market.

The demands of industrialization involved changes, not only in occupation, but in location also. To a large extent it was the same legal and customary restrictions which hampered both kinds of change, and their removal had consequently a twofold influence. But there were also some physical difficulties of movement. In Britain, where manufacturing grew rapidly in the first half of the nineteenth century, these were considerable, though not insuperable. But in other populous countries manufacturing and the railway grew more or less simultaneously, and as soon as people were free and willing to move into new industrial centres, adequate transport was available for them. In any case, much of the labour for early industrialization in Western Europe seems to have moved only quite short distances – out of villages into the nearest manufacturing town – so that transport was only a minor consideration. Inadequate transport probably retarded seriously the growth of the industrial labour supply only in those areas, notably the USA, which needed large numbers of people from overseas.

As obstacles to mobility were removed, newly mechanized industries gradually succeeded in obtaining the required number of workers by drawing in people from the countryside and by making fuller use of women and children. In achieving this, they were assisted by the rapid natural increase of population which was taking place throughout Europe in the nineteenth century. The combined populations of Britain, France, and Germany rose from approximately 66 million in 1810 to 86 million in 1840, 104 million in 1870 and 132 million in 1900.

There was the further difficulty of ensuring that this labour acquired the qualities which enabled it to carry out new kinds of work in unfamiliar conditions. There was a general problem of imposing greater regularity of working on everyone, which was tackled by the imposition of elaborate and often severe codes of discipline. And there was the further necessity for teaching each individual to do particular jobs. The old systems of apprenticeship were no longer appropriate for this purpose because they spread training over a long period. Of the great majority of factory workers it was required merely that they should learn a little in a short time, the rudiments of a few jobs which they could pick up as they went along from their overseers and workmates. There was usually little detailed instruction. The economy of training and retaining a highly efficient labour force was one which was only gradually perceived in industry. To a large extent it was, indeed, incapable of achievement in the mid-nineteenth century, for the simple reason that the heavy incidence of disease and the shortness of life among workers made a high turnover of labour inevitable. Employers provided the minimum training that was essential and a good deal of discipline. Society gradually supplemented these as elementary education, both secular and religious, was extended at varying rates in all industrialized countries. It was unavoidable circumstance as much as deliberate provision that made some labour adapt itself to the needs of a new type of work and a new way of life in the middle of the nineteenth century.

To many of the workers who changed their occupation and place of living, the dominant feature of their position must have seemed to be that they were at the mercy of circumstances quite outside their control. Rural changes deprived many of them of their security. Others grew up as members of a rapidly increasing population and, though some of them could find work on the land, many found that there was no room for them in the traditional family occupation. They were forced to move away and take some other means of livelihood. So began the steady decline in the proportion of the population engaged in agriculture, which began to be noticeable in most countries at some point in the nineteenth century. In the USA the proportion of the population engaged in agriculture, forestry, and fishing fell from 72.3 per cent in 1820 to 68.8 per cent in 1840, 53.7 per cent in 1870, and 38.2 per cent in 1900; in England and Wales the decline, which began much earlier, was from 22.8 per cent in 1841 to 14.8 per cent in 1871 and 8.6 per cent in 1901; in France from 63 per cent in 1827 to 43 per cent in 1866 and 33.1 per cent in 1901.

That an increasing proportion of the population was forced out of agriculture did not mean that an equivalent proportion was thrust into mechanized factory industries. The distressed or ambitious labourer who left his native village at any time in the nineteenth century usually went into a growing town; and in a town, merely by reason of its size and social composition, there was a far wider range of employment opportunities than elsewhere, though many of the opportunities were of a very uncertain and insecure kind. The commonest cause of the rapid growth of towns was the gathering together of factory industry or the commercial and financial institutions which expanded *pari passu* with it. Consequently, factory industry was a chief source of employment for people moving into the towns. In some towns, especially the smaller ones specializing on a single branch of production, it was predominant. But towns also needed labour for special services of their own: for local transport and messenger services, for entertainment and for catering; most of them contained some concentration of fairly affluent people with a heavy demand for domestic servants. Large towns, closely built, badly lit, and inadequately policed, also offered abundant opportunity for activities on the wrong side of the law, of which the most usual in the mid-nineteenth century appear to have been petty theft and prostitution. Factory employment was often the best paid, but it also involved the closest attention and severest discipline. Many of the other urban jobs, more casual in character, required hardly any training or special skill, and were better suited to the new arrival in town.

The urban working class, in places where industrialization was in its early stages in the middle of the nineteenth century, was extremely heterogeneous. Many of its members, especially the men who worked in factories, were receiving higher personal real incomes than their forebears had ever done. Probably few of them were aware of the fact. Most of them lived in unpleasant physical conditions; they had little leisure except between jobs; their family life was broken up because paid work for women and children was to be had by going out to it, instead of doing it at home; and, above all, most of them had grown up in a completely different environment. Some of them, practising handicrafts which were under competitive pressure from mechanical methods, also had a financially measurable grievance because their wages were forced down. Not surprisingly there were many movements of organized protest against prevailing working conditions. More trade unions were formed, and there were attempts to organize political movements on a national scale among the working class. There were intermittent strikes for limited specific objects: a rise in wages or a reduction in hours at a particular factory. There was also a good deal of effort put into various Utopian projects, which depended for most of their support on a combination of ignorance and wishful thinking – a desire for a short cut to universal prosperity and bliss, and a belief that such a consummation could be achieved at once merely by a radical change in social relationships. Yet before 1850 in Great Britain, and until considerably later everywhere else, organized labour movements gained very few lasting victories. Workers were too poor to give them much financial support and most of them were too ignorant and uneducated to be aware of what was both practicable and in their own interest; consequently, it was hard for their loyalties to survive preliminary failure. There was no unity of aim or experience among the working class, much of which consisted of a floating population passing from one job to another, its ranks constantly changing through migration and death. The first steps in industrialization, the creation of a new physical and social environment, and the formulation of new means of adapting labour to meet the changing demands of society as a whole, were achieved without much positive influence from organized labour.

But this particular experience of the shaping of the social relation-ships of an industrializing community was the outcome of conditions that were not universal but confined to particular times and places. Only in Great Britain up to about the eighteen-fifties was it a characteristic of fundamental importance to the life of the whole nation. Elsewhere until the eighteen-seventies and 'eighties something similar was happening in the few large, appreciably industrialized towns, always with local variations, and, in continental Europe, characterized particularly by a greater effort to further the interests of the old handicrafts, which were still more tenacious of their position than they were in Britain. Even the considerable industrialization of France under Napoleon III does not appear to have caused any immediate increase in the proportion of urban factory workers.

The major development of industrialization in most parts of the world came later than 1870, and took place in conditions of much more fully mechanized techniques and much more complex methods of administration in business, and of much easier mobilization of the resources of society for the purpose of modifying its established ways of life. Because of this, the kind of labour that was needed changed, and so did the opportunities which labour had of making its own abilities and interests fit in with current needs.

A higher degree of mechanization did away with the old long-drawn-out struggles for existence between handicrafts and factory occupations by bringing a swift extinction to the former. The skilled craftsman ceased to be interested in the defence of a dying industrial system. He became instead a privileged person in the most advanced forms of productive enterprise, anxious to prevent any inroads on his privilege, and conscious that he and his like were in growing demand. Increasingly elaborate methods of administration created a large demand for other types of specially skilled and trained labour: for clerks and typists and store-keepers and more specialized super-visors, and, at a higher level, for a much smaller but growing body of professional managers, accountants, company lawyers. The number of clerical and lower executive workers who were wanted was so large that they could be found only by recruitment largely from working-class families, so that labour mobility was needed in a new direction. At the same time the position of unskilled workers changed profoundly. Factories could absorb them in greater numbers in jobs which were at once more simple and more exigent; more simple because each workman had to do fewer things, more exigent because those fewer things had to be done more regularly and by more uniform methods. Many of the non-factory unskilled urban jobs also became more regularly organized, though casual work, involving native opportunism and endurance but no training, continued to employ many. So the inescapable changes in occupational mobility had a contradictory set of effects on working class life. There were more uncertainties and for large numbers there was greater insecurity, yet for many there were higher incomes and social status to be grasped. Some experienced both the economic improvement and the increased insecurity, successively or even simultaneously. The implications both for new divisions within the working classes and for new common aspirations towards self-protection were important and indicated that ultimately the organization of working life would be profoundly modified.

In a wide and expanding range of activities, a worker could not do his job properly unless he brought a new mental attitude to it. Literacy among most of their members became the basic new need of industrial communities. Its pertinence to the creation of skilled and clerical labour, which needed a foundation of knowledge on which a higher training could be superimposed, was obvious. A short experience of highly mechanized industry showed that it was no less pertinent to the efficiency of unskilled labour. Simple as were the demands on the machine-minder, he had to be capable of understanding written instructions and carrying them out precisely, and he had to be capable of grasping a simple routine in spite of the fact that it concerned something quite alien to his previous experience. It was in school where it was easiest to learn to do that. Everywhere that a large amount of highly mechanized industry was introduced, it was necessary to accompany it by expanded provision of public elementary education. Where much of the labour was newly arrived from abroad, as in the USA at the turn of the century, a larger, more efficient school system was doubly necessary, since the immigrants had to be enabled to absorb the ways, not only of a new industrial system, but of an unfamiliar national and political tradition, if they were not to be misfits and liabilities in the country of their adoption. Adaptation to the conditions of a society dependent on mechanized production was just one element in the process of the Americanization of immigrants. There the wide repercussions of basic education were obvious and intended. In other countries, too, the extension of education changed many things besides the suitability of labour to the conditions of production. Among other things it made workers better able to pursue their own collective purposes, and helped to give them different ideas of what they wished to be done with the fruits of their labour. No particular aspect of adaptation to changing technical and economic conditions remained isolated. There was a set of mutually interacting changes which together constituted a fundamental transformation of society.

But some of the adaptations within the narrow field of industrial life were delayed, often to the detriment of labour conditions. Among the most important things to every worker were the terms of the contract under which he was employed and the method of calculating and paying his wage. At the end of the nineteenth century these were often still devised in ways appropriate only to industrial conditions which had disappeared. For example, in spite of the need for more careful management, many employers had no direct responsibility for the terms of employment of large numbers of people in their works. They engaged only a limited number themselves, and these acted as subcontractors, employing and paying their own assistants. British industry, in particular, was riddled by the subcontract system. It was not confined by any means to occupations with a primitive organization and little mechanization, but was found in some of the most advanced industries, including shipbuilding and various branches of engineering, and was in force in some of the largest manufacturing establishments in the country. Irregularity of wage payments, which had been a common grievance earlier, was almost certainly declining, but payment was still not always very frequent. Many of the lowest-paid workers received their wages only fortnightly, which was a cause of some hardship. By receiving their wages unduly far in arrear, they were involuntarily contributing to the financing of the business in a way which had, perhaps, been unavoidable when it was intermittently difficult to keep up the level of circulating capital, but which was so no longer. Payment of part of the wages in kind, which in agriculture was often convenient to all concerned, and which had sometimes been a help to workers in isolated manufacturing establishments, persisted in mining and manufacture for much less laudable reasons: the over-valuation of truck was a saving to many employers. To some extent truck still prevailed at the end of the nineteenth century, though it was of declining importance.

Some of these obsolescent features were removed in the course of gradual managerial improvement, some of them gave way before the pressure of organized labour. As manufacturing and trading grew, as wages rose, and as a larger proportion of the population was gathered into towns, circumstances were rather more favourable to the maintenance of permanent labour organizations, and a lengthening experience of industrial conditions made clearer what objects such bodies could most hopefully pursue. Their path, however, was strewn with difficulties, and, though the strength of the trade union movement varied greatly from one country to another, for many years it nowhere covered more than a small fraction of the total number of working men. Yet in the later years of the nineteenth century it was clear that there were urgent functions for trade unions to perform in the social and industrial system. The small business, managed by one of its owners, was dwindling in importance and, in consequence, the relations of employer and employed were more impersonal. It was less possible for a workman to protest individually against hardship or injustice, and the imposition of uniformity of working methods on large numbers of employees meant that their position could often be improved only by a similar uniformity in the application of changes. To protect labour in its daily work and to ensure that there was little delay in passing on to labour, in the form of higher real wages and shorter working hours, some of the fruits of increased productivity was difficult except by collective action.

Collective action was also the most effective way of mitigating the influence of the characteristic insecurities of industrial life. As more of them were drawn into work in factories, warehouses, and transport undertakings, and as the physical and cultural condition of towns improved, people received many advantages, but they were exposed to new hazards; in particular to periodic unemployment, and some of them to special risks of sickness, disablement, or premature death. The financial burden of these contingencies on the individual was more than he could provide for, and it was impossible to pin responsibility for them on his employer. Insurance by pooling resources through trade unions and friendly benefit societies was the only effective means of relief. At the same time, since it was labour which suffered from these insecurities but did not create them, it became one of the tasks of its organized bodies to urge that their relief should be undertaken by the community as a whole.

To make novel, radical solutions of problems like this acceptable, and to apply them in practice, took time, however. The reshaping of industrial relations within a framework of new institutions, so as to deal with some of the impersonal and systematic problems emerging with the use of extreme mechanization in large-scale undertakings, was in progress, at first very slowly, throughout the first half of the twentieth century. Gradually a drastically changed approach to the whole question of industrial efficiency was achieved.

Something has already been said of the new methods of management which were introduced. A changed treatment of labour was an integral part of them. Some means had to be found of encouraging workers to accept conditions in which more rigorous uniformity was imposed on their work, and the amount that they produced was subject to continuous and minute measurement. Particular attention was given to experiments with the wage system so as to reward special efficiency and ensure that the substandard worker bore the financial loss of his own lack of proficiency, and so as to demonstrate that by falling in with the new methods workers could gain an appreciably increased income. The commonest form of remuneration already in existence in manufacturing establishments was the time-wage, though the precise extent to which it prevailed is uncertain. An investigation in industrial establishments (excluding the railways, tramways, and omnibuses) in France between 1891 and 1893 showed that about 70 per cent of the workers were on time-wage and the rest on piece-wage. Piece-wages appear to have been used most in some of the more skilled occupations, in which effort and output were in a fairly constant relation. In Britain, in the early eighteen-nineties, 49 of the 111 principal trade unions (with 57 per cent of the total membership) insisted on their members being paid by the piece. At the time when mechanization began to increase rapidly, the piece-wage was the only system of special incentives in existence, but its extended use was retarded by many disputes. If piece-rates remained unaltered, the whole benefit of any increase in productivity resulting from further mechanization was passed on to labour, but attempts to cut piece-rates were usually resisted. There were constant complaints that piece-rates were based on the performance of the exceptionally good, not the average, worker, and that whenever they produced higher wages than the employer had expected he tried to cut them.

Difficulty in securing the acceptance of piece-rates encouraged attempts to devise new forms of efficiency wage. Among the earliest were various types of gain-sharing, introduced, chiefly in engineering works, in Britain, Canada, and the USA in the eighteen-eighties. They provided that a proportion of the saving achieved by a workman doing a job in less than the standard time should be added to his wages. Some gain-sharing schemes were on a collective basis, the saving achieved by a group being shared among its members, irrespective of individual performance. In practice, however, most of these schemes were found to stimulate output much less than individual gain-sharing schemes. In the twentieth century many different variations on the general system of adding to the guaranteed wage a bonus for surpassing a set standard were devised and introduced. But they by no means displaced the older types of wage remuneration. Efficiency or 'progressive' wage systems were most used in the USA, as might be expected, since mechanization was carried furthest there. But sample enquiries indicated that around 1930 about 40 per cent of the workers in manufacturing industry in the USA were on time-rates, 35 per cent on fixed piece-rates, and 25 per cent on premium or bonus systems. Elsewhere time-rates still almost certainly predominated, though piece-rates were common in the industrialized regions of Central and Western Europe. Piece-rates and efficiency wages were not much used anywhere except in manufacturing and mining.

But in some of the most advanced industries the type of wage formula was becoming rather less important. Time and motion study was increasingly used to devise standard outputs and employers tried to relate the amount of wages, whatever the type of formula in which they were expressed, to these standard outputs. Workers, particularly if they acted in concert, could, in subtle ways, affect both the procedures for establishing standards and the results that could be observed. But the stronger the bargaining position of employers, the greater the influence of work measurement was likely to be. In some very highly mechanized workshops, indeed, the individual came to have little direct influence on his own rate of output, which was predetermined by the synchronization of a series of machines and the pace of conveyor systems, adjusted to conform to observed average performance. He could either keep up with the conveyor or fail to do so and lose his job. In such conditions the direct interest of labour in the attainment of maximum managerial efficiency became clear, since this determined the rate of output which formed part of the basis for negotiating wage-scales. This situation had a direct influence on the policy of some trade unions, especially in the USA, and led them to press organizational improvements on employers. Where there was less complete mechanization, the interdependence of managerial methods, productivity and wage-scales was less obvious, and it was possible for the old idea to persist, as it did in many British trade unions, that to seek for or co-operate in ways of increasing productivity was not in the interests of labour, as it was likely to force someone out of his job. Such differences in attitude were particularly important after the Second World War, when persistently high levels of employment strengthened the bargaining position of organized workers. At this time wage movements generally, though they differed from one country to another, were probably influenced rather less than before by changes in efficiency and output, and rather more by the higgling of markets in which oligopoly, not free competition, prevailed.

Another aspect of the problem of industrial efficiency which became increasingly prominent in the twentieth century was that of labour turnover. Previously this seems to have been regarded as something largely uncontrollable and perhaps not very important. But it became a serious matter if skilled men responsible for the maintenance of highly specialized and complex equipment had to be replaced frequently, and it was also a minor obstacle to full efficiency if it was necessary to be constantly fitting new recruits into groups of unskilled workers who must work together. There were also intermittent difficulties in recruiting enough suitable labour just when it was wanted. In Western Europe peacetime conscription deprived industry of part of its labour supply, and the First World War created a temporary problem of labour shortage in most of the belligerent countries. Moreover, in nearly all highly industrialized countries, the rate of increase in population was falling off. In Western Europe there were declining birthrates, and in the USA the immigrant addition to the labour force was sharply reduced after 1914.

Investigation of labour turnover began in Germany at the beginning of the century and was subsequently taken up in the USA. Studies made in the latter indicated that the labour turnover* in manufacturing industry in 1914 averaged 100 per cent, and sample enquiries during the war revealed a rate of 200 per cent in the firms studied. These were very high figures and prompted attempts to reduce them. In part the influences on turnover are social. They include fluctuations in business activity, changes in industrial structure, the level of education. But a good deal could be and was done by firms to try to encourage greater stability in their labour force. More care was taken to sift workers at the time of recruitment and to employ them in that department to which aptitude or temperament best fitted them. Some firms developed the practice of paying bonuses for long service, a few introduced pension schemes. Many of the bigger firms created a large number of welfare schemes – recreation rooms, playing fields, social clubs, entertainments, medical services – for their employees. Whether because of this or for other reasons, turnover was kept at a lower rate. In a sample of

---

* Quantitative definitions of labour turnover vary slightly, but the variations are of no significance in a general consideration of the question. A common way of measuring turnover is to express the number of persons quitting a firm's employment in a year as a percentage of the average number of persons employed by the firm during that year.

factories in 75 industries in the USA in 1929 the average rate of labour turnover was 45 per cent. In insurable occupations in Britain about the same time it was between 50 and 60 per cent. Among skilled workers everywhere, the rate of turnover appeared to be well below the average for labour as a whole. Altogether, though quantitative information is scanty, it appears that after about 1920 most industrial firms were able to retain a more stable labour force.

Stability and continuity were as vital to the highly organized firm in day-to-day matters as in the long run. The more elaborate its mechanization, the more subdivided its productive and administrative systems, the more necessary it was that the flow of work should suffer no interruption, such as might come from mechanical or administrative breakdown or from a labour dispute. Managerial systems which exercised closer control over labour were also more vulnerable to the pressure of organized labour and both employers and workers soon realized it. There were alternative ways of treating the situation. There was the way of strife, in the hope that one side would achieve a conclusive victory. Employers could refuse to deal with trade unions or to employ union labour. They could try to prevent trade unionism ever taking hold among their employees or, if it had done so already, they could try to break it. On the other hand, trade unions could use their power to call repeated large-scale strikes in order to obtain the surrender of large concessions and perhaps even of control. Alternatively there was the way of agreement, through the establishment of regular negotiating systems to deal with matters in dispute. Both ways were tried extensively at different times and places, and it is not clear that either of them at any point completely ousted the other. But eventually the way of agreement seemed to make more headway than the way of strife.

An uncompromising anti-union policy was most easily pursued by managements while labour was new to large-scale industry. Circumstances were most favourable to it in the USA before the First World War, for the constant influx of immigrants hampered the formation of a strong trade union movement. New arrivals were glad enough to accept a job as soon as they could get one, on the employer's terms, which often included the signature of an agreement not to join a trade union; and the obvious superiority of the material condition of many workers to what it had been in the recent past made a search for gains through labour organization seem less necessary. The USA was certainly not without a growing trade union movement nor free from strikes, usually for higher pay, but increasingly after 1900 for union recognition in wage negotiations.

But trade unionism remained very much a minority movement and touched very few of the masses of unskilled workers. Many of the leading businesses were able without much difficulty to carry out their policy of completely excluding trade unions from their affairs. They were able to preserve this position for twenty years after immigration began to fall off, partly because they kept up the appearance of offering more than the trade unions could do. They increased their welfare services, and some of them formed their own private 'company unions' as nominal but powerless negotiating bodies. By 1927 company unions had a membership of over 1,400,000. But it proved impossible to maintain an anti-union policy in a highly industrialized community as the labour force became more stable and homogeneous. It became possible to organize labour industry by industry instead of only on a craft basis and therefore to threaten a firm with a complete stoppage of work, and, as workers experienced reviving prosperity, the great American exponents of anti-union policies one by one conceded recognition to unions as negotiating bodies and made agreements with them in the late nineteen-thirties and early nineteen-forties.

Similar policies were never so powerful nor so long sustained in other countries, but many firms adopted an aggressive policy to break union influence before its roots struck deep. In Germany between 1901 and 1910 there were nearly 3,000 lock-outs, many of them designed to drain unions of their funds. There were plenty of individual cases where such policies achieved their object, at least temporarily; but aggressive anti-union policies never succeeded in breaking a national trade union movement, except in the few cases where they were backed by the whole civil and military machinery of the state.

The part taken by trade unions in industrial strife varied. Once industrialization had become firmly established and some years of first-hand experience of its problems had exposed the futility of pursuing Utopian schemes of overnight social transformation, most trade unions were predominantly defensive bodies. They were concerned to protect the living standards of their members by securing higher wages, shorter working hours, and pleasanter working conditions, and to enable them continuously to do this, they pressed employers to recognize their right at all times to negotiate on behalf of their members. Strikes they used intermittently as a weapon to secure specific concessions within this general range of objectives, when conditions seemed particularly favourable to them or opposition very unreasonable. Policies of this kind were followed by most

British unions in the latter half of the nineteenth century, by the German unions which grew gradually after 1868, and by the unions affiliated to the American Federation of Labor, which was formed in 1886. Some of them also participated in political activity, seeking an extension of state action on behalf of the workers' interests. But such activity was pursued peacefully. Some of it was of a piecemeal, reformist character, and, though most trade unions in continental Europe were allied with Marxian socialist parties and adopted programmes proclaiming social revolution as their ultimate aim, they were content to campaign for changes which might enable them ultimately to hasten by constitutional action the achievement of socialism. A minority explicitly turned away from political action altogether: the Roman Catholic Church, in its own defence, began to sponsor non-political unions after 1890 in order to preserve its proletarian members from the anti-religious influences associated with Marxian socialism. There were also some secular non-political unions, of which the most notable group was probably the Hirsch-Duncker unions in Germany, which in 1900 included about one-eighth of the trade union membership of that country but which were of declining relative importance thereafter. The American unions for many years after the formation of the American Federation of Labor took only a small part in politics.

But there were sections of the labour movement which were very dissatisfied with the slow progress that was being achieved through limited industrial activity and peaceful political organization. From about 1890 there was growing advocacy of more aggressive and united action, with the use of sabotage and the general strike in order to secure the surrender of all industrial property to the workers; each industry would then be run by one large union of all its workers. This general scheme was embodied in much more detail in the doctrine of syndicalism, which was accepted as the policy of most French trade unions after the formation of the *Confédération Générale du Travail* (CGT) in 1895. Soon afterwards it became the predominant influence in the Italian trade union movement, and much the same aims and methods were avowed by the small number of aggressive industrial unionists organized in the USA from 1905 onwards under the title of the Industrial Workers of the World. These various movements were able to conduct a number of large and bitter strikes which gained limited concessions. But even in the countries where they dominated trade unionism, they represented only a small minority of the workers, most of whom were completely unorganized. In these circumstances mass action such as a general strike was impracticable. In fact, before the First World War a general strike was attempted only in Sweden in 1909, where it made no noticeable difference to the social order.

About 1910 the influence of more militant trade union policies seemed to be spreading, and in the next few years large strikes with some violence were frequent in a number of countries, not least in Britain. But syndicalist doctrines were not a lasting influence. When tested by the First World War, patriotism proved far stronger than industrial solidarity. In France the CGT worked in harmony with the government and eventually abandoned syndicalism. In the USA opposition to the war in 1917 brought to an end the influence of the Industrial Workers of the World. In Italy policies of class struggle were kept in abeyance during the war, but vigorously renewed soon after it, until they were crushed by the victory of Fascism in 1922, and syndicalism was travestied by a new system of totalitarian control over industry. During the interwar period trade unions in all countries made plenty of use of the strike weapon. There was even, in Britain in 1926, a revival of the general strike. But there was nowhere a serious attempt to use direct industrial action to modify the existing economic order or to exploit the vulnerability of complex organizations by using repeated strikes to extort extravagant concessions. On the whole, neither employment conditions nor trade union finances were such as to make that a practical policy even if it had been desired.

The limited importance attached to general proletarian political aims, as compared with more specific questions, was also shown in the character of international co-operation among trade unions. The increase of international migration (some of it seasonal), the spread of industrialization, and the growing influence of international politics and commerce on the livelihood of workers in many countries all seemed by the end of the nineteenth century to make some such co-operation desirable. Unions in a few trades already had their own international secretariats, and the formation in 1889 of the Second (Socialist) International made many more contacts possible. From these arose an international trade union secretariat which in 1909, when the American Federation of Labor joined it, became the International Federation of Trade Unions (IFTU). The Catholic unions, not surprisingly, since they were under the aegis of the greatest of multinational institutions, had formed their own International Secretariat of Christian Trade Unions in 1908.

Support for the idea of international solidarity among trade unionists grew, and by 1919 unions with over 23 million members (some

60 per cent of the world's trade unionists) in twenty-one countries were affiliated to the IFTU. But, though in its early days it supported quasi-political actions such as the Swedish general strike, the IFTU never attempted to make itself a strong influence on international political decisions. Even had it developed the will to do so, renewed divisions in the international trade union movement would have incapacitated it. Within a few years of the First World War, the American Federation of Labor had left the IFTU and five separate international trade union bodies were in existence. In the nineteen-thirties the breaking of the German unions by the Nazi government left both the IFTU and the Christian International deprived of their strongest supporters. By this time the largest international trade union body was the Red International of Labour Unions, formed in 1921 by the Third (Communist) International. This body was more obviously political in character, but though its aims were international, this was scarcely true of its composition: 97 per cent of its membership was in the USSR. Later attempts at combined action between communist and other unions in a World Federation of Trade Unions ended in complete disagreement and schism after the Second World War. Unions in the non-communist countries could accept neither the subservience to government direction nor the role of ideological instruments in an international political struggle, which the communist unions took for granted. Consequently, the former broke away and formed their own International Confederation of Free Trade Unions. Trade unionism was never a consolidated power with a common worldwide policy.

The alternative approach to industrial problems by an attempt of managements and workers to seek mutual advantage through agreement was made very gradually. Its beginning was the acceptance by individual employers of the fact that a particular union had become too strong to be ignored and could make its members carry out the provisions of an agreement. When that happened, collective bargaining became possible with individual firms and, as recognition of trade unions spread, in whole industries. A further step then became possible: the creation of machinery to deal with cases of disagreement. It was in England that the first experiments of this kind were made. Though there were isolated examples as early as the eighteen-thirties, the first of permanent importance came in 1860, when a conciliation board was set up in the Nottingham hosiery industry on the initiative of three employers. It consisted of an equal number of representatives of employers and workmen, with an employer as chairman and, if it failed to agree, it called in an arbitrator. Not unless an arbitrator's award was unacceptable to one party was a strike or lock-out proclaimed. The board also had factory subcommittees which dealt with minor matters. It was a purely voluntary and unofficial body, but its decisions were regularly accepted. Similar boards were soon set up in other British industries, some of them permanent, some dealing with particular emergencies. Attempts were made to extend the system by legislation, but the first permissive Act of 1867 empowering the Home Secretary to license permanent councils of conciliation remained entirely inoperative. It was only after 1896 that official government arbitrators and conciliators began to take a regular part in industrial disputes when asked to do so by the contending parties. Conciliation boards and standing joint committees then had a frequent role in Britain in settling industrial disputes, though they did not provide a recipe for industrial peace and their effectiveness was often exerted only after a dispute had become well entrenched.

Arbitration and conciliation made slower progress in other countries where trade union strength was built up later, but they were being increasingly used in continental Europe at the beginning of the twentieth century, by which time arbitration had been made compulsory in some circumstances in Australia and New Zealand. The First World War made a great difference to the position. Belligerent governments could not afford the risk of widespread industrial disputes and compulsory arbitration became temporarily the general rule. After the war, permanent joint consulting machinery was much more common in European industry than before it and in many cases it had statutory authority. In Great Britain and Germany particular stress was put on these arrangements in the nineteen-twenties, and a large proportion of the workers had their wages regulated either by collective agreements or by the state. The range of subjects which were admitted to discussion by bodies jointly representative of management and workers was also steadily widened in many firms in the interwar period, and though the results of this discussion were often disappointing to workers because they lacked executive force, the practice of regular consultation made some contribution to the prevention of disputes. The experience of a Second World War had the effect of further extending the machinery for consultation and arbitration in industry and increasing the authority of government representatives as mediators in disputes.

During the twentieth century, experience showed the value of settling, through the work of representative bodies, many of the details of industrial life which affected at once the personal position of masses of people and the position of the community as a whole. The result was that the work of trade unions changed and their position became in most countries more secure. Almost everywhere they had first to show the workers that they could win improvements for them and to build up their strength so as to be able to carry out their promises. As industrialization spread, so did the need for some organized bodies to negotiate on specific questions in the interest of labour, and a small trade union movement spread to many countries. But much of the increase in trade union membership took place in the older industrialized countries, where the movement was already established, and this occurred although trade unions there partly outgrew their early functions. The maintenance of many of the gains which they had obtained for some workers came to be accepted as a responsibility of the state on behalf of all. But this did not mean that trade unions were superseded in their functions. It merely meant that they were freer, if they chose, to concentrate less of their attention on the defence of their members against a few major difficulties, and to deal with the whole question of labour in industry in a wider context. They could try to initiate improvements, in addition to ensuring that workers shared in improvements in the creation of which they participated at the instigation of others. It was because it had acquired these more comprehensive abilities, even though it did not fully use them, that by the middle of the twentieth century trade unionism was moving in a few countries into the rather ambiguous position of being at the same time the partisan guardian of many of the interests of labour and, as a servant of the general interest, an integral part of the functional machinery of an industrial community.

Such a change was symptomatic of a great transformation in the position of labour in society that had taken place since 1900. The whole complex body of relationships affecting labour in industry had been changed, in most ways to the advantage of the worker. Wages were higher, working hours shorter, protection against the economic insecurities of life much stronger, the opportunity to remove difficulties before they became grievances much greater. What had perhaps changed much less was the attitude of the individual worker to his job. It was by technical and administrative improvement that the material benefits accruing to labour became possible and the maintenance of a continuous expansion in realized wealth depended not least on the readiness of labour to participate in the changes which a constant improvement of methods involved and to carry out new tasks to the best of its ability. But in many cases the co-operation of labour in new methods of work was hesitant, partial, and delayed. With existing methods, security was apparently assured, and it doubtless seemed unwise to many workers to exchange that security for the mere promise of something better, particularly as much of the benefit would go, not to raising relatively the income of the individual, but to raising absolutely the incomes of a large group. Since 1900, in most highly industrialized countries, the traditional monetary incentives to work better or to work differently had diminished. More things were provided socially instead of having to be obtained by individual expenditure, and they were roughly the same for everyone, whatever work he did and however well he did it. At the same time the extra pay that could be obtained for superior skill was declining. The margin between skilled and unskilled wages intermittently but persistently narrowed in all highly industrialized countries except the USA, where such a change only began just after the Second World War. A better standard of general education and of technical training and a smaller recuitment of unskilled juveniles, owing to lower birthrates, created conditions in which it was difficult to reverse the trend. An important problem in the maintenance of economic progress thus arose: the need for a new mutual accommodation between the aims of labour on the one hand and the exigencies and benefits of the prevailing social organization on the other.

This problem had been an increasingly important feature of the changing relations between labour and industry in nearly all industrial countries in the first half of the twentieth century. After 1950 it became even more significant, for two reasons. On the one hand the interdependence of different economic activities and of different processes within the same industry became rapidly more complex, especially as rising proportions of national incomes were derived from the output and sale of types of goods produced by the most elaborate and highly capitalized methods. So it became progressively easier for some small disaffected group to upset the activity of a vastly greater number. On the other hand, greater success in operating both individual industries and whole national economies at something near to full capacity for long periods increased the loss that could be sustained as a result of interruptions which such disaffection might induce; and it might or might not impose some of that loss on those directly causing the interruption. There was thus a greater opportunity for organized groups of workers to demand concessions in return for not disrupting economic activity, and there was an increase in the price it was worth paying to secure industrial peace and continuity of work. But there was also a probability that greater industrial disruption would cause a greater loss than before in the total output and real income available for workers to share.

The opportunity to exert pressure by threatening disruption was more immediately apparent than the risk of long-term loss by doing so too often. Moreover, it was an opportunity to use in more favourable circumstances a traditional trade union weapon, whereas the experience of the nineteen-thirties, when losses of potential output and income came from quite different sources, made it more difficult to appreciate the increased risk of self-damage from strikes and other forms of industrial conflict. Greater social provision did not appear to have diminished the appetite for individual advantage, and circumstances which had strengthened the bargaining power of organized workers encouraged the pursuit of larger wage increases in the usually vain hope of restoring differentials that other influences had narrowed. There was thus a temptation for organized labour to demand more and offer less for co-operation and to minimize the risks of pushing such a policy to the extent of having frequent disputes. In general, it seems that readiness to yield to this temptation was greatest in those countries and those industries where the conduct of industrial relations, and especially the forms of trade union organization, had changed least since the nineteen-thirties. Where there had been great reorganization, as, for example, in Sweden in response to the depression or in Germany because of the destruction of the unions by the Nazis, a greater willingness was found to co-operate in maintaining a predictable continuity of economic activity. But even where this was achieved, an increased price was paid for it, especially from the late nineteen-fifties onwards, when industrial Europe had overcome the ravages of the Second World War and its aftermath. Greatly increased and continually rising real incomes were achieved where this continuity was maintained, but readiness to maintain continuity by making swift settlements involved even larger monetary payments, a situation not dissimilar to (though more productive than) that where an inflationary price was paid for temporary truces in a less smooth sequence of industrial relations. Thus the changed balance among organized bodies in the labour market was causing them to exert a more general influence on whole national economies than ever before; and some aspects of that influence, notably the contribution to a situation in which some degree of inflation became a permanent feature of the life of all advanced economies, had also great political importance.

Almost everywhere the relations between labour and management were increasingly involved with the actions of governments. In general the variety and extent of state influences on economic life were increasing, and this was true of industrial relations as of other economic matters. But in this immense pressure of the systems of industrial relations to ensure the paying out of more and more money one can see a powerful influence operating the other way round. Such a situation was possible, and difficult to reverse, because, in most industrialized countries, representatives of workers and employers were themselves free to settle most questions at issue between them, even though governments did more than before to prescribe the limits within which settlements could be made. In a liberal political system little else could be acceptable.

Yet there was also a process of mutual accommodation to opposing pressures. In the mid-seventies and the immediately following years levels of inflation rose so high as to be dangerously frustrating for governments and worrying for the conduct of daily life by a large part of the population. Counter-inflation policies became acceptable, even though they limited the capacity of labour organizations to seek higher pay, and even though, in association with other influences, they contributed to an increase in unemployment. Higher rates of unemployment than had been customary for the previous thirty years came to be perceived as normal and encouraged greater restraint in the pursuit of wage demands. This was another illustration both of the significance of labour organizations in the running of an industrialized country and of the dependence of their influence on voluntary adaptation to circumstances, which included some of the pressures of government.

Elsewhere the balance of forces was appreciably different. Countries with totalitarian *régimes* experienced many similar problems, but sought to solve them by the imposition of government decisions in the making of which many considerations, which a liberal society must respect, could be ignored. Yet even a totalitarian government had to perceive the limits beyond which at least passive non–cooperation was likely, and to adjust its decrees accordingly; and the nineteen-forties saw the replacement of totalitarianism in some highly industrialized countries. But at the same time the communist system spread and the area of its sway soon became more industrialized. The USSR had already had to cope with many of the stresses, resistances and aspirations of a new industrial labour force. Comparable problems came to be experienced in other communist countries. In all of them they were tackled with far less widespread consultation of conflicting views and with reliance on the politically or bureaucratically imposed decision, backed by reference to loyalty to an ideology that was alleged to be in the common interest. Such associations were not without political risks, for dissatisfaction with either the ideology or working conditions could spill over from one field to the other, as became particularly apparent in Poland in the early nineteen-eighties. The risks could be countered by some mixture of politically imposed restriction and relaxation. But, in communist conditions generally, the aspirations and pressures of workers, though they induced some modifications in government policies, had far less immediate and continuous effect than in more liberal countries. The contrast remained sharp, and it provides, by a particular type of example, a more general reminder of the fundamental way in which the development of economic life is affected by the political framework in which it is conducted.

CHAPTER FIVE
Government and economic life

THE APPROACH TO LAISSEZ-FAIRE

When the interaction of political and economic activity is under
consideration, it is important to remember that the subordination of
economic affairs to political direction was an established European
tradition supported by centuries of practice before Europe began to
experience that rapid industrialization which ultimately affected the
greater part of the world. There was a clear recognition that the
power of a state in a world of sharp rivalries was rooted in economic
matters, and a general belief, not seriously challenged before the
mid-eighteenth century, that it was up to the state to take direct
measures to preserve its own power, because no private institution
or person would act so as consistently to serve the interest of the
state unless he were compelled to do so. Thus, it was mainly in order
to achieve political objects that comprehensive regulation of economic affairs was undertaken by governments. But merchants,
manufacturers, and landowners, accepting this situation, tried to turn
it to their own advantage. The state could be a powerful ally or
adversary of any economic interest: it was the chief source of
patronage and privilege. Consequently, private bodies were constantly pressing for its regulations to take a form which bestowed
special advantages on them.

It was both convenient and remunerative for governments to yield
frequently to such pressure, which was commonly supported, first,
by arguments that a particular interest ought to be privileged because
it accorded with the interests of the state, and, second, by a willingness to pay for the grant of privilege. The weakness of every state in
carrying out a policy of economic regulation was that its administrative

131

machinery was quite inadequate to match the magnitude and complexity of its administrative designs. It could devise a policy and embody it, in minute detail, in laws and charters, but could make it fully effective only by working through other bodies. Consequently, a great deal devolved on local authorities, whose officers worked for the most part without pay, and on profit-seeking private enterprises which were granted protection and monopoly in return for doing specified things – which in practice usually meant that they acquired the authority of the state in seeking their own objectives. It was by regulation of the enterprise of others rather than by enterprise of their own that governments sought to direct the course of economic life. They prescribed what quality and type of goods might be produced by each industry, and on what terms new entrants might take up a particular occupation. They decided what body should conduct a particular branch of foreign trade, and whether anyone else might participate in it. To a limited extent they encouraged particular industries by the use of protective import duties or the prohibition of imports, by tax exemptions, and by subsidies. They encouraged certain lines of export by giving bounties. They prohibited exports which might directly assist other countries to become industrially stronger. By prohibitions and differential duties they diverted carrying trade into ships belonging to their own nationals.

Policies of this kind began to be called into question during the eighteenth century, especially in France and Britain. They were attacked on grounds of general theory by many writers, among whom Adam Smith was outstanding. The inconsistencies which were almost inevitable in so multitudinous a collection of regulations were held up to ridicule, and the very existence of so many regulations was claimed to be merely the wasteful application of a mistaken idea, since, as Smith put it, every individual's 'study of his own advantage naturally, or rather necessarily, leads him to prefer that employment which is most advantageous to the society'.

But the proclamation of new truth to replace old error probably had less power to change policy than had the growing strength of interests which were not served by the prevailing system. The existing body of regulations was nowhere abandoned quickly. It was whittled away gradually and in some countries very incompletely, for it was only slowly that influential opinion came to regard it as burdensome. On the whole the regulations were conceived to fit fairly static economic conditions. If all the major industries received state protection and encouragement, it was difficult for industry to make serious political complaints. If it was impossible by any means to expand some particular branch of foreign trade very much, then its preservation as a monopoly could not be held to be a denial of opportunity to a large number of potential competitors. If the occupational structure was approximately constant, then control of wages and conditions of entry could be regarded as a safeguard of the labour supply rather than as a device which hampered new enterprise by making it difficult to recruit labour. But in the late eighteenth and early nineteenth centuries economic life was becoming less static all over Western Europe and, for that reason, some at least of the existing regulations became more obviously burdensome. As population grew, restrictions on entry into particular occupations and on the establishment of new businesses became less appropriate. As technical improvements were adopted and increasing wealth opened new economic opportunities, it was necessary to obtain the means to expand industries which were denied every special privilege. So there was, in the less backward states, a steady decline in industrial regulation. Compulsory wage-fixing and apprenticeship fell into disuse, and the restrictive privileges of the gilds were removed. In England, France, and most of the Italian states the gilds were virtually powerless well before the end of the eighteenth century. But further east, reform came more slowly, because there was less ability to take advantage of new economic opportunities. It was not until 1869 that complete freedom of choice of occupation was legally established in the whole of Germany.

Indeed, in some respects the differing conditions further east caused eighteenth-century governments there not merely to delay the abandonment of old restrictions but to attempt some new economic tasks. Whereas their main economic function had been regulatory, some of them sought a more active role in directly or indirectly promoting new enterprises. Markets expanded, productive techniques improved, rising populations sought additional employment, those most responsive to change exerted new competitive pressures in some channels of international trade. In such circumstances there were new opportunities to be grasped and new risks of being left behind. In parts of Western Europe, especially Britain and the Low Countries, there was an abundance of private individuals anxious to reach for the opportunities. But elsewhere the numbers, experience and interests of the aristocracy and middle classes made them far less responsive. Rulers and their ministers, who became aware of the opportunities and feared a diminution of state power if they were completely ignored, found it desirable to try to break down or circumvent the inertia of their societies by sponsoring new schemes for production and trade. The efforts of Peter the Great, after his own observation of Western Europe, to introduce new industries in Russia provided an early example. Probably rather more effective were changed policies somewhat later in Austria and Prussia. In the former, after military defeat and loss of territory to Prussia, the government of Maria Theresa abandoned its old principle, '*Alles beim Alten lassen*' ('Leave everything as it used to be'), and set up administrative machinery to promote and co-ordinate new projects; and her son, Joseph II, set about loosening the rigidities of society by new codes of law which greatly reduced the obligations of peasants to their lords. In Prussia, in the later years of Frederick the Great's reign, and after, the government undertook an increasing number of industrial activities, in mining and iron working, as well as in the production of luxury goods. Gradually, the influence of such state actions helped the wider spread of businesslike interests and attitudes in Prussia and Austria (and there were comparable examples in some smaller German states), but it was many years before these were so diffused as to make a detailed code of state regulation feel seriously constricting.

It was in Great Britain that circumstances were most favourable to a fundamental change in economic policy in the early nineteenth century. Technical improvement, productive expansion, and the growth of markets had gone much further than elsewhere. The old framework of regulation had become quite unable to contain the existing economy. The greatest industrial achievements had been made by the cotton manufacture, which received no state assistance whatever, but had its raw material taxed. Productive capacity had been so increased and costs of manufacture so reduced that a vast increase in sales appeared to be within the grasp, provided that no unnecessary burdens were maintained in the form of taxes and prohibitions and subsidies to privileged inefficiency. It was not surprising that a strong attack should have been launched on a system of economic control whose dominant institutions were a central government representative of a comparatively unenterprising and protected landed interest, local authorities vitiated by corruption and indifference to the welfare of the people whom nominally they served, and monopolistic companies which were no longer able to supply all that was needed in areas from which they tried to exclude all interlopers. There was no other country in which so large and wealthy a proportion of the business community was outside the field of privilege created by government control, and there was none in which the international competitive position of the economy as a whole was so strong. Consequently, the demand for a relaxation of government regulation was both more powerful and more widely ranging. Whereas in most other Western countries the earlier attacks were mainly against legal obstacles to the mobility of labour and to the right to set up new businesses, against oppressive internal taxes, and against the rigidity of rural economy caused by the survival of feudalism, in Britain they extended to obstacles to the mobility of capital, and, above all, to the whole body of fiscal policy. In Britain the achievement of free trade became at least the most vociferously celebrated, if not perhaps the most important, part of the movement towards *laissez-faire*.

Mainly from about 1820 to 1860 a great deal was done in Britain to release business enterprise from government influence in the form of restrictive laws and discriminatory taxes. The Bank of England's monopoly of joint-stock banking in England and Wales, which hampered industry and commerce by preventing their obtaining as full a financial service as they needed, was abolished in 1833. The Usury Laws, which sometimes made it difficult for business to obtain capital that it required and could afford, were gradually modified and finally disappeared in 1854. The ready grant of poor relief in the parish where a person was legally 'settled', which discouraged the movement of redundant workers to places with a labour shortage, was replaced by a much more stringent system in 1834. The Corn Laws, which, at the expense of the rest of the community, gave to the landed interest a protection that was almost certainly far less than it seemed to be, were repealed in 1846. In the sphere of foreign trade the last surviving duties and prohibitions on export were removed in the eighteen-forties. The overwhelming majority of import duties were successively reduced and abolished. The great trading monopolies of the past came to an end, that of the Levant Company in 1825, that of the East India Company in China in 1833. The restrictions imposed by the Navigation Laws on the choice of ship in which goods might be consigned were modified by law and by a series of commercial treaties until they were abolished in 1849. (In the coasting trade they lasted until 1854.)

The carrying out of a comprehensive reform of economic policy was not, however, merely a matter of sweeping away a clutter of obsolete restrictions. No business man was so extreme an advocate of *laissez-faire* as to deny the state any positive function in economic affairs. In particular, its authority was necessary because it made possible the enforceability of contracts. Business needed to enter into new types of contractual relationship, and consequently it was necessary for the state to devise certain new measures of general regulation. It had, for example, to create the new code of company law, to which the necessity of limited liability gave rise, and to provide for its supervision through a Registrar-General of Companies. It also had to provide a body of financial regulations to try to ensure stability in the banking system, so that competitive business enterprises would not run much risk of seeing the rewards of superior efficiency destroyed by the errors of bankers on whom they must rely, but whom they could not control. The Bank Charter Act of 1844, providing for the ultimate centralization of the note issue in the Bank of England and tying the volume of the note issue closely to the size of the gold reserve, was the government's attempt to carry out this task, though the system did not prove satisfactory until it was supplemented by a set of conventional practices, arising not from government decree but from the practical experience of bankers.

A nearer approach to *laissez-faire* was also, paradoxical as it may seem, directly responsible for an extension of government enterprise, as well as regulation, in a few fields. The reason for this was the abandonment of the policy of maintaining privileged monopolies, which for some purposes acted as agents or substitutes for the state. When competition replaced monopoly, some functions remained necessary which the monopoly had discharged in whole or in part, but which were outside the scope of competing enterprises. In some respects the replacement of the East India Company by the Crown as the ruler of India in 1858 was the most striking example of change of this kind. Of more directly economic concern was the necessity that the government should take full responsibility for the provision of a consular service which would, among other things, assist shipping and foreign trade. The necessary reorganization of the consular service took place in 1825, and was directly connected with the termination then of the charter of the Levant Company, which had maintained consuls of its own.

In general, however, the reshaping of economic policy involved little extension of public enterprise; rather the reverse. Most activity of this kind in England had been local, not central. The chief enterprise had been water supply, but increased needs for water in the mid-nineteenth century were usually met (so far as they were met at all) by companies, and the newer types of public utility enterprise, such as gas supply and refuse collection, were at first privately operated in most cases.

In Britain in the mid-nineteenth century the functions of government, central and local, changed considerably, expanding in some directions, contracting in others. But on balance they probably became more restricted than they had ever previously been in any other state with a highly developed economy. Practical recognition was temporarily given to the view that 'he governs best who governs least', and, especially, reduces his participation in economic affairs to a minimum. Of the chief tasks left without question to the government, the maintenance of security against external attack, the preservation of internal public order, and the conduct of relations with foreign states usually influenced economic affairs only indirectly. The maintenance of civil law and of courts to enforce it was of closer concern, but was nearer to being a precondition of economic activity than an interference with it. The administration and service of the National Debt and the levying of taxation, however, gave the government a considerable economic influence. It affected directly the distribution of income and the relative opportunities of different groups of people. For about half a century after Waterloo the government played a diminishing part in economic affairs. Until 1835 its expenditure fell, and thereafter it was in general probably rising more slowly than national income. By 1860 central government expenditure was about 10 per cent of the national income of the UK, and local government expenditure only 2 or 3 per cent. But even so, at the height of the period of so-called *laissez-faire*, this meant that the government, merely because of its own expenditure and quite apart from its powers of legislative and administrative control, was by far the most important single economic institution in the country. No other body could spend anything approaching £60 million a year.

The other countries of Europe never came so near to *laissez-faire* as Britain. There was a gradual lifting of restrictions on choice of occupation and on the movement of labour and capital, and new types of regulation in the form of company and banking law were devised, as in Britain, in order to enable private enterprise to function more freely. But there was much less readiness to follow the British lead in relaxing government control over foreign trade. The British advocates of free trade had argued that if it were established in their own country it would lead to such an expansion of trade and prosperity that within a few years other countries would copy it in order to reap similar advantages. In fact, these countries were more inclined to fear that free trade would enable British competitors to crush part of their industry without their being able to expand other activities sufficiently to offset this loss. Between

1860 and 1880, however, protection was considerably reduced, though not nearly abolished, by many continental countries. Much of this was done, not unilaterally, but by means of commercial treaties. The fears of national loss from increased competition were in this way reduced by the assurance of specified reciprocal concessions. The first major step was the conclusion in 1860 of an Anglo-French treaty of commerce, by which France abolished all prohibitions on the import of British goods and lowered many duties, and Britain lowered the import duties on French wines and silk goods. This treaty included the 'most-favoured-nation' clause, which meant that each contracting party would receive the benefit of any more favourable terms which the other subsequently granted by treaty to a third party. As France negotiated commercial treaties with several other countries in the next six years and these in turn negotiated further treaties among themselves, this clause proved most efficacious in promoting a general reduction of protection in Europe. At the same time there was in many countries some tariff reduction apart from what was included in treaties. In the eighteen-seventies, though most countries retained a complex fiscal system with a large number of import duties, not many activities were restricted by heavy taxation.

In the USA the course of events was very different. While Europe was lowering tariff barriers, the USA extablished a highly protective policy. The tariff had long been one of the major issues promoting friction between North and South in the USA. The South, greatly dependent on the export of raw cotton and tobacco, was anxious that there should be as few fiscal obstacles to trade as practicable, whereas some Northern manufacturers were more concerned to have their home market protected from securely established foreign rivals. Before the Civil War there was a moderate tariff which was being gradually lowered in the eighteen-fifties. The introduction of the high Morrill tariff in the House of Representatives in the session of 1859–60 and its passage into law in 1861 was both a challenge to the South and a sign of the greatly increased strength and importance of manufacturing in the North. After this the policy of high protection was never reversed. Partly as a means of raising revenue, duties were increased every year during the Civil War, until in 1864 they averaged 47 per cent ad valorem. Minor reductions were made later, mostly on articles of common consumption, and in 1883 a general reduction of about 5 per cent was achieved. Shifts of political power caused the tariff level to change frequently, sometimes a little higher, sometimes a little lower, but after 1897, when the Dingley Act was passed, the general tariff level was well above what it had been even at the end of the Civil War.

The high tariff was, however, the one outstanding exception to a policy which carried *laissez-faire* further than it ever went anywhere else. The lofty language of the opening of the fourteenth amendment to the constitution* became a cloak for the extreme attenuation of government control over business behaviour, with the result that too often economic liberty passed into economic licence. The resources of the federal and state governments, particularly their lands, passed wholesale into private hands, sometimes by the most dubious of contractual arrangements. The raising of capital was so free of restriction that it was often done with impunity by fraudulent means. In the struggle for markets the most flagrantly discriminatory practices were adopted and were sustained by the law.

The differences in the extent to which the governments of various countries regulated economic life are probably to be explained mainly in terms of differences in their competitive position and the extent of their undeveloped resources. Britain in the third quarter of the nineteenth century had a firmly established set of economic institutions and a technical lead in the major industries which, if fully used, were bound, for the time being at least, to strengthen the country's economic position in the world. Naturally, then, the demand was for a removal of all governmental measures which might conceivably interfere with the full exploitation of these advantages, and the increasing prosperity of the time appeared to justify the maintenance of as unrestricted a system of private enterprise as possible. In the USA industrial and commercial organization and techniques were less advanced and hence there was a call for protection against foreign competition. But internally there was a seemingly limitless abundance of natural resources, fertile land and forests and minerals, awaiting development. Their rapid exploitation was the first and urgent task of the growing American nation, and the duty of the government seemed to be to stand aside and let those who were eager to carry out this task proceed with it. Wastefulness in the process hardly seemed to matter, since there remained an abundance for everyone. The continental countries of Europe enjoyed neither the internal treasures of the USA nor the international supremacy of

---

*'No state shall make or enforce any law which shall abridge the privileges or immunities of citizens of the United States; nor shall any state deprive any person of life, liberty, or property without due process of law; nor deny to any person within its jurisdiction the equal protection of the laws.'

Britain. For them, as conditions changed, the best way seemed to be to grope cautiously forward with a policy which drew on both their own traditional experience and the devices which served their successful contemporaries.

In many respects the policies of most European countries for much of the nineteenth century were still greatly affected by the kind of conditions which had persuaded eighteenth-century despots to try to initiate new enterprise. If there was a lack of private savings, or a scarcity of private individuals with business experience and the habit of acting on a rational calculation of risks, it was not much use for the state to stand aside and reduce its economic policy to 'holding the ring' for private enterprise. Where the sources of individual enterprise were few, they could be encouraged to grow by government policies of social and legal reform; but, until that happened, economic progress was likely to be very slow unless it was promoted either by foreigners or directly by the state. Where the social structure was too rigid, and the overwhelming majority of the people too poor, for there to be a large sector of private business – conditions which have come to be regarded as 'backward' – the state was left with a major role in economic development which was incompatible with a general approach to *laissez-faire*. Alexander Gerschenkron went so far in generalizing from this as to suggest that, in nineteenth-century Europe, in any country's great spurt forward, the greater the degree of economic backwardness the greater was the role of the state. The relation was probably not as uniform as that, but there were numerous illustrations of the varied ways in which governments tried to encourage developments which their subjects were not spontaneously providing. There were, for example, the attempts to attract foreign workmen and business to Russian Poland by tax concessions; there was the greater dependence in Central Europe on state support in the establishment of banks; there was the almost complete dependence on the state for transport improvements in the poorer countries of Europe.

Indeed, one of the elements in economic development was so costly, and seemed at first to involve such incalculable risks, that very few countries were advanced enough to provide it without a large contribution of finance and initiative from the state, though in the more prosperous countries of Western Europe the state found substantial partnership with private institutions. It was the provision of large railway systems that so generally demanded of the state a role at variance with the trend towards *laissez-faire*. Early experiments showed what great potential advantages might be bestowed by railways, not merely on their promoters, but on the whole of a nation's business activity and perhaps, incidentally, on government revenues as well. Since these advantages were exceptionally general, there was an unusually strong motive for governments actively to encourage railway construction if it was not otherwise undertaken. There was also the consideration that railways profoundly affected military strategy, and were therefore of direct concern to governments. But although the military value of railways was a matter of public discussion before 1850, especially in France and Germany, it was at first generally underestimated, and, until the last quarter of the nineteenth century, strategic factors probably had only a minor influence on governmental decisions to participate in railway construction. The main point was that railways were of great general economic advantage, but needed so much capital and involved so much commercial risk that unaided private enterprise could not build enough of them. In some countries the level of realized wealth was not high enough for any institution other than the state to be capable of raising the sums needed for railway construction. In others, though sufficient capital existed, it was so unaccustomed to participate in risk-bearing enterprise that government assistance or guarantee was necessary before it could be attracted to railway companies.

Governments were not in most cases responsible for the planning of railway systems, though there were instances of this, but most of them either provided financial assistance or made themselves directly responsible for some construction. In the UK, however, state assistance was practically confined to a few small lines which improved communication between Britain and Ireland. In France, most of the first railways were provided with free rights of way by the government, which also guaranteed the payment of dividends. Many German states built some of their own lines and subsidized other private ventures. The Austrian government likewise built some and subsidized others. All the first Belgian railways were built by the government. In the USA private enterprise received a great deal of public assistance. Much of the finance of the earliest local lines was provided by state governments and city councils, and the construction of long-distance lines a little later was enormously helped by lavish grants of free land: between 1850 and 1871 sixteen railway companies received 174 million acres of free land from the federal and state governments. In addition the federal government assisted some of the trans-continental lines by the issue of mortgage bonds to the extent of nearly $65 million, and there continued to be direct financial assistance to many lines from states, counties, and municipalities.

Where governments built railways, it was usual, as might be expected, for them to retain control over their operation. But even where railways were privately owned, state regulation of them increased steadily almost from the beginning of their existence, and the replacement of private by public ownership was a burning question in the mid-nineteenth century. Even in Britain the Railway Act of 1844 gave the government the option of purchasing the railways after twenty-one years, but it was not exercised. By the eighteen-seventies, however, the purchase of private lines by governments was going on gradually, notably in France and in some of the constituent states of the new Germany.

If government concern with railways was at first due primarily to economic backwardness which prevented financial resources from being commensurate with the task of creating railway systems, it was soon increased by awareness of the direct, all-pervading influence which railways were continuously exercising on the life of a whole community whose economy was rapidly expanding. Much the same was true of other forms of communication, and most governments found it convenient to take complete responsibility for the operation of postal services and to own or closely control the telegraph systems which were beginning to be developed.

In fact, the repercussions of economic advance made just as striking new demands on government action as did the need to overcome the handicaps of economic backwardness. The moderate industrialization of Britain made it possible to create a railway system without state aid, but it created problems of its own which could not be solved by private action. For example, it greatly changed the conditions of child labour. A larger proportion of employed children was working in factories instead of at home, and was thus at the mercy of employers and overseers, who were often more concerned to maximize immediate effort than to ensure that the allotted work was well within the physical capabilities of those who had to do it. Hence the demand for state regulation of the ages at which children might work and of the length of their working day, a demand which was conceded in gradual stages from 1802 onwards, though regulation was restricted to textile factories and mines until the eighteen-sixties. Most striking was the extension of positive state action by the creation in 1833 of an inspectorate to enforce factory regulation. Significant also of the trend of opinion was the agitation for the state to extend protection to adults against some of the conditions of work, especially the long hours, which they experienced and could not remedy for themselves. For male workers this agitation did not achieve anything directly for many years, but indirectly they benefited from the statutory regulation of women's work. The passing in 1847 of the Ten Hours Act, which limited the working hours of women in textile factories and laid down the hours of day between which they might be employed (thus virtually limiting the power of an employer to operate his factory at any hour he chose), presaged the extension of state control as surely as the repeal of the Corn Laws a year earlier had symbolized the triumph of *laissez-faire*.

There were other fields in which, at about the same time, the increase of industrialization was calling for the tentative extension of public regulation and activity. The growth of manufacture was accompanied by the expansion of towns, which had the effect of creating new evils and magnifying old ones. Increasing numbers of steam-operated factories led to the pollution of the atmosphere and of the canals and streams. Insanitary habits of life often had their effects mitigated by fresh air and natural water supplies in small villages, but, when transferred to large and crowded towns, became permanent threats to the well-being and life of the community and called for public remedy. So there was a gradual increase, beginning with a Nuisances Removal Act in 1846, of the restrictions imposed on individual action. For a generation the introduction and enforcement of such restrictions was timid and halting and achieved comparatively little, but though the movement was small, it was increasing.

Since industrialization had gone further in Britain than elsewhere by the middle of the nineteenth century, the emergence of new classes of government regulation to deal with specific industrial evils was most noticeable there. But in other places where mechanized industry spread, there were similar small developments. Massachusetts, the early centre of American cotton manufacture, began to regulate child labour by law in 1836 and gradually extended the scope of such legislation. France limited the working hours of children and young persons by law from 1841, and in 1848 passed an Act to limit hours to twelve a day for all workers; but these measures could not be generally enforced in the absence of an inspectorate, which was not established until 1874. In Prussia legislation to protect children and young persons in industry was adopted in 1839 but was widely evaded, despite the appointment of inspectors in 1853.

Apart from the acceptance of completely new governmental functions, there was also scope for the exercise in new fields of some established activities. Even at a time when private commercial interests were demanding freedom from interference and were vigorously trying to expand their sales, they were sometimes willing that diplomatic and military action should be used to gain new markets. While economic affairs were not a predominant consideration in the foreign policy of any great power, they were at least an occasional matter of concern, to which attention was given, particularly in dealings with weaker states. Thus the British government sought to increase the benefits obtained from earlier Turkish capitulations authorizing trade with European merchants. In 1838, by the Convention of Balta Liman, it secured the abolition of all trading monopolies and prohibitions within Turkey, the abolition of the Turkish right of pre-emption of goods, the abolition of local taxes on goods destined for export, and large reductions in national import and export duties, and 'most-favoured-nation' treatment for British trade. In the next few years other European governments took the opportunity to obtain similar commercial privileges, and as trade with Turkey grew, the British government · sought more concessions, and succeeded in obtaining further reductions in duties in 1850, especially on items of the greatest importance to British trade, such as the import of cotton goods.

In the Far East also, government action played a large part in the expansion of markets. The First Opium War of Britain with China was ended in 1842 when, by the Treaty of Nanking, China ceded Hong Kong to Britain and opened five ports to Western trade. A year later, when China granted extra-territorial rights (which by 1847 had also been extended to the USA, France, Belgium, and Sweden and Norway), Britain created a special consular service to deal with British affairs there. The American naval expedition to Japan in 1853 quickly secured the opening of the country to Western trade. The Second and Third Opium Wars, in which British troops were joined by French, and the British and French demands were supported by diplomatic pressure from Russia and the USA, led, by the Treaty of Peking in 1860, to the opening of eleven more Chinese cities to foreign trade, the opening of the Yangtse to the vessels of all nations, and the extension of various commercial privileges, as well as cessions of territory to Russia and Britain.

THE EXPANDING FUNCTIONS OF GOVERNMENTS AND INTERGOVERNMENTAL INSTITUTIONS

It is clear, from the previous discussion of what the governments of the more advanced countries actually did in the economic sphere, that although they may have been moving towards *laissez-faire* in the two middle quarters of the nineteenth century, they achieved that condition only partially; so partially, in fact, that in much of Europe the long tradition of government regulation cannot be regarded as ever having been really broken, though it was challenged and modified. Even where there was more far-reaching change, as in Britain and the USA, *laissez-faire* proved to be an elusive ideal, for in order to extend economic liberty in one way, it was necessary to introduce some new limitations, while the very conditions which seemed to increase the advantages of unrestricted private enterprise also had undesirable consequences, for which it gradually became apparent that only a collective remedy was possible. Into this condition of very incomplete revulsion from thorough government regulation there came, about 1870, fundamental new influences which led to the reversal of the previous trend towards uncontrolled private enterprise.

Most of the important influences were international in scope, though their full impact was not everywhere felt simultaneously and they were reinforced or offset by differences in internal conditions. They sprang principally from two groups of changes in industry. There was a rapid increase in the degree of industrialization of several countries which led to more intense international competition than before; and at the same time technical methods and economic organization were changing in such a way as to subject the working population to new strains. Both these factors exerted a continuous influence on every branch of social and economic policy, and in some countries they were strengthened by another change: the beginning of a sharp decline in the birthrate as substantial improvements in the standard of living came within the grasp of a larger proportion of the people and the use of contraceptives increased. Greater competition meant that, nationally as well as individually, a small variation in economic efficiency might make a considerable difference to prosperity, and changes in working conditions and the supply of labour meant that more attention had to be given to the training, contentment, and physical well-being of workers. It was to deal with this situation that drastic extensions were made in government policies, on the one hand to try to diminish waste, especially the waste of human abilities, and on the other to try to expand activity while preserving economic stability despite strong competition.

Lack of education, ill-health, and discontent were major obstacles which prevented the population from achieving its best in the economic sphere and their removal came to be recognized as an urgent need. The government of every industrial country was doing much to increase general educational provision in the late nineteenth century, and more attention was given to technical education, as other countries observed how much it appeared to have contributed to the rapid rise of industrial power in Germany. Where education had been mainly a private service, it became predominantly a public one, partly in order to make possible the raising of standards, partly in order to ensure that the entire child population could be compelled to attend school at negligible or no individual expense. How much and how new was the stress put on this particular means of improving the quality of the population may be illustrated by some figures of expenditure: the annual amount spent on education by the British government rose from £1,097,000 in 1861 to £12,662,000 in 1901, while its annual expenditure on all other civil items increased by only about £2 million over those same forty years.

A great deal of new public enterprise was undertaken, however, by municipalities rather than by the central governmental, both in Britain and elsewhere. Governmental provision to improve the minds of the people was supplemented by local services which ministered to health and convenience. Public utilities, such as gas and water supply, which in many places had been operated by private firms, and the new services, such as electricity supply and street tramways, which were beginning to be important near the end of the nineteenth century, were taken over in whole or in part by the local authorities. In these activities, also, there was concern to ensure that the service should be adequate for the whole population of the area, which was often not the case when they were privately operated. There were also various activities of the utmost importance for health and amenity – street improvement and slum clearance, for example – which private enterprise did not touch and which local authorities began to take up, though not always very vigorously. The level of expenditure illustrates the increased activities of the local authorities as of the central government: in the thirty-three years from 1871 the amount of rates raised in England and Wales rose from £17,647,000 to £56,048,000, and the extent of local authority indebtedness for capital purposes rose from £173,208,000 in 1884 to £435,545,000 in 1905. Yet at this latter time reformers were constantly insisting that England lagged behind Germany in municipal services. In Germany by 1910 the municipalities provided 80 per cent of the gas supply, had acquired shares in many electricity supply companies, operated much of the local transport, and were among the most admired agents of city improvement in Europe. In some countries other experiments were made in public enterprise; for example, in Switzerland an attempt was made in 1910 to provide cheaper food by opening municipal shops.

The increase of public enterprise was accompanied by great extensions of the regulation of private enterprise. The special problems of an industrialized and urbanized society, which had led to experiments in public control even in Britain in the days of least restricted competition, became more widespread, more acute, and more clearly recognized, and a formidable administrative system was gradually built up in many countries in an effort to deal with them. In Britain, regulation was extended to factories and workshops in nearly every industry by 1878, and there was increasing supervision of the conditions of home workers after 1891. Early in the twentieth century additional health precautions were imposed on various occupations involving contact with dangerous materials or fumes. In 1909 a new type of safeguard was introduced (or a very old one restored) when trade boards were established to fix minimum wages in some of the worst-paid industries, mostly those carried on in very small workshops or at home. Three years later minimum wage legislation was extended to one of the country's chief occupations, coal-mining.

In continental Europe also there was a great increase of factory legislation at the same time. Germany introduced a comprehensive industrial code in 1891 and France established a Ministry of Labour in 1906. In the USA less was done, but before the First World War most states had imposed limitations on the use of child labour, and there were a few provisions affecting the position of adult workers. In 1912 Massachusetts passed the first minimum wage law in the USA.

The improvement of the general urban environment also received a contribution from increased public regulation. In practically every industrial country minimum standards, of varying degrees of stringency, were imposed on private building in the interests of structural and sanitary soundness. From the eighteen-sixties onwards mild measures of town-planning control began to be adopted in Western Europe. Britain, in 1909, was one of the last countries to copy them. Innumerable matters of detail affecting public health were brought within the scope of public regulation during the late nineteenth century and the early years of the twentieth. Notification of infectious diseases, inspection of dairies and cattle, regulations concerning the preparation and sale of drugs were only a few out of the many matters which became subjects of government administration.

Many of these measures contributed not only to an improvement in the physical efficiency of the population, but also to a greater contentment with prevailing conditions and a diminution of some of the strains which they imposed. But if the conditions of a highly industrialized society were to become thoroughly acceptable to the mass of the wage-earning population, it was necessary to mitigate in some way the effects of the additional insecurities of unemployment, industrial injury, and loss of wages during sickness that industrialization and a more impersonal organization of economic life brought with them. Something had been done in the way of self-help by workers themselves, through their trade unions and friendly societies, but there were strong arguments that it was unjust for them to have to bear the whole burden of making suitable provision. The transfer of responsibility to the state was gradual. It began with the organization of compulsory insurance schemes in Germany. In 1883 a scheme of compulsory insurance against sickness, financed by contributions from workers, employers, and the government, was applied to certain industries whose workers formed about 10 per cent of the total population. It provided for free medical attention and medicine, and for the payment of a proportion of the wages lost through illness and by 1911 had been extended to 13,600,000 persons. In 1884 an accident insurance scheme was introduced. Its cost was borne by a levy on employers, except that benefits during the first few weeks of injury were borne by the sickness insurance fund. In 1888 an old age and invalidity insurance scheme, financed, like the sickness scheme, by contributions from employees, employers, and the state, was added. Thus Germany in these years dealt by means of insurance with three of the four major insecurities of industrial life. The difficulties caused by unemployment were not mitigated in a similar way, but an attempt was made to reduce the extent and duration of enforced idleness by setting up labour exchanges. The first experiments were made privately, but from 1893 onwards a comprehensive public system was gradually created.

These German innovations were steadily extended in their country of origin, and soon began to be copied in the rest of Europe. They were eventually supplemented by the introduction of other types of scheme. Small experiments in unemployment insurance were tried by local authorities in various European countries, and in 1911 Britain introduced a national scheme that at first applied to seven occupations which together had over 2 million workers. This became just as influential an example as the earlier German insurance schemes, but before the First World War the part taken by governments in relieving unemployment was fairly small. Another novel development, which was then still only in the early stages of experiment in a few countries, was the payment of family or children's allowances as an addition to wages. These experiments were made on the initiative of private employers, but it is noteworthy that in France and Germany, where they were first made on an appreciable scale, the participation of the state was repeatedly urged, especially by the trade unions, and in Germany the state governments and the municipal authorities were among the pioneers in paying allowances to their own employees.

Such innovations were the foreshadowing of later things. Before 1914 they did not make much contribution to economic life. But by that time most industrial countries had made a substantial beginning in public provision against economic insecurity, very much on the lines established in Germany. The principal exception was the USA, but even there a start had been made with workmen's compensation schemes, though not until 1911 did any state succeed in devising one which the courts accepted as constitutional.

These various attempts to minimize the adverse effects of the uncertainties of economic life on the condition of workers were supplemented by efforts to reduce the uncertainties themselves. It was repeatedly emphasized that the choice of economic policies was governed as much by the desire for stability as by the attempt to expand industry and trade. Much of the argument between protectionists and free traders in continental Europe about 1900 turned, for example, on this point of which would promote steadier conditions. In fact, however, the promotion of more activity and steadier activity were not regarded as two separate aims, for it was believed that by extending government control it would be possible to gain more nearly exclusive possession of growing markets and thereby be less dependent on the swaying fortunes of a highly competitive struggle.

The most striking change of policy was the reversal of the movement towards freer trade in Europe. As competition grew in trade in both agricultural and manufactured goods, one country after another tried to preserve its home market by raising import duties. In Germany the change came in 1879, when industrialists and farmers made common cause to support each other's claim for protection. In 1881 France increased import duties slightly, and in 1892 revised its whole tariff system and introduced higher rates of duty. Of the other larger countries Austria, Italy, and Russia all increased their tariffs in the early eighteen-eighties. The persistence of a high tariff policy in the USA has already been noted. Not until 1913 were reductions made in import duties, and even then the tariff as a whole remained highly protective. Many parts of the British Empire adopted protective policies about the turn of the century. Almost everywhere the increase of protection continued. Germany, for example, introduced in 1906 a higher and most complex tariff applying to 5,400 classes of goods. Only in Britain and a few of the smaller countries which were exceptionally dependent on foreign trade was there little change in tariff policy. Even in Britain protection became a burning political question, especially after 1903, when Joseph Chamberlain launched his campaign for tariff reform and imperial preference. By that time many manufacturers had been so worried by the experience of having duties everywhere raised against their goods that they were beginning to question the free trade policy which had received almost unqualified approval in Britain for two generations; but they were too few to be the instruments of a political triumph.

Although there was a fairly general adoption of higher tariffs, the levels reached were protective but not prohibitive. Governments could hardly afford to make them too high, since they wanted increased revenue from the duties. Moreover, it was becoming the aim of government policies, not only to favour home industry in home markets, but also to give direct assistance to traders seeking markets abroad, and tariffs were used as a bargaining weapon for this purpose. By the eighteen-nineties various countries had systems of differential duties. A higher list applied to the products of countries which had made no concessions by commercial treaty and a lower list applied to goods from countries which had done so. Tariff changes were therefore frequently followed by the negotiation of commerical treaties, which had the effect of mitigating some of the increased duties. The new German tariff of 1906, for example, was followed by the signing of separate trade treaties with seven countries before the end of the same year and with three others later.

Apart from tariff wars and commercial treaties, governments also tried to expand their countries' exports by various forms of financial assistance to producers or traders, sometimes directly, sometimes indirectly. Of the direct methods the payment of subsidies was the commonest. An outstanding illustration of the lengths to which this was carried is provided by the sugar trade. By the end of the nineteenth century practically every European country producing beet-sugar had imposed a high tariff on all imported sugars, and was paying substantial bounties on its own sugar exports, with the result that its home consumers paid high prices, while the non-producing countries, among which Britain provided the chief market, received the benefit of cheap imports. This particular piece of competitive subsidization was brought to an end by an international convention signed at Brussels in 1902, but various other products continued to be subsidized in several countries.

Some of the subsidies were devised so as to offer cost reductions to export trade as a whole and not merely to help particular industries. The offer of low transport rates for exports became a central feature in economic policy, and was achieved mainly through government assistance to shipping. Most countries gave concealed assistance to their merchant fleets by paying fairly high rates for the carriage of mail, but, partly in order to cheapen commodity exports and partly in order to reduce invisible imports in the form of payments of foreign shipping freights, much more open assistance began to be given late in the nineteenth century. The methods included bounties to shipbuilders in proportion to the tonnage constructed and bounties to shipowners in proportion to the distance run by their vessels. Some of these bounties were very generous, and contributed much to the expansion of the supply of merchant shipping. The Japanese merchant fleet was one which owed its existence to government financial aid. A navigation subsidy was introduced in 1896 and extended in 1899, and a shipbuilding bounty was given from 1896 on all iron and steel vessels of more than 700 gross tons. Many countries also used the level of railway charges as an instrument for stimulating exports. Specially low rates were offered for the carriage of commodities destined for export, and in some cases there was an additional reduction if the goods were to be shipped in vessels belonging to the home country. Germany had an elaborate system of railway charges designed to stimulate trade, and Russia between 1889 and 1893 established a state-regulated schedule of railway rates which discriminated in favour of certain commodities destined for export and in favour of particular regions which could supply a large proportion of the country's total exports.

Measures of this kind were reinforced by international political activity. Tariff wars and the more frequent negotiation of commercial treaties were not the only signs that most of the leading powers were paying more (though not predominant) attention to economic affairs in their foreign policy. To some extent the spread of industrialization and the expansion of commerce made it more urgent to secure international agreement on a larger number of matters affecting them. Some of the efforts of governments were devoted, not to the establishment of a superior position in a competitive struggle, but to securing certain conditions the absence of which would, in various degrees, be disadvantageous to all the competitors. There had been during the nineteenth century increasing attention to a few matters of basic importance to commerce, such as the removal of restrictions on through traffic along rivers which flowed through more than one country or formed international boundaries. The principle of freedom of navigation on such rivers had been affirmed in the Act of the Congress of Vienna in 1815, and was repeated and clarified, with particular reference to the Danube, in the Treaty of Paris in 1856. Numerous separate agreements gradually made the general principle administratively applicable to the chief European rivers and straits, and embodied decisions about the level of tolls. Navigational tolls on the Scheldt were abolished by international agreement in 1863, and on the Rhine in 1868. Additional international measures to regulate traffic on the Danube were taken in 1857 and 1883.

Besides the greater number of agreements of this kind, another minor symptom of change was the somewhat larger economic content of attempts to promote general political settlement. The Treaty of Berlin of 1878 did not perhaps make any more stringent economic provisions than a great power had earlier sometimes imposed on a weaker, but the limitations put on the commercial policies of Bulgaria, Romania and, to a less extent, Serbia, went considerably beyond anything previously decided by a major European peace conference. The growing clash of interests in Africa was also relieved somewhat by international economic agreement, when freedom of commercial access by all nations to the Congo region without payment of duties was established by the Treaty of Berlin in 1885, which authorized the creation of the Congo Free State under Leopold II of Belgium.

There were other matters on which it was still clearer that absence of international agreement was unlikely to benefit any individual country, whereas the achievement of such agreement might produce general advantage. Among the most important were communications, which were the subject of a number of agreements leading to uniformity in practices and in the methods of apportioning receipts.

In 1865 twenty European states signed an international telegraphic treaty. They were joined in 1868 by various Asiatic countries, and in 1869 an International Office of Telegraphy was established at Berne. In 1874 a Universal Postal Union was founded by twenty-one states with a combined population of more than 350 millions; other countries subsequently joined the Union, so that it came very near to justifying its name. Other subjects on which states co-operated for the mutual protection and advantage of their members included the international recognition of trade-marks and patent rights, which was first attempted in a convention signed at Paris in 1883 and was rapidly extended, and the international protection of copyright, established by the Berne Convention of 1886.

But such measures of inter-governmental co-operation formed only a small part of political activity. Economic affairs, so far as they impinged on foreign policy, led more often to attempts to promote national or private advantage, to the detriment of foreign competitors. As the supremacy of one country, Great Britain, in international trade declined, there was increasing pressure from private interests in all the leading commercial countries for greater government assistance in the search for markets and in attempts to secure particular contracts and concessions in foreign parts. The response to such pressure varied considerably from one government to another, but there was a general attempt to pay more attention to commercial matters in the routine conduct of foreign affairs. Of the chief trading countries, probably Britain made least change in this respect. Its government did not concern itself very much with assisting the transactions of individual firms, whereas the German consular service was very active in that way. But the British government began to gather much more information than before about foreign markets, and made considerable changes in organization so as to be better able to assist overseas trade. A Commercial Department was established in the Foreign Office in 1866 and thoroughly reorganized in 1872. The first commercial *attaché* in the diplomatic service was appointed to the Paris embassy in 1880, and another was appointed to St. Petersburg in 1887. In 1903 the number of commercial *attachés* was increased, and at the same time the consular service was almost completely reorganized. Similar developments took place elsewhere and were carried further. France combined its diplomatic and consular services by measures of 1880 and 1883, and this example was slowly followed in other countries.

In matters of high policy, economic and other factors were inextricably intertwined. Much of the content of international politics between about 1870 and 1910, and especially after 1890, has come to be summarized under the convenient, though not altogether accurate, name of 'economic imperialism'. In this period almost the whole of Africa passed under the rule of various European powers, several of which also greatly extended their territories in Asia and the Pacific Islands. In these latter regions and in the Caribbean the USA, too, was establishing an oversea empire, and at the turn of the century Japan followed the Western example by obtaining territory on the Asiatic mainland. There were also various countries in which, though foreign rule was not imposed, there was considerable political pressure (sometimes with naval or military support) which led to the grant of economic and strategic concessions to great powers. All the great powers were in pursuit of privileges in China. In Persia (Iran) spheres of interest were obtained by Britain and Russia, and the British government in 1914 became the largest shareholder in a company formed five years earlier to develop Persian oil resources. Egypt lost control of its government finances to Britain, and several Central American republics had to accept financial direction from the USA. Germany secured commercial and transport privileges in Asiatic Turkey.

Many of these developments had very strong support from the business communities of the penetrating countries and, in part, they were an extension of that policy of giving greater political support to national commercial interests, of which other aspects have already been discussed. The growth of production and the sharpening of international competition led to a more intense search for new markets in which private traders asked for the support of their own governments and private investors sought the help of their governments to safeguard their capital and insist on the payment of interest. Most strong governments were willing to give some support of this kind, and the outright annexation of additional territory was supported by economic arguments. By 1900 it was widely believed that complete political control over market areas made it easier to expand rapidly the volume of trade and ensure greater steadiness in the flow of both sales and purchases. Moreover, as industrial techniques changed and manufacture expanded, the amount and variety of raw materials needed in industrialized countries greatly increased, and it seemed prudent to try to gain control of sources of their supply. But it has also to be recognized that much of the rivalry for commercial privileges and territorial cessions in backward areas was part of an international manœuvring for position in which considerations of prestige and strategy were of major importance. Some of the economic arguments which were advanced in support of particular measures of colonial expansion were plainly ludicrous and could hardly fail to be recognized as such at the time by those unblinded by fanatical emotions. Some genuine commercial expansion was achieved; for example, British exports to Africa between 1880 and 1884 averaged between 5 and 6 per cent of the country's total exports, and twenty years later averaged 12 per cent. There were probably also exaggerated hopes because of both earlier and contemporary benefits from older imperial acquisitions. The most prominent example was the relation between Britain and India. Much of Britain's success in achieving dominance in the international commercial and financial system of the late nineteenth century was associated with its large exports to India and its ability to build up Indian exports to the rest of the world. But India was exceptional. The prospects of phenomenally rapid growth of commerce with new colonies was never bright. Their contribution to trade was small in relation to the cost of obtaining and governing them, and even smaller in relation to the total volume of international trade. There was much in the policy of 'economic imperialism' that was merely a mixture of irrational emotions disguised in the garb of economic pretension.

But whatever the motives involved, the very fact that governments extended their activities in this way had important economic effects, because of its contribution to the growth of public expenditure, which was in most industrial countries more rapid than the growth of national income, so that the burden of taxation increased. All the additional functions which governments took to themselves in order to promote and regulate economic activity cost money. Even if they did not involve government enterprise, they made it necessary to improve and extend administrative machinery. But there was more than this. Stronger government support to enterprise abroad included the threat of force as a reserve measure and was one element in the expansion of navies and armies. Thus government became more expensive both from the adoption of new functions and from the exercise of old ones on a larger scale. Expenditure was further swollen by the effects of rapid technological change, which concerned government activities just as much as private industry. There was indeed scarcely an industry in which the problem of premature obsolescence and heavier capital expenditure as a result of technical invention was so acute as it was in naval operations. Until about 1875, naval architecture and the design of guns changed only gradually, and any power which had built up a superiority in numbers of ships could feel secure at sea for years to come. But after this, invention was so rapid and far-reaching that whole fleets were becoming obsolete every ten years or so and had to be completely replaced. Disparity in efficiency between the up-to-date and the recent became so great that mere numbers of ships ceased to confer security. Competition in armaments thus became a competition in quality as well as quantity and, as might be expected, every advance in quality involved an increase in cost. The importance of increased defence expenditure in public finance may be illustrated by the growth of the British naval estimates. In 1870 these amounted to rather over £9 million. By 1900 they had reached £27,500,000, and had already been the specific cause of a complete reorganization and appreciable increase of death duties. In 1911 the estimates rose to £44,400,000 and in 1914 to £51,500,000. The rise in the opening years of the twentieth century was not so great as that in the government's civil estimates, which considerably more than doubled between 1900 and 1914. But by 1914 it was clear that the costs of armaments, public enterprise, and social services were rapidly changing the whole position of the state as an economic as well as a political institution in many countries.

Viewed in relation to what happened in the next forty years, the role of governments in economic affairs in 1914 may seem to have still been severely limited, but in comparison with the situation forty or fifty years earlier, it showed an enormous change. The great importance of this change is revealed by two of its characteristics. In the first place it occurred, with a fair degree of similarity, in nearly all appreciably industrialized or important trading countries. The chief partial exception was the USA, where conditions continued to be much closer to the old ideal of *laissez-faire* than elsewhere. But even in the USA there was a policy of trade protection and of considerable diplomatic support to commercial penetration, and there was the tentative beginning of some governmental control of internal economic activity, as shown by the widening functions of the Inter-State Commerce Commission, the closer governmental control of railway operation, and the introduction by Theodore Roosevelt of a policy designed to conserve some of the remaining natural resources, such as minerals and water power; and American municipalities in the late nineteenth century were trying to promote health and amenity in ways very similar to those in Western Europe. The second notable feature was that the development of governmental economic policies after 1914 was, on the whole, less a matter of innovation than of greatly extending what had already been begun. Many of the significant innovations, except those bound up with the existence of a totalitarian political system, had already been made.

There were, however, some important new influences which greatly accelerated the extension of government activity. Of these by far the most significant was the phenomenon of world war. Its first impact on economic activity seemed no more than a slight extension of previous growing armament expenditure which hampered civil business somewhat by causing heavier taxation but did not drastically upset ordinary business life. But early in the First World War it became clear that conditions were no longer like those of the nineteenth century, when land wars had been fought by small armies or concluded within a few months, or both, and the exercise of sea power was relatively cheap, even though its cost grew rapidly after 1875. The First World War made necessary for the first time the thorough mobilization of the productive resources of all the major belligerents, so that almost every aspect of economic life became the intimate concern of governments. The need to raise large armies and to keep up their strength for years, despite a sickeningly high casualty rate, made it essential to establish elaborate government controls over the allocation of labour, and to make efforts to ensure as great an efficiency as possible from the diluted labour force of industry. Hence an extension of measures to improve industrial welfare in order to keep workers healthy, contented, and co-operative as far as possible. The volume of military supplies needed, which proved to be far greater than any of the belligerents had made previous plans to produce, led to the application of government control to a very wide range of manufacturing industry, to the provision of government finance for the expansion of privately operated industries with an immediate military value, and to a great increase in the number of government-operated factories. Germany, in particular, organized its heavy industry very fully under government control, but all the major belligerents went a long way in the same direction. Nor was government intervention limited to industries concerned with munition production. Since the effort of the whole adult population has to be called forth in order to sustain the military and economic stresses of war, safeguards had to be provided for some of the basic items of civilian use. Thus, for example, there were attempts by regulation, subsidy, price-fixing, and rationing to ensure that war conditions did not lead to a breakdown of food supply.

Perhaps the most surprising thing about this vast extension of state economic control was that so little of it proved to be permanent in this form. In one country after another a large part of the elaborate wartime apparatus of regulation was rapidly dismantled when peace returned. But far greater technical knowledge of the means of effecting economic control had been acquired and was brought into use again when circumstances and ideas changed once more. And not all the wartime measures were abandoned. Though reponsibility for production returned for the most part to private hands, some of the provisions for improved working and living conditions remained, and, partly as a result of this, the level of government expenditure was higher than before 1914.

The abandonment of most of the wartime economic controls did not mean that war failed to alter fundamentally and permanently the role of governments in economic life. Though the problems of economic mobilization, which were in some degree peculiar to war itself, diminished and the expedients designed to meet them were dropped, other economic difficulties which arose out of the conduct of the war persisted long after peace returned, and by their magnitude and pervasiveness compelled state action. In particular, the financial strain eventually led to the complete disorganization of economic life in several European countries, so that governments had to take the initiative in trying to restore stability. They had not only to extend their normal activities in public finance, but also to provide temporary relief for unemployed workers and in some cases to take part in the operation of businesses. The economic instability which arose out of the First World War was never removed before 1939, though it was for a time reduced, and its continuance was responsible for a steady growth of government control as people demanded the provision of economic palliatives at least, if no cure was available. The emergence of heavy unemployment led to both a great extension of systems of insurance and relief in most industrial countries and the adoption of many more expedients intended to protect the industry and trade of individual countries. The familiar device of the tariff was raised almost everywhere to higher levels, and was extended even where free trade had long prevailed, as in Britain, and it was supplemented by new subsidies and by physical and financial controls over trade, in the form of import quotas for particular commodities and, in some countries in the nineteen-thirties, the rationing of foreign currency.

World war also had a lasting though less direct influence on the scope of economic policy, because it acted as a catalyst releasing revolutionary political forces. When long-established political *régimes* were shattered, all the functions of the state were subject to some degree of revision, and the administrative machinery to redirection. In this process, carried on in the midst of social turmoil, official prescription of some economic tasks and rewards became common, even if it were only for the purpose of securing enough support and enough revenue for the new *régime* to establish itself. But in fact the characteristic political change in a number of European countries was the rise to power of parties which were committed to use the authority of the state in the interest of previously underprivileged groups. Thus, for instance, the new peasant governments in most East European states carried out radical reforms of land ownership. Most potent of all was the Bolshevik triumph in Russia. The creation there of a completely centralized, state-directed economy from which private, capitalist employers had been practically eliminated, and its gradual surmounting of the material difficulties which confronted it, was an important influence on the political scene elsewhere. It did not serve as a model to be copied, because the methods by which it was established and maintained could not be introduced in quite different conditions, and because many of those methods and the human valuations implicit in them aroused widespread loathing. But, at the same time, there were many people in other countries who regarded the material achievements of the Russian experiment as evidence that socialism was an eminently practical policy and that it was by much greater extension of state direction of economic life that the well-being of the working class could be most thoroughly improved. This was a new reinforcement to old influences, arising out of the conditions of industrial life, which had already led to a considerable amount of state action on behalf of workers.

The achievements of the USSR were also used as an argument in favour of the more comprehensive change involved in the introduction of central economic planning. Earlier government measures, such as differential taxation, differential transport charges, and subsidies used in order to bias private decisions about the type and quantity of goods to be produced and sold, formed an approach to partial central planning, but until the Soviet *régime* was established, it was nowhere the practice in peacetime to centralize within the government organization itself a high proportion of the decisions that determined the distribution of national economic resources among different users. But apart from the existence of a practical example, there were other distinct influences operating in the same direction. One of these was that by the nineteen-thirties it was very clear that in existing conditions many economic resources were not being used at all, while others were being used wastefully. At the same time the changing practice of private business was providing hints for state administrative practice. As production became increasingly mechanized, as profits became more dependent on the maintenance of a smooth flow of work, as firms became larger and various branches of business more closely integrated, so there came into existence in large firms planning departments with new functions. Their task was to arrange an enormous mass of details in order to have the right amount of all the means of production in the right place at the right time to make a chosen quantity of a particular commodity by a previously determined method. They demonstrated a new technique which some people believed could be taken over and enlarged by governments as a means of regulating some, at least, of the economic affairs of a whole nation. It was the preparation and execution of large-scale war once again that gave great impetus to the absorption of this technique into the regular practice of government. But even for peacetime purposes it was adopted to a limited extent as governments came under pressure to seek some remedy for the obvious inefficiencies of contemporary economic practice, as revealed in unemployment and the squandering of wasting assets. The influences at work, even in what had been the last home of something like *laissez-faire*, were well summarized by the National Resources Board of the USA, when in 1934 it reported that

the careful inventory and appraisal of our resources, and the consideration of how we may most effectively utilize these resources, could not in any case have been long delayed, after our frontier had been closed and the progress of mechanical invention established as a permanent factor in our civilization.

In such developments the mingled pressures of immediate and recent crises and of economic changes which had been proceeding for a long time could be observed. All the major factors which had encouraged the growth of state enterprise and intervention in economic matters before 1914 persisted much later. As they became more obviously permanent and more familiar, the response to them became stronger, and as state action in a few spheres became usual, an environment was created in which opposition to further extensions of the functions of government steadily diminished.

The strengthening of old influences was seen less in the international than in the internal aspects of economic policy, but even in the international field economic life became more · dependent on political decisions than before. Intergovernmental agreement and co-operation through international institutions for the promotion of general advantages in economic affairs was not very greatly extended until after the Second World War, though it was maintained in spheres where it was already established. The secretariat of the League of Nations became a most important instrument for the collection and diffusion of economic information and the dispassionate study of some common international economic problems. The League of Nations also promoted joint governmental action on a number of the less contentious economic and social questions, and provided a means of conducting extensive inter-governmental discussions of the most fundamental economic difficulties. But on the whole its importance to economic affairs was as a source of information rather than as a strong instrument of policy.

Nor did the establishment of an international financial institution have much practical effect. When the Bank for International Settlements was founded in 1929, it was hoped that it might develop into a true international central bank, through which the mutual claims of national central banks and governments might be settled, and thus act as a useful steadying influence in international finance. But this hope was not realized, mainly perhaps because soon after the Bank was established, economic difficulties became so great that in the financial policy of every country long-term international considerations were completely ignored in an attempt to snatch at any means of immediate internal improvement. Only after 1945 did effective action in finance and trade take place through intergovernmental institutions. Some of this joint action came through the agencies and commissions of the United Nations, but the greatest influences were those of the USA, on which much of Europe depended for financial help for several years, and of the movement for the unity of Western Europe. The American influence was most evident in such a body as the Organization for European Economic Co-operation, one of the major instruments promoting the recovery of Europe with American aid. The most notable new institutions emerging in the nineteen-fifties, the European Coal and Steel Community and the European Economic Community, were deliberate contributions to Western European unity.

In the interwar years the one branch of policy in which a new international institution brought about significant action, though on a limited scale, was the regulation of labour conditions. The effect of differences in national labour legislation on international business competition had long been a source of complaint among employers, and the increase of international migration had shown workers' organizations how differences in national standards of labour conditions might affect their bargaining power. From 1890 onwards, when the first international conference on labour legislation met in Berlin, various efforts had been made to secure international agreement about labour legislation, but they had achieved little. Circumstances were more favourable just after the First World War, because the victorious governments, as one means of keeping up morale, had promised to do something to improve the conditions of workers. One measure to implement this promise was the creation of an International Labour Organization, the constitution of which formed part of each of the four treaties of peace ratified in 1919 and 1920. The Organization, to which all members of the League of Nations belonged and which was also joined in 1935 by the USA, consisted of a conference of representatives of members and a permanent International Labour Office controlled by a governing body. Its decisions, embodied in conventions, were binding only on those members which ratified them, but in fact they were instrumental in spreading various reforms quite widely. The ILO made a notable contribution, for example, in obtaining greater uniformity and justice in the terms of employment of seamen. It did much to secure further restrictions on the employment of child labour and generally to bring the standards of the more backward countries nearer to those of the rest as far as labour legislation could do so. To the improvement of working conditions generally in the leading manufacturing countries, however, it contributed only a little.

Though intergovernmental *co-operation* in economic matters did not greatly increase, every government found itself obliged to pay increasing attention to economic questions in its relations with other states. The difficulties of world trade and of discharging international financial obligations became so great that they were for long periods among the major subjects of diplomatic negotiation. Governmental decisions on external economic problems were not always by any means based mainly on an appraisal of the economic aspects of the situation, but international economic relations came to be much more closely influenced than before by the actions of governments, however these were determined. Most governments were particularly concerned to give their countries as much protection as possible from the effects of worldwide economic disturbance; but the attempt to do this involved elaborate negotiation. Moreover, as governments became directly concerned with a greater range of activities at home, they found themselves obliged to deal with the international connexions that were sometimes involved. Foreign policy had always been one of the unquestioned functions of government. In the twentieth century it acquired everywhere a proportionately larger economic content.

Nevertheless, it was in internal affairs that the extension of government control over economic life was most striking, at least wherever there was appreciable industrialization. The conditions of industrial society which had led to an extension of government activity persisted and spread. Pressure for still more collective action in the interest of the mass of dependent workers grew because the opinions and activities of women acquired political force and be-cause, as the scale of business increased, more and more people in supervisory and professional occupations found themselves in a position of economic dependence somewhat analogous to that of lower-grade labour. Measures of regulation which had been intro-duced earlier were extended to affect a greater proportion of the population. The German sickness insurance scheme was widened in 1925 to provide both for the dependants of sick workers and for members of occupations previously excluded, so that it applied to 60 per cent of the population. Other measures which before 1914 were in operation experimentally in only one or two countries were extended there and widely copied. The British system of unemploy-ment insurance had grown until it covered 12 million workers by 1930, and similar systems were introduced in the nineteen-twenties in Italy, Austria, Poland, and Germany. Where government regula-tion had been much more restricted, as it had been in the USA, there were attempts to extend it rapidly in ways already familiar else-where. During the nineteen-thirties and forties there was a great increase in social security provision in the USA. By 1937 every state had some kind of unemployment insurance scheme, though three years earlier there were none in force except in Wisconsin. The Social Security Acts of 1935 and 1939 made possible the creation of a nationwide system both of unemployment insurance and old age pensions, though it excluded various classes of workers. The Fair Labor Standards Act of 1939 introduced federal control over the minimum level of wages and maximum length of the working week.

Public regulation and public enterprise continued to increase to-gether. Indeed, when governments began to supervise and subsidize activities protecting the position of large groups of their people, they were gradually led to provide additional services with closely related purposes. Thus the growth of state-sponsored sickness insurance schemes gave governments a greater interest in positive measures to maintain health and improve the treatment of disease. It was one important influence on the increase in the public provision of hospitals and of centres of medical research. In every field where public enterprise had firmly established itself, it maintained its position and usually expanded, and additional functions continued to be taken over from private enterprise. After 1919 a large proportion of the new housing in most countries of Western Europe was provided by governments and municipalities, whereas previously it had been mainly the work of private builders. Among the reasons for this change were the acceptance of better standards of quality as necessary for the smooth working of contemporary society and the inability of private capital in some years to supply enough good housing at a reasonable profit under existing conditions of working-class income and of building costs.

For the state to step in to supply what it judged to be socially necessary when private capitalists could not meet the need was one of the earliest and most persistent reasons for the extension of public enterprise. After 1919 it was affecting other activities besides housing. The increasing burden of overhead costs made the position of various types of large-scale enterprise precarious and discouraged new investment in them. The financial difficulties of many railways, which were still vital to national economic activity, were a major factor prompting a further extension of public ownership and operation of existing lines; and where additions were still needed, they could usually be provided only with state financial assistance. The very heavy initial cost of building airports and establishing air services, reinforced by military considerations, led public enterprise to have a large share in another major branch of transport.

In the less wealthy countries, where economic development was being sought but had not yet got nearly as far, the role of government was usually wider. To some extent this was because of the association of economic progress with the assertion of national identity, which could be most completely symbolized by the government. But the principal reason was the shortage of other effective sources of developmental activity. It has been noticed that in earlier periods the more backward countries tended to lack private entrepreneurs and the ability to mobilize capital in amounts and on terms appropriate to new types of business, so that the government had to step in as a partial substitute. In the twentieth century, difficulties of this kind became more acute. Many of the most modern types of enterprise needed a larger initial capital and presented more complex problems of management than ever before, and economic development began to be attempted in societies where business experience and familiarity with the disciplines and techniques of industrial work were rarer than in the countries which had previously undergone a comparable transition. Some of the attempts at a degree of 'deliberate industrialization' in parts of Latin America – Mexico and Argentina, for example – during the nineteen-thirties and 'forties illustrated the tendency for greater government promotion of new enterprises in such circumstances. Still more central was the role of governments in the underdeveloped countries of Africa, Asia and Latin America after 1950. Many of these countries had previously been colonies of European powers and most of the local administrative experience had necessarily been gained in government service and remained concentrated there after independence had been obtained. Moreover, some key contributions of capital and skill were often needed from abroad, some of them from intergovernmental agencies, and only governments had the necessary credit, while at the same time governments felt they had a special obligation to ensure that these conditions of development brought no infringement of national independence. In these circumstances government financial assistance and control, together with some government owned and operated firms, were common features in trade and industry as well as in the provision of basic services such as transport, public utilities and credit institutions.

In some more advanced countries the reduction of private investment, especially after 1930, prompted an increase in public activity in an attempt to offset the resultant unemployment. Between 1933 and 1938 the federal government of the USA heavily increased its debt, mainly to provide relief payments and to finance public works. The German government also began public works on a large scale in 1932, and what was begun as a relief measure was found to be an admirable means of influencing the distribution of productive activities in accordance with military plans. Public investment was therefore expanded, and by 1937 54 per cent of the country's new investment was provided by the state. In Japan also, where the shortage of private persons with any surplus wealth available for investment had caused the state to take a large direct part in industrialization from its beginning, similar military influences helped to maintain and strengthen government participation in economic enterprise.

One other major change in the structure of business also affected the readiness of governments to extend their own economic enterprise. As business concentration increased, larger sectors of the economy were subject to conditions of near-monopoly. Some private firms were in a strong enough position to affect vitally the economic conditions of a large part of the nation, but had no legal responsibility towards the public. Partly for this reason there was a growing demand, springing from a concern more with social justice than with economic efficiency (though the latter was also involved sometimes), that government control or ownership should be extended to the operation of very large firms in basic industries. Here was an important source of the movement to nationalize parts of industry in several West European countries.

Even in peacetime there was a great variety of influences promoting a continuous increase in the participation of governments in economic affairs. The range, complexity, and cost of government administration and enterprise increased far beyond the point at which the state was merely the largest single economic institution. The position was reached where the economic influence of the state was almost enough to offset the influence of all other economic institutions together. By 1938 the governments of two of the wealthiest states, Canada and the UK, were already spending about a quarter of the national income of their countries, and there was a worldwide tendency for the proportion of public to private expenditure to increase. The renewal of world war greatly accelerated the change, and, as had often happened before, the return of peace did not bring a return to pre-war levels of public expenditure. Though the nineteen-fifties saw some reduction from the very high proportions of the immediate post-war years, government expenditure in 1960 in each of the industrial countries of Western Europe was from 35 to 40 per cent of the gross domestic product, except in Scandinavia, where the proportion was a little lower. Broader definitions of public expenditure would have put the figures rather higher.

Figures of this magnitude indicate a change in the relation between governments and economic life, mainly since the late nineteenth century, which was of fundamental importance. Many of the special factors involved in the change have already been noted. It might have been assumed that they had carried a trend so far that in the middle of the twentieth century it must have been near its peak, but this proved not to be so. After 1960 the increase in the governmental share of expenditure began to accelerate again even in those industrialized countries where it had already gone highest, and higher proportions became more and more characteristic of poorer countries, even though they did not adopt centrally planned economies in which the state sought to be the originator of all major enterprise. In the countries of the EEC government expenditure as a proportion of gross domestic product rose from 32.2 per cent in 1960 to an average of 39.0 in 1968–73 and to 51.1 in 1982. There were specially steep rises in Scandinavia, above all in Denmark, where the figures were 24.8 in 1960, 40.1 in 1968–73 and 60.7 in 1982. Even with a more proclaimed devotion to free enterprise, the USA, with 37.6 per cent in 1982, had a higher proportion than any member country of the OECD had reached in 1960; and so unindustrialized a country as Greece showed a rise from 17.4 per cent in 1960 to 22.4 per cent in 1968–73 and 36.5 per cent in 1982.

Some shifts were associated with changes in the ideological complexion of the government of a particular country, but this was seldom a strong influence in the long term. Even governments that thought of rolling back the frontiers of the state were likely to find most of them continuing to roll forward. So other explanations have to be sought. The spread of the rising tide of government expenditure to poorer countries was partly the result of newly independent governments seeking to assert themselves and initiate a new era, and, more generally, the manifestation of a wish to start catching up on political and economic developments which had earlier been missed. For such an attempt it often seemed that only government action was likely to be effective. There was, too, an element of emulation of more highly developed countries, in the provision of services which appeared to be sources of both comfort and prestige.

In countries already highly developed, more rapid rises in living standards expanded the long-established demand for more and more comprehensive services, which were often most conveniently organized collectively. Many of these were labour-intensive and subject to large increases in cost because of their dependence on staff accustomed to high and rising living standards. There was, too, a particularly costly impact of new technology on some of the main central functions of government, notably defence. And there was a powerful influence from the strength, closeness, and, above all, the publicity of international relationships. So rapid was communication, and so vast and miscellaneous was the subject matter of the communications industries, that anyone in any country could be instantly aware of what was going on in any other country (or, at least, believe that he was aware). So almost any activity could be proclaimed as having a representative character, or a vital public purpose, and as being appropriate for care and attention by the supreme representative institution, i.e. the government. These were perfect conditions for the opening of new channels of government expenditure.

Central economic planning and totalitarian government characterized a large part of the world and were, by definition, bound to increase the economic role of the state. But, even where liberal institutions persisted and flourished, there was an attachment to the paternally supervisory state and its disbursements, even if this encroached on roles once reserved for individuals; and bureaucracies, once entrenched, had the combined strengths of authority and ability, which made it hard to diminish them. Thus, over most of the world, many more economic and social matters passed into the care of politicians and civil servants. Non-economic motives had greater scope to influence the course of economic affairs, and political success came more frequently to depend on apparent economic achievement. Political and economic affairs became harder to separate or distinguish, and each became a larger part of the explanation of the other.

CHAPTER SIX
The growth of incomes

Each and every one of the topics already examined shows change of a radical and transforming kind, bringing, over the course of a century or so, a new character to major aspects of economic life in numerous different countries. But there was also a more general change to which all these were related in different ways. This was the continual growth of the whole economic activity of the countries directly affected. This growth is most relevantly and conveniently indicated by the level of income or product per head of population. To measure changes of this kind cannot be done with complete precision, and the longer the period and the further back in time it goes, the lower the degree of reliability usually is. There are difficulties caused by the nature and omissions of the data, and there are serious statistical problems as the components of income change over time and the relative prices of the same components differ widely at different dates. It is also impossible to match all the available data to any one concept of product with a single universally accepted definition, nor is the same concept equally appropriate as an indicator of growth at all stages in the history of an economy. Product may be stated net (when it ought to be equal to income) or gross (so as to include the replacement of depreciation of capital stock), which is more appropriate for a highly capitalized economy. Sometimes domestic product (i.e. all product created within the country) will be cited, and sometimes national product (i.e. all product created and received by nationals of the country, both people and institutions), and the data sometimes make it easier to produce one set of figures rather than the other. Thus, quite apart from differences arising from imperfections in the data, there are different absolute figures according to the concept which is being used, though fluctuations and trends are usually fairly similar without being completely identical. All conclusions based on such figures must be tentative and approximate.

Nevertheless, there is no doubt of the reality of high rates of growth and their association with recent achievements. Present-day levels of income can be assessed with reasonable accuracy for most countries and for a substantial minority of them tolerable estimates can be made for years back to the late nineteenth century. For the wealthier countries of the present day an average increase of about 15 per cent per decade in income per head since the date of these earliest estimates is not unrepresentative; some have done better, some a little worse. An increase at this rate will produce a quadrupling in a hundred years. Yet such rates of increase cannot have been occurring for very long. Had they been doing so, the levels of income prevailing not very far back in history would have been too low for subsistence, and even more recently they would have been insufficient to permit the sort of economic and social life of which there is full descriptive evidence. Economic growth at such speeds is characteristic only of the nineteenth and twentieth centuries, and even then its spread was a gradual one from a small to a larger minority of countries; but its magnitude was enough for the new dynamism of the minority to transform the economy of the world.

The achievement of high rates of economic growth was not the direct result of any one specific set of changes. All the subjects that have already been discussed, technical and institutional, industrial and non-industrial, private and governmental, had an essential part in it, in relationships subject to a great number of permutations. Of course, it is also true to say that the main *immediate* source of rising productivity (which is the counterpart of rising incomes) has been the adoption of new technologies, especially the application of power-driven machinery to innumerable processes previously done by hand or incapable of performance. But technological innovation, by its very nature, cannot be an independent act. Every such innovation is an outcome of intelligence and skill, requiring the mobilization and application of the intelligence and skill of others, and therefore related to prevailing habits of mind, to the nature of the available system of education and training, and to the state of the labour market. Almost every such innovation also embodies an act of investment and is thereby at once related to the nature of the capital market and its institutions, and to the prevailing habits of saving and all the social influences on them.

It would, however, be a mistake to think that only stagnation has been possible when mechanical innovation has been absent. Within the growing national economies of the last hundred years there have been elements of increased productivity that have had little to do with the introduction of new machinery, have required no extra labour and relatively small investments. Some of them have already been noted among the organizational changes affecting agriculture. Even before the emergence of recent high rates of growth, and before industrial technology was dominated by power-driven machinery, much more gradual but persistent and significant economic growth could be observed in some countries, especially in Western Europe and in some of the colonies it built up overseas in the seventeenth and eighteenth centuries.

Economic growth, in the absence of a mechanical technology, has usually depended on gaining command of an increasing quantity of productive resources and on the improvement of productive efficiency by means of a greater division of labour. In practice, the use of additional resources, though it also involved the working of previously neglected mineral deposits, was achieved mainly by occupying and cultivating more land, sometimes in external colonies but often within the national territory. When population was gradually increasing, as it appears to have been doing, irregularly but persistently, in much of Western Europe between about 1500 and 1750, there was a particular incentive to make these extensions of settlement. If they were mere copies of what had been done before it might well be that, though the community's output was absolutely larger, there would be no increase in output per head. But the cultivation of fresh land, the opening of new mines and quarries, or the development of a trading centre in the midst of a new settlement provided the opportunity, sometimes taken, to organize matters in a better way: to distribute land more conveniently for the needs of different cultivators, to shake off the burden of obsolete rights and dues to which non-producers were customarily entitled elsewhere. In communities where such things were happening a stimulus was also given to reforms in the older settlements and institutions, with a consequent opportunity to use existing resources more fully. The rearrangement of land-holding and the substitution of individual for communal agriculture were among the most frequent changes of this kind, but where the spirit of reform was let loose among laws and institutions it was apt to find other fields of action. New laws and public policies to repress idleness and waste, and the encouragement of additional financial organizations to assist business and the accumulation of capital were expressions of the same outlook and in their different ways made possible a more effective use of other factors of production.

Changes such as these, though seldom its sole or principal cause, often directly encouraged the greater division of labour, on which Adam Smith, reflecting on his observation of his own times, put the greatest stress as the source of increased productive efficiency. Many of them were directly associated with an expansion of the market in numbers or area or purchasing power, and this in turn could make it worth while to attempt greater specialization of function or locality – for more workers to stick to one type of productive activity in which experience and continuity fostered expertise, for production and distribution to be done by different people without either of them being left only intermittently occupied, for more of those engaged in one particular activity to congregate closely together and reap some of the advantages of sharing a common set of services and having access to a common stock of information relevant to their business. None of the new practices required a great deal of capital for its adoption, but some addition was necessary. At the very least, the fuller use of resources involved the provision of rather more working capital to cover the cost of labour and materials embodied in a bigger volume of work in progress. But the increased efficiency made it easy to provide this extra capital and might well encourage a rather greater expansion of capital in the form of more and better or more frequently renewed tools and more convenient buildings. Where this happened it was possible for economic growth to proceed a little less slowly.

It is appropriate to recall these possibilities and achievements of economic growth in a non-mechanical setting because they altered the international economic balance of the world before it was transformed by the spread of machinery; they did much to determine the conditions in which more rapid modern development took place and, indeed, in a minor way made their own contribution to it alongside the more spectacular achievements associated with a scientific technology; and they enabled some of the pioneers of rapid development to achieve more substantial reward from it by starting the process from a higher level. The earlier possibilities of growth were there, but their translation into achievement depended on initiative and intelligence and on the whole complex of social ideas and institutions and policies and accidents which granted or denied scope to these qualities. Though these circumstances always differed from one country to another, yet factors varying widely in detail often combined to produce similar inhibiting effects. As a United

Nations survey put it, 'in most underdeveloped countries, the traditional framework of political, social and economic institutions, within which economic activity was long conducted, was conducive less to economic growth than to the perpetuation of economic stagnation'. The exceptions to this generalization, mostly West European in location or origin, made their mark at an early date, as our own introductory survey of the mid-nineteenth century made clear. The superiority which the countries of Western Europe and North America then displayed in wealth, productive power and commerce no doubt owed something to the first steps which they had already taken towards a mechanized, industrialized economy, but it owed more to other types of change. Even in 1850 it is possible, though not certain, that income per head was already higher in the USA than anywhere else in the world, higher than in Britain, although the latter had run ahead of the rest on the road towards industrialization. The USA at that time was still very little industrialized. But it had unusually abundant natural resources, traditions and institutions which encouraged their use (as soon as they were accessible) to the full extent that current knowledge permitted, and a firmly established commerce to which a high proportion of its gradually accumulating capital stock was devoted and which gave a good return for it. There were other countries, notably Australia and New Zealand, which, somewhat later in date but early in their own history, enjoyed in pre-industrial conditions a level of income that was probably comparable; and they did so for similar reasons. Such countries as Britain and France, with a less rich inheritance of natural resources, relatively to their numbers, could not start their rapid development from so high a point, but their piecemeal advances, consolidated over several preceding centuries, had brought them pre-industrial incomes much higher than those of nearly all other countries, even though, by their own mid-twentieth-century standards, they were incomes that look much like poverty. The earlier superiority of these countries to the levels in the rest of the world affected both the absolute levels of income and wealth which they subsequently attained and the tasks they confronted in attaining them.

Such differences, together with differences in the speed and the degree of the adoption of the methods of mechanized industry as they became available, led to great and increasing economic contrasts between groups of nations and between different parts of the world. There were contrasts between countries that developed rapidly and those that for many decades developed hardly at all. In particular, there was a large gap, widening rapidly by the mid-nineteenth century, between a core of advanced countries, mainly in Western and Central Europe and North America, and a periphery of very poor countries which included practically all those in the tropics, but extended beyond the tropics. But there were also countries that showed something like a spectrum of development within the gap, countries that had not gone far in industrialization but had made something significant of the possibilities of non-mechanical improvement. They illustrated an intermediate state of development, observable in Eastern Europe and along the Mediterranean, which could be a foundation for something more advanced but which was slow enough to be vulnerable to severe shocks, such as a rapid change in the size of the population.

From the mid-nineteenth century, however, the emergence of new contrasts between nations depended principally on the adoption of the most up to date characteristics of industrialization. The possibility of faster development, and the rapidity of change in methods of production and organization, could put even two of the most advanced countries into different phases of development at the same time. But faster rates of change among a larger number of countries also created opportunities for catching up or overtaking in quite a short space of time. So national changes in economic leadership and rank order could occur more frequently. Yet the emergence of such divergences was the outcome of a new type of growth process which had characteristics that were broadly similar almost everywhere.

This is only what is to be expected in view of the central influence exercised by the adoption of a scientific technology and by the institutional changes associated with it. Apart from the descriptive similarities to which this must give rise it is also likely to affect the magnitude of some of the fundamental factors concerned in economic growth, in particular through the extent to which additional capital is necessarily embodied in most of the innovations. In fact, because of this, the statistics of capital formation have come to be treated very often as the best approximate indication of the extent to which an economy is equipped for rapid growth over any particular period. Other quantitative resemblances that have been noted among rapidly growing economies concern the growth of population and, though it is less clear how they may be related to the process of growth, these population trends had an important influence on its extent and on the way in which it took place. To look at the course of population and capital formation in countries of rapid economic growth throws a good deal of light on the nature of their expansion and on their relative wealth at different times. It also brings out, within the very broad similarities, striking differences in detail in the process of growth.

In nearly every country where rapid economic growth has taken place, with the one outstanding exception of France, it has been accompanied by high rates of population increase which have tended to accelerate for a time but which, in the case of those countries whose growth goes back some way into the nineteenth century, have usually dropped appreciably in more recent decades. Population increases sustained for many decades at rates from 0.75 per cent to 1.25 per cent per annum and sometimes rising even higher, and then falling back in the twentieth century near to 0.5 per cent per annum have been quite representative for economically expanding countries. Some which began their rapid expansion more recently have had rather higher rates of population increase which have not yet shown any signs of decline. High rates of population increase have not been confined to the areas of rapid economic growth and over a large part of the world they appear to have preceded it. But the acceleration of population increase during the period of growth would have been difficult to maintain without the additional product that was being achieved, and there was doubtless a direct causal link between the economic and demographic changes. Certainly the speed and the variations of population increase affected the practicable rate of economic growth in several different ways.

Unless there was a much higher level of productivity in the later years, the increase in the total output and income of a country whose population was increasing more slowly than before would also be retarded. An indefinite continuation of the rise in productivity seems, on the face of it, unlikely – how many people could be persuaded that the effort was worth while? But such a rise might be maintained for many years and there is no reason *a priori* to expect income per head to be growing more slowly in countries whose rate of population increase has declined. The high rates of population increase that have been so common have created both heavy burdens and special stimuli for the process of economic growth. Much of the effort that might conceivably have gone to provide higher average incomes for fewer people has had to go into the provision of food and homes and jobs just to keep extra numbers alive. An undeveloped country which was accustomed to save and invest less than 5 per cent of its income – a state of affairs that was probably not uncommon – was likely to find that if its population rose by 1 per cent each year practically the whole of its savings would be needed simply to keep average incomes from declining. To bring about any appreciable rise in them required much greater efforts and sacrifices. The task might be all the heavier at some periods if the increase in population was occurring in such a way (e.g. through a fall in infant mortality or a rise in the reproduction rate) as to enlarge the proportion of non-producers. It is hardly surprising that many countries with a rapid increase of population remained for long without appreciable growth of income per head. On the other hand, in a community accustomed to some degree of change and experiment, a rapid increase of population sometimes acted as a positive economic stimulus. It offered the prospect of a continually expanding market and a plentiful labour supply which, by reason of its augmentation, could readily be turned to new employments. Such conditions gave an inducement to new enterprise and investment, and an early response to the inducement might gain so high a reward as to encourage many more fresh ventures. Where a community was able to achieve a high rate of capital formation per head it could not only augment but modernize its stock of capital much more fully if it had a rapid increase of population. Given the great effort needed to get the process going, such a community could soon find that its more up-to-date equipment gave it a competitive advantage over others whose population was growing more slowly. From that advantage it could derive extra sales and income which lightened the task of maintaining economic growth in the future.

Two contrary influences could therefore make economic growth either faster or slower during an earlier period of rapidly rising population than during a later period of slower population increase. Attempts to determine empirically which sequence has usually prevailed have been hampered by the paucity of data. It seems fairly clear that for practically all countries that were experiencing rapid economic growth in the second half of the nineteenth century the rate of increase of their national income has been lower while their population has been rising more slowly in the twentieth century. Some statisticians, looking at conditions in the early nineteen-fifties, concluded (with reservations) that for most of them the rate of increase per head had also been lowered. This conclusion was never regarded as definitive. It hardly could be, in view of the appreciable differences in the growth rates calculated by different scholars for the same countries in the same periods. One worldwide study, by Dr L. J. Zimmerman, indicated that if the century after 1860 is divided into two subperiods at the year 1913, average real incomes grew at similar rates in both subperiods, not only for the world as a whole but specifically for Northwest Europe, which was one of its two chief industrialized regions, though he found some falling off in North America. Moreover, while the average long-term growth rate of real income per head in the more advanced countries had, over the hundred years, been around 1½ per cent per annum, most of the already developed countries were able to achieve annual rates over 3 per cent (and sometimes much higher) in the third quarter of the twentieth century. It appeared then that even countries with the longest history of rapid growth were able to grow faster still. Not until the late nineteen-seventies did it appear that a possibly per-manent phase of lower growth rates had begun.

The role of capital formation in economic growth appears to be more complex and full of its own uncertainties and paradoxes. A more highly industrialized economy, with the employment of machines spreading into every branch of its activities and providing the immediate source of higher productivity, is obviously dependent on the continuous provision of much more capital than one with little industry and a non-mechanical technology. But the capital needed in transforming the latter into the former and then keeping it functioning and expanding appears to have varied a good deal between one country and another. The risk that a country which devotes less than 5 per cent of its national income to capital forma-tion may be unable to escape from stagnation has already been mentioned. If it is to take care of any likely increase in population and still have a margin available to promote a perceptible increase in product per head, then experience indicates that it must be prepared to devote at least twice that proportion of its income to capital formation, and to go on doing so. Wherever data are available they show that, in countries experiencing high rates of growth, gross national capital formation (i.e. capital formation without deduction for fixed capital consumed) has over long periods usually averaged between 10 and 20 per cent of the gross national product (i.e. the product inclusive of capital consumption). In a few cases the average has exceeded 20 per cent and, very rarely, has for a few years approached 30 per cent. Where it has fallen short of 10 per cent the deficiency has merely reflected the import of capital; in other words, the ratio for gross *domestic* capital formation has exceeded 10 per cent but a portion of the additional capital assets has been owned abroad or has been offset by the realization of foreign investments. Within the range of capital formation proportions characteristic of growing economies it is also generally true that at any particular time the highest ratios have tended to be found in the countries with the highest income per head. But there have been many individual exceptions to this and the difference in capital formation proportions between countries with very different levels of income has often been quite small. Over the long period, too, the evidence does not suggest that most countries have achieved their most rapid economic growth either during or immediately after the periods when they have devoted the highest proportion of their incomes to capital formation. Nor does it appear that the maintenance of the highest rates of growth over long periods has always been the reward for those who continued to invest the highest proportions of income, though the persistence of fairly wide differences has usually meant that the economic growth of the country with the lower proportion has in the long run fallen behind that of the country with the higher proportion. Thus rapid economic growth has evidently depended on the achievement of a higher minimum level of investment than can have been usual at earlier times, but above that minimum, while one can say that high investment has usually brought its own reward, there is much uncertainty (and, it sometimes seems, almost randomness) in the relation between the amount of the extra investment and of the extra reward.

This is not really so surprising as it might seem. For one thing, much ambiguity attaches to the available data. There are manifold problems in the definition of national product or income in such a way as to permit meaningful comparisons between countries or periods with a product made up of different types of goods valued at different prices. Whatever definitions are used are bound to be imperfect and to introduce some element of bias which shows up more at some points than others; and even when common definitions are employed it is not equally easy or possible in every case to identify what items conform to them, or to be sure what adjustments should be applied to parts of one country's national accounts to make them correspond to a standard definition. Within the more general problems of the study of national product there are particular difficulties in the definition of capital and in identifying its components. All the difficulties are increased when the statistics for the past have to be reconstructed from old figures prepared with quite different purposes in mind. It is therefore unwise to attempt too precise a historical explanation of the lesser irregularities and variations observed in figures of national income and capital. Some of these irregularities may have no historical reality and reflect only errors in the original data and ambiguities in the concepts they try to represent. Another, more detectable, reason why figures of capital may mislead in comparisons is that the prices of capital goods may diverge much more from the general price level in one country or at one time than another. Thus, where the prices of capital goods were exceptionally high, as, for instance, in Italy in the nineteen-fifties, a high proportion of income devoted to capital formation represented a correspondingly less addition to capital goods than in one or two countries where the capital formation proportion was a little smaller but the prices of capital goods lower.

Nevertheless, even when full allowance has been made for the difficulties inherent in the figures, there still remain certain features of investment that make it certain that the relation between capital and the growth of income must vary a great deal in different circumstances. Most countries have found greater opportunity in the earlier than in the later years of their growth to adopt those changes in techniques and methods of organization which required a change of habits rather than the investment of capital, though the situation has altered somewhat in recent years as a deliberate search for improvements of this kind has been initiated in the most advanced countries by such practices as work study. But any easing of the early burdens of growth in this way has usually been offset in whole or in part before very long. Once a country's economy has begun to grow, its volume of business increases, the cross-currents of its trade become more complex, the functional and geographical distribution of its economic activities is subject to continual changes. Such developments create new needs involving costly investment for their satisfaction, above all for better transport, for housing in new locations, and for public utilities to serve it. Almost everywhere investment of these kinds has been the most expensive of all in relation to the increase in product to which it has given rise when brought into use. Housing, indeed, is often regarded as a category of unproductive fixed capital investment, since its contribution to the growth of productivity cannot be precisely traced and seems to be both indirect and very gradual. Transport systems have been built to yield an increment to the national output over a very long time rather than to produce a high yield at once. But though the provision of such investments, often described as 'social overhead capital', was everywhere burdensome there were great differences in the extent to which it was required. Countries such as Britain, whose economies quickly called for a high degree of urbanization, had to spend heavily on residential construction and public utility services even to maintain an unsatisfactory standard of accommodation. Some other countries could keep down this type of investment because still worse standards of housing were traditional and acceptable. Railways were built more cheaply where, as in France, they mostly preceded a high degree of urbanization than where, as in Britain, they accompanied it. Likewise, railways and roads were much more costly to construct in mountainous regions than in most others. Sometimes the capital outlay was still further enlarged in proportion to the immediate rise in income because capacity was created sufficient to cope with additional business beyond that immediately available. British railways in the eighteen-forties, Canadian pipelines and Norwegian hydro-electric schemes in the nineteen-fifties provide examples.

The differences in the expenditure on social overhead capital are only part of the story. A country which was already well equipped with social overhead capital and devoting more of its investment to the expansion of manufacturing industries normally got a bigger immediate return for a smaller outlay. For instance, in industrial countries in the nineteen-fifties the same amount of new investment devoted to manufacture produced on average more than two and a half times as big an addition to output as it did in transport, and four times as much as in public utilities and power production. At most times, too, the ratio of output to capital seems to have been higher in manufacture than in mining, so that countries have had heavy capital requirements when they have been engaged in the rapid expansion of their mineral output. Moreover, the increase of output in any sector of the economy has depended on the demand for its products as well as the amount and quality of the capital put into it. In most places the ratio of output to capital was likely to be higher in a time of brisk international trade, like the eighteen-fifties or the nineteen-fifties, than in a slack time like the nineteen-thirties. The country which indulged lavishly in capital formation during or just before one of the former periods was better situated than one which did so in the latter. Sometimes, too, the longer-lived items of capital formation were probably made more quickly and fully productive because the independent expansion of cheap supplies from abroad caused their more complete utilization. For instance, the large increase of cheap raw materials and food from other continents in the last twenty years of the nineteenth century may well have helped to increase the volume of business in several European countries so as significantly to improve the ratio of output to capital.

Other factors that need to be considered relate to the effects of a prolonged accumulation of capital. Where economic growth has been going on for only a short time the accumulated stock of capital is fairly small. If a country in that position devotes a high proportion of its income to capital formation it finds that a large proportion of its capital equipment is fairly new and this may help its investment to yield a relatively higher increment of product than is being achieved in a more highly capitalized country with just as big a proportion of income devoted to capital formation. Another effect of prolonged heavy investment is the necessity to provide more and more for the depreciation of existing assets. The proportion of gross capital formation which merely offsets the value of old capital consumed is bound to rise unless the rate of growth of gross capital formation continues to rise or the average length of life of capital assets increases. It is very difficult for the former condition to be met over any very lengthy period. The latter probably has frequently been met for a time by countries that were devoting much of their investment to the creation of social overhead capital. But countries that have the longest experience of rapid growth have in the later years almost invariably devoted more and more of their investment to fairly short-lived assets such as industrial plant and machinery. Consequently there appears to have been some tendency for the proportion of net domestic product devoted to net domestic capital formation (i.e. with both items reckoned after the deduction of capital consumed) to be rather less in the later years of growth of the richest countries, though this has sometimes been temporarily concealed by sudden widespread rises in the gross capital formation proportion (such as occurred in the nineteen-fifties) and by the inconsistent variations in the calculation of depreciation in different countries. It might seem that this was an influence making it harder for the more highly capitalized countries to maintain their rate of growth. But it has to be remembered that they were usually concentrating more of their investment on assets likely to yield a relatively high increase of output. It is also relevant that new investment used in the replacement of capital consumed, though represented by one figure which is arithmetically cancelled by another, is in practice not usually neutral in its economic effect. The new capital assets can embody the results of the most recent technological progress and their qualitative differences from the assets going out of use are unlikely to be fully represented in their respective valuations. The significance of a high gross capital formation proportion is therefore unlikely to be destroyed even though the net capital formation proportion is very much lower. For instance, in the USA the gap between the very high gross and net capital formation proportions was unusually wide even as far back as the last third of the nineteenth century, the earliest years for which there is abundant information, and it seems reasonable to regard the implicit readiness to replace existing assets by something more up to date as one influence on the very high rate at which income per head was then growing.

Another significant change that has usually marked the later rather than the earlier years of any country's economic growth has been in some of the purposes to which expenditure nominally classed as 'current' rather than 'capital' has been directed. The more advanced countries have devoted greatly increased sums to such things as the promotion of health and physical well-being, education, and scientific, technological and social research. Few countries in the early years of their growth have been able to devote comparable proportions of their income to such matters and the mid-twentieth century sees huge differences in this respect between the richer and the poorer countries. Yet such expenditure has been truly, in large part, a form of investment in human beings. Without it, inventiveness, adaptability and a general capacity to make effective use of the assets to which the term 'capital' is conventionally restricted must suffer; and to think of the relation between investment and economic growth without taking it into account is unrealistic. If capital formation is regarded in its usual restricted sense, then no clear trend in the proportion of income devoted to it, within the normal range of 10 per cent to 20 per cent or a little more, can be discerned. In all countries it has fluctuated, though in several the average over long periods seems to have been surprisingly stable; in some the slight irregular trend appears to have been upward but not, for example, in the USA or Argentina. If, however, the additional 'growth-producing' expenditure, in the wider sense, could be estimated with reasonable accuracy and added to the figures of capital formation, then it seems likely that over the long period the proportion of income used in this way has been slightly rising in most of the growing economies. This is another factor tending to make it improbable that the countries with the longest history of growth have in the twentieth century been in a lasting phase of decline in the rate of growth.

It seems clear that any significant generalizations which may be attempted about the course of economic growth cannot be carried into great detail. Everywhere there have been early opportunities to improve productivity appreciably without enormous expenditure, and everywhere, once growth has been in progress, there has been a need for heavy outlay on social overhead capital and for rising expenditure on education. But sometimes these phases have largely overlapped, so that two opposite influences have offset each other; sometimes they have come in succession to give an easier followed by a more difficult period. The burdens of the latter, however, have varied in accordance with the real cost of heavy constructional work (which has been much influenced by technological change), and also in accordance with the rate of population growth. Where the greatest need for social overhead capital has coincided with the maximum rate of population growth, the burdens have been specially heavy, unless they have been mitigated by substantial lending from abroad, as has sometimes happened. The rewards for accepting these heavy burdens have varied too and thereby made the continuing weight of the burdens themselves lighter or more onerous. The country which has succeeded at the same time in improving more cheaply the efficiency of major parts of its agriculture or industry has fared better than the one which has postponed most of such complementary improvements to a later date; but changes in the general state of world trade, independently influenced only slightly by the efforts of any one country, have also made wide differences in the immediate results of periods of heavy investment undertaken with the distant future in mind. Once a country has built up its basic equipment of social overhead capital, established the regular practice of applying the latest techniques to an appreciable part of its productive activity, and begun to spend freely enough on the education and health of its people for them to cope with complex and continually changing conditions of life, then the maintenance of further growth appears usually to have become rather easier. Social overhead capital has to be adapted and gradually improved rather than supplied almost in its entirety from scratch and more of the additions to net investment can yield their full benefit fairly quickly. But there are offsetting factors, such as the demand of a wealthier population for more of the expensive and low-yielding investment in amenity, in better housing and hospitals, or the high costs of administration and congestion in metropolitan communities. Even if these factors do not neutralize the other conditions making for easier growth – and in practice it seems probable that they usually have not completely done so – there are many others which have affected what could be achieved. The extent to which the demand for leisure has begun to catch up on the demand for goods, differences not only in rates of population growth but in the age-division of the population into producers and dependants, the very varied costs which wars and military needs have imposed, on different countries – all these have helped to decide whether basically easier economic conditions have been translated into greater or less growth.

Moreover, the easier conditions may not last indefinitely. Even the most abundant supply of social overhead capital needs continual gradual adaptation and modernization. If this need is neglected there will eventually be an accumulation of inefficiencies and obsolescence that can be put right only by a new phase of heavy investment. Technological changes, or drastic changes in the relative costs of alternative types of service, perhaps especially in transport, may also produce a comparable effect in a country that has regularly dealt prudently with its stock of social overhead capital. Automobile and air transport, for example, may not only demand vast new investments for their establishment and continual growth but may also cause the abandonment of, say, dozens of small railway sidings while these still have many years of unexhausted physical life. Specialized types and larger sizes of ships may not merely be replacements for other ships but the means of rendering obsolete much of a country's port equipment. Even so, however, it would be unusual for drastic changes of this kind to impose on a country's economy a burden relatively as heavy as that imposed by the initial establishment of the infrastructure of an industrialized economy.

Given all these various possibilities and the multitudinous ways in which they may be combined, it is to be expected that the growth of incomes will have proceeded very differently in different countries over both long and short periods. The available data clearly bear out this expectation, even though they need to be regarded as tentative and approximate, particularly as for several countries the alternative estimates differ enough to suggest slightly different conclusions. There are series of national product figures, on bases as nearly comparable as is practicable, for France from the eighteen-forties, Germany, Ireland, Italy, Sweden, and the UK from the eighteen-sixties, and Canada, Denmark, Russia, and the USA from the eighteen-seventies. From the beginning of these national series to the mid-nineteen-fifties the decadal rate of growth of product per head ranged (when appropriately weighted for changes in political boundaries) from just over 10 per cent for Italy and about 12½ per cent for the United Kingdom to about 20 per cent for the USA and over 27 per cent for Sweden. The rates were about 14 per cent for France and 15 per cent for Germany and perhaps 15 per cent for Russia also, though the last must be a dubious figure because of the deficiencies and obscurity of the data.

The comparative impression conveyed by these figures is much modified by looking at what was happening at different times within the long period. The relative lowness of the rate for the United Kingdom was the result almost entirely of the poor progress in the first quarter of the twentieth century, and, to some extent, of a few years at the end of the Second World War and just after. In the eighteen-eighties the rate went well above 20 per cent and in the rest of the period, too, was much higher than the long-term average. The apparently rather better performance of Germany was attributable almost entirely to the achievements of the eighteen-seventies and eighties, when the heavy industries were making great strides and decadal growth rates of more than 30 per cent were attained in product per head. At most other times, except for a brief span in the late nineteen-thirties and the beginning of very rapid revival in the Federal Republic in the nineteen-fifties, the German growth rate was rather low. France, unlike Germany and the United Kingdom, maintained a high growth rate, with a maximum approaching 30 per cent, in the early years of the twentieth century as well as in the late nineteenth, no doubt to a large extent because it was later in building up a substantial sector of heavy industries and in mechanizing an appreciable range of its manufactures. But the French long-term growth rate was brought down by absolute decline in the nineteen-thirties and the Second World War. The USA which had been very adversely affected by the Civil War, really established full recovery and renewed rapid growth in the late eighteen-seventies and the eighteen-eighties when income per head rose by about 50 per cent in ten years. As in France the rate of growth was also very high at the beginning of the twentieth century (though the peak was earlier than in France) and became negative in the thirties. But unlike France and, indeed, most of Europe, the USA derived a great stimulus to its economic growth from the Second World War. So, too, did a few other countries that had great reserves of unused resources which could fairly readily be brought into production; likewise those which already possessed an advanced industrial economy and were able to remain neutral. Canada, Australia, Sweden and Switzerland all experienced high growth rates in the nineteen-forties. In the nineteen-fifties and sixties rates of growth were, by the standards of previous experience, exceptionally high in the great majority of countries, though there were wide divergences between the rates for different countries. Among the advanced countries which have just been discussed, Canada and the USA increased their product per head at only modest rates in the fifties but both achieved much higher rates in the sixties, Canada particularly so. For France and Italy there were very high and steady rates over the twenty years and for Germany also, though the phenomenal rate of the fifties was appreciably reduced in the sixties, it was still very high. The United Kingdom had the slowest growth in this group of advanced countries in the nineteen-sixties, yet even for this country between 1950 and 1970 product per head was growing at rather more than 20 per cent per decade, which was well above the previous long-term average. After 1973, however, and still more after 1979, there was a slowing down nearly everywhere. Two per cent per annum was then near the top of the range for product per head, though Japan kept appreciably above this, and at the start of the nineteen-eighties few of the most advanced countries showed much growth. If the experience of these years were prolonged, the general rate of growth of product per head, except in Japan, would be below 10 per cent per decade.

In general, there has been a good deal of irregularity in the course of growth among almost all those countries that have maintained a high average for a long time, though periods of more than two or three years when growth has been interrupted by absolute decline have been rare. The steadiest expansion has been that of Sweden, and the exceptionally high long-period growth rate there owes much to the entire or partial avoidance of most of those interruptions to the process that have affected the other growing economies from time to time.

Another way of looking at these different growth rates is by consideration of their effects on the relative incomes of various countries at different times. To the uncertainties and ambiguities of any one series of national income calculations, however, international comparisons add their own manifold complications, which include both differences in the accounting treatment of what should be comparable items and dissimilarities in the course and structure of national prices. Such comparisons must therefore be regarded as even more tentative than comparisons of incomes within the same country over a long period. The comparative estimates of different statisticians have shown such wide discrepancies, especially for the period down to the First World War, that it seems unwise to put much weight on them. Even for more recent years, when there is more agreement about the figures for individual countries, any comparative tables need to be viewed with great caution. The official statistics of communist countries, for instance, are related to such different concepts of national product from those used elsewhere that it is very difficult to devise a reliable common basis for comparison. Even where comparable concepts are being used there is always the problem that the expression of all figures in terms of one currency by the application of current exchange rates does not accurately represent comparative purchasing power. Conclusions about relative incomes in different countries may easily be unreliable unless the relevant data consistently show fairly wide differences. So only a few very rough indications will be attempted here.

For the eighteen-sixties the USA, Australia and Britain have each been suggested by different statisticians as the country with the highest income per head. There is comparable uncertainty about the proportionate size of the average incomes of other countries. One set of estimates suggests that both Belgium and France had achieved somewhat higher average incomes than Britain by 1860 and that this superiority has been maintained by Belgium ever since and by France except during the nineteen-thirties and forties. Another set of estimates puts average incomes in Spain at a level fairly similar to those in France down to 1900. Figures have been put forward to indicate that average incomes in the USA were already double those in Britain by 1913. All these are honestly made efforts which, in the light of general historical knowledge, look very implausible and seem unacceptable when other calculations produce very different results. But they illustrate the difficulties of this kind of exercise.

Whatever the position in Australia in 1860, it seems fairly certain that average incomes there did not keep up with the American level. The probability is that throughout the last third of the nineteenth century Britain, Canada, and the USA were the three countries with the highest average incomes, that Australia and New Zealand came next, and that in all the industrial and industrializing countries of continental Europe the level, though steadily rising, was somewhat lower. After about 1890, and particularly in the early years of the twentieth century, the British level rose more slowly. It may well be that average incomes were higher in the USA and Canada than in Britain by 1913 and it seems certain that the income gap between Britain and other European countries had been reduced. Denmark, of the smaller continental countries, and Germany, of the larger, probably had the highest average incomes. After the First World War the USA had an appreciably higher level than any other country and increased its advantage in the twenties but fell back relatively in the thirties, so much so that some estimates have suggested that it was temporarily overtaken by New Zealand. France also shared the experience of improving its relative position in the twenties, when its average incomes were well above those of Germany, and falling behind in the thirties. The probability is that in 1938 income per head was highest in the USA and New Zealand, with Britain, Canada and

Denmark not a long way behind. The USSR and Japan, despite the rising productivity of industrialization, still had average incomes well below half the West European level.

After the Second World War the position was very different. The USA and Canada had enormously raised their income levels; Australia and Sweden had made substantial, though smaller, increases; and most of the European belligerents, except Britain, had experienced an absolute decline. In Germany, Italy and Japan the extent of the decline was huge. By 1950 average incomes in most European countries were again approaching pre-war levels or had surpassed them, but Britain was in no better position than in 1945. Countries physically undamaged by the war, notably Australia, New Zealand, Sweden and Switzerland, had been able to advance rapidly and raise their average incomes much above those of most European countries. The ensuing quarter century of high but widely dispersed growth rates produced appreciable changes in relative income levels. The USA had gone so far ahead that it easily remained the country of highest income per head, but average incomes in many European countries were becoming a rather larger fraction of the American. Among the most striking changes were the continued rise of Sweden to income levels near those of the USA, the phenomenal increase of incomes in a few small oil-producing countries, with Kuwait as the outstanding example, the astonishing rise of income levels in Japan, and the relative decline in the position of Britain and New Zealand. Immediately after the Second World War average incomes in Japan may have fallen as low as one-sixth of those in Britain, but by the early nineteen-seventies the Japanese level was only a little below the British. In 1957 income per head, at current prices, averaged $2,100 in the USA and only in Canada did it come within two-thirds of that level. Indeed, the only countries where income per head was more than half as much as in the USA were, in rank order, Canada, Sweden, Switzerland, Iceland, New Zealand, Australia, and Luxembourg. The United Kingdom, Belgium and Norway came next, just below this level. In 1971, again at current prices, income per head in the USA averaged nearly $4,600 and it exceeded $4,000 in Sweden also. The countries with an average over $3,000 were, in descending order, Canada, Switzerland, Denmark, Kuwait and West Germany. Next, still above half the level of the USA, came Norway, Belgium, Australia, France, Luxembourg, the Netherlands, and New Zealand. Also with average incomes over $2,000, but just below half the level of the USA, were the United Kingdom, Finland and Iceland. Just below them came Austria, Japan, Israel, Italy and Libya. If a reasonable basis for comparison could be found, it is likely that the USSR and East Germany might also appear in this list of countries for 1971, probably somewhere near the bottom.

After 1970 international comparisons became even more difficult because of the adoption of floating exchange rates, the fluctuations of which at any particular time were often well out of line with relative national price levels, however they were measured. There was no common denominator which would be thoroughly satisfactory for expressing the income or product of different countries. But statisticians did the best they could and produced figures which might have the occasional serious individual aberration, but which offer reasonable approximations for most comparative purposes. Subject to these reservations, it appears that some of the most striking developments of the recent past were carried further. Japan went on overtaking more and more countries, continental Western Europe continued until 1983 to gain on the USA, yet the USA had such a high level of product that even a relatively low growth rate provided large absolute increases. The UK and New Zealand continued to fall further behind most of the other advanced countries. Attempts were regularly made to express incomes and product in US dollars. In 1982 GDP per head in the USA was $13,152. Among the developed countries this was exceeded by Switzerland ($14,928) and Norway ($13,648). Other countries with a figure over $10,000 were, in descending order, Canada, Sweden, Iceland, Denmark, West Germany, Australia, and Finland. Others which exceeded $7,500, and were thus over half the Swiss figure, were (also in descending order) France, the Netherlands, Luxembourg, Japan, Austria, Belgium, the UK and New Zealand. Some alternative calculations would put Italy in this list, at the bottom, and, if national income were used instead of GDP, Luxembourg would appear appreciably higher, above Iceland and Denmark, which would also be surpassed by West Germany. A year later the rank order was much the same, though the differences in the level of product per head had changed somewhat, with the UK, Belgium, Japan and Denmark reducing the gap from those above them, and Luxembourg experiencing a reduction.

The whole process of growth, commonly seen in terms of national units, thus had the most important international connotations. Among nations that had achieved high rates of growth the appreciable variations that were possible in rates could and did bring about fairly frequent and substantial changes in relative incomes and wealth, and hence in trading ability and requirements and in general economic power and influence. Over a span of no more than two generations they effected fundamental shifts in the international economic balance of the world.

Nor was the international significance of economic growth derived only from its results. The whole process is scarcely conceivable except in an international context. For most of the countries that achieved the greatest growth the task was lightened and speeded because in an early and onerous phase some of the necessary capital could be borrowed abroad. Australia, Canada, New Zealand, Sweden, and the USA all benefited substantially in this way. Still more widespread was an early reliance on the purchase of essential capital equipment abroad, even if it had to be financed at home, and over and over again expanding exports played an essential part in obtaining a high increment of income from recent productive investment. Above all, growth depended on an international exchange and diffusion of ideas and information – about resources and techniques and the design and operation of institutions. Those who were unable to share in this continuous interchange, because of ignorance or extreme poverty or physical remoteness, had only a slender chance of participating in economic growth.

It was because this gradually became more obvious that the achievement of economic growth became a matter of conscious international concern. The shifts of wealth and economic power among the growing countries were not the only ones. Even more striking was the increasing differentiation of these countries, as a group, from the rest of the world. In the early nineteen-seventies, when income per head in the wealthiest countries ranged between $2,000 and $4,500, there were other countries with more than half the world's population in which they were of the general order of only $225 or less. There had doubtless been large international disparities of income in the early nineteenth century and long before, but nothing to compare with this. While little is known in detail of the past course of income in most of the poorer countries it seems fairly clear that this situation arose because most of them had continued to stagnate. Indeed, there are signs that in the twentieth century when some poor countries found their populations increasing faster, total national income could not keep pace with it. It is, for instance, not impossible that income per head in India may have been lower in 1940 than at the beginning of the century. But one of the fruits even of very imperfectly distributed economic and technical advance is the wider diffusion of knowledge. After the Second World War a widespread awareness both of the disparities in economic growth and of the innovations and practices on which it depended became part of the international environment. Knowledge of the past results of growth came to be an additional cause of attempts to initiate it in new places and so eventually to bring about yet more possibilities of shifts in the international economic balance, which could already be so much more quickly transformed than in earlier centuries.

CHAPTER SEVEN
The emergence of an international economy before 1914

Many close international relationships were of the greatest import-ance in economic affairs in the middle of the nineteenth century and long before. It would be unrealistic to suggest that the second half of the nineteenth century saw the appearance of something appropriate-ly called 'an international economy' which was entirely new. The continuous and varied activity in international trade, the sophisti-cated markets in foreign exchange and the wide assortment of business done by international merchant bankers were all symptomat-ic of an economic life which transcended national boundaries as a matter of routine; and they had all proved capable of much expan-sion before 1850. Yet there was quite a wide difference between what seemed characteristic then and what was happening in the ordinary daily course of business half a century later, a difference which showed itself in the scale and comprehensiveness of international dealings and in the extent of their influence upon domestic transac-tions. Even though there was no clear break in practice to indicate a change in kind, the completeness of international financial arrange-ments and the pervasiveness of international considerations in all sorts of transactions were such as to make the world of 1900 one in which the merchant, the banker or the finance minister of 1850 would have felt out of place.

Despite the rapid changes of the first half of the nineteenth century there were some large restrictions on the extent of economic interdependence among the nations, and though they were lessening they were slow to disappear. There was the limitation imposed by the shortage of specialized productive power; above all, the pre-ponderance of agriculture among productive activities, in conditions where most communities had a fairly high degree of self-sufficiency

in food and where manufacture gave rise to a far greater proportionate amount of international trade than agriculture did. There was
the limitation that showed itself in the confining of a large part of
international trade within several mainly distinct commercial areas or
groups, defined by physical proximity or political association.
Western and Central Europe had long formed one such area, Russia
and the Baltic another, the North Atlantic a third, India and the Far
East a fourth. Within each of these areas trading accounts had usually
been more or less balanced, leaving only relatively small settlements
to be made by transfers of bullion or credit between one area and
another. With the expansion of trade in the later eighteenth and early
nineteenth centuries some of the barriers between these separate areas
were reduced, as is shown by the increase in the number of foreign
currencies regularly quoted in such centres as Amsterdam and
London; but they did not quickly disappear altogether. In the
eighteen-fifties a great part of both the imports and exports of most
countries (even a country with so large a foreign trade as Britain) still
followed similar channels and, though a strict bilateral balance may
seldom have been approached, a fairly complete settlement of mutual
obligations was often possible within a group comprising quite a
small number of countries.

The changes that characterized the later nineteenth century involved the removal of these earlier limiting influences. Most obvious
of all was the sheer increase in the volume of international trade as
certain key areas became more productive and more industrialized,
with an associated diversification of both output and demand. The
third quarter of the nineteenth century was probably the time when
international trade grew fastest of all (the imperfections of the data
preclude complete certainty) and though it seems likely that the rate
of growth afterwards fell off a little, the absolute increase between
1875 and 1914 was far greater than in any previous period of similar
length. As this was happening there took place a gradual fusion of
the trading areas and groups which hitherto had remained at least
partly distinct. To a diminishing extent did the major countries,
Britain in particular, seek most of their imports where most of their
exports were concentrated. The area within which a multilateral
settlement of international obligations was a routine practicality
became ever wider until it was normal for a great part of the world
to be involved in balancing the international accounts of each individual country. As the regular, easy transfer of debits and credits
between most parts of the world became commonplace, so too did
other types of transfer take place with greater ease and frequency.

The factors of production, both labour and capital, moved internationally in much greater volume than before and often along new channels, and as they moved they helped to build up new specialized centres of productive power, with rapid repercussions on the amounts and direction of international trade. It was this complex of associated changes in the movements of trade, capital and labour which gave to the economic life of the late nineteenth century a predominantly international character. The most obvious outward sign of that character was the completion of a set of commercial, banking, and monetary institutions which served and controlled international economic purposes, giving them priority over purely domestic matters.

Such changes were not accidental or arbitrary. They did not spring from any determination to think and act more in international terms than before. The resulted from demographic and economic influences that were concentrated in a small but increasing minority of countries. Populations grew larger and where the output of goods could be efficiently diversified, especially by industrialization, it was often helpful to be less self-sufficient. If diversification was not immediately possible, then it sometimes became advantageous for some of the extra population to migrate to places where it was. Where industrialization took place there were new products on offer, new materials in demand, rising incomes which created a market for a greater number of goods drawn from a wider variety of sources. Technical advances associated with those that helped to make industrialization possible rendered accessible vast new areas where production, at first particularly of food and raw materials, could be expanded cheaply. These new areas were in many ways the commercial complement of the industrializing countries elsewhere, just as their early emptiness was complementary to the growing population density in other parts of the world. Their accessibility not only to trade but to settlement, from poor as well as wealthier areas, so that they were open to rapid economic development, was an essential feature of the growth of an international economy. Greater economic interdependence among the nations was directly associated with changes in the international distribution of productive power, and this in turn involved changes in the distribution of the factors of production, through international transfers as well as domestic effort and reorganization. It is thus evident that the emergence of an international economy depended on a wide variety of related factors and that its course and its nature can be most fully revealed only by a closer look at the changes in these factors both separately and in relation to each other.

The most striking of the international transfers of productive resources was the migration of labour. Its importance came from the directions which it followed rather than from its magnitude, for though in absolute terms this was many times greater than at any earlier time it was still a fairly small proportion of the total natural increase of population in most of the countries from which the emigrants departed. For a country to increase its population faster than its neighbour was no guarantee of achieving an economic superiority. In the absence of complementary assets a bigger population could be a drag on economic progress and in both the nineteenth and twentieth centuries some large and increasingly populous countries have remained among the poorest. But there were in the nineteenth century several vast areas with a rich natural endowment and too small a population to make effective use of more than a small part of it. Most of them had a nucleus of basic equipment (even though they soon outgrew it) and a sufficiently stable and adaptable society which made it possible for extra workers quickly to prove themselves more productive there than in most other places. It was to such areas that the majority of migrants moved. They thus contributed to that more complete harnessing of some of the world's richest productive resources and to that building up of new regions of unusually wealthy commerce which distinctively characterized the international economy of the late nineteenth century. It is true that there was an offsetting influence, since many of the migrants were drawn from the most advanced countries of Europe, where productivity was higher than in most other places. But it is doubtful, even in these cases, whether most of the migrants were doing a more productive job at the time of their departure than they found in their new homes. It is certain that even more of the migrants came from very poor areas that were likely to derive positive relief from the departure of some of their increasing population. The migration of labour was not exclusively economic either in origin or effect and its economic aspects were far from uniform. Yet its economic significance is undeniable and it is hard to escape the conclusion that, on balance, it wrought an international economic advantage in at least two ways: it more frequently moved workers from conditions of lower to higher productivity than it did the reverse, and it helped to concentrate a disproportionate share of economic development in areas where the potentialities were unusually great.

These generalizations need the support of a rather more detailed account of the extent and direction of migration. Unfortunately, from the nature of the available data, such an account is bound to have serious deficiencies and to leave a wide margin for speculation. Statistics of migration are far from perfect and their comparability is difficult because of differences in classification among different countries. They are good enough to give a fairly clear account of the magnitude, direction and timing of gross migration, i.e. the total movement of people, whether temporary or permanent; but, because figures of the numbers of emigrants who returned to their old homes are very scanty, they reveal much less about net migration, which in the long run was of greater economic significance. There can be no doubt that the permanent transfer of labour was very much less than the figures of gross migration might suggest. This is indicated by the few continuous statistics of net migration that were collected: in New Zealand from 1853 to 1930 net immigration was only 22 per cent of gross and in Argentina from 1857 to 1926 it was only 53 per cent. Further confirmation comes from census material in countries both of emigration and immigration. The net loss by migration that can be calculated for some countries of emigration was much less than the excess of recorded departures over arrivals; and the numbers of foreign-born persons enumerated in countries of immigration cannot be closely matched to the numbers of immigrants arriving. But though migration statistics cannot be taken at their face value they still give a useful rough indication of the direction and variations of a movement which, even after undergoing some fairly drastic arithmetical deflation, was big enough to have a strong economic impact.

The greatest migrational movements were from Europe and Asia (especially the former) into the Americas. This is what would be expected since, despite the great natural resources of the Americas, they contained in 1850 only about one-twentieth of the world's population in one-third of its land area, whereas Europe and Asia had about 85 per cent of its population in 40 per cent of its area and were multiplying their people rapidly. The principal effect of migration on the distribution of population was partly to offset this rapid multiplication. The unevenness of distribution was prevented from becoming appreciably worse but there was not enough migration to reduce it significantly. In 1930 Europe and Asia still contained about four-fifths of the world's population and in Europe alone the proportion was a little higher than in 1850.

Between 1820 and 1930 the recorded gross intercontinental migration, which must have greatly exceeded the number of permanent transfers, totalled about 62 million. Most of it – not far short of three-quarters – took place in the half century preceding the First World War. In the first half of the nineteenth century migration was difficult and small in amount. Transport was limited, slow and relatively dear. Many of the areas potentially most suitable for settlement were inaccessible or virtually unknown. Legal restraints on emigration still survived in many parts of the Old World. Population increase had not reached its maximum rate. But these conditions changed. The railway and the steamship transformed the physical problem of movement. The reports of the earlier emigrants inspired more of their compatriots to follow them. Serfdom was abolished over more and more of Europe and thus made millions free to move for the first time, while restrictions on the movement of Asiatic labour were relaxed as a result of diplomatic and military pressure from the West. The continued rapid growth of population threatened still more grinding poverty in those unindustrialized regions, starved of capital, where more land for the masses to cultivate was the only hope and ambition and was not available, because of either natural limitations or the social and political structure. So, in the second half of the nineteenth century, migration increased irregularly but rapidly until it reached a peak between the opening of the twentieth century and the outbreak of the First World War.

Most of the intercontinental migration was directed to seven countries, the greater part of whose area had previously been only very thinly occupied. Over the period from 1820 to 1930 the proportionate distribution of recorded immigrants among these countries was: USA 61.4 per cent, Canada 11.5 per cent, Argentina 10.1 per cent, Brazil 7.3 per cent, Australia 4.5 per cent, New Zealand 3.0 per cent, South Africa 2.2 per cent. In these figures Australia and South Africa are somewhat under-represented because of the deficiencies of their nineteenth-century migration statistics. The earlier Australian figures, for instance, have to be omitted from a comparison of this sort because it is impossible to exclude from them the movement of people between the separate Australian colonies. The detailed figures for the most active period of migration are set out in Table 8. Though they are slightly swollen by the inclusion of international migration within the Americas, any exaggeration of the total is probably offset by the omission of the minor flows of intercontinental migration, to such countries as Chile, Uruguay, Tunisia, and Rhodesia.

TABLE 8   GROSS IMMIGRATION INTO THE CHIEF RECEIVING COUNTRIES,
1861–1920 *(thousands)*

Country	Total 1861–1920	1861–70	1871–80	1881–90	1891–1900	1901–10	1911–20
Total	45,525	3,051	3,709	7,655	5,998	13,702	11,410
USA	28,593	2,315	2,812	5,247	3,688	8,795	5,736
Canada	5,138	283	220	886	321	1,453	1,975
Argentina	4,879	160	261	841	648	1,764	1,205
Brazil	3,481	98	219	531	1,144	691	798
Australia	1,823	n.a.	n.a.	n.a.	n.a.	652	1,171
New Zealand	1,394	195	197	150	197	347	308
South Africa	217	n.a.	n.a.	n.a.	n.a.	n.a.	217

N.B. The figures for the first four countries include immigration from each other
and from the rest of the Americas, but this overweights them only a little in
comparison with the remainder.

There was some other migration on a scale big enough to have a
substantial influence on economic development. That which most
resembled the intercontinental migration was the movement of
people into the empty spaces from other parts of the same continent
or the same country. Even in countries overseas to which many
European emigrants went, much of the settlement of the more
distant interior was accomplished by the movement of those born
within the country, perhaps the second or third generation of
immigrant stock, rather than by recent immigrants themselves.
Comparable movements occurred in other potentially rich areas
which had been only thinly occupied. In Russia, though some regions
were densely inhabited, others offered scope for greatly increased
settlement, and the area which presented this opportunity gradually
expanded with the acquisition of piecemeal additions to Russia's
Asiatic empire. Between 1828 and 1915 4,200,000 foreigners settled
in Russia. Two-thirds of them came from Europe, mainly from
Germany and Austria, and one-third from Asia, especially China,
Japan, Persia, and Turkey. Most of this movement came from
countries bordering on Russia and many of the settlers did not
penetrate far beyond the border. Statistically it was more than offset
by the exodus of people from the Russian Empire in the same
period, mainly to the USA. But there was also a great extension of
settlement as a result of long-distance internal migration. Between
1828 and 1915 over 7 million people moved from European to
Asiatic Russia, most of them into Siberia and most of them after
1890. Some 1,300,000 of these were prisoners and exiles, the rest
mostly peasant settlers.

The remaining type of migration was different. This was the

movement of labourers, usually under contract, to tropical areas where plantation agriculture or mining enterprises were being extended and the local population was small in number or unwilling to man the new operations. Most of this movement was intended to be only temporary for periods up to about ten years, but a minority of the labourers stayed in their new countries after they had completed their contracts and their numbers appear to have been augmented by a certain amount of spontaneous movement in minor trading activities. There is only a very imperfect statistical record of this sort of migration. It is clear that it never approached the scale of the great movements between Europe and America, but along a few channels it was very substantial in the late nineteenth and early twentieth centuries. The largest numbers apparently went from China to the East Indies, Malaya, and some other parts of Southeast Asia. Between 1881 and 1915 the arrival of an annual average of about 170,000 Chinese was recorded in the Straits Settlements, while for a shorter period of twenty-one years the records of departures (almost certainly very defective) averaged only 40,000 a year. Where migration statistics are lacking, population censuses sometimes give a clue to the direction of movement. In 1922 over 8 million Chinese were living abroad, more than a million in each of Formosa, Java, the East Indies other than Java, and Siam. Although these figures doubtless included many born locally of Chinese stock, they suggest that these areas were among the chief receivers of immigrants, except that the large number in Formosa could be attributed to its having previously belonged to China. Other similar movements took place from India to Malaya and Ceylon. On what was probably a smaller scale there were comparable transfers of workers among some of the French tropical colonies, in Oceania as well as Southeast Asia, and there was a little within tropical Africa, for instance the recruitment of workers in other Portuguese territories for the plantations of Guinea and São Tomé. Some of the relatively small movements of contract labour took place over longer distances between continents. Thus there was some migration from both China and India to the West Indies and from India to South Africa.

The sources of migration were even more dispersed than its destinations. As is evident from Table 9, there were few countries of Europe that did not provide a substantial number of emigrants. Many more came from Asia. No country ever occupied a dominant place in emigration comparable to that of the USA as a receiver of immigrants, though there were several which at different times lost an exceptionally high proportion of their people by emigration.

TABLE 9   GROSS INTERCONTINENTAL EMIGRATION FROM EUROPE, 1861–1920 (*thousands*)

Country	Total 1861–1920	1861–70	1871–80	1881–90	1891–1900	1901–10	1911–20
Total	40,064	2,672	3,124	7,279	6,745	12,396	7,848
British Isles	12,831	1,572	1,679	2,559	1,743	2,841	2,437
Italy	8,575	27	168	991	1,580	3,615	2,194
Austria–Hungary	4,441	40	111	436	724	2,342	788
Spain	3,779	6	13	572	791	1,091	1,306
Germany	3,494	634	626	1,342	527	274	91
Russia	2,268	1	58	288	571	1,100	250
Portugal	1,388	80	131	185	266	324	402
Sweden	1,068	122	103	328	205	224	86
Norway	718	98	85	187	95	191	62
Others	1.502	92	150	391	243	394	232

N.B. 'Russia' includes Russian Poland. 'Others' covers Belgium, Denmark, Finland, France, the Netherlands and Switzerland. Greece, Turkey and the Balakan states are excluded. The very imperfect quality of migration statistics should be borne in mind when using both this table and Table 8.

Ireland, the one country whose population was permanently and drastically reduced by emigration, was the outstanding example. For half a century after the famine of 1846 there was scarcely a year in which less than 1 per cent of the total population emigrated. In sixty years Ireland sent to the USA half as many people as it contained at the time of its maximum population. In the decades 1840–9 and 1850–9 more immigrants to the USA came from Ireland than from any other country, and in every decade up to and including 1900–9 Ireland was one of the five largest suppliers of immigrants to the USA. The next highest ratio of emigration to population was in Sweden and Norway, but it was considerably lower than in Ireland. Emigration from Sweden never quite reached 1 per cent of the population in any year and the peak proportion for Norway was 1½ per cent in 1882, only about half the Irish maximum. After the predominance of the Irish in the middle of the century, Germany briefly became the biggest supplier of emigrants to the USA until about 1890. Then the movement began to come increasingly from Southern Europe. The largest immigrant-supplying countries to the USA were Italy in 1890–9 and 1910–19 and Austria-Hungary in 1900–9. Altogether there were eight countries which each sent more than a million emigrants to the USA between 1820 and 1930. They were, ranked in order according to the number of emigrants: Germany, Italy, Ireland, Austria-Hungary, Russia, Canada, England, and Sweden.

For most European countries the extent of emigration to the USA gives a rough indication of the importance of emigration in their life, but there were some from which there was a large movement in other directions as well. One of the chief sources of migrants was Italy, especially in the last quarter-century before the First World War, when agricultural over-population in the south was being increasingly felt. Between 1876 and 1926 over 16 million people left Italy, many of them only temporarily. Of these, nearly half went to other European countries and, of those who crossed the Atlantic, nearly as many went to Argentina and Brazil as to the USA. But in the twentieth century the latter became the principal destination of emigrants from Italy, which provided not only the second largest national group of immigrants to the USA but also the largest in both Argentina and Brazil. To Argentina were admitted 2,718,000 Italians (nearly half the total immigration) between 1857 and 1926, and between 1820 and 1930 Brazil admitted 1,480,000.

It appears that the chief countries of emigration were the eight which each sent more than a million people to the USA, together with China, Japan, India, Spain, and Portugal. Chinese and Indian emigration, as has already been briefly mentioned, was mainly to other parts of Asia, though there was some to other continents. Japanese emigration was insignificant until after 1885, when it was first legalized, but it grew fairly quickly. In the next twenty years about half a million people left, the largest group (over one-third of the total) going to Hawaii, where the Japanese became the dominant racial element in the population. Subsequently a larger number went to the USA, but Asiatic Russia became the chief destination of Japanese emigrants in the early years of the twentieth century. From Spain between 1820 and 1930 gross recorded emigration was well over 3,500,000 and from Portugal over 1,500,000. Most of the Portuguese emigrants and half a million of the Spanish went to Brazil, but the majority of the Spanish went to Argentina. The figures for these countries were appreciable but they were much less than those for the United Kingdom and Italy, which were the greatest sources of international migration in the period from the middle of the nineteenth century to the First World War.

The value of the migrations is suggested by the economic character which the chief receiving areas fairly quickly attained. All of them came before 1914 to occupy an important place in international trade, often out of proportion to the size of their population. In most of them the average level of income of the population as a whole was much greater than in most of the rest of the world, and this was one immediate reason for their commercial importance. Even in South Africa and Brazil, where average incomes were low, there was (particularly in the former) a large sector of the economy into which the immigration from overseas was fitted and in which higher incomes were obtained. Only if it could be shown that the labour supply and productive development of these countries are explicable largely in terms of internal influences would it be justifiable to deny an important economic, as well as social, role to international migration. Some writers have inclined towards such an interpretation of the economic development of the USA which, because of sheer numbers, must be a major test of the economic influence of migration. But, even when full allowance has been made for the high ratio of native to foreign born at nearly all times, for the rapid natural increase of population, for the vast internal movement of population and the great activity of native born Americans in exploiting the unworked resources of their own country, it seems unrealistic to accept this interpretation completely. The domestic market and the labour force of the USA would have grown a good deal more slowly and been less varied in the absence of immigration, for immigrants brought not only their own numbers but added to the rate of natural increase. Had there been no immigration after 1870 the population of the country would have been perhaps 12½ per cent lower, and the labour force 14 per cent lower, than it actually was by 1920, and with fewer people much of the natural wealth of the country would have waited longer for effective use. Moreover, the bunching of immigration in waves, with each wave usually bigger than its predecessor, helped to give the whole economy a powerful push forward from time to time. In the other principal receiving countries the influence of immigration was relatively even stronger. Their populations were much smaller before the great migrations towards the end of the nineteenth century. From this time onward the proportion of foreign born in their population was often higher than in the USA. Immigration had a greater effect on the size of their labour force and home market and therefore on their supply of worthwhile trading and investment opportunities.

The complementary value to some of the countries of emigration can be seen clearly in Ireland, where a reasonably rapid growth of incomes did not come until the population had been reduced, though it may be that the reduction went further than any economic necessity required. Both sides of the picture appear if the output which the agricultural worker could achieve in Ireland is compared with what he could produce in a similar occupation at the same date in, say,

New Zealand or the USA, to which so many of his number departed. If the same contrast is made between the USA and some of the emigrant areas of Southern and Eastern Europe it is still sharper. But many emigrants took on non-agricultural jobs in the countries to which they went. In Argentina, for example, the proportion of immigrants in the population of the cities was always very much higher than in the country as a whole. Some of the urban jobs open to immigrants, whatever country they came to, were insecure, poorly paid and only slightly productive. They brought little economic gain to anybody. There were also some regular flows of migration, such as that into Jamaica from India and China, which were used to try to stave off decay rather than to promote expansion and which merely exchanged low productivity in one region for low productivity in another. But movements of this kind were only a small part of the total amount of migration, and the occupational changes encountered by many agricultural emigrants to the major receiving countries were not just an unhelpful transfer from over-populated land to the casual wastefulness of a slum labour market. In some regions, above all in the USA from the later years of the nineteenth century, the economic function of migration was changing. It became one instrument in the process of expanding world production by shifting resources out of agriculture into secondary and tertiary industry. Peasants and agricultural labourers from the Mediterranean and Slav lands of Central and Eastern Europe, with little alternative employment at home, became not more productive farmers but part of the labour force of expanding mechanized industry in the New World and of the ancillary urban services which its changing economy required. For large numbers migration meant a direct change from participation in one of the less productive agricultural economies to the manufacturing economy in which labour had attained its highest productivity.

Such advantages could accrue from the migration of labour only because much else was involved; in particular, because, for the most part, workers moved to places where far more of other resources was at their disposal than they had had at home. The contrast between the abundance of good land in all the principal countries of immigration and its greater scarcity in most of the countries of emigration obviously had much to do with the increase in agricultural output and earnings which migrants could achieve. But even in agriculture the difference usually depended also on a greater supply of capital per head in the countries of immigration; and when it was manufacture, construction and mining, rather than agriculture, that absorbed more and more of the immigrants in increasingly productive employment the significance of this factor was all the more evident.

The accumulation and mobility of capital affected the development of the international economy differently from the accumulation and mobility of labour. A straightforward increase in capital formation, at more than the rate generally prevailing in the world, almost invariably strengthened the country in which it was achieved and enabled it to expand its trade and play a large part in international economic affairs. An unusually rapid accumulation of population did not necessarily have any such effect. A country which proved capable of rapidly increasing its stock of capital but was, for the time being, relatively short of labour was a strong attraction to workers from abroad, and the international mobility of labour could readily help it to achieve and maintain a more productive balance among its economic resources. But a country in which a rapid increase of population was outrunning the supply of capital and other resources had little hope of redressing the balance by attracting capital from abroad. Foreign investors were much more likely to be repelled by its low productivity than allured by the possibility of more fully employing the abundant but underutilized human resources. The most significant feature of the international mobility of the factors of production was that both labour and capital tended to flow to areas where they might be expectd to become more productive. This meant that workers moved to countries where capital was already abundant or could most readily be augmented either from domestic savings or foreign investment and that their choice among such countries was guided by a rational preference for those that were still fairly lightly populated. On the whole, international capital moved to areas with similar economic characteristics, but was certainly without any preference for those that were still fairly lightly capitalized.

The great and continuous increase in the world's stock of capital and its very uneven international distribution were among the most powerful influences on the growth and character of the international economy in the second half of the nineteenth century. The supply and distribution of capital depended on international disparities in the rates of domestic capital formation more than on international investment. International economic conditions were moulded by the same influences as underlay the emergence of a sustained rapid growth of national income in a small number of countries which most others were unable to emulate. The decisive investment influence on the world's economic growth and on its need for an expanding and more varied international commerce was the achievement of higher rates of saving (and their application to the exploitation of technological advances) in much of Europe, especially Western, Central, and Northern Europe, and in areas of European settlement overseas, most of all in the USA. It was an achievement for which much of the explanation must be sought in the internal history of the countries themselves and in the regular cultural and economic contacts among this small group. But its influence was worldwide for, by increasing industrialization and by raising productivity in economic activities more generally in these countries, it made each of them a better market and a source of cheaper and more abundant goods for the outside world.

The main international influence of the large changes in domestic investment is therefore to be found directly in the history of international trade. But the greater wealth and larger commercial interests which they helped to bring to some countries enabled a few of them to exert a further influence on the international economy by exporting capital. Though the effects of international investment were, as far as the supply of long-term capital is concerned, only supplementary to those of the differential rates of domestic capital formation, they were by no means negligible. On the whole, both sets of influences probably worked in the same direction, but some distinctive developments resulted mainly from the international mobility of capital.

Although some international movement of capital had gone on for a long time within Western Europe and between European countries and their colonies, it had been on a small scale. After 1815 British investors gradually began to make more purchases of foreign securities, but even then the British stock of foreign investments was being built up only slowly and not much foreign investment was being undertaken elsewhere. The main period of capital export was the fifty or sixty years preceding the First World War. The chief sources of capital were the United Kingdom, France, and Germany, though, relatively to their small size, there were appreciable sums from Belgium and the Netherlands. From about 1890 the USA also exported capital, though the sums involved were much less than the value of investments in the USA that were owned by foreigners.

The magnitude of international investments at any date can be estimated only by indirect means, though there is usually the safeguard of comparing results reached by different methods. So figures are bound to be less certain than they appear and from time to time attempts are made to revise them. Some recent revisions suggest that some foreign holdings may have been over-estimated, but there are grounds for suspecting that some appreciation of foreign-owned assets was not fully recorded. It may well be that the weaknesses in figures commonly used are of differing kinds which tend to offset each other. It seems safe to suggest that a reasonable approximation of the course of international investment can be given, in terms of magnitude as well as direction.

The United Kingdom was much the largest exporter of capital. In 1914 probably somewhere around half of the international investments belonged to the British and for much of the nineteenth century the proportion must have been a good deal higher. British investment abroad went on somewhat irregularly. In the first half of the nineteenth century the accumulated total was gradually pushed up to a little over £200 million. In the third quarter much more was done and the accumulated total was over £1,000 million at its end. This was followed by a very quiet period for foreign investment in the later seventies, a rapid revival in the eighties, and lower investment again in the nineties. At the end of the nineteenth century British foreign investments stood at about £2,400 million and a remarkable burst of activity in the years just preceding the First World War took them to £4,000 million by 1914. Foreign investment by the French became significant in the eighteen-fifties and early sixties and, though it slackened for a time thereafter, it had reached about 15 milliard francs (£595 million) by 1880. A subsequent strong though irregular revival, with particularly heavy investment early in the twentieth century, brought about a threefold increase in the accumulated total between 1880 and 1914. German foreign investment developed much more slowly until the eighteen-eighties, partly because interest rates within Germany were permanently higher than in the United Kingdom and France, partly because of the later and more sudden economic expansion of Germany itself. In 1883 the accumulated total was only about 5 milliard marks (£245 million) but in the next ten years it more than doubled and by 1914 had reached 25 milliard marks (£1,223 million). The beginning of foreign investment by the USA in the preceding quarter of a century had accumulated a gross total of about $2,600 million (£534 million) by the end of 1913.

The directions taken by these international capital flows varied at different times. Until about 1870 much of it went from one European country (usually Britain or France) to another, especially within Western and Central Europe. British capital participated in the earlier phases of industrialization in France and Germany and was subscribed for government loans in various parts of Europe, and French capital took a large part in new ventures in Spain and Austria. Of the investments placed outside Europe, much the greater part at this time went to the USA. In the last third of the nineteenth century the situation changed, mainly as a result of a change in British investing habits and of the creation of many more opportunities in new places. Some of the former chief importers of British capital had become wealthy enough to raise, chiefly at home, all the capital they needed without offering as high rates as British investors thought they could safely obtain elsewhere. Much investment continued to go to the USA, but the rest turned increasingly to the British Empire and to the new areas of immigration in South America. From the sixties to the eighties India received a large share of British foreign investment and from the very end of the century there was some modest increase in the tropical African and Asian colonies but, in the period as a whole, much the greater part went to the regions of white settlement. At the end of 1913 47 per cent of British foreign investment was in the Empire, Canada having the largest share, 20 per cent was in the USA and another 20 per cent in Latin America, nearly half of it in Argentina. Foreign investment from other sources also tended to withdraw from Western Europe (except for Scandinavia) but still found outlets in other parts of Europe, especially in Russia, and to a less extent in the countries of Southeastern Europe, to which a good deal of German capital was directed for political ends. In 1914 60 per cent of French foreign investments and just over 50 per cent of German were in Europe, and in 1900 the French proportion had been 70 per cent. Nearly a quarter of all French foreign investment was in Russia alone in 1914, and the Russian economic development since 1890 had depended a good deal on the supply of capital from France and Belgium. Since 1900 France and Germany had both increased the export of capital to their own empires overseas, but this was only a small proportion of their foreign investment. Outside Europe their investors, like those of Britain, had been attracted most by the regions of white settlement. In 1914 17 per cent of German foreign investment was in the USA and another 17 per cent in Latin America, to which there had also been a large flow of French capital since 1900. The early capital exports of the USA also went mainly to other, later-developing American countries. In 1914 roughly 40 per cent of the total was in Mexico and nearly 30 per cent in Canada.

A high proportion of the export of capital was made through the purchase of foreign government securities. Some of the proceeds were used by the borrowers for their own fiscal purposes, which might have no element of genuine investment. But the governments often applied them immediately to productive enterprises and much that was initially applied in other ways gave an indirect stimulus to developmental expenditure. In addition, even before 1850, some British foreign investment had been made by setting up or taking shares in private transport, mining or manufacturing concerns. After 1870 British investors turned increasingly to this kind of activity and were less attracted than before by government securities. From this time until 1914 the greatest object of capital exports came to be the provision of railways in newly developing areas. In 1914 40 per cent of British investments abroad were in railway companies, 30 per cent in government and municipal loans (and some of these had been partly devoted to railway finance), 10 per cent in raw material production, chiefly mining, 8 per cent in banks and finance companies, and 5 per cent in public utility undertakings other than railways.

The main direct effects of the international investment can readily be discerned. In the first place, it did a little to provide basic items of capital equipment, such as railways, and some up-to-date industrial enterprise in a number of European countries in the early stages of their industrialization. What these countries obtained by the import of capital was usually very small in proportion to what they provided out of their own savings, though Russian economic progress depended on an unusually large amount of borrowing from abroad. But in most European countries foreign capital probably had rather more importance from the originality and priority of what it did than from its magnitude. The provision of early railways with the aid of foreign capital and enterprise when most investors at home were still unwilling to risk their savings in such a novelty was a particularly useful contribution. Much larger in scope was the influence of foreign capital in speeding up settlement and productive development in thinly populated areas which had great natural resources, governments able and willing to uphold civil contracts, and a potential rapid inflow of white settlers. Even in the USA, where the ratio of foreign to domestic capital was generally low, the capital imports made an invaluable contribution. They made it practicable for the country to press on with its own development without being inhibited by the persistence of a balance of payments deficit for many decades. They were concentrated particularly on the provision of internal transport, which was the most fundamental physical requirement in preparing the whole country for economic development of any kind. And at certain times of particularly rapid growth they came forward in unusually large amounts. In the other extensive countries of white settlement capital imports had a similar type of influence and were even more significant because they formed a higher proportion of the total investment than they did in the USA.

A lesser influence of international investment came in some countries (often with some sort of colonial status) in which domestic capital formation remained very low. Foreign investment sometimes came to these places to provide what was needed to develop a few lines of trade with Europe and America and also to provide effective government. Capital imports were devoted to such things as harbour works at international ports; plantations and mines, with railways to connect them with each other and with a port; roads and some public utilities in the centres of government and foreign trade. In these cases foreign investment usually created no more than a highly capitalized commercial enclave in a country which otherwise remained economically underdeveloped. It was the sort of activity on which was based the idea that foreign investment was primarily an instrument of economic imperialism; but, in fact, it absorbed only a small proportion of international capital and made only a minor contribution to the trade of the countries which supplied it. More rarely, something more comprehensive and of wider commercial influence was done. The most notable instance in the second half of the nineteenth century was the large British investment in India which, among other things, provided the subcontinent with such a fundamental requirement as an extensive railway system by no means limited to giving access to British-owned undertakings. This investment was not sufficient to set the whole Indian economy on the way to continued rapid expansion, partly because it was spread over so huge a population, partly because it slackened after the mid-eighties, above all because, unlike almost all the other chief capital-importing areas, India was not in a condition where it was practicable to accompany capital imports with greatly increased domestic savings. But at least the British investment was enough to raise India's commercial capacity, as both exporter and importer, quite substantially.

India was, in fact, exceptional in its experience of international investment, which for the most part was directed towards areas which had other prominent assets to encourage them, including a capacity to help themselves with their own investments. Other undeveloped areas usually remained in a position where it was very difficult for them to obtain extra capital at all. International investment thus tended to reinforce the other factors which helped to concentrate the world's productive power and commercial influence in a small number of countries. But, by seeking out, more or less at the same time, the areas of natural wealth and adaptable institutions to which migrants were also moving, it ensured that the dominant points of the international economy were geographically more widespread and that wealth and commercial influence were extended beyond those countries that had raised themselves up by industrialization.

One other important consequence of international investment was the increase which it provided in the foreign earnings of the leading countries, especially Britain. Throughout the nineteenth century Britain had in most years an adverse balance of merchandise trade, but it was not until about 1870 that dividends and interest on foreign investments became the major item among the 'invisible' exports which for a long time had turned this into a regular (though sometimes small) surplus on the balance of payments as a whole. Thereafter this growing item, which in the years just before the First World War was supplying more than 20 per cent of Britain's total income from abroad, ensured that, whatever the vicissitudes of trade, Britain was certain to have a substantial surplus on current international account. Sterling was therefore a currency of unquestionable strength and, because that strength was derived in part from its regularly being spent on new enterprises overseas, it was also a currency that was always readily available. This combination of security and availability enabled sterling to play a unique part in the financing of international trade.

The supply of short-term capital for the needs of international trade did not need to be on anything like the scale of the long-term capital stock employed by businesses concerned with foreign trade. Most of it was turned over and put to fresh use every few months and, as credit institutions became more highly organized and communications improved, it is probable that some economies were effected in the stock of short-term capital relatively to the volume of trade which it financed. It was therefore practicable for a much bigger proportion of the short-term capital to come from one or two wealthy centres, if other circumstances made this convenient. The London money market was an important source of international finance throughout the nineteenth century, though in the first half of the century the financing of international trade was considerably dispersed. From about 1860 the share of the London market substantially increased and it is likely that in the late nineteenth century the greater part of international trade was conducted in sterling, which was even used to finance some of the internal trade of non-British countries. Before 1914 there was little modification of this state of affairs, except for a slight increase in the use of international credits in German marks in the early years of the twentieth century.

Both commercial and institutional influences were responsible for this dominant role of the London money market. The United Kingdom had a bigger foreign trade than any other country and, for this reason alone, sterling was bound to be specially important and London was assured of exceptional opportunities for international banking business. In the first half of the nineteenth century a number of international merchant bankers, most of whom had originated elsewhere, established themselves in London and built up a large business which included the acceptance of bills of exchange, drawn on foreign merchants and banks, and dealings in foreign exchange. In the same period the elements of the London market were further augmented by the development of specialist firms of bill-brokers who borrowed the surplus funds of the banks and applied them to the discounting of bills of exchange, at this time mostly bills used in internal trade. During the third quarter of the century the situation changed in various ways that were favourable to the international use of sterling. The English banking system grew so rapidly that it mobilized more funds than could profitably be lent out at home, so that a bigger surplus was available to be employed, through the bill brokers, in the finance of international trade. Britain's own foreign trade and long-term foreign lending grew faster than before, with the result that it was easier for other countries to obtain sterling than it had been – easier for them to pay for British financial services as well as goods. Sterling itself became a more reliable currency after the eighteen-sixties. Earlier it had been subject to some serious crises and there had been times when the Bank of England had had to seek temporary assistance abroad. But, partly because of improved banking practices and partly because of Britain's greatly increased exports, these weaknesses were overcome. While London grew stronger, some other centres failed to keep up with it. In particular, its greatest rival, Paris, was seriously and permanently damaged as an international financial centre by the Franco-Prussian War. For the rest of the century the conditions which by 1870 were bringing about the international pre-eminence of the London money market became all the stronger. The safety and expertise of the firms making up the market grew with experience. The further increase of Britain's earnings abroad added still more to the security of sterling, which was more readily available than ever as the destinations of British payments, both in return for imports and in the making of long-term investments, became more widely dispersed and less closely tied to the destinations of British exports. Sterling thus had the supreme merit for international trading purposes that, while it had the high degree of security originating in the regular earning of a large international surplus, it was not constantly reverting to the exporters of the home country. The surplus, in effect, always went back into an international pool, and sound businesses all over the world could at all times earn or borrow as much sterling as they needed.

The ability of the London money market to exercise its decisive influence on the finance of international trade depended not only on its own virtues and those of sterling, but on the preference of governments and businesses in many parts of the world for the exercise of those particular virtues, rather than any of the various alternatives (including vices) that were conceivable. In particular, in the late nineteenth century there was a general acceptance of the view that the maintenance of exchange stability should be the chief immediate aim of banking policy. Governments and business circles agreed that they had more to gain than to lose by stabilizing their financial relationships with each other, submitting to a common international discipline in monetary policy and not upsetting trade by arbitrary, unilateral actions which must create uncertainty about the future value of mutual debts and credits. In the late nineteenth century nearly all currencies came to have a value fixed in terms of a defined content of gold and therefore, within narrow limits, fixed in relation to each other. Governments accepted the duty of regulating currency and credit so that the demand for and the supply of their currency were balanced around the par value in gold. If too much of their currency was being spent, so that they were threatened with the possibility of maintaining equilibrium only at a lower exchange value, it was the expenditure that had to be cut, even though this involved immediate hardship, not the currency value and the gold content that had to be reduced.

It was not new in the late (or, indeed, any part of) the nineteenth century for standard coins of different currencies to have nominally fixed relations to a specified amount of a precious metal and therefore to each other. But in practice the limits of exchange variation had been fairly wide, partly because the transmission of coin, bullion, and market information was slow and fairly expensive and partly because of variations in the content and physical condition of coin. The latter influence had ceased to be important for the major currencies by the early nineteenth century and the former was more gradually overcome. But after 1850 further difficulties were threatened because some countries used gold as standard money, some used silver and some used both; and the price relation of gold to silver, which had been nearly constant, began to vary. In the 'fifties recent discoveries caused a slight excess of monetary gold and a relative shortage of silver but, with the assistance of some international co-operation in monetary policies, this was gradually corrected without ever having gone very far. But from the late sixties there was a growing divergence in the opposite direction. This was eventually countered by the almost universal adoption of a gold standard, to which Britain had adhered in practice since 1821. The changeover was led by the new German Empire in 1873 and virtually completed in 1897 when Russia went over to gold. In effect the world then had something very near to an international currency, divided up in different proportions in different countries.

Such a provision might appear to make the maintenance of exchange stability almost automatic. In practice it was not as simple as that. Without the development of an elaborate institutional framework and a firm adherence to certain lines of policy there could be no assurance that it would not be necessary to alter the gold content and exchange value of particular currencies from time to time. One requirement for stability was that any country that lost foreign exchange or gold, or whose exchange rate was falling towards the point at which it would become cheaper to make payments abroad in gold than in currency, should contract credit, and vice versa. But this by itself could not necessarily restore equilibrium to a country's external financial position. It could be effective only in a community where business was sufficiently dependent on bank credit to be restricted or encouraged by changes in the cost of borrowing. Even then, monetary policy would not be fully effective unless commodity markets were also highly organized. It was necessary that commodity prices should vary quickly as the conditions of demand and supply changed and that producers and merchants should vary their commitments in accordance with changes in the price of commodities as well as credit. If these things did not happen, if prices were sticky or merchants and producers ignored their trend when placing new orders, the intentions of credit policy would be frustrated. A demand for imports and therefore an outflow of currency, for instance, might be maintained for an appreciable time after a tightening of credit which had been intended to stop it.

In the forty years preceding the First World War, the years of the partial or complete international gold standard, these favourable conditions for the maintenance of equilibrium were present over a wide area and to a high degree. All the countries with a large foreign commerce developed some kind of integrated banking system, though its internal connexions and the directness of its influence on business varied from one country to another. The diffusion of market information to every part of the world that was commercially concerned became very rapid and complete, thanks especially to the telegraph and cable. Moreover, for many of the chief commodities of international trade it became practicable for world prices to be established in one or two centres on the basis of grading and sampling and information about forthcoming supplies from every source. Even if in some of the most advanced countries there was a good deal of business that was independent of bank credit and therefore partly insulated from the workings of credit policy (at any rate temporarily), the markets for commodities which formed a large part of international trade operated in a way that made them extremely sensitive to all kinds of both financial and commercial influences.

There were also important ways in which the activities of the London money market and the pursuit of stable financial conditions in the rest of the world reinforced each other. It was far easier for London houses to extend trade credit plentifully and widely when they were operating in an environment where all in authority were co-operating to maintain conditions in which the uncertainty of the future was reduced to a minimum. Risks were reduced, fewer enquiries needed to be made, less was wasted on bad debts, financial business was cheaper to operate and probably more funds could be attracted to it. On the other hand, because such a high proportion of international finance was provided in sterling the task of maintaining general stability was greatly eased. So much was regulated through the elaborate and experienced institutions of London that the completion of equilibrium through national credit policies, the foreign exchange markets, and the subsidiary gold markets (London itself was the greatest gold market) involved much less drastic operations than it might otherwise have done. Conditions were thus unusually adapted to the maintenance of a combination of order and abundance in international finance, so that other factors making for the promotion of international trade might be expected to have full scope.

That the influences encouraging trade were strong and had plenty of play is evident from what happened. Statistics of trade for the world as a whole continue to be rather approximate until the last quarter of the nineteenth century, when their reliability began to improve greatly. But they are good enough to indicate that trade grew very fast. The total value of international trade (i.e. the exports of all countries plus the imports of all countries, every commodity thus being reckoned twice but transport costs only once) has been estimated at £800 million for 1850. More reliably it can be put at £2,700 million or £2,800 million in the late seventies. In the last quinquennium of the nineteenth century it was averaging about £3,800 million, a figure that would have been some £200 million higher if prices had been the same as they were twenty years earlier. By 1913, when the price level was fairly close to what it had been in the mid-seventies, international trade had increased to a little over £8,000 million.

Within the long-sustained general expansion there were various important changes and irregularities. One of these was in the growth of trade in different classes of goods. Though the data are defective it is highly probable that during the third quarter of the nineteenth century, because of the continued growth of population in countries that were devoting more and more of their resources to industry, trade in foodstuffs came to be a bigger proportion of the total. This, in turn, helped to ensure that, despite the growing exchange of manufactured goods as these became more varied, trade in primary products was persistently much larger than that in manufactures. After about 1880 it seems unlikely that the leading industrial countries became relatively much more dependent on imported foodstuffs though, of course, as these countries grew in size their food imports increased absolutely. In so far as there was any further switch from home production of food to imports, its effect on the commodity structure of international trade was counterbalanced by the growing demand of the wealthier industrial countries for some of each other's manufactures. By the later seventies international trade in primary produce was about 70 per cent higher than that in manufactures and over the long period the proportion fluctuated around this level. Some of the fluctuations were, however, quite wide. The growth of international trade as a whole was by no means regular. In the third quarter of the nineteenth century expansion was apparently faster than at any subsequent time until after 1950, and within this quarter it seems likely that the early fifties and the early seventies were years of particularly rapid growth. Thereafter the most striking variation was a falling off in the rate of growth of trade, with a minimum in the nineties, followed by a renewed acceleration. These variations were largely concentrated in trade in manufactures. Indeed, from the mid-eighties until the outbreak of the First World War the rate of increase of international trade in primary produce was, in terms of volume, astonishingly steady, at about 17 per cent per quinquennium. In the early nineties it was a little less, but even then the variation was slight. In terms of value the growth was not quite so steady. On the other hand, international trade in manufactures grew at widely fluctuating rates. In the nineties there was very little growth at all and then in the next decade the rate of expansion rose very high, far higher than for trade in primary produce. Thus there was a tendency for trade in manufactures to fall behind that in primary products and then catch up again, though the divergence was less wide in terms of value than in terms of volume. The contrast can be seen in the figures of Table 10.

TABLE 10   QUINQUENNIAL INCREASES IN VOLUME OF WORLD TRADE,
1876–1913 (*percentages*)

Period	World trade in manufactures	World trade in primary products	Total world trade
1876–80 to 1881–5	24.4	21.8	22.8
1881–5 to 1886–90	12.9	17.1	15.5
1886–90 to 1891–5	1.7	15.5	10.2
1891–5 to 1896–1900	4.7	17.1	12.9
1896–1900 to 1901–5	31.8	17.6	22.1
1901–5 to 1906–10	23.3	17.4	19.5
1906–10 to 1911–13	22.7	16.7	18.8

These fluctuations, and the different degree to which they were reflected by the different constituents of international trade, appear to be connected with changes in prices, and these, in turn, were much influenced by changes in the volume and direction of investment. In the third quarter of the century, when the prices of most things were everywhere rising gradually but irregularly, prices of manufactures and primary goods kept fairly closely in step with each other, save that in the boom of the early seventies the exceptional demands for manufactures caused their prices temporarily to rise much the faster of the two. But this was soon redressed. Prices in the last quarter of the century fell considerably and in the later 'seventies and early 'eighties it was the prices of manufactures that fell most, partly because heavy investment in their production during the preceding boom had now made them very plentiful, partly because the demand for primary products was growing rapidly as industrial countries sought to import more food, particularly at a time of bad European harvests. But by this time the greatest field of investment was coming to be in the opening up of new regions of primary production, with the result that by the mid-eighties food and raw materials were becoming more and more abundant. For the next twenty years, therefore, the terms of trade moved against primary producers; i.e. the prices of their goods fell more or rose less than those of manufactures. By about 1900, however, the world's demand for primary products had greatly increased. Investment in their supply was not rising so markedly as it had been and was being outpaced by investment in manufactures, with the result that during the next decade the terms of trade began to move slightly in the opposite direction. Renewed heavy investment in primary producing areas was only starting to reverse this trend just before the First World War.

These price movements altered the growth of incomes in ways which reacted on the course of trade. Thus in the eighteen-seventies the large investment in industrial countries enabled them to import more of both manufactures and primary goods and the buoyant market for the latter enabled primary producers to go on into the eighties expanding their imports of manufactures. But when primary producers found their incomes affected by an adverse movement of the terms of trade, without any offsetting acceleration in the growth of their export volume, they could no longer afford to increase their imports of manufactures so fast. The effects of this were probably being enhanced in the early 'nineties by some slackening of industrial investment as well as by one or two sharp tariff wars, both of which may have retarded the growth of trade among industrial countries. The deceleration in the growth of international trade was reversed at the end of the century by more active investment and business in industrial countries. Within a few years primary producers found themselves getting better prices and receiving bigger investments. Both contributions helped them to purchase more manufactured goods, so that there was a stimulus to international trade which was sustained almost until the outbreak of the First World War.

Although the long-term increases in the sales of both manufactures and primary goods were very similar, there were considerable changes in the direction of trade and the way it was shared among different countries. The dominant influence was that of the larger countries which had become highly industrialized by the end of the nineteenth century. Naturally, as new areas of supply were opened and the most advanced productive techniques became more widely diffused, the commercial pre-eminence of these few countries became a little less marked, but it diminished only slowly. In the first half of the eighteen-eighties 50 per cent of the world's visible international trade was done by France, Germany, the United Kingdom, and the USA. Twenty years later their share had fallen to 46 per cent and in the years 1911–13 it averaged 44 per cent. The reduction had come entirely in the share of France and the United Kingdom, and for Germany the trend had been slightly in the opposite direction. But the United Kingdom, with 14 per cent of the world total in 1911–13, still had a bigger foreign trade than any other country, though its share had been 19 per cent in 1881–5.

The continued leadership of the United Kingdom as a trading nation, together with the increased strength of its international financial position, gave a special importance to changes in the directions of its trade in the late nineteenth century, even though most of these were relatively fairly small. They both resulted from, and helped to push further, the increased area specialization that was associated with the spread of industrialization and the opening of new regions of agricultural production. The most notable change was that UK trade showed rather greater regional imbalances than before. In particular, a declining proportion of exports went to the rest of Europe, without much change in the proportion of imports which was drawn from there; and an increased proportion of imports came from North America without that market showing as big an increase in the proportion of UK exports which it took. For the world trading system to work well there had to be offsetting shifts which involved more elaborate multilateral dealings. For the UK these shifts showed in a substantial drop in the proportion of imports bought from Asia, while the proportion of exports was maintained; and, on a smaller scale, by expanding exports faster than imports in the African market. The UK was, in effect, able to have a bigger adverse balance of trade with most of the world because it achieved a bigger surplus with India and some African countries. These, in turn, were able to find non-British markets for additional exports, especially in the growing industrial areas of continental Europe and North America.

Thus new lines of international specialization matched the simultaneous creation of a payments system in which internationally acceptable currency and credit were readily available all over the world and debts incurred in one area could be cancelled by credits earned anywhere else. In this way the effects of international trade, which generally brought economic benefit to those who participated in it, were more varied and more widely diffused than they could otherwise have been; and the expansion of world production was made easier and more orderly by the diversion of some of the frictions and rivalries, which it potentially involved, into safer channels. Newly industrialized areas were freed from any pressure to concentrate their exports in the regions from which they sought more food and raw materials and thereby to come into acute competition with the United Kingdom where its trade was strongest. They were able instead to build up their exports in other areas and to pay for their increased imports with funds of which a large part came, directly or indirectly, from the United Kingdom itself, by the way of the import surplus which it had with most other countries – a surplus which trebled in amount in the last forty years of the nineteenth century. It was the combination of immense productive and commercial expansion with the binding of the whole world into something very close to an economic unit, by means of a network of commercial and financial transactions, that was outstandingly characteristic of the late nineteenth century. And the two elements in this combination were not fortuitously associated. Each was a necessary condition for the full development of the other.

The existence of such a state of affairs is perhaps the strongest reason for suggesting that before the end of the nineteenth century it had become appropriate to speak of an 'international economy' with much less hesitation and qualification than would have been necessary in the early part of the century. If such a phrase is to have any significance it would also seem necessary that the international economy should show some signs of having acquired a common history of its own; and, in fact, such signs do appear to have become increasingly numerous in the late nineteenth century. The international economy did not begin to move consistently as a whole, with each of its constituents sharing the same economic experience as the rest and varying its activity in step with all the others. There were times when countries with many economic links found their fortunes quite at variance. But, on the whole, economic influences in any commercially active part of the world spread more quickly and more widely than before, and many different and widely separated countries found themselves more or less simultaneously affected by the same factors, to which they reacted in similar ways, though often in very different degrees.

One indication of greater international similarity was the course of business cycles. Earlier in the nineteenth century it had been usual for severe financial crises, which seldom lasted very long, to be transmitted from their centre to other countries with appreciable foreign trade. But other fluctuations in economic activity often had quite a different course and timing in different countries, and sometimes even within different regions of the same country. Dr W. L. Thorp's long and detailed study of business conditions showed, for instance, that between 1790 and 1857 England and the USA were in diametrically opposite phases of the business cycle almost as often as they shared the same phase. But from 1857 to 1925 the phases agreed in 49 per cent of the years and were directly opposed in only 21 per cent. England and France shared the same phase in only 28 per cent of the years from 1840 to 1882, but in 65 per cent of those between 1882 and 1925, while the proportion of years of diametrically opposite phase fell from 33 per cent to 9 per cent. Of seventeen countries whose business activity Dr. Thorp examined from 1890 onwards, ten had recessions in 1890–1, fifteen in 1900–1, fifteen in 1907–8, and twelve in 1912–13; and the exceptions were not always very significant. For instance, Japan and South Africa failed to show recession in 1900–1 only because they were already plunged in economic depression. In most years, by this time, the movement of business activity was in the same direction in the great majority of countries. Its course was most individual in predominantly agricultural countries such as South Africa, China, Brazil, and Russia. Closest conformity to a common international pattern was found in countries that were predominantly industrial or engaged to an unusual degree in international trade, or both: England, France, Germany, the Netherlands, Sweden.

It is possible, however, for similar short-term fluctuations to be superimposed on very different longer-term trends and it is by no means clear whether a course charted for the international economy as a whole can be adequately representative. Much common experience was provided by similar movements of price. Most countries with appreciable foreign trade found prices rising between 1850 and the mid-sixties. In the USA, where prices had been particularly affected by currency inflation during the Civil War, they began a prolonged fall at that point. In most other countries the fall was temporary and prices rose still higher in the early seventies. Thereafter falling prices were almost universal until the late nineties, after which came a period of rising prices which lasted until 1920. Common movements of prices were accompanied by a good deal of similarity, though not uniformity, in the course of interest rates, and there were many suggestions that the same was true of profits – that they rose generally or, at least, were more easily obtained whenever and wherever there was a sustained rise in prices, and vice versa – but on this there is no conclusive evidence. What seems more certain is that similar price movements had similar effects on business psychology. Where there was much industry or trade, business was generally thought to be in a favourable condition for most of the third quarter of the nineteenth century, though with some sharp setbacks which differed from one country to another, and with rather more gloom for much of the 'sixties. The early 'seventies saw a very widespread boom but all the wealthier countries experienced a break in these conditions at some time varying from 1873 to 1875. After this, during the prolonged price fall, there were mounting complaints of depression in industry and trade, and by the eighties one government after another was instituting enquiries as to what had gone wrong – enquiries which produced the most varied and often unconvincing explanations. Not until near the end of the century, when prices were rising again was the widespread belief that there was general depression shaken off. On the whole the twentieth-century years before 1914 enjoyed with contemporaries a reputation for fairly good business. If there were ills in one place they could be attributed to the successes of competitors rather than to a general blight which hung over all.

The main additional support for this highly subjective, though widely held, version of the general course of the world's business is to be found in some of the irregularities already noted in the history of international trade, especially international trade in manufactures. Although this was growing almost continuously, its rate of growth was faster (in terms of volume and not merely of value) in times of rising than in times of falling prices. In particular, its growth fell off most markedly towards the end of the late nineteenth-century price fall, when complaints of depression were becoming most widespread and intense. It does, indeed, seem likely that those engaged in activities producing a large proportion of their output for direct sale in international markets experienced many difficulties in the last quarter of the nineteenth century and easier conditions before and after. This applies to both agricultural and manufacturing activities and to highly commercialized countries in whatever part of the world they were situated, though it certainly does not apply equally to all activities which turned increasingly to international markets. Those European regions of coal-mining or of dairy farming, for instance, which began to produce more for export in the last quarter of the nineteenth century probably fared very well, on the whole. But they were hardly typical of the great export activities.

It is, however, equally true that the great export activities were not completely representative of business generally. It is quite possible that in the third quarter of the nineteenth century international trade grew faster than production in the world as a whole. The data are not good enough for certainty one way or the other. But even then there was scarcely any country that did not consume much more of its own produce than it exported. After 1975 there is no doubt that, though international trade grew fast, industrial production grew faster. In other words, the most usual case was for industrialists to become relatively rather more dependent on home and less dependent on foreign markets. The same may also be true of agriculturists, though perhaps not to the same extent. Of course, in any country with appreciable foreign dealings, particularly in a period when credit policy was dominated by international considerations, the producer for the home market was bound to find that his supplies, his investment opportunities, his sales, and his profits were all affected by external factors, the cumulative influence of which could be very powerful in the long run. But at any particular time these were intermingled with all sorts of domestic factors that retarded or reinforced or distorted their effect, so that for several years together particular groups of activities, or particular countries, might display economic trends which diverged widely from those of international trade.

Many such divergences can readily be found. For instance, the growth of manufacturing output in the world was particularly rapid in the later eighteen-eighties when the growth of international trade was decelerating, and after a few years of slightly slower growth it was again accelerating in the later 'nineties while international trade, especially that in manufactured goods, was still growing at very little above its minimum rate. The years from 1891 to 1905, in fact, saw the fastest growth of all in the world's manufactures but only the last five years of this period experienced a rapid expansion of international trade. Doubtless this divergence was due in part to the recent emergence of the USA, which sold an unusually high proportion of its manufactures on the home market, as the biggest manufacturing nation: in the later nineties its output of manufactures was more than 50 per cent greater than the United Kingdom's, whereas in the early eighties the two had been about equal. From 1906 to 1914, though world trade and manufacturing both continued to grow fast, there was some falling-off in the growth rates and this was much more marked for manufacturing than for international trade.

Other discrepancies can be found in the experience of individual countries. During the last quarter of the nineteenth century, which was relatively poor for international trade and heard so much talk of depression, most industrial or industrializing countries enjoyed lengthy spells when their output and income rose unusually fast. Few of them grew so much in the more vigorous trading years just before the First World War. Yet the precise timing of their periods of great expansion varied a good deal from one to another. Sometimes the difference may in part have been directly caused by international dealings, as when large international transfers of capital and labour offered an immediate stimulus to the recipient country and perhaps only a delayed benefit to the sender. The economic growth of Canada and the USA in the first decade of the twentieth century, when the growth of many European countries showed no such spurt forward and was in some cases severely retarded, probably owed something to an influence of this kind. But many of the differences must have had a much more complex origin. Countries on either side of the Atlantic sometimes made their major economic advances in antiphase, but not always. So it was, too, for agricultural and industrial countries. Even the economic progress of near neighbours showed similar characteristics. France and Germany both progressed rapidly in the early 'eighties, but in the 'seventies Germany was advancing much faster than France and in the early twentieth century the opposite was the case.

All these examples illustrate the endless variety of economic experience in the period and show that any very rigid and stereo-typed version of the course of the international economy must be qualified almost out of recognition. But they do not show that the international economy lacked any unity of its own, with common characteristics that spread their influence persistently throughout the world. From the mid-nineteenth century to the First World War the outstanding feature of the world's economic history was the presence of conditions facilitating expansion to an unprecedented extent and over a very wide area. And from the 'seventies onward the conditions were being modified in such a way that the expansion could proceed with remarkably little friction. Naturally the extent and timing of the benefits gained by different countries varied greatly. They had different natural resources to employ, social traditions and institutions with different degrees of adaptability; they began industrialization at different dates and in different ways, or they did not begin it at all. The international influences themselves, besides operating in a different setting in every country, had their own unevenness. Some

international channels of trade and investment were far more efficiently developed than others. The general influences were, on the
whole, more advantageous to countries that concentrated on industry than to those which concentrated on even the most efficient
agriculture. But the striking thing was that, however unevenly in
extent and with whatever irregularities in timing, over the long
period the economic expansion was in some degree shared in almost
all countries that came significantly within the scope of international
commerce. Even the poorest areas usually had some share, though it
often showed itself more in an increased population than a higher
standard of living.

The factors that gave this period its favourable character were of
many kinds. One of the most fundamental was the possibility of the
much wider application of basic technological advances: the use of
the steam-engine, for instance, as a source of energy for an enormously increased number of productive processes and, perhaps even
more important, its general use in transport, making cheaply accessible much bigger markets and sources of supply. Associated with this
was the bringing into use of huge reserves of previously neglected
productive resources. Far more of them became accessible for the
first time than had ever become newly available in so short a period
before. Rapid settlement and heavy investment soon put much of the
best of them to effective use, with an influence on supply that spread
throughout the world. It was the development of the regions of
white settlement, the USA above all, and their immediate linking
with the whole international trading system, that was the chief
means whereby this transformation was accomplished. The increase
of investment and foreign trade in India added significantly to it. The
opening to trade of some newly acquired colonial territories added a
little more, though from this source the gain was usually small and
sometimes indirect; some of these territories, in fact, required more
external resources for their running than they themselves made
available for trade. But altogether the expansion of the world's
productive area was on a scale impossible at any earlier or later
period. It was assisted by favourable political conditions, especially
after 1870. Despite diplomatic rivalries that were often tense, there
was between 1871 and 1914 neither war nor subversion on a scale big
enough to hinder the growth of production and trade to any significant degree; and new political barriers to international trade, though
often irritating, were not generally high enough to cause great
difficulty. Governments paid more attention than before to meeting
the needs of business, not just by assisting in the search for new

markets but more fundamentally by modernizing the framework of law and administration within which business must operate and by increasing the flow of commercial information. Most influential of all in the administrative and institutional field was the fact that bankers, and to a considerable extent politicians also, in all the chief trading countries shared a common belief that international stability was to be sought before all else in economic affairs, and were prepared to act in accordance with their belief even in the face of difficulty.

The intensive development of production by the application of a wider-ranging scientific technology, its extensive development by newly exploiting the resources of vast and richly endowed areas of the world, the spread of the fruits of development through a worldwide, multilateral system of trade and payments. operating in conditions of economic and political stability – these were the fundamentals of the late nineteenth century economy, giving unity both to a particular period and to the economic history of a large part of the world. On any comparable scale they had never existed together before, nor did they continue a full existence together very far into the twentieth century. The sudden increase in the world's productive area was a once-for-all gain and by the early years of the twentieth century the best of the gain had been made. For this reason alone the conditions of further economic development in the world could never again be as they were in the half-century before 1914. And, besides this, the international political stability was subject to increasing strain. World war destroyed it and with its overthrow much of the smoothness and cohesion of international economic arrangements were bound to be put in jeopardy. The kind of international economy that had grown up since the mid-nineteenth century was thus both unique and mortal. The needs that it served went on, but the means of serving them could not continue un-changed. After 1914 there still was an international economy, but it was something different from what had been built up before, and in a real sense the First World War divided one economic era from another.

CHAPTER EIGHT
International economic relations 1914–1933

Just how sharp a division 1914 brought in international economic affairs became apparent only in fairly long retrospect. To contemporaries there appeared to be a sequence of upheavals, arising mainly from non-economic causes, and some of these disturbances were so deep and prolonged that they left behind permanent changes in important but limited sections of economic life. The immediate upheavals were countered by whatever improvisations were readily practicable and some account was taken of their legacy of more permanent change when modifications were made in the regular practices and institutions of economic life. But an inescapable pre-occupation with these matters distracted attention from the deeper economic changes that were beginning to appear before 1914 and became gradually more pervasive. The need for adjustment to these changes was inadequately met and became ever more serious. There was thus a continual, though submerged, conflict between the organization of international economic affairs and the conditions in which it had to operate.

Because of this conflict, more than anything else, international economic history for at least thirty years after 1914 was much less coherent than before. It cannot realistically be presented as anything like an orderly evolution along lines generally recognized and encouraged throughout the commercial world. It appears rather as a series of short phases marked out by alternations of partial breakdown and repair, with the repairs proving always so impermanent that eventually it become obvious that patching was not good enough and only reconstruction would do. The first phase was one of increasing dislocation, with some permanent losses, during the First World War and its immediate aftermath. This was followed by a period in which great efforts were made to remove the recent dislocations and restore the international economic system as nearly as possible to its pre-1914 condition. From 1925 to 1931 the restored system can be seen at work, at first with apparent success but from 1929 under increasing strain which led to virtual collapse in 1931. For two more years there were attempts to prop up the ruin, but they failed and 1933 marked the end, for the time being, of a fully organized international economic system. After this there was a brief era, which obviously could not last, when, despite the maintenance of international trade and payments as an integral part of economic life, only truncated media of international economic co-operation were in use. International considerations were almost completely subordinated to national financial and recovery policies in this period. It was brought to an end by the Second World War, which did sufficient destruction to leave the way clear for an effort to rebuild an international economic system on rather different lines from before and to bring it gradually into use.

The first inroads into the smoothness of the pre-1914 system could scarcely have been expected to introduce so long and troubled a sequence. They began as minor repercussions of war on finance and trade. Some capital tied up in international trade and foreign enterprises became, temporarily at least, irrecoverable, and some of the most useful channels of short-term investment were closed or made unattractive by commercial uncertainty. The international gold standard was abandoned, and international financial dealings became a less stabilizing influence than they had been. The division of the world into opposed camps had a similar effect on the movement of commodities. International trade was forced to change some of its channels and to draw part of its finance from new sources.

As the scope of the war increased, the problems of recasting international economic relations became more difficult. At first the main need seemed to be to find new markets and sources of supply to replace those in enemy hands. But soon the chief belligerents were in a position where they could not adequately supply foreign markets, old or new. Productive resources had to be diverted from manufacture for export to turning out war supplies; by 1918 the proportion of the industrial production of the UK which went for export was little more than half what it had been in 1913. At the same time the countries which had been the chief sources of foreign investment could be so no longer, because all their savings were absorbed by their own military activity. In fact, the main international movement of capital ceased to be from Western Europe to primary producing areas in order to develop unused real resources, and instead was from the USA to Europe and from the UK to its Continental allies in order to finance the work of destruction.

So what had seemed in 1914 to be a situation in which business could continue as usual with some rather difficult but still relatively minor changes had become vastly more intricate and serious by the end of the war. The chief European powers had suspended some of their previous economic activities, temporarily as they thought. But that suspension had encouraged permanent changes elsewhere. When the customers of the belligerents could no longer obtain the goods which they were in the habit of importing, they tried to produce them for themselves or to obtain them from countries which were expanding their output of civilian goods, as Japan was. Some of the markets to which European countries expected to return had been firmly occupied by others. Moreover, the power of Europe to resume normal economic activities was somewhat impaired. The physical destruction of war was one cause of this though, outside Russia, probably not of major importance. The physical capacity of the world to produce had not been greatly reduced, though in the battle areas of France and Belgium, where some important industrial assets were located, the task of reconstruction lasted four years, and the yield of agricultural land in various parts of Europe suffered because it had gone short of fertilizers for two or three years.

More serious was a breakdown of economic organization, which showed itself in the haphazard working of the transport service in Central Europe and, above all, in the existence of financial chaos in many countries. The origin of this last phenomenon was the huge budget deficits which formed part of war finance. Among the chief effects of the resultant inflation was the destruction of the value of monetary savings, so that the revival of investment, which was necessary for recovery, was greatly impeded. Inflation also brought a great element of uncertainty into business deals. For the re-establishment of commercial relationships short-term credit was essential, but there were some currencies in terms of which no one knew how much a debt would be worth in a few months when it would be due for repayment. Business therefore became increasingly speculative and economic recovery was retarded, because it was difficult to borrow capital in order to revive production, and it was difficult to achieve a balanced budget and stabilize the currency until production revived. The financial difficulties were just as acute in international dealings. Inflation and the interruption of many branches of international trade had the effect of upsetting the relation between the internal price levels of some countries (including France and Italy as well as those of Central and Eastern Europe) and the exchange value of their currencies. Though such countries needed large supplies of imports, they were unable to pay for them because of their high price relative to the price of exports, and the low level of production made it impossible to remedy this situation by expanding the volume of relatively cheap exports. In these conditions foreign loans were necessary if supplies of goods were not to fall very low, and the activities of the American Relief Association saved Europe from much greater hardship than it actually experienced. Altogether the Association supplied food to the value of $1,415 million (£291 million), most of it in late 1918 and 1919, and of this sold only 29 per cent for cash.

There was thus great economic disturbance in Europe at the end of the war and, though many of the difficulties were of a temporary kind, the problem of recovery was complicated by the necessity for adapting national economies to changes in the international distribution of wealth. Countries whose affairs had for a long time been adjusted to the regular receipt of interest on foreign investment found this income reduced. Former debtors had become creditors, and former creditors, notably Germany, had come to have an acute need to borrow abroad. During the war the USA had ceased to be an international debtor, and by 1922 had become a net creditor for about £1,200 million, apart from the large sums owed by foreign governments on account of loans for war finance. On the other hand, British foreign investments had been reduced by about 15 per cent in value and French by 55 per cent, and the total German foreign investment remaining at the end of the war was worth only about £100 million.

Further difficulties were introduced by some of the political decisions in the peace settlement. The division of the old Habsburg Empire by the Treaties of St Germain and Trianon involved the drawing of frontiers which had little relation to established commerce. Some main roads and railways passed repeatedly from one new country into another and back again; the great city of Vienna was left without visible means of support; and the very increase of separate governments in Central Europe, each with a national consciousness to assert, not least by measures of protective economic policy, was an obstacle to the speedy revival of commerce.

Equally serious was the decision to exact large sums as reparations from the defeated powers. This was taken without consideration of the effect it would have on world economy, by causing international capital movements that had no relation to current commercial transactions or to opportunities of profitable investment, and by reducing the ability of Central Europe to participate in ordinary international trade. In the disturbed economic condition of Europe it was particularly unfortunate that the amount demanded was left unspecified, though with indications that it would be huge, for two years after the signing of peace treaties. The relatively small amount demanded from Bulgaria and the method of its payment were defined in the Treaty of Neuilly, and large deliveries in kind by Germany were specified in the Treaty of Versailles, but all other sums were left to be fixed by a reparations commission by 1 May 1921, though provisional payments were to be made before then: Germany in this interim period was to pay 20 milliard gold marks (about £1,000 million) and to give bonds or a promise to issue bonds for a further 80 milliard gold marks.

The reparation question was an important element in the background of European economic affairs just after the war, when the major problems were those of transfer from a war to a peace economy and the restoration of a sound financial system. Western Europe had not become nearly so disorganized economically as Eastern and Central Europe, and though inflation occurred, it did not become unmanageable. For a year after the spring of 1919, Western Europe seemed to be well on the way to recovery, as it shared with the USA in a strong boom, while stocks of goods, which had run down during the war, were replenished and arrears of maintenance made good. But in the later part of 1920 and throughout 1921 a severe depression ensued which delayed the restoration of Europe's full productive power and which was partly due to the inability of Central and Eastern Europe to take much part in international trade. Political changes and economic collapse had for the time being taken Russia almost completely out of international economic affairs and this disrupted many important commercial and financial connexions. In Central Europe financial chaos and productive stagnation persisted, and governments, too insecure to risk offending vested interests and perhaps a little inhibited by the belief that any fruits of recovery were likely to be swallowed up in reparations, failed to take vigorous action to improve matters.

The reparations commission announced its decisions on 30 April 1921. The total amount demanded was 132 milliard gold marks (about £6,500 million), and Germany was alleged to have made less than half of the interim payments agreed upon. No figure was named for sums to be obtained from the other ex-enemy states, and

Germany was ordered to give three sets of bonds for 12,38, and 82 milliard gold marks respectively, to pay 1,000 million gold marks in the summer of 1921, and thereafter an annual sum not exceeding 3,000 million gold marks, made up of a fixed amount of 2,000 million gold marks, plus the yield of a 26 per cent tax on exports. Faced with the alternative of submitting to an allied occupation of the Ruhr, Germany accepted these terms.

But by this time the practical question was how soon economic activity in Central Europe would collapse altogether. Germany, Austria, and Hungary were all in the grip of acute inflation. The value of the German mark, which at par was 4.20 to the dollar, fell from 8.50 in the middle of 1919 to 270 by November 1921. When in July 1922 it was rapidly falling again, Germany asked for a two-year moratorium on reparation payments in order to avoid financial collapse, but the French government refused to agree to this. Austrian inflation had gone further and the value of the currency (which at par was 5 crowns to the dollar) fell to 83,600 crowns to the dollar by August 1922. At this point the League of Nations sponsored a loan to Austria on condition that finances were subject to international control. This supervision lasted until 1926, and achieved a balanced budget, the stabilization of prices, and the introduction of a new currency, the schilling. Meanwhile, the German financial situation rapidly worsened. By the end of 1922 it was threatening complete dislocation of economic activity, and Germany defaulted on reparation deliveries to France and Belgium, who responded by sending troops to occupy the Ruhr in January 1923. Germany in turn retaliated by working the Ruhr industries as little as possible and pouring out new money, partly as payment to those whose livelihood was diminished by these events. By November 1923 the value of the currency had fallen to the meaningless level of 4,200 milliard marks to the dollar. It was then withdrawn from circulation and replaced by a new rentenmark at the rate of 1 for every 1,000 milliard of the old marks.

This financial collapse was due primarily to the continued refusal of the German government to make any approach towards a balanced budget and not to the demand for reparation payments, though this, of course, affected what was politically possible, and helped both to destroy confidence and to increase the strain on foreign exchange. But the collapse of the mark made it necessary to reconsider the whole reparations question. However unfortunate had been the attempts to exact reparation payments, it was for the time being impracticable to abandon them, because the allied powers needed the receipts from this source in order to discharge the intergovernmental debts arising from the war and its aftermath. As a result of loans to finance the conduct of the war, the post-war sale in Europe of American surplus war stores on credit, the continuance of American 'Liberty Loans' for reconstruction up to 1921, and the grant of relief supplies on credit, all the allies were in debt to the government of the USA, and all except the USA were in debt to the British government. The latter had lent to its allies about twice as much as it had borrowed from the USA, but nevertheless pressed unsuccessfully at the peace conference in 1919 for a cancellation of all war debts. American policy was to regard these loans as business transactions and to demand repayment, though no payments were made before 1922. In the Balfour Note of 1 August 1922, the British government made a new effort to dispose of the question by declaring that it would demand from its debtors no more than it was itself required to pay to the USA. But this policy merely aroused hostile criticism in the USA. and induced no co-operation by the American government, which was pressing for the funding of all war debts owing to it. During 1923, agreements were signed which settled the terms on which the debts of the UK and a number of smaller powers to the USA were to be repaid, and regular payments by these signatories began. No settlement had then been made of any of the debts owing to the UK or of those owed by the other major debtors, including France and Italy, to the USA, but it was clear that large regular transfers of money on this account were not likely to be avoided much longer.

The American government consistently refused to admit that there was any connexion between war debts and reparations, but the absence of any prospect of avoiding the financial burden of inter-allied debts was an important part of the background to the re-examination of the reparation question at the end of 1923, though the settlement eventually reached made no admission of the relationship. This settlement, known as the Dawes Plan, came into operation on 1 September 1924, and embodied a schedule of annual payments which were secured on specified revenues. The payments were to rise gradually from 1,000 million marks (£50 million) in the first year to a standard amount of 2,500 million marks which would be reached in the year 1928–9. A virtual moratorium was granted for the first year, as 800 million marks could be paid out of the proceeds of an internationally sponsored loan. Of the total reparation payment, 50 per cent was to come from certain federal taxes, 11.6 per cent from a tax on the gross revenue of the German railways, 12 per cent from bonds secured by a first mortgage on the capital equipment of German industry, and 26.4 per cent from bonds secured by a first mortgage on the German railways. Germany was permitted to pay in marks, and a Transfer Committee was appointed with power to suspend the transfer abroad of reparation payments if this seemed likely to upset the German currency or exchange stability. In addition, the shares of the various allies in reparation receipts, which had originally been fixed at a conference at Spa in 1920, were slightly revised. France was to receive 52 per cent, the UK 22 per cent, Italy 10 per cent, Belgium 8 per cent, and the remaining 8 per cent covered small amounts due to other claimants.

The introduction of the Dawes Plan was a useful contribution to a marked improvement in both the economic and political aspects of international relations about this time. While it was being prepared Germany had at last achieved a balanced budget, and at the end of 1924 was able to replace its temporary rentenmark currency and return to the gold standard, and the country was apparently far better able to meet its obligations and take a major part in international trade than at any time since the war. Financial disturbance was also being reduced elsewhere. The combination of an international loan and financial control by the League of Nations, which was proving successful in Austria, was also applied to Hungary in 1924, and there, too, the outcome was a balanced budget and a stable currency. In the same year there was a general improvement in currency conditions throughout Europe, and Sweden was the first of a series of countries to return to the gold standard. In 1925, there came a major sign of a return to a more stable financial situation when sterling went back to the gold standard at the pre-war parity in relation to the dollar.

Much was also done in 1925 to settle the question of inter-allied debts. Funding agreements in respect of their debts to the USA were signed by Belgium, Czechoslovakia, and Italy during the year, and negotiations for similar agreements by Yugoslavia and France were begun, though not completed until 1926. A beginning was made with funding agreements for the debts owed to the UK, though the major agreements, those with France and Italy, were not signed until 1926, and some others not until 1927. With the USSR, neither the USA nor the UK was able to make a settlement.

The introduction of a set of large and arbitrary additions to normal international payments was not a fruit of economic common sense, nor was the wide variation among the terms granted to different debtors a contribution to political justice. But the settlements did show some recognition of practical needs. Some attention was given to the debtors' capacity to pay. The capital sum to be repaid was reduced in every case, usually by a large amount; the annual payments were kept down by spreading the discharge of the debts over sixty-two years; and provision was made for remissions (varying greatly from one agreement to another) of a considerable part of the standard annual payments during the first few years that the settlement was in operation. The UK, in spite of receiving from the USA much more onerous terms than any other debtor, eased the situation by making greater concessions to its own debtors than a strict interpretation of the Balfour Note would have required. For the year 1927–8 the UK was paying £33 million to the USA while receiving only £25 million in respect of war debts and reparations combined. When the maximum level of payments was reached in 1933, the UK expected to be receiving about £33 million and paying £38 million a year. It would undoubtedly have made international dealings easier if both war debts and reparations had been abolished, so that international payments might be regulated by contemporary needs and conditions. But the debt settlements were at least not quite so bad as the previous uncertainty. The financial commitments which they involved were known in advance and provision could be made accordingly, even if it involved economic strain: and the acceptance of settlements of a vexed question lessened for a few years one particular piece of political irritation. There was, indeed, a reduction of tension in international politics, which was further helped by agreement on new security arrangements, embodied in the Treaty of Locarno in 1925. It had become possible for governments to concentrate their efforts more on economic affairs, both by improving the institutions of the international economy and by diagnosing and correcting weaknesses of structure and policy which impeded prosperity.

In 1925 it seemed that the world could at last restore the economic organization and resume the smooth progress which it had abandoned in 1914. For Europe in particular this year witnessed a marked change in economic affairs. Since the beginning of the war the less industrialized continents had been steadily increasing their share in the world's production. In each of them output had risen by at least 20 per cent, whereas in Europe it had declined. But in 1925 European output was for the first time as great as it had been in 1913. Rapid expansion continued; the European output of crude products rose by an annual average of 4.5 per cent up to 1929 – nearly twice as fast as output in the rest of the world – and by 1929 the relative European share in world production was as great as before the war.

The revival of production took place in a setting of closely woven international relationships which, superficially at least, resembled those of the late nineteenth century. International trade, which had been stagnant, again began to expand steadily: between 1925 and 1929 the volume of international trade rose by 20 per cent, though, owing to falling prices, its value increased by only 5.5 per cent. Its transactions were smoothed by the same financial institutions as before 1914. Indeed, so successfully had the pre-war system of international economic arrangements operated and so sharply did its efficiency contrast with the chaos of the immediate post-war years that, as a major part of the recipe for prosperity, an attempt was made to reproduce the old system as closely as possible, without much attention to changes in the conditions in which it must function.

But however great an effort was made to return to what was tried and true, circumstances prevented the new international economic system from being an exact copy of the old. Many exchange rates had been drastically altered and corresponded less closely to relative costs and purchasing power. The French franc, for example, was seriously undervalued from the time of its stabilization in 1926 and so was the Belgian currency. France had devalued the franc by 80 per cent in terms of gold, whereas the pound had gone back on gold with the pre-war parity against the dollar; but French prices, in terms of gold value, were far below British. Indeed, national prices in the late nineteen-twenties, when converted to gold values, showed wide variations in the amount of the increase over the 1914 level. Some of the difference might be related to changes in competitive strength, but more appeared to be determined by the choice of exchange rates at which different currencies were stabilized. The UK was the most prominent example of a country with relatively high prices (though its prices were probably not greatly out of line with those of the USA and Germany), but some others showed still larger discrepancies, notably nearly all the British Commonwealth and the Scandinavian countries, which had also kept the pre-war parities. There was a general problem that relative national prices and international exchange rates were very imperfectly related and this seriously disturbed competitive conditions in international trade.

The gold standard was not what it had been. Gold coins were no longer in circulation, and the internal convertibility of paper currency into gold was almost everywhere little more than nominal. There had, in fact, been both a reduction in the output of newly mined gold and, because of heavy international borrowing, a major redistribution in the ownership of the world's gold stocks, which left most European countries with smaller reserves in proportion to their liabilities and compelled them to adopt various expedients to economize in the use of gold. Withdrawal of gold from circulation was only one of these, but it had the important effect of making it easier to pay less attention to what had been an axiom of monetary policy before 1914: that the internal volume of credit should be varied in accordance with the external movement of gold. Equally important was the widespread adoption of the gold exchange standard, which meant that some countries, instead of holding gold as the basis of their currency and credit structure, held claims on gold standard countries in the form of currency, bank deposits or securities. In Europe alone, Austria, Czechoslovakia, Estonia, Finland, Italy, Romania, and Yugoslavia adopted a gold exchange standard.

This clearly made international finance more vulnerable than before 1914. Any serious strain in a country on the full gold standard was liable to cause great difficulties in many other countries almost immediately, and the shortage of gold made it less easy for many gold standard countries to withstand for long a loss of gold in times of economic difficulty. It was also potentially dangerous that the UK was no longer earning as big a current surplus as before, for sterling continued to be a major international currency, on which the gold exchange standard relied heavily. Still, despite these incipient weaknesses, the restored international financial system seemed likely to work satisfactorily as long as no very acute disturbances arose in other branches of economic activity, and the experience of many years before 1914 suggested that such disturbances need not occur.

One important cause of this freedom from disturbance in the earlier period had been the continuous international redistribution of productive resources, roughly in accordance with current economic needs as indicated by the market. In the nineteen-twenties, with a less secure international financial system, the resumption of a large and prudently directed international migration of capital and labour was as necessary as ever.

International long-term lending was in fact undertaken on a large scale by the USA, Britain, and France. In money terms British foreign investments had risen beyond the pre-war figure by 1927, if not earlier, and in the later 'twenties their total value was probably in the region of £4,300 million. The gross foreign investments of the USA (apart from war debts) rose to $15,170 million by 1930, and, though there was still plenty of foreign capital invested in the USA, the country was a net creditor for about $8,370 million (roughly £1,700 million). French foreign investments in 1928 were estimated at 50 milliard francs (£400 million), of which 15 milliard francs had been added since the end of the war. The old investments which survived the First World War had declined in value, partly as a result of further sales, but mainly because of currency depreciation.

But neither in volume nor in the uses to which it was directed was this international investment suited to the removal of current economic difficulties. The USA had replaced the UK as the largest international creditor on current account, but its combined long-term and short-term lending was much less in proportion to its current surplus than that of the UK had been before 1914. The result was that until 1924 gold and foreign exchange were going to the USA in large quantities. From 1925 to 1929, however, though the previous inflow of gold was not appreciably reversed, American foreign lending was as great as the current favourable balance of payments, and the disturbing search for foreign exchange in which to pay the USA was for the time being suspended. Once again, international investment was making it possible for balances of payments to be adjusted without great difficulty. But investment committed the borrowers to making larger payments in the future, and the trouble was that much of the international investment of the nineteen-twenties failed to contribute to an increase of saleable output, which was the only practicable way of helping them to do this. What happened before 1914 presented a striking contrast in this respect. Most international investment then went into transport and productive enterprises in relatively undeveloped areas, whose exports were in growing demand. In the nineteen-twenties a far larger proportion went into European countries, much of it going to governments, municipalities, and other public bodies which used it for the improvement of public works and amenities rather than in ways which immediately improved their power to earn foreign exchange and so meet interest payments. There was still appreciable investment elsewhere, notably in Latin America and the British Empire, which contributed to a real increase in production. This did not always, however, mean an increase in earning capacity. Some of the international investment merely led to a greater output of commodities (coffee was a notable example) with which the world's markets were fully stocked.

International investment thus did not contribute as much as in the past to the continuous diffusion of productive power and smoothing away of long-term difficulties. It was even more serious that the same could be said of domestic investment in many countries. Too little new capital, unwisely distributed, was a common situation reflecting shortcomings in both home and foreign investment and making it more burdensome to meet the higher interest charges which prevailed generally. Moreover, some of the characteristics of international investment imparted new dangers to the economic situation. In particular, the great increase in the proportion of short-term borrowing made the position of debtor countries far more vulnerable to sudden changes in world financial conditions, and the fact that many short-term loans were used to finance long-term capital projects made larger-scale default, with all its spreading effects, very likely if general stringency ever developed. The position of Germany, which between 1924 and 1931 borrowed £465 million on long-term and £586 million on short-term threatened considerable economic disturbance.

But in the later nineteen-twenties these potential difficulties were not generally recognized. Though international investment did not make the contribution which it could have done to steady economic expansion, it certainly gave a few years' respite from financial uncertainty. As long as a country continued to receive new foreign loans, it had a source of foreign income (even though it was called capital) out of which it could pay interest on previous loans, whether these had been put to productive use or not. And that is what happened in many cases. Part of the interest on foreign loans was met, in effect, out of the capital of later loans; for several years investors received the expected yields and the precarious nature of their transactions was concealed. It was not only commercial dealings which were thus wrapped in a blissful veil of illusion. The reparation and war-debt settlements were made to seem economically sound in just the same way. From 1924 to 1929 Germany made the payments required under the Dawes Plan without any sign of difficulty while considerably expanding its economic activity; but in the same period it borrowed abroad nearly three times as much as it paid in reparations. The USA lent money to Germany which enabled it to pay reparations to the European ex-allies, which enabled them to make war-debt payments to the USA – and so the circle continued.

Difficulties in connexion with the international migration of labour were more obvious. The problem of areas of dense population with a low level of productivity did not disappear; on the contrary, it became more serious. But less was done to relieve it by migration to other areas where labour could produce more. There was some international migration during the nineteen-twenties, but it was on a much smaller scale than at the beginning of the century, and its sources and destinations changed appreciably. In what had been the chief immigrant-receiving countries, much less unoccupied land was still available and new immigrants were coming to be regarded less as a means of bringing the natural endowment of the country into productive use and more as competitors who might undercut existing wages, especially if they came from countries of low living standards. It became the rule for the receiving countries not only to restrict the total of new immigrants but, by means of quotas and literacy tests, to exercise discrimination as to the countries from which they might come. The result was that most of the areas where population was increasing fastest, Southern Europe, the Far East, and South America, were less able to find outlets for emigration than before. In South America no problem arose, for there was still much unsettled land. Argentina and Brazil continued to receive many immigrants from Southern Europe, and Peru was one of the few countries in which Asiatic settlers were permitted to gain a firm foothold. But the USA, which had been the greatest magnet, was no longer freely open. Under the quota system more immigrants were admitted from the countries of Northern than of Southern Europe, whereas up to 1914 they had flooded in from Italy and Austria-Hungary. The most important source of immigration to the USA was no longer any of the old overcrowded countries, but Canada. Some relief to the pressure of population in Southern Europe was given by the need for labour in France, which during the nineteen-twenties received more immigrants than any other country except the USA, but there was little relief by emigration for the swelling populations of the Far East. Indians still went to Ceylon and Malaya, and Chinese labour also continued to go to the latter; some Indonesians left Java for the thinly populated island of Sumatra; some Japanese settled in their colony of Korea and in other parts of the mainland. But such movements were small in proportion to natural increase. The result was that the increased population remained where it was, and produced, at the cost of great effort, a larger supply of goods, some of which the rest of the world decided that it did not want. In this also there was a marked contrast with the nineteenth-century situation. Then the main threat of population pressure had been in Europe, and it was averted partly by heavy investment and industrial progress at home and partly by the departure of large numbers of people to other continents where they produced cheaply goods which found a ready market.

The restored international economic system of the later nineteen-twenties was in many ways a sadly weakened version of the pre-war system on which it was modelled. Its faults were to be found both in the design of its institutions and in its economic structure – the functional distribution of its resources, the pattern of its production and trade, and so on. Both sets of weaknesses were continuously present even while there seemed to be rising prosperity, and their persistence and interaction were primarily responsible for the eventual deep depression which undid all the repair work of the nineteen-twenties.

Many symptoms of these weaknesses could be observed, even at the best of times, without going far below the surface. One was the prevalence in most industrial countries of higher rates of unemployment than had previously been associated with expanding activity. There were great differences among the unemployment rates of various countries, but in several of them the proportion of workers unemployed at the top of the boom was similar to that in previous depressions. In the UK the lowest annual average rate in this period was 9.7 per cent in 1927, and in Sweden the rate at the end of each year was never below 10 per cent.

Another disturbing symptom was the failure to adjust the output of a number of the basic commodities of international trade to the level of demand prevailing at acceptable prices. There were examples of this among both primary and manufactured goods, but it was more striking among the former. One clear indication of it was the accumulation of unsold stocks. World stocks of wheat, which were 9,300,000 tonnes after the 1925 harvest, began to rise steadily thereafter, despite light harvests in 1926 and 1927, until they reached 21,300,000 tonnes after the 1929 harvest. Much the same happened to supplies of sugar. During the First World War the European output of beet-sugar had declined and cane-sugar production was expanded, especially in Java, to replace it. But after the war the production of beet-sugar revived with the assistance of import duties and government subsidies, until by 1927 it was back to the pre-war level, while the expanded output of cane-sugar was still maintained and had, indeed, been increased by the development of new strains with a higher sucrose content. The output of coffee was also raised far beyond the amount which the world market could absorb at a price remunerative to growers. There was a general difficulty that the labour force engaged in primary production for the market was increasing much faster than the population of the major consuming areas, that supplies were further augmented by the use of better technical methods, that increases of income in the wealthier countries were not devoted to the purchase of large quantities of basic food-stuffs, and that in other countries which were physically in need of more of these foods, incomes were not growing enough to make it possible to purchase the available supplies. The creation of monopolistic associations of producers, trying to keep up prices by holding stocks off the market without taking any action to reduce output, aggravated the difficulty. Canadian wheat producers and Brazilian coffee producers were doing this, and similar practices affected various raw materials, including rubber, copper, and nitrates. Iron and steel was almost the only raw-material industry which attempted to adjust output to demand. In most others some degree of over-production persisted.

In manufacturing industry, surplus output was a less common problem than surplus productive capacity. Expansion to meet temporary wartime needs, the spread of industrialization to new areas, and the failure of demand for some major items to expand as rapidly as before, all contributed to this situation. The demand for manufactured goods in general was growing relatively to that for other types of goods, but it was spread over a wider range of commodities, and the increase was concentrated mainly on more highly finished goods which could find a mass market only in the wealthier countries. Where goods of this type formed a high proportion of a country's industrial production and trade, as in the USA, they contributed to the maintenance of a high level of industrial activity; where older and on the whole less elaborate types of manufacture predominated, as in Britain, industry was less prosperous. But the weakness of countries which could not fully employ their industrial resources, because they were not adapted for the production of those goods for which demand was growing fastest, was offset and partly concealed by changes in the relative prices of different classes of goods. In the nineteen-twenties the prices of manufactured goods fell more slowly than those of primary produce. So countries that were highly industrialized were able to maintain a relatively strong international economic position by obtaining cheaper imports, although some of them failed to expand their own activity as much as was possible.

Thus the relative expansion of primary and manufacturing production in the world was not so well adjusted to current needs as it had been before 1914. In general, the expansion of production and incomes in primary producing areas then had enabled them to supply fairly closely what the manufacturing areas needed and to provide markets which absorbed the surplus output of the latter. But now the primary producing areas were supplying rather more of some things than the manufacturing areas wanted, while the incomes of the former were not growing fast enough for them to be able to buy all the surplus output which the full capacity of the manufacturing areas could produce. The disharmony was not very great, but it could easily make worse any disturbance that might arise in international economic relations.

The actual course of events only gradually came to reflect the strength of these various difficulties and dangers. For a time, moderate prosperity seemed widespread. The restoration of financial stability and the revival of international trade and investment had the effect of making the movement of business activity throughout the world much more uniform than it had been since 1914. By 1927 a considerable degree of uniformity had returned, and the dominant position of the USA as international creditor and investor caused the world economy to be greatly influenced by American conditions. In the USA the expansion of both production and profits was particularly marked. The manufacture of producers' goods and of durable consumers' goods, especially automobiles and everything connected with them, grew rapidly, and there was tremendous activity in the constructional industries as roads, factories, and houses were built in great numbers. By 1928 there were signs that some commodity markets in the USA were approaching saturation. The average level of wholesale prices began to fall and the volume of new construction declined. But financial dealings continued to expand, and a strong speculative boom developed. A fairly steady price level at a time when real costs of production were generally falling had helped to swell profits for several years, and an easy credit policy made more money available for the stock market. A rise in security prices, which at first reflected an increase in profits, was continued as a result of speculative buying for the purpose of reselling at a higher price. In the summer of 1928, the monetary authorities tried to check this wave of speculation by tightening credit policy, but they were unable to do so. Higher rates of interest attracted more money in private hands, both at home and abroad, to the stock exchange, and the price of securities soared without any relevance to the earning power of the assets which they represented. Such a situation could not last, particularly when industrial activity was declining, and in October 1929 security prices came tumbling down. Business confidence was badly shaken, economic activity declined, and the underlying weaknesses of the international economic system were exposed to strains such as had not previously tested them.

The financial situation in the USA had already had repercussions abroad. The attraction of money to New York by high interest rates, the expectation of a financial crash in the USA and some strain on gold reserves had caused several central banks to restrict credit and thus accelerate a decline in economic activity which had already begun. The situation was worsened by a reduction in the international investment on which the world had again become dependent. From late in 1928 France, which had returned to a full gold standard, was using its current surplus mainly to buy gold as a basis for the currency instead of investing abroad, and the opportunities of profiting by speculation were drawing capital into instead of away from the USA. Debtor countries were able to carry on for a time by using up the floating assets which they held abroad, but their position became increasingly difficult as American lending further declined after the stock exchange crash and contracting foreign trade forced a reduction in British lending abroad. The fact that some debtors had been able to meet their obligations only by continuing to receive foreign loans was at last exposed when the supply of loans fell off.

Indeed, the position was even worse because many of the debtor countries had still less income than before, apart from the absence of foreign loans, out of which to meet their commitments. This was particularly the case in countries overwhelmingly concerned with primary production. The caution induced by the financial crash late in 1929 caused merchants temporarily to draw on stocks instead of renewing orders, and this, together with previous overproduction of many primary commodities, brought prices down very rapidly. Primary production did not fall off, and prices remained low even though orders increased again. Countries whose exports consisted mainly of food and raw materials therefore found their incomes from foreign trade contracting quickly and, in the absence of sufficient foreign credit to compensate for this, they were forced to reduce their imports, which in turn reacted on the economies of industrial countries. By the first quarter of 1931 the value of international trade was rather less than two-thirds of what it had been two years previously.

The financial implications of these changes were serious. While primary producers were nearly as busy as before, they received lower incomes in return for their efforts, and while manufacturers had to accept at first only relatively small reductions in the price of their goods, they could sell much less of them, so that in manufacturing countries there was both a sharp fall in incomes and a heavy increase in unemployment. Everywhere government revenues declined, while in some countries the need for relief payments and attempts to create work introduced new items of government expenditure and increased the difficulty of balancing the budget. At the same time most countries, except France and the USA, had difficulty in balancing their external payments, though many of them succeeded by introducing severe restrictive measures. The credit of many debtor countries suffered, and in some cases confidence was so shaken that capital fled from countries which needed it to countries which could not use it. In these conditions the financial shortcomings of the international economic system, as it was restored in the nineteen-twenties, became a menace to recovery. The weakness of its institutions, the unproductive use of many foreign loans and the creation of a network of reparation and war-debt payments with little reference to commercial conditions left much of the world, and especially Europe, with a burden of debt that there was no immediate means of discharging, and with no recognized instrument for mitigating the difficulties. By 1931 the decline of activity had gone on so long, so many adjustments had been made in the form of lower costs, and so many arrears had accumulated in the maintenance of equipment and stocks that there was some incentive to place new orders and thus arrest the decline. But, instead, these influences were completely overwhelmed by the emergence of an acute international financial crisis which dealt new blows at commercial institutions and business confidence.

Though there were powerful economic causes underlying this crisis, its course was much affected by political decisions. Not all of these were taken with the solution of economic problems as their primary objective. Moreover, the problems were so severe that the search for immediate palliatives, without arousing political unpopularity, made it less likely that the main emphasis would be given to economic rationality. The new crisis became apparent in Austria in May 1931, when the largest commercial bank, the *Creditanstalt*, was found to be insolvent, mainly as a result of the depreciation of its assets, but partly also because of some withdrawal of foreign short-term securities. This last development was partly due to lack of confidence arising from the opposition of other powers, especially France, to a proposal for an Austro-German customs union, which, they feared, might be the first step towards an *Anschluss*. In spite of the unfavourable political situation, however, the *Creditanstalt* was preserved by the Austrian government, with the assistance of loans from the Bank for International Settlements and various foreign central banks. In order to prevent a renewal of the difficulty, restrictions were imposed on the withdrawal of Austrian banking assets.

The immediate effect of this was to move the centre of financial crisis from Austria to Germany. The latter's financial position had been deteriorating for some time, despite a reorganization and reduction of its reparation payments from 1929, when the Young Plan replaced the Dawes Plan. The cessation of foreign long-term loans in 1929 had brought difficulties which were tackled by a policy of severe deflation leading to a decline of economic activity, and the heavy poll of the Nazi Party at the elections in September 1930 caused a sharp drop in confidence abroad, which expressed itself in the withdrawal of about £50 million of short-term assets. Though this drain temporarily ceased, the dispute about the proposed customs union and the events in Austria set it going again. When Austrian banking assets were frozen, foreign holders of them sought to protect themselves by realizing those others of their foreign assets that they felt were least secure, especially those in Germany, which experienced large foreign withdrawals. On 5 June 1931 the German government issued a memorandum which expressed an extremely gloomy view of its financial position and mentioned the impossibility of continuing to pay reparations. This convinced the outside world that financial disaster was imminent and hastened the withdrawal of foreign short-term funds. In the first fortnight in June, £50 million of gold and foreign exchange left Germany, and in the third week, despite a rise in the discount rate from 5 per cent to 7 per cent, another £17,500,000 was withdrawn.

Germany's financial troubles in 1931 were coming to a head just before the next instalment of reparations was due for payment on 1 July. The threat of default called urgently for international action, and the initiative was taken by the American President Hoover who, on 21 June, announced his proposal for a one-year moratorium on all reparation and war-debt payments. This announcement immediately caused a slackening of the withdrawal of capital from Germany, but by no means ended it, as it was very uncertain whether the French government, in the midst of its disputes with Germany, would agree to the proposal. In fact, it did not make known its willingness to do so until 7 July, by which time the German financial position had become still weaker. Germany had, however, been saved from complete disaster by foreign assistance in the form of loans of $25 million (just over £5,100,000) each for three months from the Bank for International Settlements, the Bank of England, the Bank of

France, and the Federal Reserve System. The London Conference of
ministerial representatives of the USA, Belgium, France, Germany,
Italy, Japan, and the UK, from 20 to 23 July, agreed that when these
credits expired they should be renewed for another three months,
that the financial institutions of the various countries concerned
should take joint steps to maintain their existing volume of credits to
Germany, and that the Bank for International Settlements should be
asked to convene a committee of representatives nominated by the
governors of central banks for the purpose of considering Germany's
needs of credit. These measures of international assistance, together
with the relaxation in the drain of funds abroad in July and the
imposition of severe financial restrictions, including control over
foreign exchange dealings, limitations on bank withdrawals, and an
increase in the fiduciary issue, enabled Germany's financial activities
to continue in a somewhat improvisatory way. The Committee
appointed at the suggestion of the London Conference secured an
extension of commercial credits to Germany until the end of
February 1932, and on 18 August 1931 issued its report at Basel. This
document pointed to the necessity for new long-term loans to
Germany to replace the short-term capital that had been withdrawn;
without this there could be no sound financial system, but long-term
lending could take place only if confidence were restored by a great
improvement in international political relations. It also urged that the
reparations payments to be made by Germany should be fixed at a
level which would not imperil the maintenance of its financial
stability. This was an accurate diagnosis, but there was little chance
of the suggested remedies being applied in full. Something might be
done about reparation payments, but the political preconditions for
the revival of long-term international economic transactions simply
did not exist. Germany, and many other nations, would have to
carry on with the aid of a series of *ad hoc* expedients.

Though in the summer of 1931 Germany was preserved from
financial collapse, the general position of international finance rapidly
became worse. In July there were large withdrawals of capital from
London. The chief reason for this was the shortage of funds to meet
immediate commitments in many European countries. The absence
of reparation receipts, the depreciation of foreign assets and restrictions on the withdrawal of many of them, all contributed to this
situation, in which the easiest way to make up the deficiency was to
withdraw funds invested in London. But there was also declining
confidence in the soundness of sterling, which increased the drain. In
July the Bank of England borrowed £50 million from the Bank of

France and the Federal Reserve System, but this was soon exhausted, and by the middle of August British reserves of foreign exchange had fallen very low. No new foreign loan was obtainable and the government resigned on 23 August. Its successor obtained a year's credit which enabled it to borrow up to $200 million (£40 million) in the USA and 5,000 million francs (£40 million) in France. But the withdrawal of funds continued as many foreign creditors sought to restore the nominal level of their reserves, which had fallen because of the continued decline of stock exchange values on the Continent; and exaggerated reports of naval mutiny at Invergordon led other creditors to move their funds elsewhere. By late September the London money market had lost more than £200 million in two months, nearly all of it by transfer abroad, and, as no more large foreign loans could be obtained, Britain suspended the gold standard on 21 September.

The decision was the result mainly of temporary difficulties arising from the British position in international finance. Many British short-term assets abroad were unrealizable while London remained an open financial market on which every creditor could draw. But the events of 1931 showed clearly the vulnerability of an international system which made such extensive use of a gold exchange standard, and the inadequacy of British reserves to support the country's functions as one of the two chief centres of trade and finance. The proportion of its reserves to its international commitments, which had seriously declined as a result of the First World War, had not been sufficiently built up in the years of revival from 1925. This failure reflected the slowness with which British exports grew, and was thus bound up with the fact that a large proportion of the country's capital was invested in declining industries.

The British abandonment of the gold standard removed one of the main pillars of the international economic system, which by this time was so distorted as to be no longer recognizable as a means of promoting orderly material improvement. For the time being the nations could conduct their economic relations only by a variety of improvisations, which might carry them on until a combination of economic recovery and political wisdom should make it possible to rebuild an international system.

Something was achieved merely by playing the game of follow-my-leader. When Britain left the gold standard and sterling depreciated, an increased strain was put on the foreign balances of many countries, which they could ease only by depreciating their own currency. Up to April 1932, the gold standard had been suspended in twenty-four countries and, though legally in force, was in practice inoperative in seventeen others. By this time large-scale financial upheavals were almost over and, by one means or another, most governments had temporarily been able to adjust their affairs to the new circumstances. The exchange value of the pound had ceased to fluctuate much, and a group of currencies was being managed so as to keep a stable value in relation to it.

Much of what was done to achieve some degree of stability was the result of unilateral decisions by governments. Its effect on the international scene was to prevent things from becoming worse rather than to offer any prospect of general improvement. Indeed, the usual object of such decisions was to restrict international dealings in some way and, if possible, to take advantage of this restriction in order to improve the internal economic position. The abandonment of the gold standard made it easier to do this. Among other effects it not only made easier but, for a time at least, made necessary government control over the use of foreign exchange. Several countries were able to remove restrictions of this kind after a few months, but in the middle of 1932 they were still in operation in thirty-one countries. In most cases they were an influence reducing the volume of international trade. Other devices with a similar effect continued to be applied rigorously. Tariffs had increased almost everywhere since the onset of the depression and were still rising. The Import Duties Act passed by the UK in 1932 was a notable symptom of the change, for it ended three-quarters of a century of virtual free trade by introducing a general 10 per cent tariff and protective duties up to 33⅓ per cent on some manufactured goods. In some countries, including France and Germany, tariffs were supplemented by the imposition of quotas for certain classes of imports.

But probably a greater source of relief than restriction of imports was the familiar remedy of default on debt payments. Some debtors simply imposed moratoria on debt service; others were able to negotiate agreements with their creditors for some postponement of payment. The most important debtor of all, Germany, was able to renew the moratoria on most of its payments until the end of February 1933. In the summer of 1933, after Germany had imposed unilaterally a new partial moratorium, an agreement was made under which, on nearly all its borrowing, it was excused from transferring abroad any amortization payments and half the interest due. The unpaid half of the interest was replaced by bonds which could be retained or negotiated for marks in Germany or exchanged at the

Golddiskontbank for foreign currency at half their face value.

Although so many of the decisions of economic policy everywhere were made nationally, as part of a desperate scramble for self-protection, it was realized that the fundamental difficulties were common to a large part of the world, and that international agreement on mutual concessions and assistance might make it easier to overcome them. In 1932 and 1933 various attempts to improve the economic situation by international action continued. One matter which obviously had to be treated in this way was the payment of reparations and war debts. The Hoover moratorium was a most useful emergency measure, but by itself it did no more than provide an interval in which the problem might perhaps become less difficult. In fact, the problem showed no sign of solving itself. The German government in November 1931 asked the Bank for International Settlements, as it was entitled to do under the Young Plan, to appoint an advisory committee to investigate its capacity to pay reparations. This committee reported on 23 December that Germany would be unable to make the full payments due in July 1932. If Germany was not in a fit financial state to pay reparations, neither were other countries able without great difficulty to make war debt payments to the USA. But American opinion, not least inside Congress, had hardened against waiving claims or offering further financial assistance to Europe. The only practicable course for the European powers concerned was to recognize the obvious by bringing reparations to an end and to do it in such a way as to create as strong a political case as possible to put to the USA for a final settlement of war debt payments. After much preliminary discussion and haggling, this is what was done by an international conference which opened at Lausanne on 16 June 1932. As the resumption of war-debt and reparation payments was due on 1 July, the participating powers declared on the first day of the conference that all such payments would be reserved while the conference was in progress. Agreement was reached on a permanent settlement, which provided for the payment of a final lump sum of 3,000 million marks (£150 million) by the German government in the form of negotiable 5 per cent bonds which the Bank for International Settlements would, at its discretion, issue to the public after a lapse of at least three years. Any bonds unissued after fifteen years would be cancelled.

As the reparation creditors could not easily afford to dispense with income from this source if they had to go on meeting war-debt claims, the Lausanne Agreement was not brought into force, but payments due from Germany and war-debt payments due to the UK continued to be reserved until it should be ratified; and Belgium, France, Italy, and the UK declared that they would not ratify the Agreement until they had reached a satisfactory settlement with their own creditors. But in spite of negotiations lasting through the rest of 1932 and 1933, it was impossible to obtain from the USA any appreciable concession about war debts, and in the end the whole question was ended by the default of the debtors. Most countries never resumed payments after the expiry of the Hoover moratorium, and after December 1933 no country except Finland made any war-debt payments. The Lausanne Agreement was never ratified, but no attempt was made to abolish the reservation of reparation payments. Reparations, in fact though not in law, were ended.

The removal of this major element of economic weakness and disturbance was in a way a notable achievement of international co-operation, but it could hardly be regarded as an augury promising success in the treatment of other economic problems by international negotiation. To end reparations and war debts involved only the destruction of an arrangement which to almost every country concerned had become both burdensome and unworkable, and even this piece of healthy destruction was accomplished in spite of the opposition of the USA. Where the need was not for destruction but reconstruction, involving the sacrifice of individual advantages by various countries, internationally agreed action was far more difficult to obtain. The financial weakness and commercial stagnation which had afflicted Central and Eastern Europe were a serious obstacle to economic recovery for the world in general, and could not be overcome without assistance from outside in conformity with a common policy. But political rivalries and an unwillingness to abandon temporary economic props destroyed all attempts to secure international agreement on this question. Various proposals in the winter of 1931–2 for a Danubian customs union were firmly opposed by Germany, and a plan put forward at a four-power conference in London in April 1932, providing for uniform tariffs and mutual preferences among the Danubian states, the renunciation of most-favoured-nation rights in these countries by other nations, and a small foreign loan to meet immediate needs, was rejected absolutely by Germany and Italy. Another attempt to deal with the same problem at the Stresa Conference in September produced superficially a greater show of agreement but, though recommendations were adopted for the balancing of budgets and the removal of trade restrictions, little was done to implement them. The result was that the reorganization of commercial activity in Southeastern Europe was left conveniently ready to be fitted into the economic pro-gramme of Nazi Germany in the next few years.

Attempts to promote a revival of trade within defined regions were also either frustrated or only moderately successful. An agree-ment by Belgium, the Netherlands, and Luxembourg in 1932 to make successive annual reductions in their tariffs on each other's goods was never put into effect, because the British government objected to the infringement of its most-favoured-nation rights. The Ottawa Conference, called in the same year to discuss the lowering of tariffs within the British Empire on imperial goods, produced instead a set of agreements, the most important effect of which was to raise British tariffs on non-imperial goods. These agreements were followed by an expansion of trade within the Empire, but this appears to have been largely offset by the failure of British trade in some other channels to revive when the world began to climb out of the depression.

One last attempt was made to secure by international agreement concerted action to promote economic recovery, not within any limited area, but for the world as a whole. In 1933 the League of Nations summoned a World Economic Conference, to which the USA agreed to send a delegation. But the prospects of success, never bright, were destroyed at the outset by American financial policy. On 19 April, just before the Conference was due to meet in London, the USA went off the gold standard. Just when an effort was to be made to restore international monetary stability, the world's most important currency was left to fluctuate unsteadily for an indefinite period with no indication of what its value would eventually be. The reason for this curious policy was not any weakness in the foreign exchange position of the USA, which was, in fact, far stronger than that of any other country, but the hope that it might cause a rise in the internal price level. Early in 1933 there had been a wave of bank failures in the USA, which led to the grant of vast emergency financial powers to the new government of President Roosevelt. The prolongation of severe depression and political pressure, especially from the farming interest, made the government ready to experi-ment with inflationary methods of raising incomes by raising prices. The idea behind the departure from the gold standard seems to have been a naïve belief in the automatic adjustment of the purchasing power of a currency to its foreign exchange value. The external value of the dollar was deliberately forced down in the belief that its internal value would go down correspondingly and the prices of those goods which had a world market would rise. Since in fact in the first half of

1933 the external value of the dollar fell by 30 per cent and the internal prices of various primary products did rise and industrial activity did increase a little (almost certainly for quite different reasons), the USA was unwilling to abandon its financial experiment for the sake of the World Economic Conference.

In spite of the chronic addition to financial uncertainty thus created, the Conference was held and dragged on until 25 July, but the failure of the USA to decide what it eventually wanted to do about the value of the dollar made it impossible to introduce any very effective measures to strengthen international finance and expand world trade. Somewhat ironically, the only part of the work of the Conference which had much influence on future practice was that concerned with devising new restrictions on the supply of primary commodities. Several important international restriction schemes began there and provided an example which was quickly followed: schemes for wheat, nitrates, rubber, sugar, tea, tin, copper, diamonds, and potash were in operation by 1935, as well as nationally or privately operated schemes for many other important internationally trade commodities.

By 1933 the problem of rebuilding an international economic system was so difficult that even if American policy had been quite otherwise, the World Economic Conference might still have achieved little. There were in many countries fundamental difficulties of a structural and social kind, which had been building up for a long time, and which could be overcome only over an extended period. They could not be cured by international institutions alone, but they were a source of weaknesses that would have hampered a much stronger international system. For the time being, however, attention was concentrated on the international institutions, although it was an attention accompanied by so many inhibitions that there was little chance of agreement on effective action. Most countries had become so conscious of dependence on their own protective economic devices that they dared not risk abandoning them for the sake of a share in promised but unproved international benefits. Conditions were such that the introduction of any scheme which would provide some continuous and partially automatic means of regulating the economic relations between different countries had taken on the appearance of a daring experiment rather than a return to normality. Such an experiment could be begun only in an atmosphere of general political confidence or else as part of a radical remedy after a complete collapse of the existing international order. In 1933, when military aggression had reaped its first fruits in Manchuria and Hitler had just come to power in Germany, general political confidence was neither present nor in prospect. A collapse of the international order was beginning to appear as a future possibility, but it had not arrived. To restore international economic co-operation to its full former extent was for the time being politically impossible, and, since in most countries the economic situation began to improve about this time, the urge to attempt it diminished. Save in comparatively small things, there were few efforts to improve economic relations by international action after 1933, until another world war left once again the problem of rebuilding a shattered international economy.

CHAPTER NINE
International economic relations
1933–1945

The subordination of international to national considerations did not
mean that the intricate economic interdependence of nations had
been destroyed or even very greatly diminished. From 1933 onwards, most industrialized countries underwent a gradual revival of
internal economic activity and, though one element in this was the
use of previously unemployed men and equipment to produce things
which had formerly been imported, a slower revival of international
trade grew out of it. Productive resources available at home had to
be supplemented by imported materials in order to sustain increased
internal activity. Even where self-sufficiency was most thoroughly
pursued, as in Nazi Germany, it was impossible to build up home
industry without increasing imports of raw materials, and to pay for
these an attempt had to be made to expand exports. At the same time
a reduction of unemployment in many countries made it possible to
sell greater quantities of imported food. The result of these changes
was a modest revival of international trade in primary produce, the
volume of which, in the later nineteen-thirties, was higher than
before the depression. But the increase was less than proportionate to
the growth of world population. Moreover, although there was
some rise in current prices, which meant that the nominal value of
the trade rose rather more than the volume, the price increase was
less than sufficient to offset the currency devaluations that had taken
place. It did not add, in real terms, to the purchasing power of the
primary producers. This was probably one, though by no means the
only, reason why international trade in manufactured goods failed to
recover to its pre-depression level, although its volume revived
appreciably after 1935. As in the case of primary produce, the value
in current prices rose a little more than the volume, though values in
relation to gold were declining.

While the maintenance of the volume of trade showed how closely interlinked the economic affairs of nations remained, changes in the way in which international trade was financed showed how far the old arrangements for settling those affairs had deter'orated. The late nineteenth-century system of multilateral payments, centred on the United Kingdom, continued to function with some modifications until the world economic depression, but from 1931 onwards it was severely restricted. There was still a good deal of short-term capital available, especially in London, for financing trade in many parts of the world in the old way, but far more trade was conducted on a strictly bilateral basis than before. This was especially so in the case of totalitarian countries, which subjected trade to close central control. Ever since the cessation of foreign loans, Germany had had great difficulty in obtaining sufficient foreign exchange to pay for essential imports. To avoid this problem it tried increasingly, particularly from 1934 onwards, when all imports were made subject to licence, to draw imports from countries already in its debt on current account or to pay for imports in marks which could not be taken out of Germany. Much German trade, notably with the countries of Southeast Europe, was governed by bilateral agreements of various types, the effect of most of which was that Germany's suppliers were under strong pressure to buy as much there as they sold, because if they did not do so they merely accumulated currency or bank balances which could not be used for any purpose except making purchases in Germany.

But even where there was not so much direct government control of trade, changed financial circumstances encouraged a nearer approach to bilateral balancing of payments in international commerce. While it was still exceptional for imports and exports exchanged between two individual countries to be roughly equal in value, an approximate balance of this kind was achieved within the trade of various groups, each containing only a small number of countries. A change in the direction of British trade was an important factor in this development. A much higher proportion than before of the imports of the UK came directly from countries in which a large amount of British capital was invested. The surplus of exports from Britain to the tropics, which had been a permanent feature of international trade since the late nineteenth century, changed to a surplus of imports, and the surplus of imports which the UK received from the white British Dominions greatly increased. Consequently the UK bought less from the rest of Europe, and continental Europe as a whole bought less from the tropics and from the white British Dominions. Within these areas, however, those other European powers, notably France and the Netherlands, which had tropical empires, established or increased an import surplus from them.

The importance of bilateral settlement of international payments was openly recognized in such attempts as were made to expand world trade. Almost all of these took the form of agreements between two countries (though larger groups participated in a few) to lower certain duties, increase import quotas, or relax the exchange restrictions included in earlier agreements. The USA took a leading part in these attempts, and between 1934 and 1938 negotiated some twenty foreign trade agreements. But the lessening of restrictions in agreements of this kind was invariably very slight and made little contribution to the revival of international trade.

The growth of bilateral payments was closely associated with two other economic characteristics of the time: the absence of a world-wide monetary standard and the cessation of international long-term investment. For a few years an attempt was made to keep the international gold standard in operation in an appreciable minority of the world's commerce. France, Italy, Switzerland, the Netherlands, and Belgium remained as an important group of gold standard countries in Western Europe. The USA continued throughout 1933 the policy of trying to raise internal prices by allowing the currency to depreciate externally. But before the end of the year the price level was showing little response to this policy, and in January 1934 the USA returned to the gold standard with the dollar devalued to 59.06 per cent of its old parity. This was, however, not of great assistance in easing the difficulties of international payment. There was no certainty that the experiment of depreciation might not be tried again if it seemed convenient for internal reasons, though there was a minor safeguard in an agreement of France, the UK, and the USA not to vary their exchange rates without mutual consultation. The new exchange value of the dollar was, moreover, much too low in relation to its internal purchasing power, and helped to make the excess of American exports over imports still greater than before. The result was a very large transfer of gold and currency to the USA from the rest of the world, which made it increasingly difficult for many countries to maintain exchange stability.

The drain of gold abroad gradually weakened the position of the remaining gold standard countries, though France, the chief of them, had built up such large reserves that it could go on losing gold for a long period without monetary disaster. Equally important was the necessity for restricting credit at home in order to force down prices in an attempt to compete with countries which had depreciated their currencies. Lower wages and considerable unemployment were an incidental accompaniment of this policy and were a source of political unrest. By 1935 there were signs of growing weakness among the European gold standard countries. In that year Belgium devalued its currency, though still staying on the gold standard, and Italy's Ethiopian war imposed a great financial strain which resulted in a reduction of the country's gold and foreign exchange reserves by a third in six months; but by this time the working of the gold standard was little more than nominal in Italy. When, in the autumn of 1936, the new Popular Front government in France found that, without devaluing the currency, it could not carry out its policy of trying to promote greater activity by increasing wages, prices, and public expenditure, the gold standard came practically to an end. In agreement with the UK and the USA, the franc was devalued, and the maintenance of its new parity entrusted to the operation of an exchange equalization fund. Other countries immediately put restrictions on the use of gold, and only Belgium kept an open market for gold in exchange for currency and vice versa. After this the movement of gold had little part in maintaining the fixity of exchange rates, and seldom took place except in official transactions to rectify deficits in international balances of payments.

A reasonable measure of international monetary stability was still maintained without the gold standard. Various groups of countries kept the values of their currencies in a fairly constant relation to each other, and individual countries, each attempting to keep the exchange value of its own currency steady, contributed to international stability. But attempts to stabilize exchange rates were not always successful. The French devaluation of 1936 was not followed by currency stability as intended, but by more than eighteen months of continual depreciation. And there was little certainty that the relation between different currencies would not be suddenly and arbitrarily altered. This uncertainty was one of the monetary obstacles to the revival of trade. The other, more relevant to the growing practice of bilateral settlement, was the fact that, in the absence of an international monetary standard, there was no obligation for all currencies to be made freely exchangeable for each other. The extent of this restriction should not be exaggerated. Many countries did not exercise very tight control over the use of foreign exchange, and earnings in some currencies could still be used to finance trade with third countries, even though they belonged to a different currency group.

But by the later nineteen-thirties the currencies of the totalitarian countries could be exchanged only under the strictest regulation, and surpluses or deficits in trade with these countries could not be offset by deficits or surpluses in trade with others. Consequently, multilateral payments even outside the totalitarian economies were restricted, because the exclusion of receipts from trade with these left the payments to be made among countries with mutually convertible currencies appreciably unbalanced.

The almost complete absence of new long-term international investment during the nineteen-thirties increased the difficulty. In the past, international investment had not only contributed to the growth of the world's productive capacity, but had also made available a regular addition to the supply of foreign exchange beyond what was earned in current trade. It thus provided a margin for the adjustment of international payments, and was particularly helpful to debtor countries which needed foreign exchange in order to pay interest and dividends abroad. When international investment ceased, debtors, even though they were quite solvent, had some difficulty in obtaining all the foreign exchange which they needed except by increasing their direct exports to their creditors. Changes of this kind made it possible for debtor countries to meet their obligations to one of the two chief creditors, Great Britain, but the necessity of paying the USA had to be met mainly by drawing on reserves of gold and dollars. This was an expedient that could not go on indefinitely, and was one more sign of incipient weakness in international economic affairs. Economically, the rest of the world was becoming more dependent on supplies from the USA than the USA was on supplies from outside.

The cessation of international investment removed an instrument which, for three-quarters of a century, had helped to smooth the course of world economic development. Changes in international migration reinforced the effects of this removal. The old receiving countries took few new immigrants. Some of them indeed (Australia for example) had for a time during the depression lost more people than they received. France, which had welcomed many foreign workers during the nineteen-twenties, began to send some of them home again when it was overtaken by depression. The appearance of racial persecution in Germany and the preparation of schemes for the exchange of minority groups between neighbouring countries gave increased importance to population movements in which economic factors were of little influence.

The great reduction in the international movement of the factors of production was one element in a lessening of the unity of the world economy. The most important influence in that change was the greater emphasis put on the treatment of internal problems in the economic policies of almost every country, an emphasis carried so far in a few cases as to involve a deliberate exclusion of outside economic contacts which were not absolutely indispensable. The result was a rather greater divergence in the course of economic activity in different countries than for some years past. Production recovered earlier and expanded more quickly in Germany and the UK than in France and the USA. From 1936 onwards, the two former were producing considerably more than ever before, whereas the USA was only just able to restore its output to pre-depression level and France failed to do that. France, in fact, lingered in depression when most other countries were recovering and hardly shared in the general revival of prosperity until the autumn of 1938. The USSR, dependent only to a very small extent on dealings with the outside world, experienced almost uninterrupted industrial growth throughout the nineteen-thirties, and Japan, exercising strict financial control over a large part of Far Eastern trade, underwent similar, though less rapid, growth.

But in spite of these disparities, there still was an international economy sharing a considerable amount of common experience. The temporary cessation of international investment left untouched the intricate network of indebtedness on which world production and trade depended. The growth of bilateral settlements restricted the volume of trade moving in some channels, but still left most channels at least partially open. Everywhere the same overwhelming influences of international politics affected the course of economic policy, and at the end of the thirties a common concern with rearmament was helping to restore greater uniformity to the world-wide movement of economic activity.

The problems involved in reconciling inescapable interdependence with different national economic interests were fundamentally much the same as they had been a decade earlier and were still unsolved. Individual industrialized countries had learnt a good deal about the way in which monetary policy could be used to shield them from the worst effects of external depression, but had done little to lessen the chances of depression arising in the rest of the world. Primary producing countries which had seen their markets collapse catastrophically had discovered the extreme vulnerability of their position in the existing state of international specialization, and were anxious to remedy it in the most obvious possible way, by diversifying their economy with some industrialization. But they lacked the finance which was essential before much could be done towards achieving this, and the cessation of international investment meant that they could not obtain it abroad. Little was done to create larger incomes in these countries by higher production; the main contribution to their well-being came from attempts, some by governments and some by private international combines and cartels, to ensure a stricter regulation of output and sales in order that prices might not fall further. Nor, despite the recovery of the later thirties, did most industrialized countries succeed in using their productive resources to their full capacity or anything near it. Britain in its recovery never had less than a million unemployed, and in the USA about 5 million remained unemployed at the peak of activity in 1937. The incentive to improve this state of affairs was not as strong as it might have been. Internally, things were undoubtedly getting better, and internationally it was not difficult for industrial countries to remain solvent, as they were favoured by circumstances similar to those which helped to conceal their weaknesses in the nineteen-twenties. The great fall in primary produce prices during the world depression enormously cheapened the imports of industrial countries, and though the subsequent increase of trade and operation of restriction schemes arrested this development, they reversed it only to a small extent. The relative prices of exports and imports remained more favourable to industrial countries than in the previous decade, and it was possible for these countries to produce as much for export as solvency required, without working at full capacity. Full adjustment to changes in the relative productive power of different countries could be temporarily postponed.

Yet there was a whole series of related economic weaknesses spreading throughout the world. Most of the industrial countries were able to keep their foreign trade reasonably balanced because their demand for imports was kept down by failure to employ all the available labour and plant. To work at full capacity would have made it necessary for practically every such country except the USA to expand its exports in order to pay for greater imports, and that could have been done only by introducing more efficient methods of production, by changing the proportion of different types of goods produced, and by the creation of higher incomes elsewhere. But because the imports of industrial countries were kept down by commercial policy and under-employment, the incomes of other countries were prevented from expanding much. And because the latter had for the time being little opportunity to increase their earnings from foreign trade, they seemed to be unfavourable fields for foreign investment, which might otherwise have helped to create bigger incomes there. Moreover, because of difficulty in building up large excesses of exports over imports, few countries were in a financial position which enabled them to invest heavily abroad. Of the former chief lending countries, the UK, in the later nineteen-thirties, could never achieve an appreciable surplus on current international transactions, and net British investment abroad, which was certainly small, may have been negative; and the USA had experienced so much loss on earlier investments that there was no hope of more American capital being invested abroad for the time being without far rosier prospects than appeared.

These conditions were in many ways frustrating, especially because there were so many current possibilities of a much more prosperous world. There were new industrial products and new techniques of production, which had proved themselves, mainly in the USA, and which most industrial countries had adopted to only a small degree. Technology, particularly in chemistry and electrical engineering, was indicating the immediate opportunity for further advance in productive efficiency and in the variety of final products available to the public. A better organization of the institutions of the market was needed, and so was bigger investment, resting on more secure financial conditions and on greater confidence, which, once established, might be sustained by higher sales and incomes. Not everyone was conscious of the extent of the unfulfilled potentialities, not everyone was uncomfortable enough to feel frustrated by contemporary conditions. But there were signs of a search for a change. They could be seen in the intellectual quest for more productive economic policies. They could be seen more worryingly in the readiness of large numbers not to stop at protests against immediate hardships but to adhere to alternative systems of political philosophy and government. Quite quickly these last manifestations of frustration contributed to a growing sense of political insecurity and threat. But, despite these social and political pressures, the frustrations of the defective economic arrangements were not sufficient to induce immediate vigorous measures to overcome them.

In the course of the nineteen-thirties, the world established in economic affairs a new *modus vivendi* which was much less unpleasant than the state of chronic depression that preceded it. But it rested on very shaky foundations and had no prospect of permanence because it postponed treating long-standing problems without solving them. One of its characteristics was that highly industrialized countries maintained or improved their material standard of life only in part by their own efforts, but made up for failure to make the most of their own natural endowment by obtaining some of what they needed at very low prices from the rest of the world. The appearance of growing prosperity was in part the illusion of a transient moment, achieved at the expense of many countries where the diminution of poverty, which at best had been very slow, was interrupted, and at the expense of the future of the wealthiest countries themselves, who kept up their standards of consumption by using for this purpose resources which needed to be devoted to investment if the rising trend of consumption was to continue.

Before the difficulties inherent in this situation had time to come to a head, the whole scene was changed by the outbreak of war and its subsequent spread over most of the world. In some respects economic conditions were completely reversed. The world in the nineteen-thirties had kept down its production because it had not discovered how to organize itself so as to consume all that it could create. In the Second World War, even those who had previously consumed as much as they wished had to go short because it was impossible to produce enough. Some countries, notably Britain, which had been favourably placed because they were among the best markets for overabundant supplies, soon found themselves in the difficult position of being instead the hardest pressed customers for scarce goods. On the other hand, some characteristics of the immediate pre-war economy were intensified for new reasons. The neglect of new investment at home continued in order to make more resources available for defence and destruction, not in order to increase the level of current consumption, which fell sharply almost everywhere. Failure to invest abroad continued, and the realization of existing foreign assets accelerated under the same pressure to devote as much as possible to the prosecution of the war. Control over the use of foreign exchange became much more stringent and bilateral trading arrangements still more common, less in order to preserve financial security than to enable some of the chief belligerents to ensure that they squandered their precious financial reserves as slowly as possible and obtained in return the maximum benefit to their war supplies.

The administration of economic affairs became much more detailed and complex everywhere in the attempt to cope with the immense demands which war imposed, but in one respect the complexity of old relationships was greatly reduced. Though international trade and finance were subjected to the most rigorous government control, the essential international economic relationships underlying all the minute administrative detail were far simpler than in peacetime. The reasons for this were the division of the world into two large opposed groups, whose economic relations with each other were merely those of mutual blockade, and the vast extent of conquests by the axis powers which made it temporarily possible for economic purposes to ignore old political boundaries. By the summer of 1940, most of Western and Central Europe was under German domination and by the end of 1941 most of Eastern Europe had been added. It was possible to attempt the economic organization of almost the whole continent by methods of centralized direction which were mainly extensions of what had been in operation within Germany before the war. The needs of the German government were paramount, and there was no longer any necessity to safeguard the financial interests of the individual subject states. The conquest of a large part of the Far East by Japan in 1942 created an analogous situation there. Matters which previously involved international dealings were settled instead by arbitrary decisions made on behalf of a single dominant government or its representatives.

Outside the area of axis domination, international transactions between states whose sovereignty was unimpaired still went on. The major question of international economics was at first how the UK obtained its overseas supplies and later how the USA supplied the rest of the United Nations. A very large proportion of the international transactions during the Second World War was covered by the arrangements for payment within the sterling area and by Anglo-American arrangements.

The sterling area was an informal grouping of countries that kept a considerable proportion of their monetary reserves in the form of sterling in London and had a common interest in coordinating their respective financial policies. Its membership was very nearly the same as that of the British Empire; the only British countries that did not belong to it were Canada and Hong Kong. A few foreign countries, including Egypt and Iraq, were also members. The great influence of the sterling area on wartime supply came from the fact that its members pooled their receipts of foreign currency and withdrew from the pool only what was needed for their own immediate needs. They were prepared to go on providing supplies for the UK without receiving immediate payment in full for all of them. Instead of demanding cash they simply allowed the amount of sterling credited to them to go on accumulating in London. By the end of the war, although £564 million had been realized by the sale of British investments in the sterling area and was used to finance purchases there, the balances of the sterling area countries in London had been built up by £2,723 million, of which £991 million had been spent on supplies to the UK and the rest on the contribution of the UK to the defence of India, Burma, Egypt, and the Middle East. Arrangements which made possible large supplies from Canada to the UK under similar conditions of deferred payment were also made at the beginning of the war, and it proved possible to agree on terms of deferred payment with some neutrals, of whom the most important was Argentina.

The financial relations between the USA and the belligerents presented very difficult problems at first. As a sequel to the default on war debts the USA in 1934 had passed the Johnson Act, which forbade Americans to lend money to any foreign government that remained in default on its payments to the USA; and the Neutrality Act of 1935 forbade the export of arms to belligerents, forbade American ships to enter combat zones and forbade belligerent purchasers of American goods to take them out of the country until they had obtained legal ownership of them – which meant, in effect, until they had paid for them. The embargo on the export of arms was removed in November 1939, but the obligation of the belligerents to pay cash and provide their own shipping remained. For a time the main influence of the financial restrictions imposed in this way was to cause the British and French governments to restrict their purchases of war supplies in the USA to a fairly small amount in order to conserve their gold and foreign exchange. But as Britain and France were greatly in need of additional sources of supply, they soon became willing to spend their dollars more quickly, while attempting, in the early part of 1940, to offset part of this expenditure by increasing exports at the cost of cuts in civilian consumption at home. After the defeat of France, the desperate British situation made it necessary to seek supplies without reckoning the effect on the long-term financial position, and by the end of 1940 orders had been placed in the USA which, when paid for, would leave the UK practically without dollars. The American response to the exhaustion of normal means of financing purchases was the introduction of lend-lease, which became law on 11 March 1941.

Lend-lease meant that a great variety of goods was supplied to the belligerents, chiefly to the UK, without immediate payment. Nominal title to the ownership of the goods remained in the USA, and the whole question of financial settlement was left until after the war, though provision for some direct or indirect repayment was explicitly made. Lend-lease supplies at first were small because of the time needed to establish an effective administrative system, but after the entry of the USA into the war, their volume grew rapidly. The arrangements were supplemented by agreements on mutual aid between the USA and its allies, of which the first, that with the UK, was made in February 1942. As a result, the flow of lend-lease supplies was partly offset by a smaller reciprocal flow of goods and services to the USA, also without immediate payment. The enormous importance of lend-lease and mutual aid is shown by the value of the supplies exchanged under these schemes. From its inception to its termination in August 1945, lend-lease aid amounted to a total value of $43,615 million, of which $30,073 million (£5,628 million) was supplied to the British Empire (most of it to the UK) and $10,670 million to the USSR. Reciprocal aid from the British Empire to the USA totalled $7,567 million (£1,605 million).

The vast scale of lend-lease not only greatly reduced the amount of payments among the allies, but also made it possible for international trade and payments in other channels to decline. In particular, the UK, which until the outbreak of war was still the largest international trader, was assured of its necessary imports by lend-lease, and temporarily freed from the necessity for earning by exports enough to pay for them and to prevent the reserves of gold and dollars falling further below their already inadequate level. The export drive was called off, and a far larger proportion of the total British effort than would have been possible in other circumstances was devoted to military operations and war production. In the first half of 1940, British exports were still about 90 per cent of their pre-war volume. Thereafter they declined rapidly, until in 1944 they were, apart from munitions, less than a third of what they had been before the war. British reserves of gold and dollars, which were just over £600 million at the outbreak of war, almost disappeared by 1941, and though they gradually recovered, mainly as a result of the expenditure of the American armed forces stationed in the sterling area, they were only about £420 million at the end of 1944.

Thus permanent sources of economic strength were sacrificed to present emergencies, and the means whereby international transactions were normally maintained and, indeed, made possible were allowed to slip further and further into disuse. The financial and commercial methods which were part of the strength of wartime effort were also plain symptoms of the weakness which would need to be overcome when peace returned. On the allied side they were rooted in growing dependence on American supplies. The disparity in economic achievement between the USA and the rest of the world, which was already a source of serious difficulty in international commerce in the interwar years, was enormously enhanced by the Second World War. While destruction stalked the earth and the economies of many rival nations were ruined, the USA, simply by exerting full effort and without detriment to current standards of material consumption, was able vastly to increase its productive ability. During the war the size of the productive plant within the country grew by nearly 50 per cent and the physical output of goods by more than 50 per cent. At the end of the war more than half the total manufacturing production of the world took place within the USA, which, in fact, turned out a third of the world production of goods of all types. The USA by this time owned half the world supply of shipping, whereas in 1939 it owned only 14 per cent. Even two years after the war it supplied one-third of the world total of exports while taking only one-tenth of the imports. The change in the international position wrought by the war is clearly shown by contrasting the experience of the USA with that of the UK, the only other victorious major country to escape enemy occupation. The USA met the cost of the war entirely out of larger output, but the UK, covered only 40 per cent of it in this way, and met no less than 35 per cent of the cost by consuming capital and thereby putting future prosperity further into jeopardy.

Of the many economic difficulties arising from the war, this division of the world into one great creditor and a host of impoverished debtors was among the most serious. It completely transformed the position of international trade and finance. So many countries had incurred such greatly increased financial obligations, while their capacity to meet them had deteriorated, that they could not quickly resume their old place in commerce. They were forced to seek what assistance they could from outside, and to protect themselves by the imposition of multitudinous stringent controls over trade and finance, in comparison with which those of the nineteen-thirties seemed slack and incomplete.

The changed position of the UK at the end of the war was particularly important, because it had been the greatest international market and one of the two chief sources of international finance, and because its whole economic life had for a century been adjusted to an abundant flow of imports. The sale of foreign assets and the accumulation of debts to foreign suppliers, which together amounted to more than the total foreign assets which Britain held at the outbreak of war, made it impossible for her to take much part in international finance except by the gradual repayment of the sterling balances held by creditors. The loss of income from investments overseas and the reduction of earnings from the carrying trade, as a result of the sinking of 11,800,000 gross tons of shipping, made it impossible for the UK to import on the pre-war scale; and, in order to prevent the reduction of imports being too drastic, to offset the rising prices of essential food and raw materials, and to meet the claims of creditors, it was necessary to expand exports greatly beyond the pre-war level. Britain thus had to undo the effects of four years, in which export industries were diverted to other uses and foreign markets deliberately allowed to disappear, and then to seek a new commercial position in relation to the rest of the world.

Other countries were affected equally or more drastically by the war. France, like Britain, had ceased to be a creditor nation, and had a formidable task of industrial re-equipment in order to be able to compete internationally when the disappearance of immediate shortages made price an important consideration. Germany and Japan, previously important suppliers of goods to other countries in Europe and the Far East respectively, were completely knocked out and, far from being able to resume their old economic position, they became a charge on the finances of their conquerors.

The influence of physical destruction was far greater than in the First World War. The vast increase in the range and power of aerial attack resulted in damage to the principal centres of production over a very wide area and in serious interference with transport, on which commerce no less than armies depended. The area over which destructive ground fighting took place was also very much greater. It was particularly significant that heavy fighting took place in the Far East as well as in Europe. During and just after the First World War increased production of some goods in the Far East made up for some loss of production and export capacity in Europe. But the Second World War left some important Asiatic export areas with little surplus production of the goods for which the outside world was clamouring and with serious difficulty in raising the means of subsistence for their own inhabitants. This loss of production meant that the rest of the world became still more dependent on supplies from the Americas, and made still more difficult the balancing of international payments.

Physical destruction was only one cause of this upset. The administrative and social disorganization which came with it was equally potent and less easy to remedy. In many parts of the Far East the defeat of Japan did not lead to the restoration of stable, secure conditions, helpful to production and trade. Aspirations and passions released by wartime experience continued to sway the actions of large populations. In Burma, Indo-China, and Indonesia many men turned their attention away from peaceful production to political agitation and guerrilla warfare, and output suffered accordingly. Nor were unrest and disorganization confined to the Far East. In much of Europe there was severe political turmoil which reached its most destructive expression in the Greek civil war. On the whole, however, the economic effects of internal political cleavages and social unrest were probably less in Europe. One feature that was of some help to recovery was that though inflation was universal, it never reached the fantastic proportions of the period just after the First World War. The techniques of monetary management acquired in the nineteen-thirties had a useful influence here.

But the fundamental international political disagreements which emerged after the war undoubtedly had a great influence on the economy of Europe. The political division of the world into communist and non-communist, most strikingly exemplified in the effective partition of Germany, was also a commercial division. Important pre-war channels of trade were closed with little prospect of being reopened. Nazi Germany had deliberately sought to make the economies of Southeast Europe subsidiary to its own, but after the war trade between the western zones of Germany and this area had practically ceased. The fact that Southeast Europe had already been organized by Germany as a satellite economic *bloc* simplified the task of the USSR in subordinating it to Russian economic needs, which was done with great thoroughness. Though it was Germany that was most drastically affected by this change, the other countries of Western Europe were also forced by it to seek fresh channels of trade. After the war trade between Western and Eastern Europe was approximately balanced at a low level, whereas before the war Western Europe had had a large surplus of imports from Eastern Europe. For Western Europe this meant a loss of supplies which caused further dependence on trade with America.

There was thus an unexpectedly difficult political situation within which a solution to the problems of physical supply and economic organization had to be sought. But the nature of the economic problems was well known, for some had been left over from the breakdown of world economic organization in the 'thirties, and war had simplified some as well as exacerbating others. Attempts at long-term reconstruction were being planned before the end of the war and these plans were well advanced when peace came. When immediate emergencies had been dealt with, there was a prospect of creating a more orderly system of international economic relations than had existed for the last dozen years.

CHAPTER TEN
International economic relations 1945 to the early 1980s

RECONSTRUCTION AND NEW INTERNATIONAL INSTITUTIONS

In 1945 the seriousness of the split between the communist and non-communist worlds was not fully appreciated. Plans for economic revival and reorganization were made with as little regard to it as possible. Whatever the degree of comprehensiveness that was attainable, and whatever the extent of the geographical area that could be included, the requirements from a system of international economic organization were essentially the same. Any enforced adaptation to political constraints could be left until later. When the war ended there was an urgent twofold task. Temporary means had to be found to assist war-torn countries to repair the worst of their physical devastation, to turn their economies back to full production for peacetime needs, to resettle their uprooted populations, and generally to fit their commerce into a changed international setting; and an attempt had to be made to establish some form of permanent and stable international economic system to replace that which had foundered in the post-1929 depression.

It was impracticable to concentrate on only one of these objectives and let pursuit of the other wait upon the attainment of the first. Both were matters of pressing necessity, and neither could be fully achieved unless the other were at least partially secured. Few countries had sufficient internal strength to give them hope of regaining and maintaining a prosperous national economy if it had to be conducted amid confused and wildly fluctuating international economic conditions. On the other hand, the operation of a reliable international system was impossible without the complementary and co-operative actions of individual countries, and the ability and will of any of them to assist international purposes were likely to be slight until steady economic revival was being experienced. A successful international system required the creation of new institutions that would work less arbitrarily and with less nationalistic discrimination than those of the thirties, but less rigidly and with a more careful adjustment of financial resources to the likely demands upon them than those of the later twenties. But however carefully designed such new institutions might be, they would not last long unless some of the major countries using them could keep them healthy with ample reserves and a large flow of trade and payments, such as could originate only in efficient domestic production accompanied by widely spread and worthwhile opportunities of exchange and investment. In 1945 there were too few countries in a fit condition to make a contribution of that kind.

But although it was still too early to put them in full working order, the institutions of a new international economic system were by that time clearly taking shape. The design of these institutions was intended to ensure three important contributions to the maintenance of expansion without friction in the world economy. First, there was to be a return to a system of stable exchange rates, but with safeguards to ensure that purely temporary difficulties need not compel a country to choose between abandonment of the system and the imposition of serious damage on its domestic economy, and with other safeguards to enable exchange rates to be adjusted in the most orderly way in cases where permanent unbalance had arisen. Second, there was to be some assured supply of international long-term capital, such as had almost disappeared since 1931, and an attempt was to be made to keep it to more permanently productive purposes than after the First World War. Third, international trade was, as nearly as practicable, to be opened on similar terms to all nations, with the gradual abandonment of the manifold discriminatory restrictions which had been built up, especially in the nineteen-thirties, though there was less concern for the removal of general tariff protection of domestic industries against foreign competition.

The design of institutions to serve the first two of these three purposes was under discussion from 1942 onwards and agreement was reached at a United Nations Conference at Bretton Woods in 1944. To promote the restoration and maintenance of stable exchange rates an International Monetary Fund was created and was intended to operate in such a way as to help the return to a system of multilateral international payments, unhampered by foreign exchange restrictions. The Fund was an international currency pool from which members might be allowed to borrow in order to correct temporary deficiencies in their balances of payments, thus (it was hoped) avoiding the need to impose exchange restrictions or to seek a remedy through depreciation, either of which might cause general damage to international trade and finance. The size of the Fund was intended to be $8,800 million at the outset, but some of the countries for which provision had been made did not join, so the total subscribed fell rather short of the target. The quota to be paid was prescribed separately for each country, according to its size and resources. The greater part of a member's subscription could be paid in its own currency, but each member had to pay in gold 25 per cent of its quota or 10 per cent of its net official holding of gold and dollars, whichever was the less. A member which was allowed to borrow from the Fund was thus, to a large extent, obtaining the foreign currency it needed in exchange for its own domestic currency. A member's borrowing rights were limited to 25 per cent of its quota in any one year and in total to the full amount of its quota. The exchange rates in operation on 1 July 1944 were fixed as the par values for the future, but each country was allowed one initial adjustment of its rate up to a maximum of 10 per cent. Thereafter the exchange rates of members were to be varied only at their own request and with the consent of the governing body of the Fund.

The full strictness of the Fund's principles could not be applied in the disturbed conditions of the immediate post-war period. The Fund was too small and its formal principles had too little latitude for it to be a suitable instrument to deal with conditions of acute difficulty. It offered a means of combining security with reasonable flexibility in international commerce and finance, once the unbalance in international payments had been reduced to fairly small proportions. Until this reduction was achieved there was a risk that membership of the Fund might compel some countries to impose excessive strains on their internal economy in order to preserve exchange stability. In practice this danger was avoided. In the early post-war years the International Monetary Fund made some loans of currency to meet difficulties that were more than mere temporary disturbances in the balance of payments, and most requests for permission to use exchange control devices were granted. There was thus only gradual progress towards the establishment of the kind of monetary arrangements envisaged when the Fund was established. But a considerable degree of exchange stability was eventually achieved without constricting international trade or many countries' internal economic activity. To this achievement the existence and the activity and rules of the Fund made a useful contribution, though it was too small and too restricted in function to be the dominating element in international exchange and payments.

The second basic institution established as a result of the Bretton Woods conference was the International Bank for Reconstruction and Development, which was concerned with long-term investment for productive purposes. This body proclaimed that one of its objects was to conduct its operations so as to effect a smooth transition from a war to a peace economy. But inevitably its main preoccupations were less immediate. In fact, it was not in a position to begin operations at all until 1947 and, though it had an authorized capital of $10,000 million, shortage of funds restricted its loans to $700 million in the next two years. The great virtue of the Bank was that it provided a means of mobilizing international capital and directing it to productive projects the technical and economic soundness of which was thoroughly investigated in advance, but which were situated in areas where the raising of sufficient capital at a reasonable price was difficult or impossible. A project was unlikely to receive the approval and assistance of the Bank unless, when complete, it had extremely good prospects of strengthening the economy of the country in which it was located. On the other hand there were two severe limitations in the position of the Bank. One was that its available funds, though they grew, remained small in relation to needs. The other was that it could not tie up too much of its capital for too long, but needed to recover it and re-lend it for fresh purposes. The strain on the borrower was increased because of the need to provide for repaying the principal of the loan, and the assistance to development was thus rather less than might have been derived from a lender who was content to accept an equity shareholding. The first limitation could be mitigated by the influence of the Bank as a stimulus to the revival of private international lending, which was even more important than its own direct financial operations. Apart from setting an example of successful investment which others might like to copy, the Bank could provide such an influence both by making small loans for specific projects, in the hope of encouraging private investors to join in the same or related enterprises, and by acting as a guarantor of private loans. The other limitation became steadily more apparent and an attempt was made to deal with it in 1956 when the International Finance Corporation was set up in close association with the International Bank. The new body was an investing rather than a lending agency but was operating on a relatively small scale. By September 1959 it had accepted commitments totalling $25 million. Even more significant for the poorer countries was the foundation in 1960 of the International Development Association as a very close affiliate of the International Bank. The IDA had larger funds than the International Finance Corporation and it provided developing countries with loans on easier terms than they could otherwise obtain. The standards of creditworthiness which it applied were much less rigorous than those which the International Bank, by its charter, was obliged to use, and it charged only low rates of interest.

The restoration of non-discriminatory multilateral trade was an aim which proved to be less easily embodied in formal institutions. Even before 1939 the USA, which previously had been foremost in the erection of barriers to international trade, had begun to pay lip-service to more liberal methods, though its practical contribution at that time was slight. During and after the war it sought to use its influence more powerfully to end discrimination. The mutual aid agreement between the USA and the UK in 1942 contained a significant article pledging both governments to work for the elimination of discriminatory practices and the reduction of tariffs and other trade barriers. Discussions on ways of liberalizing commercial policy took place among officials of the American, British and Dominion governments from time to time during the war, and in the final settlement of lend-lease obligations account was taken of the pledge in the mutual-aid agreement. The American government was then in a strong position to press other countries to accept its views on future trade policy. The sudden ending of lend-lease with effect from 2 September 1945 presented immense difficulties to countries whose wartime external payments position had been dependent on its existence. The UK, in particular, had cast away most of its export trade as part of the common war effort and needed financial aid until it had greatly increased its export capacity. It also needed to ensure that the general obligations which it had incurred in accepting lend-lease were not now turned into specific burdens. To meet the difficulties the American government granted to the British government a credit of $3,750 million (£937.5 million) at 2 per cent, repayable in 50 annual instalments from the end of 1951,and the net liability of the UK to the USA in respect of lend-lease supplies was fixed at $650 million (£162.5 million), to be repaid on the same terms as the new loan. This rather limited assistance was given only on conditions that were intended to assist in liberalizing trade but were in practice not only onerous but unworkable. The UK undertook to remove, within a year of first drawing on the credit, all restrictions arising from the pooling of the dollar receipts of the sterling area, so that each country in the sterling area might have its current sterling and dollar receipts available for current transactions anywhere. It also undertook to repay its sterling debts to foreign countries as soon as possible and to support the American plan for an International Trade Organization of the United Nations, which would be a permanent institution to bring about and supervise a non-discriminatory system of world trade. This last undertaking involved, as a corollary, British membership of the International Monetary Fund.

Thus the attempt to create a truly liberal system of international trade was being pursued both by pressing potentially influential countries to change their own practices and by setting up international machinery that should work on clear principles to which all would adhere. But, with the best will in the world, no major country just after the war had the means to act in accordance with the precepts preached by the USA. The terms offered in connexion with the American loan to Britain showed no recognition that the latter, as part of its war effort, had drastically reduced both its international capital assets and its current international earning power, or that hardly any country in the world could currently earn enough dollars to meet its commitments to the USA. When, in fulfilment of the conditions of the loan, sterling was made fully convertible the easily foreseeable result followed at once. Anyone with capital claims on sterling and current obligations in the dollars that were so hard to earn had an obvious incentive to realize the former in order to meet the latter. In five weeks the British reserves fell by $700 million and in order to prevent the rest from melting away the absurdly premature experiment had to be terminated. From that time it was recognized that non-discrimination in international trade and payments (and especially the ending of discrimination against the dollar) must be approached very gradually and by means of close international co-operation. Even the International Trade Organization, on which the USA had set such store, proved unacceptable because, though it provided for international co-operation, it was not nearly gradual enough. Agreement in principle to the establishment of such an organization was reached at the Havana Conference on Trade and Employment early in 1948. The Final Act of this conference included a most comprehensive code for the removal of discrimination in every branch of international trading relationships. Despite the qualifying provisions and escape clauses in this document, so many precariously placed countries saw in it a threat to their economic defences that it was impossible to obtain the minimum of twenty ratifications in eighteen months, without which the International Trade Organization could not come into existence. Even the United States Congress, much less liberal than the executive, refused ratification. So in the autumn of 1949 this cherished project passed into limbo.

The one permanent piece of machinery which then survived for the liberalization of trade was the General Agreement on Tariffs and Trade (GATT) which had resulted from a conference of 23 nations at Geneva in 1947. The main purpose of this conference was the simultaneous negotiation of a set of bilateral agreements for tariff reduction and the diminution of mutual preferences, and no less than 123 such agreements were made. But the contracting parties to the GATT also pledged themselves not to increase existing preferences or to create new ones save in certain specified circumstances. The most significant exception was that the signatories were permitted to give increased preferences if this was done in the course of a scheme by which tariffs among the group receiving preferential treatment would be reduced to zero within a reasonable time. Thus the way was cleared for the creation of larger free trade or common market areas. The GATT remained in existence as an instrument for promoting simultaneous tariff concessions over a wide area in accordance with agreed principles. The number of countries adhering to it quickly increased and its administrators arranged combined tariff negotiations among the contracting parties at frequent intervals. In this way trade policies were gradually eased in the later nineteen-forties and the fifties, though it was only one type of obstacle to a non-discriminatory, multilateral system that was being reduced.

By 1948 there were important institutions of a new international economic framework not only in existence but in regular operation. They had a most useful, and perhaps essential, part to play in a combination of orderly economic expansion and reasonably stable international economic relations thereafter. But such institutions neither made up a complete international system nor guaranteed its success. Even in the most favourable conditions there were many gaps and vulnerable points that had to be dealt with in other ways. The International Monetary Fund was not big enough and flexible enough to be an effective regulator unless there were other plentiful sources of international liquid assets and ready access to them through growing trade and investment. Production in new areas and markets to absorb it were not likely to grow fast unless the activities of the International Bank were supplemented many times over from other sources. The more liberal trade policies promoted by the GATT could not go very far without something to assure rather shakily situated nations that better trading prospects were being opened before them and that something could be provided for them to fall back on if things went wrong.

In practice, most of these gaps were made good, to some extent, from the same source: the activities of the USA. Not only was the USA much the biggest contributor to the formal international organizations, but American loans and gifts, American spending abroad for non-commercial purposes and the liberalization of American trade policies together made possible a necessary increase in international liquidity, assisted long-term schemes of development and enlarged the opportunities of international trade. As other countries recovered and became more wealthy some of them were able to make a contribution of a similar kind, but the role of the USA in an international economic system remained dominant and central. Without it, international economic activity must have faced stagnation and breakdown, and new institutions and policies would have had little chance to display their virtues.

Even three years after the end of the war, however, conditions were still too disturbed for the new institutional arrangements to work satisfactorily, whatever assistance they received from outside. Until the acute disturbances caused by the war were greatly reduced, the new institutions were bound to meet both economic obstacles and intangible mistrust with which they were never intended to cope. Efforts to deal with immediate pressing difficulties had been in progress continuously since before the end of the war. Individual countries did a good deal by way of self-help. The victorious Western powers put money and administrative effort into the avoidance of starvation, the resettlement of the population and the re-starting of production in the territories which they occupied, and gave help to others which they had liberated. There were also specially organized international efforts. Most notable was the work of the United Nations Relief and Rehabilitation Association (UNRRA) which arranged the supply of essentials such as food and clothing to devastated allied countries immediately after their liberation. During nearly four years of existence, from November 1943 to June 1947, UNRRA spent about £1,000 million, of which about two-thirds came from the USA. Invaluable, too, though more for its humanitarian than its economic achievement, was the International Refugee Organization which from July 1947 to the end of 1951 was at work resettling the homeless and destitute, uprooted by the war and its aftermath, but which came to an end with its task far from completed. Some of the more permanent 'specialized agencies' and commissions of the United Nations also made a contribution. For example, the Economic Commission for Europe, established early in 1947, had, among its specified duties, 'to initiate and participate in measures for facilitating concerted action for the economic reconstruction of Europe'; and it did much practical work in improving the international distribution of essential commodities that were, for the time being, very scarce.

Yet, despite all these efforts, economic recovery in Europe and the Far East was distressingly slow and this had important effects on the world as a whole. The continued weakness of Europe, in particular, completely upset the world's trade and greatly reduced what had been one of the most influential factors in its politics. It was probably a changed and threatening political situation which did most to induce greater and more co-operative efforts to overcome the persistent weakness. The political arrangements in Europe at the end of the war had been framed on the assumption of co-operation among the victorious allied countries, but this co-operation had never been forthcoming from the USSR, which from the beginning would have nothing to do with a common policy in Germany and set out to make the countries of Eastern Europe an unchallenged sphere of influence for itself. Within two years it had gone very far, though not quite the whole way, towards securing this last objective and showed no symptoms of a sated appetite. The USSR, though it had not made good its great economic losses, still had immense military power and its political pressure at this time was directed almost entirely towards Europe. For European countries, continued economic misery not only reduced their military potential but threatened disaffection among many of their people, as the large support for the communist parties in France and Italy seemed to suggest. The possibility loomed by 1947 that, if things went on as they were, not only would there be an economic breakdown but most of Europe might be swallowed up in a communist empire. It was in these circumstances that efforts at recovery began to be concentrated most heavily on Western Europe, where success would have the most far-reaching influence, and to be directed in a more concerted way, with the aid of greater American resources.

In June 1947 the American Secretary of State, George Marshall, suggested that the European countries should agree on joint measures to overcome their economic difficulties and consider what aid from the USA in the next five years would enable them to carry out these measures and become solvent again. Every country in Europe needed such help, but the USSR, after hesitating for a brief time, evidently concluded that its acceptance would concede to the USA a degree of political influence that was not to be borne. The USSR not only refused to join in any scheme of the kind suggested but used all pressure to ensure that the whole of Eastern Europe also kept out. This was a most significant decision. It ended the possibility of both political and economic co-operation within Europe as a whole. It delayed the economic revival of the USSR and Eastern Europe and ensured that when it did come it would be within a tightly closed *bloc*, sharing to only a very small extent in the international economic activities of the rest of the world. And it served as a warning that helped to strengthen the co-operation and speed up the efforts of the rest of Europe and the USA – all the more so when the next twelve months brought further threats from the communist *coup* in Czechoslovakia and the Russian blockade of Berlin.

The immediate effective response to the American offer was a conference of sixteen European countries in Paris. These countries were able to submit a joint programme for consideration by the government of the USA in October 1947. An emergency credit of $537 million to help Austria, France, and Italy was appropriated in December and the machinery for the full scheme was set up in the following spring. The USA set up the Economic Co-operation Administration to deal with the programme of aid and the sixteen European countries concerned, together with the western zones of Germany, established the Organization for European Economic Co-operation (OEEC) to be the permanent administrative body for their part of the scheme. The aid programme came into operation on 3 April 1948 and was designed in the way most likely to be effective – heaviest and most general at the beginning, then more limited and selective as European recovery gathered momentum. In the first fifteen months aid amounted to $4,278 million, most of it in outright grants, not loans. In the following years it was gradually reduced.

This European Recovery Programme achieved some of its objectives with gratifying speed. By 1950 most of the participating countries were producing at least 20 per cent more than in 1938. The major exception was Germany, whose utter collapse had hampered economic recovery elsewhere and who had to begin again from a lower level than the other countries. In Germany the grant of American aid needed to be supplemented by political and financial reforms at home. These were forthcoming in 1948 when the attempt to maintain agreement among the four occupying powers was abandoned, the three western occupation zones were merged and most internal matters handed over to the Germans, and a new currency was introduced. Though West Germany remained behind the others for a time, its recovery soon gathered speed and in September 1950 output there was for the first time as great as in 1938. Neither there nor elsewhere, however, was internal revival matched by an equally rapid strengthening of the external position. In 1948 the members of OEEC paid for less than two-thirds of their imports out of the proceeds of current merchandise and 'invisible' exports, and with the USA alone they had collectively an adverse balance of $3,600 million. Their efforts to remedy this were hampered by the continued movement of the terms of trade against manufactured goods, and they also found that among their own increased ouput there was at first very little that could be sold competitively in the USA. Nevertheless a revival of foreign trade followed more slowly in the wake of expanding production. Until the end of 1952 the current deficits of the OEEC countries were rather more than covered by the receipt of aid from the USA and their reserves were higher than they had been when the European Recovery Programme began. From 1953 they could, as a whole, pay their way without aid and accumulate bigger reserves by ordinary commercial transactions. Even the special difficulty of earning, within the total surplus, a sufficiency of dollars was a little more gradually overcome.

Thus in the early fifties the European Recovery Programme successfully accomplished its main purpose, and through the great increase of production and trade in Western Europe helped to spread an expansion of economic activity in a large part of the world, as well as contributing to the greater political and military strength of Western Europe itself. The European Recovery Programme also provided both the example and some of the means for further co-operative organization, which altered the framework of both economic and political activity. The OEEC itself remained in existence after the ending of the aid programme until in 1961 it was transformed into a new Organization for Economic Co-operation and Development, to which the USA and Canada were added as full members. The OEEC in its later years was a useful medium for the discussion and co-ordination of matters of common concern in economic and social policy. It supplemented some of the work of the GATT by promoting the multilateral easing of the system of import quotas. Of the institutions associated with its earlier work the most important new one was the European Payments Union, established in July 1950. This was an arrangement which helped to liberalize the finance of trade among European countries and to use the greater financial strength of some of them to assist those who temporarily had greater difficulty in paying for their imports. Each member was allotted as a quota 15 per cent of its trade with other members in 1949. While debts above the quota usually had to be paid in full, only 40 per cent of those within the quota needed to be paid in gold or dollars; the rest could be left on credit. The 40 per cent was raised to 50 per cent in 1954 and to 75 per cent in 1955, a sign of the steadily returning strength of Europe. The European Payments Union was wound up in December 1958 when its members at last felt strong enough to permit full external convertibility of their currencies. Their example was simultaneously followed by many other countries, including those of the sterling area. Thus the European Payments Union had played its part in edging the world nearer to that state of non-discrimination in international finance and trade which had been sought ever since the end of the war.

As European recovery came within sight, there was growing interest in associated activities for wider and more permanent purposes. One early fairly small scheme was for a customs union of Belgium, the Netherlands, and Luxembourg. Agreement on this was reached by the exiled governments in 1943, but it did not come into force until 1948, when internal customs duties were abolished and a common external tariff was established. In 1949 the progressive reduction of quantitative restrictions among the three countries was begun. At the same time there was a growing body of opinion in favour of something at least equivalent, or preferably more comprehensive, for a much wider area. The chief motives of the advocates of such schemes were political – to end the old conflicts between France and Germany and to raise the political strength of Europe in the world – but they knew that their political objectives needed the support of economic as well as political changes. The first new proposal, made explicitly in 1950, 'as the first step in the federation of Europe', was the Schuman plan to combine the coal and steel production of France and Germany under a common High Authority, open to other European countries. Britain declined an invitation to join in the negotiations, but an agreement to set up a European Coal and Steel Community was reached in 1951 by France, Germany, Italy, Belgium, the Netherlands, and Luxembourg. The agreement came into force in 1952. The Community was given an obviously political organization: an executive body, a court of justice, and a parliamentary assembly. But its existence involved appreciable changes in two of the greatest industries. The reduction of tariffs and the gradual abolition of quotas were a start in the process of creating a balanced market matched by a balanced production. This in turn required the regulation of competition on agreed lines, which included openness in the publication of prices and freedom from the statutory regulation of product prices by individual governments. It also involved a concerted investment policy and provision for the retraining and resettlement of workers displaced by changes made in order to implement agreed policies. Such arrangements might have made the Community act as a rather restrictive international cartel. But this did not happen to any significant extent for the time being, probably because both the member countries and the outside world experienced shortage rather than excess of both coal and steel. It may have been this situation which caused the Community (unlike the later European Economic Community) to refrain from establishing a common external policy to deal with imports of coal and steel. This was a matter on which member governments were free to differ, and it left open the possibility of freer international competition. The Community and the UK signed a treaty of association in 1954, but its purposes were only consultative, though it kept the UK fully in touch with the detailed development of Community policies.

Quite apart from its political influence, the Coal and Steel Community quickly showed evidence of economic success. Trade across national boundaries within the Community increased much faster than production, and production grew more than in the rest of Europe. For coal this expansion was rather precariously based and soon proved impermanent, but this was not evident in the mid-fifties, when the whole outlook was promising. Such success was an encouragement to take the experiment further. For some time the objective of greater consolidation was pursued in attempts to build a European Defence Community; but after these efforts had been destroyed by France's refusal to participate in 1954, economic action was again given first place.

The new idea was to extend arrangements comparable to those for coal and steel to the whole of economic activity and thus to build up a European Economic Community, more frequently, though inadequately, described as 'a common market'. Such an arrangement offered scope for a new scale of industry and trade, for more efficient lines of specialization and for the liberalization of policies within the Community. But it was also bound to involve some measure of discrimination, perhaps a large one, against the rest of the world.

There were numerous countries, led by the UK, which wanted neither to make so great a political merger as an economic community implied nor to encourage so much economic discrimination. They sought to ensure that if a European Economic Community were created it would be within a much larger group of countries forming one great free trade area. But France would have none of this and, in the interest of political reconciliation, the other members of the Coal and Steel Community were not prepared either to forgo a European Economic Community or to shape it in a fashion unacceptable to France. So these six countries in March 1957 signed the Treaty of Rome, which provided for the new Community to come into existence at the beginning of 1958. It was an attempt not merely to achieve a common trade policy with no mutual barriers but also to make the whole range of economic and social policies and organization fit ever more closely together, so that in every member country there might be comparable opportunities of development in fair competition with the rest. The UK, the Scandinavian countries, Switzerland, Austria, and Portugal, disappointed of their hope of wider free trade, joined in the Convention of Stockholm in November 1959, by which a European Free Trade Association was instituted in July 1960. The object was to proceed by stages to secure complete free trade in industrial products within the area before 1970 and an attempt was made to keep the early tariff reductions in step with those made in the European Economic Community.

The European Free Trade Association seemed rather small for its purpose and some of its members soon showed a hankering for equality of access to the larger market of the EEC, which they could obtain only by swallowing their previous objections and becoming members of the Community, if they were acceptable. In fact, additional would-be members, of which the UK was much the largest, did not prove acceptable until Denmark, Ireland and the UK were admitted at the beginning of 1973. Norway, which had also successfully negotiated for membership of the EEC, then decided, after a national referendum, not to take it up. So until 1972 the European Free Trade Association continued to carry out its agreed programme of trade liberalization and succeeded in expanding the trade among its members somewhat faster than their international trade as a whole. It was noticeable, however, that the countries of the EFTA found that the proximity and prosperity of the EEC countries stimulated a specially rapid rise in their trade with them also.

Thus in Europe in particular (and there were in other parts of the world smaller and less elaborate attempts to create some sort of regional community of economic purpose among neighbouring states) there was the establishment of wider organization to secure greater co-ordination of economic policies for common benefit. The EEC above all, the EFTA to a less extent, offered a large area in which a bigger market was available on favourable terms and in which more efficient production might be achieved; and also presented the possibility that these characteristics might be a barrier to the trade of the rest of the world, which could enter the market only on less privileged terms. In practice, it looks as though the forms of organization were only partly responsible for the trading benefits conferred both on and by their constituent countries. The trade of both the EEC and the EFTA with outside countries grew rapidly and continuously, and this probably had less to do with the limited and falling external tariffs and the special arrangements negotiated with particular countries than with the rapidly rising prosperity and purchasing power of nearly all the members of both organizations. That rising prosperity must have been aided by the improved market opportunities that had been deliberately created within the organizations. In the EEC there was also the cumulative indirect influence of the habit of working together on some common policies, so that it could gradually be taken for granted by more and more businessmen, even outside the giant companies, that any firm could plan its affairs with a multinational horizon in view. But there were also many sources of economic stimulus that were felt in similar fashion by countries both inside and outside the new organizations. From 1961 to 1970 the exports of the EEC countries grew in volume at the remarkable rate of 10 per cent per year, those of the EFTA countries at the historically high rate of 6.3 per cent per year, despite the rather sluggish economy of the UK, the largest member. But it has to be noted that the rate for the whole world (heavily influenced, it is true, by its EEC component) was 8.0 per cent; and the EEC rate was less than two-thirds of that which Japan achieved without membership of any regional commercial association. Clearly, a capacity for vigorous growth was widely spread in the world and not confined to any particular kind of organization.

THE QUARTER CENTURY OF BOOM

From the time that European recovery was well in progress, the world entered a spell of unusually rapid economic growth that was sustained without significant interruption for a quarter of a century. The increase in world production of agricultural goods was 32 per cent between 1948 and 1958 and 30 per cent between 1958 and 1968; of minerals 40 per cent in the first of these decades and 58 per cent in the second; of manufactures 60 per cent in the earlier and 100 per cent in the later decade. The volume of exports of the non-communist countries grew even faster: 83 per cent from 1948 to 1958 and 113 per cent from 1958 to 1968. In the early nineteen-seventies, at least down to 1973, growth was somewhat more erratic but still generally of similar orders of magnitude. The growth of aggregate production of goods and services fell below the rate for the sixties in 1970 but recovered again from the latter half of 1971 to 1973, despite a slight fall in agricultural production in 1972. The growth of the volume of exports also fell temporarily and recovered again in 1972. All these figures suggest a widely diffused economic expansion over a long period, but one in which manufacturing countries took a disproportionate share. The distribution of international trade bears this out. The exports of the industrial countries of North America, Western Europe and Japan doubled between 1948 and 1958, while those of the rest of the world rose by 52 per cent. In the next ten years, in value terms, the former group increased their exports by 136 per cent, the rest by 92 per cent. In 1968 70 per cent of all exports, by value, came from the countries with developed market economies and 11 per cent from the centrally planned economies, several of which were substantially industrialized. A further illustration of the growing influence of manufactures is provided by their rapidly rising share in international trade. At least since the eighteen-seventies trade in primary produce had regularly far exceeded that in manufactures, but during the nineteen-fifties this old relationship was upset and by 1957 world trade in manufactures was slightly exceeding that in primary produce. Thereafter the divergence in favour of manufactures became greater. Between 1958 and 1968, in the non-communist countries, exports of manufactures grew in volume by 139 per cent, of fuels by 125 per cent, but of raw materials other than fuels only by 63 per cent and of foodstuffs only by 52 per cent. The rising international sales of manufactures were clearly not attributable to a relative decline in their price. On the contrary, the terms of trade which had swung heavily against industrial countries since 1939, began to reverse themselves after the end of the Korean war in 1951. Not until 1971 did they again start to move in favour of primary producing countries.

Yet it would be a mistake to assume that the rising proportionate strength of industrial countries and the trend of the terms of trade left primary producers with little chance of progress. Had this been so, the outlook for most of the world's poorer countries, which relied overwhelmingly on primary production, would have been bleak indeed. But in fact, although the exports of primary produce grew more slowly than those of manufactures, their absolute increase was large in comparison with the growth achieved at most times in the recent past. This increase was a source of extra income and of increased importing capacity, which could provide the means for some acceleration of general economic development. Already in the fifties some relatively poor primary producing countries were adopting policies which explicitly sought to initiate economic growth by means of larger investment and a diversification of output, including some industrialization. It became fairly common for 12 per cent or more of the gross domestic product of an under-developed country to be devoted to gross domestic fixed capital formation. One result in the 'fifties was that many such countries increased their gross domestic product at an average of at least 4.5 per cent per annum. Indeed, the primary producing countries as a whole, excluding those few (such as Australia and New Zealand) that were already highly developed and the special cases of large oil producers, increased their national incomes at an average rate of 3.8 per cent per year between 1950 and 1958. This was much higher than anything known in the second quarter of the twentieth century. Though the figures to support the suggestion do not exist, it was probably higher than the primary producing countries as a whole had ever known before.

What was demonstrated in the 'fifties as attainable by some was adopted in the sixties as an objective for all. The United Nations designated the 'sixties as the First Development Decade and suggested that what it classified as 'developing market economies' should aim to increase their total production by an average of 5 per cent a year. In fact, the 'sixties proved to be a decade of more rapidly growing trade than the 'fifties, and this large group of countries as a whole succeeded in increasing production at an average annual rate of 5.5 per cent. There was a fairly wide dispersion about this average, the rate for African countries falling somewhat short of the 5 per cent target, while that for West Asia, where several countries relied on oil production, rose above 8 per cent. Nevertheless, the achievement was encouraging enough for the 'seventies to be designated as a Second Development Decade, with the target increase in annual total production raised to 6 per cent. The results in the early 'seventies would have been thought remarkable by any earlier generation but appeared to be falling short of what was wanted. The group as a whole still surpassed the 5 per cent target of the 'sixties but did not improve on its performance then.

There were, in fact, several ways in which the maintenance of the rapid advance of the poorer primary producers always appeared vulnerable. One problem, not likely to be insoluble as long as the world economy enjoyed sustained prosperity but threatening in other conditions, was that of finance. The rising international earnings of the developing countries provided less than enough to pay for those essentials of further development which they could obtain only from abroad. In the ten years ending in 1959 the external expenditure of primary producing countries exceeded their income from abroad by at least $33,000 million, and probably more. Their imports averaged about 10 per cent more than their exports and their accumulated borrowings built up their debt service liabilities to another 6 per cent of their export earnings. In such conditions the rapid economic growth of primary producers could continue only because wealthier, more industrialized countries were able and willing to finance this fairly wide gap. Despite a more rapid growth of exports the same sort of situation persisted in the sixties and seventies. Some of the help came from international institutions established to assist development. From their inception until the middle of 1971 the International Bank for Reconstruction and Development made effective loans totalling $9,980 million, the International Development Association issued effective development credits of $3,013 million, and the International Finance Corporation made operational investments of $528 million. Well over one-third of the IDA credits went to India and about one-third to Pakistan. Mexico, Brazil, India, and Colombia were the largest borrowers from the IBRD, together receiving over one-quarter of the total loans, and Brazil, India, Turkey, and Pakistan received the biggest share of IFC investments, together about 30 per cent of the total. The change in the character of this group of associated institutions after 1960, when they began to function less on banking principles and more as agencies of development, was particularly helpful because it meant that their activities imposed less of a burden of debt service. This was vital because most of the finance to make up the balance came from individual governments and private sources, and, though a good deal of the government aid was in the form of outright grants, much was on commercial terms or something near to them. By the early sixties India and Pakistan were so much indebted as to be in danger of exhausting their credit and some Latin American countries were spending 20 to 25 per cent of their export receipts on debt service. A continuance of complete reliance on orthodox methods of bridging balance of payments deficits would, in such cases, have been likely to bring economic improvement to a halt. The provision of aid and 'soft' loans strengthened the power of the borrowers to take on other commitments on commercial terms and the deficits of developing countries continued to be sustained.

Other potential points of weakness remained more evident. One was that, although the developing countries relied predominantly on agriculture and, despite all their success in diversification, were likely to need to do so for a very long time, their efforts at advancement were much less successful in agriculture than in industry. For instance, in the decade 1961–70 their average annual rate of increase of production was 7.1 per cent for industry but only 2.8 per cent for agriculture, and in the early 'seventies the rate for agriculture went lower, and for 1972 even became negative. This was all the more disquieting for countries whose rate of development fell appreciably below the average for the developing countries as a whole. At the beginning of the Second Development Decade about half the developing countries were falling short of the growth rate suggested for the First Development Decade. By 1972 about one in five of these countries was experiencing, temporarily at least, a decline in income per head. Among the countries in this unhappy situation was one of the biggest, India, which had been among the largest recipients of intergovernmental finance. In India the level of food production per head, which had been rising steadily in the later 'sixties, fell in the early seventies below what it had been in the early 'sixties. Any such setbacks to the expansion of food production in large areas were particularly serious because of the accelerated growth of population. To produce enough food for the vastly increased numbers of people was a task which involved the whole world, for the whole world, in differing degrees, would share in the suffering if it were not accomplished; but the burden of providing for bigger populations tended to fall first and most heavily on some of the developing countries. Many of these had rates of population growth appreciably higher than any ever experienced by the countries that are now well developed. The effort to feed the extra population had to absorb a large part of the resources available for economic expansion and was a distraction from the pursuit of other activities in which more productive techniques were available. Thus the best estimates of the agricultural population suggest that, as a proportion of the total population, it fell between 1950 and 1965 only from 66 per cent to 64 per cent in Asia (excluding China and the USSR) and from 76 per cent to 74 per cent in Africa. When the provision of adequate food ran into difficulties despite this continued concentration of labour on its production the whole programme of economic development became more precarious. Moreover, the fruits of the achievement in expanding production dwindled significantly when they were considered as contributions to individual living standards. It was a common experience in the developing countries for average annual increases in income per head to fall 2.5 to 3 per cent below the rates for total national production. In countries whose growth rates fell significantly below the targets set for the Development Decades that could mean very little economic advance for most individuals.

There were, then, both brighter and darker sides to the economic achievement of the poorer primary producing countries. A few of them, especially some of those which became large producers of petroleum, took giant steps forward out of poverty; and a greater number, including some without the advantage of oil reserves, moved into a much less uncomfortable economic position. Most of them increased their activity and output at a rate unknown before. In this respect they shared substantially in what was probably the greatest phase of economic expansion the world had experienced. But for most of them there was no advance in their relative position in the world. In the 'sixties the developing countries increased their aggregate production by 5.5 per cent per year, compared with 5.0 per cent by the developed countries. But differences in population growth took away that small advantage when it was translated into increases per head; and, even if this had not been the case, to have grown only 0.5 per cent per year faster than countries whose product was already many times higher merely meant that the absolute increment achieved by the developing countries fell far short of that achieved by the already developed. In absolute terms the developing countries, despite having speeded up their growth, fell further behind the developed, year by year. Even in agriculture, in which many of the developing countries had long had a role as specialist suppliers in the world economy, their position in terms of relative efficiency was becoming somewhat weaker. In the 'sixties the developed countries increased their agricultural production at an average of 2.5 per cent per year, which was nearly as fast as the developing countries. But the former group achieved this expansion with a sharply reduced labour force, unlike the latter. Between 1950 and

1965 the agricultural population as a proportion of the total population fell from 33 per cent to 23 per cent in Europe and from 14 per cent to 6 per cent in North America.

All this suggests that the engine of growth of the world economy was located in the developed industrial countries. In looking for an explanation of the great surge of economic growth that characterized the third quarter of the twentieth century, one is bound to concentrate attention on factors that originated with them. But it is necessary also to take into account some conditions which they shared with other types of country and some which were transmitted between them and others, for rapid economic growth occurred in this period in economies of all types. It was equally prominent in the centrally planned economies. Indeed, the communist countries of Eastern Europe and Russia claimed higher growth rates than the rest, though differences in national accounting practice made comparison very difficult: in the decade 1961–70 their net material product rose at an average of 6.7 per cent per year. And, when all the reservations about the outcome have been made, the developing countries had a continuous rise in output that hardly any observers in 1950 would have thought was anywhere near attainable.

The strongest and most universal stimulus to growth was probably the rapid progress in technology, above all in chemicals and engineering, which developed new products and new processes for the needs of every branch of activity. Agriculture, mining, transport and communication, and services were just as much affected as manufacture. It was a continual progress in which the dominance of the mechanical was increasingly supplemented by the electrical and the electronic. Most of the innovations originated within a few already industrialized countries, and some were only improvements (more widely adopted, and developed with a greater number of variations for different purposes) on what had been done before 1945 in the most technologically advanced regions. But they soon spread their influence, through foreign sales, licence agreements, the establishment of foreign subsidiaries, to take advantage of potential new markets, and through the international movement of trained men. Yet technological progress also had outside help. One source was the emergence of apparently ever-increasing and cheaper supplies of energy, especially in the form of oil and natural gas. This was, of course, an advantage attributable in part to the application of new technical expertise in mineral exploration and extraction; but it owed something to the readiness of owners of finite fuel resources to dispose of them without regard to the covering of long term depletion costs. There was some possibility that greater immediate growth was being sought at the expense of future resource supplies. But the greater ease obtained in this way was itself a stimulus to the exercise of further ingenuity and to higher investment, in the confident belief that lower costs brought in a constantly growing number of consumers. Such conditions facilitated the maintenance of both a high level of employment and a high rate of economic growth. These were objectives which intellectual enquiry had placed more plainly within what was regarded as the manageable ambit of governmental policy. Both the Keynesian theory of employment (often adopted in a somewhat crude way by politicians) and the detailed analysis of the historical statistics of economic growth played their part. The achievement of nearly full employment in practically all industrial countries, whether by deliberate policy or good fortune or a mixture of the two, stimulated the whole world economy. These countries became richer markets and their sustained activity enabled them to achieve longer runs and a more economical scale in many types of production. This, in turn, helped them to become bigger and more efficient exporters.

But domestic full employment policies alone were not enough, nor could they be maintained indefinitely without other aids. In particular, they needed to be supplemented by stable and expansive international commercial and financial arrangements. Full employment created, among other things, a higher demand for imports; and, sooner or later, there was bound to be a hiatus if these could not be paid for out of income earned abroad. So there had to be a general widening of export opportunities and the provision of regularly available finance for the expanding volume of international trade. Even centrally planned communist economies felt this need. As well as orthodox trading activities their answer to it involved exchanges or one-way transfers of goods in accordance with political decisions that reflected both mutually agreed plans and a very uneven distribution of power within the communist *bloc*. For other countries the response came partly through the normal readiness of businessmen to grasp enlarging opportunities, and partly through the succession of international agreements which progressively liberalized commercial policies; but it also had to come to a great extent through the continual adaptation of the international financial system to changing conditions. In many ways the characteristics of that system were not only the most important means of smoothing out any potential frictions in the process of worldwide economic expansion but also the clearest indicators of the extent to which the underlying conditions for continued expansion still remained.

The most important requirements of international finance were that it should be abundant and secure. There was a need for internationally acceptable liquid funds to be always readily available on a scale adequate to finance all current needs for sound trade and investment, and for transactions with those funds to be regarded with confidence, both because the exchange value was predictable and because there would be no risk of government action preventing the full transfer of what was due. These needs had been met fairly well by the arrangements, built up after the Second World War and in the 'fifties, which have already been described. The commitment, under the Bretton Woods system, to fixed exchange rates, adjustable only in special circumstances, gave the desired degree of stability. The readiness of the USA, while it was still heavily in surplus, to return dollars to the international pool through gifts, loans and investments, kept the supply of international money adequate though not over-flowing; and in the 'fifties liquidity was further aided by the sterling which the UK's import surplus helped to make available, and by the arrangements in the European Payments Union which enabled coun-tries temporarily in deficit to economize in the use of convertible foreign exchange. And the rapid reconstruction of the European economy, with gradual moves towards currency convertibility, brought steadily increasing confidence in the security of international transactions.

From 1958, however, a number of important changes began to come into the situation, on the whole making things easier for the time being, but some of them carrying the possibility of eventually bringing serious instability into the whole system. The International Monetary Fund had pursued a rather passive policy in its first ten years and had done nothing to increase its resources except to accede to a gradual trickle of additional applications for membership. In 1956, when sterling was seriously affected by lack of confidence at the time of the Suez crisis, it started a much more active lending policy to ease the maintenance of exchange stability and this change of policy was maintained. In its second decade the IMF was lending approximately as much each year as it did in the whole of its first decade. In support of its enlarged role it augmented its resources in 1958 by raising members' quotas by 50 per cent and at intervals thereafter it raised the quotas further. Some of the later changes also included extra increases in the quotas of some of the more prospe-rous members. A further strengthening of the powers and resources of the IMF came from an agreement, called the General Arrangements to Borrow, which was made in 1962 with a group of ten of the wealthiest member countries. These countries undertook to provide standby credits of $6,000 million 'to forestall or cope with an impairment of the international monetary system'. Drawings from these credits were restricted to members of the Group of Ten itself.

Other major changes of the late 'fifties were particularly important for liquidity as well as stability. Although the USA maintained a positive, but generally diminishing, balance of payments on current international dealings until 1971, it was paying out for capital purposes so much more than these current earnings that through the 'sixties its basic international balance was running more and more heavily into deficit. In 1971, when even the trade balance became negative, the basic adverse balance became huge, at over $10,500 million, and in this year there were other payments which greatly increased the total. The dollar was the central currency of the international system, with gold maintained at a fixed price in dollars for all official transactions. The deficits of the 'sixties and early seventies ensured that this key currency, which ten years earlier had been kept available only by special arrangements, was in constantly enlarging supply. Furthermore, many of the dollars found their way into European banks, which redeposited them with other banks, where they became the basis of loans to non-bank borrowers. Thus an additional pyramid of credit was built up in what came to be known as Eurodollars. These changes greatly added to liquidity and eased the provision of short-term finance for the exceptionally rapid growth of international business. The USA had previously accumulated such enormous reserves and its currency was backed by such immense and rising productive power that the reversal of the 'dollar problem' from one of scarcity to one of superabundance seemed unlikely to cause much worry for a long time. Yet there was the question whether *any* country could indefinitely maintain its exchange rate in the face of such long continued deficits, and if the dollar lost its value one of the central pillars of the international financial system would be demolished. There were also risks in the rapidly growing use of Eurodollars, since the governmental and banking authorities in neither the USA nor the countries in which the transactions were made could regulate dealings as effectively as they could if they were conducted in their own currency. It was harder to safeguard the international system against the recklessness of individual institutions if they chose to be reckless in Eurodollars.

In 1958, with the increase of IMF quotas as a gesture towards minimizing any risks of balance of payments difficulties, there came also the restoration of convertibility of the currencies of Western and Central Europe. By this time most of these currencies were backed by strong economies which became stronger still in the 'sixties. They were subject to some embarrassments from an outburst of speculation in the London gold market in 1960, and again in 1961, when a 5 per cent upward revaluation of the mark was wrongly assumed by speculators to be the prelude to a more drastic realignment of exchange rates. But thereafter the central banks took care to safeguard the stability of the system by arranging in advance a system of swap credits among themselves, so that any major currency which was subject to temporary strain could immediately be assisted by loan.

The convertibility of the currencies of so many more countries which had large and growing output and trade added greatly and continuously to the available supply of international short term finance. All these countries had to increase the quantity of their own money to serve the needs of their rapidly expanding business, and they were inclined to yield (some countries a little, some rather more than a little) to pressures to increase their money supply somewhat more than that. Some of this increased supply of money went into the international system. Most European currencies had only a small direct part in the financing of international trade – in the mid-sixties probably about one-third was financed in dollars and one-quarter in sterling – but they were abundantly available to buy the currencies in which settlements were made. Increased international dealings also necessitated the keeping of larger international reserves and here again the usual practice was to accumulate more foreign currency, mainly dollars, in the official reserves as one gain from thriving external trade. Gold as a proportion of international reserves fell from 69 per cent in 1951 to 60 per cent in 1965 and 45 per cent in 1970. As long as currencies were convertible to dollars, and dollars were as good as gold, and gold had a stable value, this was a happy enough situation; but if any break were to occur in this chain of equivalence, there was trouble in store. One other feature associated with the sustained rise in demand, growing more rapidly for internationally traded goods than for others and supported by a rising supply of internationally convertible money, was the diffusion of some degree of inflation through the whole international system. Indeed, had there not been this diffusion, the readiness of some countries to inflate their domestic demand by monetary and fiscal policies would fairly soon have made exchange rates much less stable. As it was, the developed market economies of the world found consumer prices rising at an average rate of 3.4 per cent per year in the decade 1961–70, with rates for particular countries ranging from 11.9 per cent for Iceland to 1.1 per cent for Cyprus and those for the main economic powers of Europe and North America being between 4.1 per cent and 2.7 per cent. These, by the standards of historical experience, are fairly high rates if maintained unbroken for any length of time, though the events of the 'seventies caused this important fact to be forgotten.

On the whole, throughout the 'sixties, the benefits of the international financial system were far more prominent than its weaknesses. Finance was amply available in the forms in which it was wanted and, despite frequent minor disturbances, exchange stability was maintained. Inflation brought additional problems of adjustment in a whole range of business practices, but in most cases it was possible to keep inflation at a fairly steady rate, and what was approximately predictable was not too difficult to live with. The weaknesses of the system were well known and the subject of much discussion, but when the world as a whole was enjoying such exceptional economic growth there seemed little urgency about applying a remedy for them.

In fact, however, the inherent weaknesses were almost certainly increasing progressively beneath the surface of events. The most obvious symptoms of weakness were the basing of the international system on the currencies of countries that were repeatedly or continuously in balance of payments deficit and the imperfection of the mechanisms for restoring the international balance. The succession of sterling crises, which eventually led to devaluation, provided a clear warning, but sterling was only a minor reserve currency, and the international system was partly protected by the diminution of its role, so perhaps the warning was not taken seriously enough. One great problem about maintaining the conditions of international equilibrium was that all the pressure for adjustment had to be placed on the deficit countries. They needed the help of supporting measures from other governments, and of loans and credits from the IMF and foreign central banks. Such assistance could be conditional on the adoption of measures to reduce the deficit, though if it were a reserve currency that was concerned, the common interest in its preservation reduced the pressure that could be exerted for policy changes. But the restoration of international balance also needed suitable measures from countries persistently in surplus and, since they were asking no help from anyone, little pressure could be put on them beyond an appeal to enlightened self-interest. Little was done to provide reserves that were less in need of protection from the disequilibrium of powerful individual countries. The one step of possibly eventual significance was the decision of the IMF, made in 1967 and implemented from 1969, to establish Special Drawing Rights (with each SDR originally equivalent to a US dollar) and issue them to members in accordance with their quotas. This established the principle of international reserves being created by an international institution. But in their early years SDR formed only a very small proportion of the reserves of individual countries and there was disagreement about the basis on which they ought to be allocated. The developing countries urged strongly that they should receive a much larger share of the SDR as a means of enlarging their financial resources for development.

By 1970 there had been no fundamental change in the international financial system and some of its features were becoming too unrealistic. The rise in the market price of gold well above the official level made it look more and more uncertain that the dollar was as good as gold, even though the leading central banks pooled their dealings in gold and operated a two-tier market in which official transactions were separated from the rest and carried out at the official price. The system was kept going only by the willingness of central banks to refrain from converting into gold the mounting supply of dollars which flowed into them as a result of the continuing US deficit on international account, for the USA no longer had enough gold to cover its official liabilities. In the end, not all the improvisations of central banks could maintain the exchange rate of the dollar. The collapse came in 1971, after the USA had sustained an outflow of $12,500 million in six months and the rate of loss had gone higher still in August. On 15 August 1971 the convertibility of the dollar was suspended and the USA imposed a temporary surcharge of 10 per cent on a large proportion of its imports. The other main trading countries produced no common policy but only a series of individual improvisations in immediate response. In December, however, after useful adjustments had been made by transfers of gold and SDR, an attempt was made to patch up the system. The exchange rates of the chief trading nations were realigned, with the dollar depreciating by about 12 per cent against the major currencies and the mark and the yen appreciating against the rest. To lessen the strain of temporary disturbances it was agreed that currencies might in future be allowed to fluctuate within a wider range (2.25 per cent) on either side of the central rate.

These arrangements could not be more than temporary as they

neither fundamentally changed the mechanisms of adjustment nor tackled the deeper causes of disequilibrium. In fact, they proved more transitory than had been expected, without their failure stimulating a more urgent search for fundamental reform. For the developed countries 1972 and 1973 were years of rapidly growing industrial production and trade, partly because of their simultaneous adoption of expansionary domestic policies in order to get back nearer to full employment. Apparent prosperity lessened the urge for institutional reform; but it was also associated with conditions which threatened its continuation. The long divergence between industrial and agricultural growth rates now became much wider and mining production also fell further behind manufacturing than before. It was thus becoming harder to meet the rising industrial demand for many commodities and their prices rose and stocks diminished. With lower stocks, temporary changes in demand were likely to produce disproportionately large fluctuations in price. Rising and volatile commodity prices fed back rising costs and financial uncertainties to the industrial producers; rising costs and prices provoked rising wage demands; and all these influences reinforced the expansionary policies already in force and accelerated the rate of inflation. As an example of the extraordinary change, market prices in sterling of staple commodities other than oil rose on average about threefold between the end of 1971 and the spring of 1974, most of the rise coming after the autumn of 1972; and in the course of 1973 British retail prices rose by 9.2 per cent, with the rate of increase still rising fast. Rising real costs of commodities foreshadowed a check to the growth of industrial production and trade, and such high average rates of inflation almost inevitably involved wider divergences of national price trends than before, with greater difficulty in maintaining external equilibrium.

Thus there was a variety of signs which began to cast doubt on the continuance of the long period of prosperity and smooth expansion which had proceeded with only minor interruptions since about 1948 or 1950. The cracks in the institutions were the most obvious, but the institutions could be repaired or replaced if there were a strong enough agreed common purpose. Common purpose, however, was harder to achieve when other features of the economy were changing in unexpected ways. The experience of the early 'seventies indicated that the technical and managerial capacity to sustain high rates of economic growth was still abundantly present. But the rapid rise in the price of industrial inputs threatened to remove one favourable factor that had come to be taken almost for granted; and the change from the sort of predictable inflation that could be tolerably lived with to a phenomenon that was more powerful and more erratic brought new anxieties. Among them was a weakening of the faith that the determinants of economic activity were readily susceptible to government management. Such blows to confidence, together with distortions to the expected pattern of costs and demand, made it less likely that the business and political behaviour, which by assuming prospective expansion had helped to achieve it in practice, could continue as before. So a new era was emerging, in which the continuing technological forces and the social aspirations, pushing towards continuous economic expansion, were restrained by the re-emergence of temporarily ignored limitations of resources and techniques in some fundamental activities, and by limitations of the powers of economic management. In these conditions a good deal of economic progress was still practicable, but it was likely to be slower and more irregular than in the preceding quarter-century.

WEAKENED INSTITUTIONS AND REDUCED ECONOMIC MOMENTUM

During 1973 the evidence that an important transition had been reached was so mixed that it appeared very uncertain. In various ways this was a year of great and seemingly growing prosperity. Unemployment in most countries was low in absolute terms and lower than in the preceding year. The 24 countries of the OECD increased their gross domestic product in real terms by 6.1 per cent, a rate rarely reached before, and this growth was led, among the larger members, by countries of such recently differing performances as Japan and the UK. The same 24 countries increased the volume of their exports by 12.7 per cent. There was perhaps too little of a contrary kind to indicate that, in the foreseeable future, there was never going to be another year anywhere near as successful as this. But there was enough to show that there were basic weaknesses. Price levels, which for two years had moved rather erratically, began to rise at an accelerating rate nearly everywhere and, among the larger industrial countries, reached particularly high rates of increase in Japan and Italy. Retail price indices rose by over 10 per cent in both these countries in the course of 1973. And the recent repairs attempted to the international financial system showed their inadequacy.

Institutional problems were, indeed, the most obvious immediate sources of worry. Only six months after the agreements of December 1971 international financial pressures were again growing. The trade of the UK was moving rapidly into deficit, so in June 1972 the pound was floated and its exchange value fell erratically. A large volume of disturbing capital movements was taking place in the latter half of 1972 and it became still larger in the early months of 1973. New defensive measures were inevitable. First the Swiss franc and then the lira and the yen were floated, and in February 1973 the USA, experiencing renewed weakness in the balance of payments, devalued the dollar by a further 10 per cent. The extreme uncertainty caused the world's foreign exchange markets to be closed for the first half of March, but this breathing space was used for further adaptations. The value of the Deutschemark was increased by 3 per cent against the dollar. This prepared the way for the adoption of the policy, known as 'the snake', by which the main EEC currencies (except sterling) were floated together. The essence of the arrangement was that the currencies in the snake would be managed so that, within narrow limits, they would all have similar movements relative to the dollar. Shortly afterwards the Norwegian and Swedish currencies were linked to this policy. 'Managed floating', in fact, became the exchange rate policy of almost all industrial countries, though they did not all share identical criteria of management.

These changes facilitated others. The management of other currencies mainly in relation to the dollar strengthened the case for treating the dollar, despite all its recent tribulations, as the principal reserve currency, and most countries with substantial foreign commitments made large additions to the holdings of dollars in their reserves. Such developments appeared to confirm the reduction in recent years in the monetary significance of gold. So it seemed rational that more and more countries withdrew from their agreement to operate a two-tier system for gold, and made themselves free to deal in gold in the private market. This was the prelude in the next five years to the revaluation, at market prices, of the gold in national currency reserves; so even gold was a less stable element than before in the valuation of currencies. A system of floating exchange rates, related to a somewhat insecure dollar, ran the risk of meeting many shocks which, if not countered, might seriously complicate the operation of the system and alter some exchange rates drastically and suddenly. As one safeguard against this risk the members of the Group of Ten almost trebled the size of the stand-by credits which, since 1962, they had always kept available in order to cope with impairments of the international monetary system.

It would be a misleading exaggeration to regard these innovations of 1973 as a conscious redesigning of the international monetary system. They were improvisations in response to immediate pressures. But they were improvisations that fitted together in a rough and ready way and they were the most influential and lasting of the institutional changes of this time. Managed floating remained the norm. It did not prevent some very severe disturbances but it continued to provide a moderately orderly framework and, within it, a fair degree of responsiveness to market forces, though sometimes even more to the irrational than the rational forces. The snake arrangement continued until 1979 and then provided much of the model for the European Monetary System, which was introduced (still without sterling as a member) in that year, with its own unit of account, the European Currency Unit. The dominance of the dollar remained, and dollars were abundantly available for international purposes. Its changed treatment gave gold also a renewed influence on international reserves and liquidity, which was very noticeable at the end of the 'seventies, when the market price of gold rose rapidly.

The persistent reliance on improvised expedients was not quite what had been intended. As a sequel to the agreement of December 1971 the IMF had set up a Committee on Reform of the International Monetary System and Related Issues, which represented 20 countries, but its achievements were small. It did not get round to holding a meeting at ministerial level until March 1973 and it was never able to overcome the differences of interest between debtors and creditors, or between developing and developed countries, so as to reach agreement on major questions. In 1974 it decided that priority had to be given to arrangements which would deal practically with short-term problems (which was what was already happening independently) and wound up its own work in June with a generally useful but limited set of recommendations, which were soon implemented. They included guidelines for the management of floating exchange rates; the setting up of another 'Interim' committee to go on with proposals for monetary reform, but only in a step-by-step way; and another of the many measures by which the IMF vainly tried, for many years, to swim against the tide and promote the SDR to dominance in international reserves instead of the dollar. This time the SDR was disconnected from its original equivalence in value with the dollar, and its value was made to depend on that of sixteen currencies in pre-ordained proportions.

Such limited conclusions left the field clear for the *ad hoc* arrangements that have been described, though the Interim Committee of the IMF kept open the possibilities of further reform. The latter body's main achievements came at the IMF meeting in Kingston, Jamaica, in January 1976, when its recommendations were adopted as the basis of the second amendment of the Fund agreement, which came into force in April 1978. To an appreciable extent, however, the provisions did more to define and give authority to the prevailing *ad hoc* arrangements than to introduce radical changes. The floating of the currencies of member countries of the IMF, and the right of central bankers to involve themselves in the management of the floating, were legalized, and the IMF assumed general surveillance of the managed floating and the liquidity position of the member countries. The main complementary change was an increase in the quotas of members. This was not done on a uniform basis. The quotas of the wealthy oil-exporting countries were increased by much more than the average and the quota of the UK, the second largest contributor, by much less than the average, but the total quotas increased by just over one-third. The IMF sought again to enlarge the role of SDR by increasing the amount in issue year by year and by encouraging the downgrading of gold. This was done by returning one-sixth of its own gold holdings to the contributing members at the old official price, and by selling another sixth in the market, with the proceeds going into a trust fund to help very poor countries with balance-of-payments problems. The attempted boost to the SDR did not make much difference, but the increase in the resources of the IMF (which were increased again in 1979), together with its resumption of an international supervisory function, improved the chances of operating safely the potentially vulnerable arrangements which had emerged from the improvisations of 1973.

The monetary reforms were not the only institutional changes of 1973. The most prominent of the rest, which has already been noted, was the enlargement of the EEC at the start of the year, when Denmark, Ireland, and the UK became members, though Norway, which had also negotiated membership, found the agreement rejected by its electorate and stayed outside. The enlargement of the EEC and the consequential loss of members by EFTA ended the general significance of the latter. A bigger EEC appreciably enlarged the area of preferential trading within Europe and also imposed some new protective disadvantages, particularly on countries of the British Commonwealth, to whom easy access to the UK market had been a valuable stimulus to trade. Over the next few years there were some significant shifts in the directions of international trade and the

bigger Community had an increased attraction for foreign investment, with some change in its distribution within Europe. But, on
the whole, enlargement of the EEC was not a major influence on the
next ten years of international economic affairs. It came too late. The
forces making for rapid economic growth over a very wide area
were passing their peak. The EEC, on its own, had no policies
which would prolong them, or substitute for them, not least because, for a Community of predominantly industrial states, it devoted an extraordinarily high proportion of its financial and administrative resources to the promotion and protection of agriculture.

A more immediate and much more powerful influence came from
the policies of OPEC which, in the latter part of 1973 and the early
months of 1974, brought about a revolution in oil prices. In this
short period the price of crude oil roughly quadrupled. Different
refined products underwent different price increases, but the general
order of magnitude was approximately a doubling. The immediate
motivation was a wish to demonstrate the political power of the oil
producers of the Middle East, but such a demonstration was possible
only because of economic factors. Above all, there was the current
high level of demand for oil throughout the world and the expectation, shared by users and suppliers, that it would go on rising. Only
in such conditions was it possible for a cartel, which controlled a
good deal less than the total supply, to maintain its chosen prices.
There was also an element of delayed adjustment to cover total long-
term costs. It appeared that many resources were being depleted at a
rate for which the current flow of revenue was not adequate compensation, on any reasonable assumptions about the future. But, in
any case, poor countries, that were not concerned with fine calculations of the appropriate rates at which to discount the future, were
anxious to increase their oil revenue as much as the market would
bear, in order to speed up their development and improve their
consumption.

Such circumstances indicate why the oil price rise was such a
severe shock to the whole international economic system. In the very
short run there was no way to escape. Oil users had to pay up or
suffer a loss of supplies and a decline in economic activity. In time,
there were possibilities of fuel economy and of switching to other
sources of energy, but this could not happen immediately and could
not restore the *status quo*, for the whole structure of the energy
market had been altered. The assumption of an abundant supply of
cheap energy (with oil as its principal component) for all foreseeable
needs was one of the confidence-building expectations which under-

lay investment and other policy decisions that assisted rapid economic growth in the nineteen-sixties and early seventies. By 1974 this basic assumption had been falsified by events and there was no prospect of its early reinstatement.

Adverse effects of several kinds were to be expected and were likely to have their heaviest impact very early. Prices, the pattern of international trade, balances of payments, exchange rates, the location of international investible funds and investment opportunities – all were exposed to substantial alteration. The difficulties were enhanced because these were changes superimposed on conditions in which stronger inflationary pressures had already been induced by other influences. They were less likely to be contained because they were experienced within a financial system in process of very incomplete reconstruction and relying more than ever before on the judgement of financial managers who had to operate without very clear guidelines. Differences between nations in economic policy, in financial resources, in the will to exert control in the face of political pressures, and in short-term interests were together likely to cause large changes in the relative national financial positions.

What was so obviously likely came to pass very quickly. Proportionately the heaviest burdens fell on those poor countries whose supply of energy came almost entirely from imported oil and whose hopes of development would come to an end without it. They received some consideration from their creditors and were helped by a special oil facility which the IMF established for their benefit in June 1974, but their economic prospects were damaged. It was, however, the large oil producers and the wealthier industrial countries whose activities mainly determined the course of the world economy.

Higher costs of transport and of inputs to production led to higher prices of finished goods, which were already on a rising trend. Higher prices led to higher wage demands, which were further exaggerated because the assumption began to be built in that prices would be still higher before the next wage rise could be obtained. Employers and governments were disposed to concede a large part of the wage demands, both for the sake of good relations and in the belief that the alternative would reduce real incomes, and therefore reduce demand, and therefore reduce business activity and employment. So costs and prices went on rising. The mid- and later seventies became the world's most general era of high inflation. But the structure of costs and the extent of the concessions on wages and salaries differed widely from country to country, so there was great divergence in rates of inflation, as can be seen from Table 11.

TABLE 11   ANNUAL INCREASES IN RETAIL PRICE INDICES, SELECTED
COUNTRIES, 1971–1980 (*percentages*)

Country	1971	1972	1973	1974	1975	1976	1977	1978	1979	1980
United States	4.3	3.3	6.2	11.0	9.1	5.8	6.5	7.7	11.3	13.5
Japan	6.1	4.5	11.7	24.5	11.8	9.3	8.1	3.8	3.6	8.0
France	5.5	6.2	7.3	13.7	11.8	9.6	9.4	9.1	10.8	13.6
West Germany	5.3	5.5	6.9	7.0	6.0	4.5	3.7	2.7	4.1	5.5
Italy	4.8	5.7	10.8	19.1	17.0	16.8	17.0	12.1	14.8	21.2
United Kingdom	9.4	7.1	9.2	16.0	24.2	16.5	15.8	8.3	13.4	18.0
Switzerland	6.6	6.7	8.7	9.8	6.7	1.7	1.3	1.1	3.6	4.0
Turkey	19.0	15.4	14.0	23.9	21.2	17.4	26.0	61.9	63.5	94.3
Australia	6.1	5.8	9.5	15.1	15.1	13.5	12.3	7.9	9.1	10.2
All OECD	5.3	4.7	7.8	13.4	11.3	8.6	8.8	7.9	9.8	12.9

The oil price rise had an immediate and huge impact on inter-national trade and payments. In effect, most of the world moved into deficit and most of the world's surpluses were concentrated in the hands of a few wealthy oil-producing states of low population. First estimates of the international re-distribution of surpluses were some-what exaggerated. Nevertheless, it was on a scale which had never been experienced before, and presented a very difficult financial problem. Nearly all international investment had been made by the OECD countries and together they found that between 1973 and 1974 their current balance of payments deteriorated by $39,000 million. After that first enormous swing some fairly large correction was practicable as the prices of finished goods were adjusted to the higher cost of inputs, and the more efficient economies achieved savings in other costs and improved their competitive position. Adjustments in exchange rates also helped to strengthen the trading position of some non-oil producers, though the tendency of ex-change rates to be slow in adjusting to the effects of divergences in the rates of inflation was a limiting factor. The payments position of the main industrial countries as a group improved markedly after 1974 and some of them were well situated: West Germany main-tained a remarkably healthy condition throughout this crisis, and Japan, which had been severely affected by higher payments for imported oil, was back in current surplus by 1976. But the wealthy oil exporters continued to receive large surpluses, which their domes-tic economies were too small to use at all fully, and many developing countries stayed in deeper deficit than before. There was a major task of recycling international funds if their new distribution was not to act as a damper on international trade and therefore on the general growth of economic activity. This recycling was accomplished with a fairly high degree of success, by both direct and indirect means. The wealthiest oil exporters became large foreign investors and the world's international banking system negotiated loans in many parts of the world. Most of the international capital went into the industrialized countries, which offered the most productive use for it, but enough went into loans and grants to enable the developing countries to cover their commitments for the time being.

It took a couple of years for these activities to start showing positive benefits. The loss of foreign exchange by so many countries in 1974, because of the large rise in the cost of their imports, had a constricting effect on trade and in 1975, for only the second time since 1950, the volume of world trade declined. But the adjustments then in progress began to take effect and the expansion of world trade was resumed for the rest of the seventies, though at a slower rate than had prevailed until 1973. Just as it had done for the preceding quarter century, international trade continued to lead production, so this recovery of trade after 1975 was particularly important for the prosperity of the world economy.

Not all was keeping free of trouble. The continued concentration of surpluses in a small number of countries meant that in some quarters the search for foreign investment outlets was exceptionally strong, while the corresponding diffusion of deficits created a very widespread desire for foreign funds without the would-be borrowers always being able to show that they deserved a high credit rating. Thus the conditions existed for the creation of a large and growing volume of international debt, some of which was likely to be difficult to service and still more difficult to repay. The signs were that this was happening, although it was not until the early 'eighties that it was obvious that it had built up into a threat to international financial stability.

Another problem was the very divergent degree to which different countries recovered from the shocks of 1973–4. It was particularly serious that, when the world had gone over to a system of floating exchange rates all related to the dollar, the dollar itself again became a generally depreciating currency. The USA showed remarkable economic resilience in 1975 and achieved a large international surplus, but thereafter its relative performance declined. By 1977 there was a large international deficit on current account and this was always increased by an outflow on capital account. It was not surprising that the exchange rate of the dollar declined against most other major currencies except sterling, which suffered from a very high rate of inflation (by the standards of industrialized countries) at a time when the UK balance of payments was not strong. In 1974 a US dollar exchanged on the average of the year for 292.0800 yen or 2.5878 Deutschemarks or 2.9793 Swiss francs. In 1979 the yen weakened a little but the dollar declined further to 1.8329 Deutschemarks or 1.6627 Swiss francs. Even against sterling the dollar declined rather quickly after 1977, with a drop only just short of 20 per cent in two years.

These changes seriously reduced the international purchasing power of anyone whose income came in dollars. The oil-producing countries were particularly affected because oil was priced throughout the world in dollars. One result of the fall in the dollar was a reduction in the price of oil in real terms, which producers had not intended. Moreover, the slower growth of output throughout the world and some successful price resistance, which showed both in the achievement of fuel economy and switches from oil to other fuels, contradicted expectations of continuing steady expansion of oil sales for a period with no foreseeable end. All these influences combined to keep down the revenues of the oil producers. A few of them, nearly all in the Middle East, were still left with enormous surpluses in proportion to the size of their populations and were extremely rich. But other oil-producing countries, particularly in Africa and Latin America, were much poorer and had commitments to development in the hope of lessening their poverty. These commitments were made on the strength of optimistic expectations about their future oil revenue, and the basis was weakening. As a result of the price rises of 1973–4 the share of mineral fuels among the imports of all countries practically doubled, in value terms, and remained steady at the new figure until 1978, when it dropped in one year from 22.1 to 19.6 per cent. This was an alarming change for OPEC. The world seemed to have adjusted to the first oil-price revolution and trade was still growing steadily, even though more slowly than a few years earlier. In these circumstances the device of trying to restore oil revenues by another series of large price increases looked both attractive and realistic to producers and was adopted by OPEC in 1979. Over a two-year period the effect on consumers' pockets was slightly greater than the first time round, though the difference was due more to secondary repercussions on the costs of the energy industries and not to greater leaps in the price of crude oil. The weighted average retail index of energy prices for all OECD countries rose by 16.2 per cent in 1979 and then by 24.5 per cent during 1980. The corresponding figures in the previous episode had been 26.8 per cent in 1974 and 12.3 per cent in 1975.

The initial effects looked favourable for the oil producers. The share of mineral fuels in the value of world imports rose to 22.4 per cent in 1979 and 26.5 per cent in 1980, and in 1979 the members of OPEC had collectively a balance-of-payments surplus of more than $100,000 million, though most of it accrued to the small number of wealthy countries among them. But it was a temporarily better result from a volume of international trade which, in absolute terms, soon began to turn down. Signs of serious disorder in the world economy quickly appeared, and it was disorder which the oil producers, in the not very long run, could not avoid sharing.

The second oil-price revolution, compared with the first, came when world trade (however secure a growth had been anticipated) was, in fact, less buoyant; when the quiescence of international debt problems depended on the maintenance of conditions in which enough could be earned internationally to service the debts; and when inflation, though improving, remained higher than before 1973 and had persisted so much longer at high levels as to be harder to correct and a greater cause for alarm. In every respect things turned for the worse in 1979. All oil importers found their foreign expenditure soaring, their domestic costs rising, and the inflationary pressures (which would drive costs higher still by unpredictable amounts) increasing, and their international competitive position threatened. Most countries were in a position where they could either buy rather less or run into debt, and the small minority enjoying higher revenue were in no position to compensate for this. The entire international financial system was affected by greater uncertainty and insecurity. The greatest source of international demand, the countries of the OECD, started to reduce the volume of imports in 1980 and continued to do so for three successive years. It was a reaction to weakened finances. Their collective international balance of payments on current account worsened by nearly $41,000 million in 1979 and a further $39,000 million in 1980. Poorer countries, which had to pay more for imports, found rather more unfavourable export conditions facing some of them. Within a couple of years the threat that some large debtors would be unable to meet their foreign obligations had begun to loom. From 1970 to 1980 the debt service ratio (i.e. debt service payments as a percentage of export earnings) for developing countries as a whole had hardly changed, a serious deterioration in Latin America having been offset by an improvement in Asia, where the largest borrowing had hitherto taken place. But the ratio rose from 13.6 in 1980 to 16.3 in 1981 and 20.7 in 1982, and in the latter year it reached the frightening figure of 53.2 for Latin America. There had been heavy lending to Brazil and Mexico, in particular, and there were fears of defaults that might seriously damage some large financial institutions in the industrialized countries.

Stronger inflationary pressures produced domestic as well as international financial problems and stimulated corresponding attempts at corrective action. Permanent expectation of high inflation rates led to practices which tried to anticipate future price rises when remuneration of the factors of production was settled, though such practices were carried much further in some countries than others. The effect was to increase expenditure on production prior to (and usually more than) any increase in output. So the volume of output per head was restricted and costs were raised in ways that altered the competitive position. As financial uncertainty increased, and slower or non-existent growth of trade put a premium on competitive strength, more and more countries tried to tackle the problem either by restrictive financial policies or by direct measures of control to limit the power of particular groups to secure much larger money revenues. Such policies took time to reduce inflation and change competitive strengths, but they had an immediate effect on expectations about future levels of incomes and sales. In association with all the other influences that pressed for reduced expenditure in the interests of financial solvency and more competitive costs, they tended to inhibit the growth of activity and, still more, to restrict the level of employment. So the world economy, having slipped after 1973 from boom to slower growth, started the eighties by sliding from slower growth to recession. There was no great employment-creating set of innovations to attract a cumulative wave of productive new investment, which might give a stimulus spreading throughout economic life, for the general trend of current technological ingenuity was to control productive and administrative processes much more precisely, with savings in energy and labour. The increased capital needs of the new controlling methods were not so great as to compensate for those no longer needed for provision of the displaced energy and for equipping the displaced workers. So the restoration of economic expansion had to be left to the provision of greater abundance by higher efficiency and the hope that some of the fruits of abundance would set up demand for some more labour-intensive products, rather than simply be offset by more unemployment.

This was not a dynamic economic condition for the world of the early nineteen-eighties. It was not surprising, though it may have seemed ironic, that the lack of dynamism had particularly adverse effects on the oil-exporting countries whose policies had been the catalyst for the influences that brought it about. Slow growth generally, and in some industrial countries a year or two when output contracted, and the general pursuit of energy-saving and of alternatives to oil, seriously affected the demand for oil. Although in 1981 and 1982 OPEC was still heavily in surplus (over $80,000 million for the two-year period), its poorer, heavily populated members were already in deficit, and OPEC as a whole started to run into a current trading deficit in 1983, though the wealthy states still had a large foreign investment income as an offset. In 1984 the world output of crude oil was 2.4 per cent *lower* than in 1974 and the share of OPEC in the total had been reduced by the development of new oilfields. The reduction was attributable mainly to the slower growth and successful adaptation of the industrial countries: the oil imports of Europe and the USA fell from 19.8 million barrels per day in 1974 to 13.0 million in 1984.

The institutions for dealing with the more difficult economic conditions after 1979 were much the same as before. The additions to international debt, especially among developing countries, led to greater and more frequent difficulties of servicing and repayment. In these conditions the acceptance of general responsibility for surveillance of managed currency policies gave the IMF a renewed importance. More and more countries became so pressed by foreign debt that they had to seek financial help. The IMF provided it on a short-term basis, but only after governmental acceptance of stringent conditions about budgetary and other financial policies, which were specific and on strict anti-inflationary lines and were subject to regular monitoring of performance. In some cases, especially in the early 'eighties, much of the indebtedness was to commercial banks, which were unable to impose changed policies on the borrowers, and which at times faced the prospect of having to withdraw from their investments with what they could rescue from them. In years of debt crisis, such as 1982, when difficulties in Poland were followed by much larger problems in Mexico, there was a real possibility of losses so heavy as to weaken the international banking system. Where practicable, in such cases, there was concerted action by the IMF and the commercial banks. The IMF obtained government undertakings of financial reform, in return for a loan, and then, on the strength of the improved chances of solvency, helped to persuade the banks to reschedule the commercial debt and interest payments. It was helpful that these tactics in 1982 brought particularly quick improvements of the desired kind in Mexico, and it was not apparent until much later that they were less sustained than had been hoped. Thereafter banks were more ready to be convinced that patience, and the postponement of pressure while adjustments were made, was the lesser evil from their own point of view. But it was characteristic of such measures that they were directed at improving financial stability and not, in any direct way, at promoting economic growth, and this was a source of complaint among developing countries.

It was, indeed, notable that the IMF had come to have greater prominence than the International Bank for Reconstruction and Development, although the latter had invested heavily in developing countries throughout the seventies, and to a greater extent than before (especially through the IDA) on rural schemes in poor regions. Such investments still continued but it was becoming harder to persuade member governments to provide more money for such purposes. It was a sign of the times that in 1980 the IBRD began devoting part of its resources to loans to support long-term structural changes in the economies of developing countries, the kind of purpose to which IMF short-term loans were devoted in the effort to increase solvency and financial stability. After five years' experience there were proposals that the proportion of the Bank's portfolio devoted to this purpose (so far 10 per cent) should be very substantially increased.

A sound economic structure and a stable financial framework had come to be seen as both foundations and continuing conditions for sustained economic growth, which would otherwise be repeatedly checked or reversed by the threat of insolvency and the consequent discouragement of investment and enterprise. There was room for doubt, however, whether the existing institutions and policies did as much as was required to ensure that the necessary growth-producing activities were likely to develop within the framework, and also whether international financial conditions were being made as stable as was wanted for a steady expansion of international trade. The latter doubt was the more striking because it concerned imperfection in the achievement of the objective to which the greatest importance was attached.

The international monetary system which had emerged by the mid-seventies was not fundamentally changed. Though the IMF hoped to make SDR the centre of the system, and the amount of SDR was increased, the hope was never realized and by the mid-eighties was fading. The creation of the European Monetary System was a help in providing certainty and stability in the relations between most members of the EEC and in the large block of international trade conducted within the Community. But neither the European Monetary System nor any of the currencies within it sought to play any major role in the international payments of foreign countries or as an important component of their monetary reserves, and no one tried to push them into acting otherwise. Japan, although it built up a foreign trade as big as that of West Germany, the largest European exporter, played even less of a general role in international payments. What remained was still a system of managed floating exchange rates dominated by the dollar, and in the eighties the system began to work more erratically.

On the whole, though hampered by the depreciation of the dollar, it had done better in the mid- and late 'seventies than might have been expected. Countries that were careless about above-average rates of inflation, or declined in competitive strength for other reasons, usually found their balance of payments deteriorating and then their exchange rates falling. To maintain their international creditworthiness and the level of trade necessary for their living standards they had to modify their financial and economic policies in order to become more competitive again. If things had been allowed to slip too far, or the country had few reserves, help from the IMF or foreign banks, or both, was likely to be needed, and the adjustments would be called for in a rather severe fashion. Thus, in a rough and ready way, there was a continual, partly self-correcting, mutual adjustment of competitive power, foreign trade, and exchange rates.

The most notable change from about 1980 was that exchange rates appeared to respond more to capital movements than to variations in current balances of payments, and capital movements depended increasingly on the expectations of dealers about the probable behaviour (speculative or otherwise) of the rest of the market in the immediate future, and less on the demand for productive investment. There were two main reasons for this. One was the advance in the technology of communication and information. Projections of current trends, and their price and profit implications, could be made almost instantaneously on the basis of up-to-the minute information from every major financial market in the world, and funds switched between investment centres just as quickly on the basis of those projections. The second was that the currency most affected was the dollar. This currency was so special and so central as to be assumed to be exempt, not from variations in value, but at least from the most drastic adjustments of economic policy and behaviour which had been common elsewhere immediately before. The USA went back into current account deficit in 1982. It had then a very large internal fiscal deficit, which continued and which helped to make the country decreasingly competitive. So the international deficit on current account became enormous, reaching $40,000 million by 1983. But foreigners continued to send capital to the USA in huge amounts and more than covered the current account deficit and provided some of the means in this way for a couple of years of recovering domestic output. The dollar appreciated substantially against every major currency.

In relation to all recent experience, and all perception of current underlying trends in real economic factors, the international financial system was behaving perversely. The exchanges between non-dollar countries still showed a response to current trading conditions, but movements produced in this way were superimposed on the stronger influence of the dollar exchange, sometimes offsetting it a little, but sometimes reinforcing it. So the world as a whole experienced substantial swings in exchange rates which were not easy to predict or relate rationally to current conditions. Adjustment to exchange-rate depreciation was less easy to achieve than it had been. Because so much of the difficulty was associated with capital movements, governments and central banks were led to defend themselves by keeping interest rates high – a policy for which they often had internal reasons also. Because it had become more difficult to correct trade imbalances through the exchange rates, there was a growing temptation to seek correction through political pressure for specific measures of protection in commercial policy. This was perhaps a more serious threat as, since the nineteen-sixties, there had been less success than before in further liberalizing the conduct of international trade through successive rounds of GATT negotiation. The combination of influences associated with the more erratic working of the international financial system was unhelpful to the needs of a world seeking a way out of the most severe recession since the nineteen-thirties. It appeared that there was a need for new attempts to reform financial institutions if uncertainty about the operation of the essential framework was not to remain a continuing drag on economic progress.

As the institutional changes, from the early 'seventies on, were associated with more fundamental economic factors affecting the supply of resources, costs, and markets, it was more or less to be expected that other aspects of adaptation would show a comparable mixture of well-directed ingenuity and increasingly influential omissions. This expectation proved to be well founded, so conditions for continued progress under greater difficulty were established. In most important respects the characteristics and achievements of world economic activity after 1973 were, in their broad features, on similar lines to those they had followed before, but everything advanced more slowly and the deceleration was more marked after 1979. The most obvious change was in the structure of international trade. In terms of value, the proportion of total imports which consisted of mineral fuels rose from an average of 11.0 per cent in 1968–73 to 27.0 per cent in 1980–2, and the corresponding loss of import share was more or less evenly divided between the food, drink, and tobacco category and raw materials other than mineral fuels. Trade in manufactures underwent little relative change. Developing countries as a group continued to achieve higher rates of economic growth than developed countries, although the former, of course, still had much the lower absolute increase of output. But developing countries are not a homogeneous group and the maintenance of their average growth came mainly from the favoured few who either were oil exporters or were industrializing rapidly. Poor countries that were oil importers and remained overwhelmingly agricultural mostly had a difficult time. Low growth rates were particularly common over much of Africa.

The main influence on the performance of the world economy, however, continued to be the advanced industrialized countries of North America, Europe, and East Asia, nearly all of which were in the OECD, the only exceptions being the communist countries. In 1981, 63.4 per cent of the world's total output came from only six countries: the USA, the USSR, Japan, West Germany, France, and the UK, in that order of magnitude. Whatever indicator is used, the progress of these dominant economies shows a serious falling off after 1973, yet it was still at a rate which in most periods before 1950 would have been regarded as encouraging and symptomatic of a fairly high degree of prosperity. Only after 1979 was there such a setback as brought comparisons with recessions which, in the fifties and sixties, were coming to be regarded as relics of a past that had been banished for ever. The accompanying Tables 12 and 13 show some of the indicators of declining performance in successive periods.

There were various related changes that are worth noting. In all these countries there was some switch towards services, which by the early eighties were responsible for three-fifths of the GDP of OECD countries, but the better maintenance of productivity in service occupations meant that there was not so large a change in terms of full-time employment. The proportion of GDP devoted to

TABLE 12   ANNUAL AVERAGE GROWTH RATES OF REAL DOMESTIC
PRODUCT, 1960–1982 (*percentages*)

	1960–7		1968–73		1973–9		1979–82	
	Total	Per head	Total	Per head	Total	Per head	Total	Per head
USA	4.5	3.2	3.3	2.2	2.6	1.6	0.1	−0.9
Japan	10.5	9.4	8.8	7.3	3.6	2.5	4.1	3.3
EEC	4.4	3.6	4.8	4.1	2.4	2.2	0.4	0.2
All OECD	5.1	3.9	4.8	3.7	2.7	1.9	0.9	0.2

TABLE 13   ANNUAL AVERAGE GROWTH RATES OF VOLUME OF IMPORTS AND
EXPORTS, 1960–1982 (*percentages*)

	1960–7		1968–73		1973–9		1979–82	
	Imports	Exports	Imports	Exports	Imports	Exports	Imports	Exports
USA	9.5	5.7	7.2	8.9	4.5	5.0	−3.5	−1.8
Japan	13.9	16.5	15.0	12.8	1.8	7.8	−2.9	8.0
EEC	8.1	8.2	11.0	10.5	4.0	5.0	−0.7	1.5
All OECD	8.6	8.1	10.2	10.0	3.7	5.1	−1.4	1.6

gross fixed capital formation remained fairly steady nearly everywhere, but, as GDP was growing more slowly, the rate of increase
in the total amount of fixed capital also slowed. This may have been
one reason for a much slower increase in value added per person in
both industry and agriculture, though this trend was reversed for
agriculture after 1979. Such changes in occupational structure and
productivity, together with much reduced opportunities as the
growth of exports decelerated and the restrictive financial policies
(which many countries found necessary in the face of higher inflation
and balance-of-payments problems), presented some threat to the
maintenance of employment. Gradual increases in unemployment
rates, and their acceleration after 1979, were widespread.

Comparative national statistics of unemployment were often
somewhat misleading, partly because of large differences in the
proportion of people who made themselves available for employment, as well as differences of demographic structure. Within the
EEC, for example, the proportion of the population aged 15–64
who were classed as within the labour force was consistently well
over 70 per cent in the UK and Denmark, but below 65 per cent in
Belgium, Italy, Luxembourg, and the Netherlands. Indeed, from
1970 it remained below 60 per cent in the Netherlands and fluctuated
around 60 per cent in Italy. On the average for 1980–2 Denmark had

TABLE 14 ANNUAL AVERAGES OF EMPLOYMENT AND UNEMPLOYMENT, 1960–1982
EMPLOYMENT (E): *PERCENTAGE EMPLOYED OF POPULATION AGED 15–64*
UNEMPLOYMENT (U): *PERCENTAGE UNEMPLOYED OF TOTAL LABOUR FORCE*

	1960–7		1968–73		1974–9		1980–2	
	E	U	E	U	E	U	E	U
USA	62.5	5.0	63.8	4.6	65.2	6.7	66.6	8.0
Japan	72.5	1.3	71.0	1.2	69.6	1.9	70.5	2.2
EEC	66.4	2.1	64.7	2.7	63.1	4.6	61.6	7.2
All OECD	66.4	3.1	65.6	3.4	65.0	5.2	64.3	7.2

the second highest unemployment rate but also had the highest proportion of those aged 15–64 in employment, whereas the Netherlands had the third highest unemployment rate but the lowest proportion actually in jobs from that age group, 53.8 per cent against 72.9 per cent for Denmark. Thus some, but not all, aspects of economic performance were better indicated by employment figures than unemployment figures. But the striking thing was the general increase in the proportion of those who sought work and could not get it. As a persistent trend (which showed no sign of reversal in the first half of the 'eighties), rather than an occasional brief aberration, this had great significance because it was a departure from one of the main objectives of policy, adopted in the post-war world and sustained with a high degree of success in most countries for a quarter of a century. In the early 'eighties the general upward trend of unemployment figures seemed to symbolize a bleaker world.

By this time the most prominent characteristics of the long post-war economic success story had been left behind. The Bretton Woods financial system, the maintenance of nearly full employment, the continous experience of economic growth at rates never long sustained before, and the resulting confidence to plan and invest for a future with more of the same – all had gone. The wide sharing of economic advance, though not ended, had been greatly modified. There had been remarkable success in increasing total food output in line with population increase, but the abundance of food production and the abundance of mouths were sometimes located far apart. Figures could still be produced to show the rapid growth of the 'Third World' of developing countries. But the Third World was really several worlds, some of which continued in poverty that was being exacerbated not only by rapid population growth but by mounting debts. For a time it was possible to assume that all these changed features were only temporary, and activities were always in train to control and limit their adverse consequences. But palliatives were no cures, and the most common experience was that economic difficulties became greater and the rewards in the form of rising incomes and more varied and secure living conditions came more slowly, less abundantly, and less generally. The conclusion gradually forced itself that there had been not just an interruption of economic success but a move into a different phase of economic history.

An extended experience of rapid economic growth had not destroyed the appetite for more of it but had strengthened an understanding of many of the qualities and conditions needed in order to sustain it; and it had also fostered some illusions. There were restraining influences on economic growth, which had been assumed to be no longer operative but which reasserted themselves and showed that they had to be lived with. In the early nineteen-eighties there was still an immense technological power that could be directed to economic growth and there was large capacity for the control and co-ordination of complex economic undertakings that could perform tasks of great wealth-creating potential. But there were higher costs and new difficulties to be faced in acquiring productive resources and applying them in the most economical and useful way. There were limits to the power of human institutions to prevent chaotic consequences from the continuous release of extra finance into a system where all formal controls were increasingly flexible, simply in the hope of encouraging ever higher growth of economic activity. There were limits also to the range of low-skilled occupations that could be retained in economies which based their progress increasingly on the provision, by capital-intensive and low-energy techniques, of goods and services with a low material content. Even as recently as the early 'sixties these constraints had seemed either not to exist or not to matter. Twenty years later they were inescapable.

The performance of the world economy was certainly less expansive after 1973 and showed every sign of continuing at a lower level. But, despite the post-1979 depression (a recurrence of a not unfamiliar historical phenomenon), it was a standard of performance that was not distinctively low if put in the context of the longer period of around a century and a half in which common economic influences, under the impetus of industrialization, had been more and more thoroughly embracing the whole world. The difference was more in the criteria by which it was judged. 'The revolution of rising expectations' was one of the tags which was popularized in the third quarter of the twentieth century and it was a more accurate label than many others. Before very long the expectations began to be disappointed, and one of the needs was to discard the illusory element in them. But retrospect shows how immense was the achievement of the period during which there was an international economy adequate to justify the name. Observation of the present and very recent past indicates the continuing strength of the forces making for economic advance and suggests, indeed, that the links which could spread common influences throughout the world were probably stronger than ever. The third quarter of the twentieth century was probably an exception rather than the first act of a new norm. It was a period with unusual opportunities for catching up with a backlog of known technologies that had previously been inadequately applied, resources that had been under-used, and latent demands that better organization could satisfy; and, partly for these reasons, it could temporarily ignore some things that must exert constraint in the long run. But if normality – which in economic affairs can never be more than an inconstant approximation – has to be sought in earlier and later times, it shows a record of continual, though somewhat fluctuating, economic advance that in only four or five generations had cumulated into a transformation of the economic world. Even if more extravagant hopes had been abandoned, there was nothing to suggest that this process had ceased to exert its power

Bibliographical Note

Almost anything in economic history anywhere since the mid-nineteenth century has some relevance to the history of the international economy. Much of it has a supporting rather than a central significance for international changes; but the reader who has already built up a special knowledge of the history of one major country's economy, or of one theme which may be influential in the internal economy of several large countries, will often find this a convenient starting point for a more international study of economic history. He or she will be able to fit into the international context the material on particular countries and themes which is already familiar. This note concentrates on works which deal with general and specific themes in international economic history, including some which study the course of the world economy as a whole, and comparative studies that range very widely.

There are few works which try to deal comprehensively with the international economy over a long historical period. Probably the most useful are F. Mauro, *Histoire de l'économie mondiale* (Paris, 1971) and J. Foreman-Peck, *A History of the World Economy: international economic relations since 1850* (Brighton, 1983). A shorter work, which in most respects takes a narrower view of the subject than is given in the present book, is A. G. Kenwood and A. L. Lougheed, *The Growth of the International Economy 1820–1980* (London, 1983). There are valuable studies of shorter periods. Much the best is W. A. Lewis, *Growth and Fluctuations 1870–1913* (London, 1978) which, in its presentation and detailed analysis of the evidence, is quite outstanding. For later years there is the projected six-volume *History of the World Economy in the Twentieth Century*, edited by W. Fischer, with a different single author for each volume. This is of variable quality, but two volumes are particularly helpful: C. P. Kindle-berger, *The World in Depression, 1929–1939* (London, 1973) and A. S. Milward, *War, Economy and Society, 1939–1945* (London, 1977). A good introduction to part of the period is still provided by W. A. Lewis, *Economic Survey 1919–1939* (London, 1949) and, for a longer period over a lesser area, but in more detail, by I. Svennilson, *Growth and Stagnation in the European Economy, 1913–1950* (Geneva, 1954). For later years there are W. M. Scammell, *The International Economy since 1945* (London, 1980) and A. J. Brown, *World Inflation since 1950* (Cambridge, 1985).

Interest in the nature and causes of economic growth has been pursued on a worldwide scale and the best of the resulting studies are essential to anyone interested in the history of the international economy. Some of them have built up a large body of statistical material and tried to present it on as uniform a basis as practicable and all of them have sought for general explanatory principles which can embrace the many contrasts in levels of achievement. The great pioneer in this work was S. Kuznets, whose contribution is best assimilated from two large works of synthesis, *Modern Economic Growth: rate, structure and spread* (New Haven, 1966) and *Economic Growth of Nations* (Cambridge, Mass., 1971). An important attempt to systematize the subject has been made by W. W. Rostow in a sequence of books. The most stimulating is still *The Stages of Economic Growth* (2nd edn, Cambridge, 1971), though there is additional material in several later works. In particular, his large book *The World Economy: history and prospect* (London, 1978) presents a huge array of comparative statistics, but keeps them within explanatory categories that appear to have become stereotyped. Explanations of comparative growth in different types of society and economy, with a carefully constructed quantitative basis, come in three books by A. Maddison: *Economic Growth in the West* (London, 1964), *Economic Growth in Japan and the USSR* (London, 1969) and *Economic Progress and Policy in Developing Countries* (London, 1970). Other helpful works include C. Clark, *The Conditions of Economic Progress* (3rd edn, London, 1957), B. E. Supple, ed., *The Experience of Economic Growth* (New York, 1963), E. D. Denison, *Why Growth Rates Differ* (Washington, 1967), J. D. Gould, *Economic Growth in History* (London, 1972), and P. Bairoch and M. Lévy-Leboyer, eds, *Disparities in Economic Development since the Industrial Revolution* (London, 1981). Important collections of essays by individual authors are A. K. Cairncross, *Factors in Economic Development* (London, 1962) and two volumes by A. Gerschenkron, *Economic Backwardness in Historical*

A short history of the international economy since 1850

Perspective (Cambridge, Mass., 1962) and *Continuity in History* (Cambridge, Mass., 1968). Some of the basic comparative statistics are examined in detail and revised in a long article by P. Bairoch, 'Europe's gross national product, 1800–1975', *Journal of European Economic History*, vol. 5 (1976).

All the main elements in international economic relations have an abundant literature, though most of it relates to limited themes and fairly short periods. Only works with a broader or more extended subject matter are noted here. A very illuminating brief introduction is given in two lectures by W. A. Lewis, *The Evolution of the International Economic Order* (Princeton, 1978). Much fuller information is provided by S. Grassman and E. Lundberg, eds, *The World Economic Order, Past and Prospects* (New York, 1981), which includes an important chapter by W. A. Lewis, 'The rate of growth of world trade 1830–1973'. Another long-term study of a large part of world trade, which tries to improve on previously available figures, is P. Bairoch, 'Geographical structure and trade balance of European foreign trade, 1800–1970', *Journal of European Economic History*, vol. 3 (1974). The period since the First World War is much better served with abundant figures, subjected to detailed analysis, than earlier periods. P. L. Yates, *Forty Years of Foreign Trade* (London, 1959) and the much more elaborate A. Maizels, *Industrial Growth and World Trade* (revised edn, Cambridge, 1970) are leading contributions. One important study which goes back into the late nineteenth century is League of Nations, *Industrialization and Foreign Trade* (Geneva, 1945). Its examination of the interwar period should be supplemented by League of Nations, *The Network of World Trade* (Geneva, 1942).

International investment has been studied for a long time and some of the older works remain very useful, in particular H. Feis, *Europe the World's Banker 1870–1914* (New Haven, 1930) and L. H. Jenks, *The Migration of British Capital to 1875* (London, 1938). Important later works include A. K. Cairncross, *Home and Foreign Investment 1870–1913* (Cambridge, 1953), R. E. Cameron, *France and the Economic Development of Europe 1800–1914* (Princeton, 1961), and J. H. Adler, ed., *Capital Movements and Economic Development* (London, 1967), of which the first of the three parts is historical. A major problem has always been that most of the historical evidence is indirect. This has given special importance to attempts to check the reliability of estimated figures by relating them to what is known of the statistics of international trade and balances of payments. The most valuable work of this kind is A. H. Imlah, *Economic Elements in the Pax Britannica* (Cambridge, Mass., 1958). But the indirectness of

320

the evidence has also led to attempts to revise both the figures and their interpretation. Among works which guide the reader through the resulting controversies are A. R. Hall, ed., *The Export of Capital from Britain 1870–1914* (London, 1968) and P. L. Cottrell, *British Overseas Investment in the Nineteenth Century* (London, 1975). A further stage in the controversy is marked by D. C. M. Platt, *Foreign Finance in Continental Europe and the USA, 1815–1870: Quantities, Origins, Functions and Distribution* (London, 1984). For the history of the subject in the mid-twentieth century, J. H. Dunning, *Studies in International Investment* (London, 1970) is useful.

The most comprehensive information on the history of international migration is still to be found in I. Ferenczi and W. F. Willcox, eds, *International Migrations* (2 vols, New York, 1929–31). An attempt to improve, collate, and reinterpret many of the figures is made in a long article by J. D. Gould, 'European intercontinental emigration', *Journal of European Economic History*, vol. 8 (1979). A detailed attempt to relate migration to the whole development of the economy on both sides of the Atlantic is B. Thomas, *Migration and Economic Growth* (2nd edn, Cambridge, 1973). The closely related subject of change in the size and composition of the population is studied in A. M. Carr-Saunders, *World Population* (Oxford, 1936), United Nations, *The Determinants and Consequences of Population Trends* (New York, 1953) and United Nations, *The World Population Situation in 1970–1975* (New York, 1974).

Some of the works already mentioned discuss the major institutions and the governmental policies which influenced their subject matter. It is helpful to supplement them by specialist studies of institutions and policies central to international economic affairs. Probably the most thoroughly explored branch of policy is tariff history. Earlier years are treated in P. Ashley, *Modern Tariff History* (3rd edn, London, 1920), which may be followed by League of Nations, *Commercial Policy in the Inter-War Period* (Geneva, 1942). A wider range of international economic policies is considered for the period after the Second World War in G. Myrdal, *An International Economy: problems and prospects* (London, 1956). An important institutional element in the later commercial policies is examined in K. W. Dam, *The GATT: Law and International Economic Organization* (Chicago, 1970). Institutional studies are more fully available for the years since the Second World War than for earlier periods. Useful works include M. A. G. van Meerhaeghe, *International Economic Institutions* (London, 1966). For the most influential financial institutions of the nineteenth and early twentieth centuries W. T. C. King,

History of the London Discount Market (London, 1936) is helpful. It may be supplemented by W. M. Scammell, *The London Discount Market* (London, 1968). The large financial institutions of more recent years are dealt with in great detail by E. S. Mason and R. E. Asher, *The World Bank since Bretton Woods* (Washington, 1973), J. K. Horsefield and others, *The International Monetary Fund 1945–1965* (3 vols, Washington, 1969), and M. G. de Vries, *The IMF 1966–71: The System Under Stress* (Washington, 1976). Other works deal with the institutional framework of international financial and commercial policy in the nineteen-sixties and seventies without concentrating on the history of a single institution. Among them are F. Hirsch, *Money International* (London, 1967), J. Williamson, *The Failure of World Monetary Reform* (Sunbury-on-Thames, 1977), and R. C. Amacher, G. Haberler and T. D. Willett, eds, *Challenges to a Liberal International Economic Order* (Washington, 1979).

One theme running through the history of both international finance and economic development since 1945 is that of international aid. A helpful general study is W. G. Friedmann, G. Kalmanoff and R. F. Meagher, *International Financial Aid* (New York, 1966). Others which deal with particular phases or aspects are W. A. Brown and R. Opie, *American Foreign Assistance* (Washington, 1953), H. S. Ellis, *The Economics of Freedom: The Progress and Future of Aid to Europe* (New York, 1950), H. B. Price, *The Marshall Plan and its Meaning* (Ithaca, 1955), and W. W. Rostow, *The United States in the World Arena* (New York, 1960).

Finally, it should be stressed that statistical reference works which permit comparisons among a wide variety of countries and for extended periods are essential in order to reduce the inevitable imprecisions of international economic history and to give it clearer shape. Some of the books already mentioned, especially those dealing with economic growth, contain a great many statistical series on at least a roughly comparable basis. There are also some much wider ranging collections of statistical material. For the nineteenth century, comparative material of this kind is less fully available than it became later. The most useful collections are in three books by M. G. Mulhall, *The Progress of the World* (2nd edn, London, 1880), *Industries And Wealth of Nations* (London, 1896), and *The Dictionary of Statistics* (4th edn, London, 1900). Most of the historical collections which go back into the nineteenth century but cover the twentieth century as well are concerned with a single country, though they can be used together for comparative purposes. Particularly useful examples are US Bureau of the Census, *Historical Statistics of the United States* (revised edn, Washington, 1960), B. R. Mitchell and Phyllis Deane, *Abstract of British Historical Statistics* (Cambridge, 1962), and B. R. Mitchell and H. G. Jones, *Second Abstract of British Historical Statistics* (Cambridge, 1971). There is, however, one valuable, long-period international collection: B. R. Mitchell, *European Historical Statistics 1750–1970* (London, 1975; abridged edn 1978). It is also helpful to consult P. Bairoch, *International Historical Statistics,* vol. 1, *The Working Population and its Structure* (Brussels, 1968).

For the later twentieth century, international economic statistics are much more abundant, though few collections cover very long periods. OECD, *Historical Statistics 1960–1982* (Paris, 1984) is useful and W. N. Peach and J. A. Constantin, *Zimmermann's World Resources and Industries* (New York, 1972), though mainly contemporary, has some historical tables. The principal international institutions, such as the United Nations Organization, the OECD, and the secretariat of the Contracting Parties to the GATT, all regularly publish statistical information which is updated annually and often retrospectively corrected. Many of these publications include a large selection of figures for earlier dates, for comparative purposes. This is a valuable feature of what is perhaps the most useful of all such works, the United Nations *Statistical Yearbook* (New York, annually); but almost any of these collections can be helpful for reference.

Index

Africa, 41, 48, 65, 152, 154, 165, 199, 207, 218, 286, 289, 306, 313
agriculture: generally, 15–16, 17, 18, 35–51, 52–3, 103–4, 108, 109, 111, 171, 192–3, 202, 203, 222, 223, 228, 285, 288–9, 290, 297, 302, 314; British, 9, 20, 35–7, 111; collective, 42–3; communal rights in, 18, 36, 171; dairying, 37, 40, 221; decline in proportion of population employed in, 37, 111, 288–9, 290; enclosure and, 36, 38; extensive, 43–6; French, 38, 39; great estates in, 35–6, 39; machinery in, 36, 38, 42, 45–6, 47–8, 49; peasant, 39–42, 50; plantation, 47, 48–9, 199; protection for, 38; ranching, 44–5; and soil exhaustion, 46, 50; tropical, 16, 46–50; in USA 14, 44–6, 111
air transport, 75–6, 164, 184
aircraft industry, 31, 56
aluminium, 54–5, 56
American Relief Association, 229
Anglo-American Loan Agreement (1945), 274–5
Anglo-French Treaty of Commerce (1860), 138
apprenticeship, 12, 110, 133
arbitration, 124–5
Argentina, 43, 45, 165, 182, 196, 197, 198, 201, 203, 207, 239, 264
Asia: generally, 2, 41, 63, 65, 70, 72, 77, 154, 165, 196, 197, 198, 199, 207, 267, 289, 307: Central, 69; East, 313; Southeast, 50; Western, 286
atomic energy see nuclear physics, applications of
Australia, 3, 44, 59, 65, 77, 125, 173, 185, 187, 188, 189, 190, 197, 198, 258, 286, 304
Austria, 11, 20, 67, 134, 141, 150, 163, 189, 200, 207, 231, 236, 244, 245, 279; see also Habsburg Empire
Austria-Hungary see Habsburg Empire
automobile industry see motor industry

Babbage, Charles, 83–4
backwardness and economic growth, 140, 164
bakery industry, 24
Balta Liman, Convention of (1838), 144
bananas, 47, 50
Bank for International Settlements, 161, 244, 245, 246, 249
Bank of England, 135, 136, 245, 246
Bank of France, 245–6, 246–7
banking, 18, 40–1, 91, 92, 136, 140, 192, 194, 208, 213, 214, 225, 287, 304, 309–10
Belgium, 7, 10–11, 20, 57, 66, 67, 141, 144, 187, 188, 189, 205, 207, 228, 231, 233, 235, 250, 251, 256, 257, 281, 314
Berlin: Treaty of (1878), 152; Treaty of (1885), 152
Berne Convention, 153
biological research, 33
Bohemia, 11, 20; see also Czechoslovakia
book-keeping, 86
boot and shoe industry, 25
borax, 54
Boulton and Watt, 8
brass, 56
Brazil, 43, 45, 59, 197, 198, 201, 202, 220, 239, 241, 287, 308
Bretton Woods Conference, 271, 273, 315
brewing, 8